The Canadian Federal Election of

2011

The Canadian Federal Election of
2011

EDITED BY
JON H. PAMMETT & CHRISTOPHER DORNAN

DUNDURN
TORONTO

Editor: Andrea Waters
Project Manager: Shannon Whibbs
Design: Jennifer Scott
Printer: Marquis

Library and Archives Canada Cataloguing in Publication

The Canadian federal election of 2011 / edited by Jon H. Pammett and Christopher Dornan.

Also available in electronic formats.
ISBN 978-1-4597-0180-9

1. Canada. Parliament--Elections, 2011. 2. Canada--Politics and government--2006-. 3. Elections--Canada--History--21st century. 4. Voting--Canada. I. Pammett, Jon H., 1944- II. Dornan, Chris

JL193.C3584 2011   324.971'073   C2011-903806-4

1   2   3   4   5   15   14   13   12   11

 Conseil des Arts du Canada Canada Council for the Arts   Canadä    ONTARIO ARTS COUNCIL CONSEIL DES ARTS DE L'ONTARIO

We acknowledge the support of the **Canada Council for the Arts** and the **Ontario Arts Council** for our publishing program. We also acknowledge the financial support of the **Government of Canada** through the **Canada Book Fund** and **Livres Canada Books**, and the **Government of Ontario** through the **Ontario Book Publishing Tax Credit** and the **Ontario Media Development Corporation**.

Care has been taken to trace the ownership of copyright material used in this book. The author and the publisher welcome any information enabling them to rectify any references or credits in subsequent editions.

J. Kirk Howard, President

Printed and bound in Canada.
www.dundurn.com

Dundurn	Gazelle Book Services Limited	Dundurn
3 Church Street, Suite 500	White Cross Mills	2250 Military Road
Toronto, Ontario, Canada	High Town, Lancaster, England	Tonawanda, NY
M5E 1M2	LA1 4XS	U.S.A. 14150

CONTENTS

CHAPTER I

From Contempt of Parliament to Majority Mandate
Christopher Dornan

In the end, did the earth move?

We were assured in the run-up that this would be a dull election. And it was. Right up until the outcome.

The outcome was not simply a majority government, the prize to which the Conservative Party of Canada had devoted itself from its inception. The results overnight rewrote the Canadian political landscape in ways not even the vaunted Conservative machine had anticipated.

Going into the writ period, the question was whether the Conservatives could swing a majority mandate. Although the Liberals were certainly not the powerhouse they had once been, they could be expected to perform better than they had in 2008. The NDP would presumably take their usual mid-teen slice of the vote — perhaps even less if they bled support to the Greens or to the Liberals. And the Bloc would carry the majority of seats in Quebec. At best, the seat projection arithmetic made a Conservative majority a close-run thing, and few among the pundits and pollsters thought it overly likely.

On the morning of May 3, the country indeed had a majority government. But more than that, the Liberal Party, the once natural governing party, was broken, leaderless, routed. The Quebec separatist party on the federal stage had been not just defeated but crushed. Doubly delicious for the Conservatives, the stronghold of Quebec fell not to the Liberals — who once owned the province and its seats — but to the NDP, whose electoral apparatus in the province was largely gestural. A party with no machine to speak of took fifty-nine seats. Together, the three parties with hopes and expectations of carving Quebec up among themselves returned a grand total of sixteen Quebec MPs.

That is the crucial contrast of the 2011 federal election. The Conservatives won their majority through superior political calculation and the professional implementation of long-prepared plans. The NDP took Quebec and rode into Stornoway on a wave of support that surprised even them. Both parties mobilized their bases and expanded beyond them, but where the Conservatives did so through political technocracy, the NDP did so on the basis of a populist surge in which the party became the magnetic pole for opposition to the Conservatives. The Conservatives methodically turned out their targeted vote; the NDP, to the detriment of the Liberals and the Bloc Québécois, galvanized anti-Harper sentiment.

Never let it be said that leadership — or the lack of it — is not a determinant of Canadian federal politics. Plainly, the success of the Conservatives in attaining their long-sought majority was very much the work of Stephen Harper, who guided the party behind closed doors with discipline and authority. By the same token, the success of the NDP in attracting the votes of those opposed to Harper was owed to the performance of Jack Layton, particularly in the French-language leaders' debate. These are two very different types of leadership. Harper's is managerial; Layton's was charismatic. One runs a tight ship. The other delivered almost sixty seats on the spark of a single television appearance conducted in his second language. The index of leadership is whether you can get people to follow you.

The Conservatives used the strategy of incrementalism in plotting the party's course to majority rule. They would inch their way to a plurality and then to a majority mandate by acclimatizing the electorate to the party and its priorities. They would champion nothing too radical, nothing that might rankle the great middle of the Canadian public. Instead, they would implement so-called pocketbook initiatives, intended to lessen the tax bite on families and put more discretionary income in their hands. But the aim, ultimately, was not simply to make the country comfortable with Conservative rule. It was to shift the centre of gravity of mainstream thinking, to make Conservative values and priorities the new common sense.

To those not persuaded by Conservative blandishments, its designs on power looked less like the politics of incrementalism and more like the politics of unvarnished invective. It wasn't that the Conservatives pursued anodyne policies most of the electorate could find no fault with. It was that they pursued next to no policies at all, beyond the vilification of their enemies in the Commons. The signature feature of their government was their visceral hostility to opponents. Parliamentarians on the opposite side of the chamber were not honourable adversaries who differed from the government on matters of principle or policy. They were foes to be treated with contempt and prejudice.

And so, from the Conservatives' first major act after winning their 2008 majority — the attempt to eliminate the per-vote subsidy to political parties, clearly intended to cripple their opponents' party machines — to the vote of no confidence that toppled the government in March 2011, the fortieth Parliament was toxic in its hyper-partisanship. The Commons the public saw on the nightly news was seemingly just one fight after another over whether and to what extent the government had to honour the institution of Parliament and its ancillary agencies.

The issue that most vividly captured the government's rancour toward the House — and vice versa — had to do with Afghans captured or detained by the Canadian Forces and delivered into the hands of the Afghan military, police, and prison system. The Military Police Complaints Commission had been investigating allegations that such detainees had been maltreated, but the government had simply refused to co-operate. Eventually, the chair, Peter Tinsley, discontinued hearings in the face of the government's refusal to release pertinent documents to his commission.

This piqued Commons interest in the issue, and in late 2009 Canadian diplomat Richard Colvin testified before a House of Commons special committee that he had attempted to alert the government in 2006 and 2007 to allegations that Afghan detainees had been routinely tortured once delivered to the Afghan prison system. Colvin's superiors testified that his memos contained no such warnings, and the committee demanded to see the relevant documents. The government again refused, prompting Parliament to pass an extraordinary motion ordering the government to produce all documentation related to Afghan detainees.

Facing a firestorm of criticism over its conduct and plummeting approval ratings in opinion polls, the government again prorogued

Parliament for two months, from December 30, 2009, until March 3, 2010 — the second time in a year the Conservatives had resorted to this extraordinary measure. The pretext was the Vancouver Olympics, but it was clear that the measure was intended to cool the Afghan detainee controversy and allegations that the government had misled the House. As a tactic, it worked. An issue that could well have boiled over into an election — and what government would prefer to go to the polls defending or denying complicity in torture? — was managed. It was bad government, perhaps, but it was inarguably good politics.

Almost as soon as the Afghan detainee controversy subsided, however, the government invited another. In its periodic censuses of the Canadian population, Statistics Canada issued two versions of the census. The so-called short form went to 80 percent of recipients, while 20 percent received a much longer and more detailed questionnaire. Under law, all recipients had to complete and return the form they received. In late June 2010, the government announced that the long form would no longer be mandatory, a move that was seen by statisticians as simply baffling. The census, they protested, provided the government with the information essential to formulating sound policy. Without the long-form census, future governments would be informationally impoverished. They would have to rule on the basis of hunch, ideology, and wishful thinking. The Conservative measure was opposed, not simply by the government's political adversaries, but by people and agencies as varied as the chief economist of the TD Bank, the Toronto Board of Trade, and the United Way. Munir Sheikh, the country's chief statistician, resigned.

The Conservatives argued that the mandatory long-form census was intrusive and authoritarian, since failure to comply could lead to fines or jail terms. But again, what was seen by their opponents as bad government was intended by the Conservatives as good politics. It was apiece with their get-tough-on-crime measures (stiffer sentences, more prisons), which had been roundly denounced as wrong-headed by almost every criminologist in the country, and their cuts to the GST, which had similarly been decried as bad economic policy by almost every economist in the country. Speaking at McGill University in 2009 on the role of evidence in policy-making, former Harper chief of staff Ian Brodie (himself a former university professor) argued, "Politically, it helped us tremendously to be attacked by this coalition of university types."[1] The new hegemony, presumably, would no longer bow to the groupthink of academics, the public service mindset, or the reflexive cant of people such as the Auditor General, the Veterans' Ombudsman, and the Parliamentary Budget Officer.

And then there was International Cooperation Minister Bev Oda, who catapulted into the spotlight in February 2011. In 2009 she had rejected the renewal of a Canadian International Development Agency grant to Kairos, a multi-faith umbrella group devoted to "ecological justice and human rights." It was perfectly within the purview of the minister to do so, but she said that the decision had been made by CIDA bureaucrats. An Access to Information inquiry lodged by Carleton University journalism student Bev Mackreal revealed that the memo from CIDA to the Minister had in fact recommended that the grant be renewed, but the memo had been amended when someone inserted the word "not" in handwriting.

Oda testified before a House committee that she did not know who had inserted the word "not," only to subsequently admit that she had ordered the memo amended. The government defended the right of a minister to ignore or override the counsel of public servants, but this was not what was at issue. The issue was whether the minister had misled the House. The Speaker was asked to rule on an opposition motion that Oda had violated MPs' privileges by misleading them. The Speaker found that there was sufficient evidence to warrant further investigation by a Commons committee, but the government fell before the matter could be pursued.

Meanwhile, the House of Commons Standing Committee on Finance had been attempting since October 2010 to discover the cost of the government's plans to buy F-35 jet fighters, the cost of its proposed crime and prison legislation, the cost of hosting the G8 and G20 summits, and the cost to the treasury of its reduction in corporate tax rates. Again, the government had refused to comply. On the same day that he delivered his ruling in the Oda case, the Speaker referred the matter to the Committee on Procedure and House Affairs. This committee delivered its report on March 21, finding the government in contempt of Parliament — not only the first time that a government in Canada had been found in contempt of Parliament, but the first government in the history of the Commonwealth to be so found. This set the stage for the vote of no confidence four days later.

The opposition parties, appalled at the bullying comportment of the Conservatives and their disdain for rules of Parliamentary conduct, no doubt thought that Canadians would be similarly appalled. In a country in which rule of law is paramount, who would want a government that ignores, defies, or exploits the rules of parliamentary procedure according to its political interest? Who would want a government that angry at people who disagreed with it?

The Conservatives, for their part, judged that the partisan theatrics of the House of Commons could be dismissed as just that — partisan theatrics that bore little relevance to the day-to-day concerns of voters and citizens. And they were right. Though the Conservatives formed the government, as long as they were in minority the opposition parties together held more seats on many House committees. The opposition properly tried to use this to hold the government to account — to use the parliamentary committee structure to raise legitimate questions (as they saw it) or to thwart, harass, or undermine the government as best they could (as the government saw it).

The finding of contempt of Parliament is only damning if one accepts that Parliament speaks with unimpeachable authority and without partisan interest. If, instead, one sees Parliament as a viciously partisan arena in which the goal is to cause one's enemies as much grief as possible, then the historic finding of contempt is just a political use of a procedural ordnance, on the order of proroguing Parliament when things get overheated.

So the government fell, not on its budget or its crime legislation, its foreign policy or its proposed military purchases, its handling of the constitutional file or any other substantive policy. It lost the confidence of the House because Parliament said it could no longer trust it to honour the rules of government.

The ethical conduct of the government never ignited into an election issue, although the come-from-nowhere surge of support for the NDP suggests that sizeable elements of the public were motivated as much by their opposition to the Harper Conservatives as by the appeal of NDP policies. Mid-campaign, Liberal leader Michael Ignatieff urged those who wanted the Harperites stopped to "rise up." Large numbers of them did, but they flocked to the orange banner.

Why to the NDP and not the Liberals? Now there's a question. The outpouring of national sentiment on the occasion of Jack Layton's death in late August, four months after the vote, provides part of the answer.

At a party conference in Ottawa mere weeks after the election, the triumphant Conservatives congratulated themselves not simply on the success of their campaign but on a new prevailing hegemony. The victory, they averred, signalled not only the success of their electoral calculus but the coming to pass of their true and long-term goal: to bring the national ethos in accordance with conservative principles. The country, they felt sure, had been changed. The earth had moved.

But had it? This book explores the conduct of the campaign and the import of its outcome. Why did the Liberals implode and the Bloc self-destruct? How did the Conservatives engineer their majority and what accounts for the rise in fortune of the NDP? What does this mean for conservatism in Canada, as well as for progressivism? What future for those demonized by the prime minister at the onset of the campaign as "arch centralists"? How did the media play in the contours of the campaign, and why did the plethora of polls still manage to miss the most crucial results?

But perhaps the most telling question is whether the Conservatives are correct that the centre of political gravity has shifted, or whether their victory was the result of electoral technique, not a national mood swing. The consequences for the country are very different depending on the answer, but either way Canada will have a Conservative government until 2015, meaning that the party of Stephen Harper will have been in power for almost a decade. Certainly long enough to make an imprint on the country, mood swing or not.

NOTES

1. John Geddes, "Cracking Eggheads," *Maclean's*, August 16, 2010, 21.

CHAPTER 2

The Conservative Campaign:
Becoming the New Natural Governing Party?

Faron Ellis | Peter Woolstencroft

When viewed through the lens of the primary objective — securing a stable, national, majority government — the Conservative Party of Canada's (CPC) 2011 election campaign was an unqualified success. Organizationally superb, it efficiently achieved maximum seat gains out of marginal gains in voter support. Most importantly, it executed the most recent stage of a long-term plan that has assembled the most ideologically and geographically stable, winning electoral coalition that any Canadian conservative party has had in generations. Indeed, only eight years after successfully merging the feuding factions of Canadian conservatism and five years leading a minority government, Prime Minister Stephen Harper has built the most formidable political machine in the country. In achieving a majority he has taken the latest steps in fulfilling the long-term goal: ensuring the Conservatives replace the Liberals as Canada's natural governing party.[1]

In each election since he created the CPC, Harper has expanded the party's organization, its policy appeal, share of the national vote, and number of seats in Parliament. Although disappointed by their 2011 showing in Quebec, the Conservatives increased their share of votes in every other province. Save for a one-seat decline in British Columbia and five lost in Quebec, they maintained or increased their seat total in every province. Crucially, they won more than two-thirds of the seats in Canada's most populous province, Ontario, furthering their urban growth strategy by making major gains in Toronto. Stephen Harper did not achieve his victory alone. But he established, led, managed, and effectively controlled the party that did the work. There is little doubt that this is his victory, and his restructuring of Canadian party competition with the Conservatives in the dominant position will likely be one of his most important and lasting legacies. It is certainly among the most important outcomes of the 2011 Canadian federal election campaign.

After the disappointment of failing to secure a majority in the 2008 election was followed by the near-death experience at the hands of the Liberal-led coalition, Harper, his government, and his party intensified their "permanent campaign" efforts throughout the entire fortieth Parliament, directing nearly all of their organizational, public policy, and legislative efforts towards securing a majority in the next contest. They meshed their parliamentary agenda with their electoral agenda by focusing on growth in Ontario, while holding seats and making marginal gains where possible in the West and the Maritimes. While not overtly abandoning Quebec, they recognized that their route to majority would run through urban Ontario — not rural and suburban Quebec. The strategy was locked in early when Conservatives determined that the best way to save the government in late 2008 was by demonizing the separatists' participation in the proposed coalition. What followed were two and a half years of clear and conscious legislative and organizational efforts to secure growth in areas outside of Quebec. By framing an electoral dynamic that pitted their party against all of the others, they defined the 2011 ballot question as a choice as between the stable, familiar, competent economic management of the Conservatives and the instability and economic ruin that would follow from a Liberal-led coalition backed by socialists and separatists. When the late-campaign dynamics changed the order of the players by vaulting the NDP ahead of the Liberals, the ballot question and its underlying logic remained the same, and indeed became more focused: vote for a strong, stable, national Conservative majority government or prepare for bad things to come.

During the "permanent campaign" that existed throughout the fortieth Parliament (and indeed since the 2004 Liberal minority),[2] the Conservatives kept their electoral machine operative while they worked on implementing their long-term strategy of incrementally inching themselves closer to the median Canadian voter while at the same time nudging Canadian voters closer to conservative values. The party knew its base was solid and loyal. So they embarked on a strategy of identifying what they believed were already naturally conservative voters, aiming to convince them to recognize the similarities between their values and the pragmatic, moderately conservative policies of the CPC. In government, its legislative program was designed to provide the evidence. By the time the government was defeated, it had survived long enough to be credited with having successfully managed the economy through the worst of the recession and had sufficiently inoculated itself against the well-worn accusations of harbouring an extreme right-wing hidden agenda. They consistently branded themselves as the familiar, stable, democratically legitimate alternative to the fractious collection of all the other parties that was conspiring to "steal" power by way of a sinister coalition. As they had done to his predecessor, they ruthlessly and relentlessly undermined the credibility of Liberal leader Michael Ignatieff. In doing so they provided voters with a plausible narrative that positioned the Conservatives as the only party focused on the economic issues that mattered most to Canadians, and therefore the only party they should trust with a majority government that would end the parliamentary instability.

The plan succeeded. Conservatives were rewarded with their majority, thereby ensuring an uninterrupted decade of Conservative rule. One or even three consecutive election victories do not necessarily make a dynasty (see Chapter 12). But results from the 2011 election intimate a considerable amount of stability in the new Conservative electoral coalition. If they continue to maintain and develop their organizational machine, it is likely the Conservative Party of Canada will be the dominant party on the Canadian federal scene for years to come.

THE LEADER AND PARTY

The term "permanent campaign" aptly describes the dynamics of Canadian federal party competition during the string of three minority parliaments from 2004 to 2011. All parties were forced to be constantly on a campaign-ready footing. Conservatives excelled in this environment. Although he inherited some operational and institutional capacity from the merger of the Reform and Progressive Conservative (PC) parties in 2003, Harper has essentially been building a new party. This has afforded him the luxury of establishing an organizational structure that ensures the extra-parliamentary party and the party in government work in unison and under the control of the leader. This organizational capability allowed the Conservatives to face down the opposition at every turn, knowing that when the government was eventually defeated, they would be in better shape than any of their competitors to effectively contest for power.

THE LEADER

Stephen Harper's journey towards becoming one of Canada's longest serving prime ministers is unique. Few prime ministers have worked tirelessly for a new federal party before voluntarily retiring after one term as MP, only to return as leader of the rebranded party he helped create. In becoming Alliance leader, Harper immediately set about the task of creating a permanent, professional political institution capable of earning the trust of Canadians and eventually governing the country. His immediate challenge was to bring order to the chaos that had become the official opposition. He succeeded beyond expectations, even settling differences with members of the Democratic Representative Caucus who had split from the Alliance caucus and were sitting in a formal parliamentary working coalition with Progressive Conservatives MPs. When Peter MacKay replaced Joe Clark as PC leader in 2003, Harper relentlessly pursued MacKay in attempting to achieve a merger of their two parties. Despite MacKay's initial resistance, having just secured his leadership by agreeing to never accept a merger, Harper prevailed and in 2004 easily won the party's first leadership contest.[3] He then began building a political organization that suited both his leadership style and the permanent campaign circumstances into which his party had been born. Despite his history with Reform-Alliance, the result would resemble the traditional parties that Harper used to criticize much more than it would resemble Reform.

In bringing order to the CPC's parliamentary operations, in building the new party organization, and in his strategic manoeuvres — first to achieve government and then to hold onto power — Harper developed a reputation as both overly controlling and at times bitterly partisan. He never went out of his way to challenge either characterization, repeatedly stating that his long-term goal was to have the Conservatives replace the Liberals as Canada's dominant federal party while dismissing the former characterization as a simple fact of political leadership. Stating that there are only two kinds of prime ministers — those who are too controlling and those who are not in control — he was eminently more comfortable being one of the former. And after initially being perceived as more the angry, young opposition leader than a PM-in-waiting, upon assuming prime ministerial responsibilities in 2006 Harper was transformed into the party's single most important asset. He appeared comfortable on the international stage, no more so than during his second term when he revelled in the leadership opportunities provided by the government's comparatively enviable fiscal position and the country's stable financial institutions. As the Canadian media dutifully reported all the foreign media praise of Canada, his leadership scores consistently hovered well above those of his federal competitors, creating an image as the most competent and trustworthy economic manager. Back home within the often frustrating confines of a minority Parliament, his behaviour was more sharply partisan and antagonistic. But many of the rough edges were being smoothed by his willingness, at the urging of wife Laureen, to show the public more of his private persona by making public appearances playing the piano, singing Beatles tunes, and entertaining pop music stars at the prime minister's residence. In framing the leadership choice for the 2011 election, Conservatives were confident that their branding of Harper as familiar, stable, moderate, and competent, when combined with his experience, would carry the day.

THE PARTY

The combined effects of the "permanent campaign" and the CPC's novelty created conditions whereby the party and its campaign operations were essentially fused.[4] After a brief but intense internal power struggle, Harper prevailed and centralized most of the party's national operations under the authority of its national director, the chairman of the party's financial arm, or the permanent campaign chairman, all of whom either report directly to or are significantly controlled by the leader. The party's organizational structure is flat and highly centralized, consisting only of the local Electoral District Associations and the three primary national entities: the National Council, the Conservative Fund, and the National Office. It has no regional or provincial organizations and no formal special interest associations such as youth, women, or ethnic associations. Each of the national and local levels is for the most part financially self-sustaining.[5] Party members continue to meet at national conventions,[6] but their deliberations and the resulting policy positions contained in the Conservative Policy Declaration are not binding on the leader and caucus. In fact, given that the leader is free to develop new positions and alter existing declarations for more immediate political purposes, the status of formal policy within CPC resembles that of the Progressive Conservatives and other traditional parties rather than the more populist Reform-Alliance.

The sophisticated outreach program that the party established in its first term was expanded as Conservatives targeted heavily ethnic urban ridings outside Quebec. Citizenship, Immigration and Multiculturalism Minister Jason Kenny continued to tirelessly promote the party at ethnic events, while Harper met with community leaders and directed a variety of legislative and international diplomatic efforts toward securing support from voters who until recently had traditionally shunned conservative parties. Inroads amongst these voters would be crucial to securing urban seats and had the additional benefit of easing doubts about the party's lingering anti-urban reputation among non-immigrant urbanites. After securing government in 2006, the party tried to expand its base by simultaneously targeting new Canadians while attempting to expand in Quebec. But the Quebec initiative stalled in the 2008 campaign when the Conservatives misjudged how cuts to cultural grants, something they perceived to be relatively minor, could be effectively spun by their opponents as an attack on Québécois national pride and identity. Recognizing that further building efforts could just as easily be derailed by something as trivial as the funding of hockey arenas, Conservatives determined that even their best efforts in Quebec were unlikely to produce a stable enough base to supply the seats needed to obtain and sustain majority governments. Over time, Quebec would be treated much more like any other province, which fit the Conservatives' national approach to campaign organization that rarely makes operational concessions to accommodate Quebec's uniqueness. Although careful not to appear antagonistic towards the province and its interests — because that narrative can also impede progress in other parts of the country, particularly Ontario — they would campaign hard in Quebec but shift their focus to the urban outreach strategy. The 2011 election results indicate that those efforts were largely successful.[7]

Like all of the federal parties, the Conservatives' fundraising operations were impacted by the changes to party financing initiated by the Chretien government (2004) and furthered by Harper in 2006.[8] However, the Conservatives vastly outperformed their competitors via their superior Direct Voter Contact operations (DVC). They also benefited more from the per-vote subsidies and election rebates. Their enviable financial position allowed them to purchase large amounts of broadcast advertising, on an ongoing basis, making this a reoccurring feature of the "permanent campaign." During the 2011 writ period, the national campaign would spend its $21 million limit and finish with no debt and money in the bank. Early estimates suggest that its 2011 national campaign expenditures will resemble those from 2008,[9] where slightly over half was spent on paid TV and radio advertising, with less than 3 percent on other advertising. The leader's tour accounted for a further 13 percent of the total, while 16 percent was spent paying for professional services, office expenses, and other salaries. As was the case in 2008, the party had conducted most of its research prior to the formal writ period and therefore spent very little on polling during the 2011 campaign, concentrating that amount locally in targeted ridings.

Table 1. Conservative Party Revenue, 2004–2008 (in thousands)

	2004	2005	2006	2007	2008	2009	2010
Contributions	10,910	17,847	18,641	16,984	21,179	17,702	17,420
Number of contributors	68	107	109	107	112	101	145
Mean dollar value per contributor	160	107	171	158	189	175	120
Transfers from candidates, associations, leadership contestants	39	225	287	92	152	65	20
Total contributions and transfers	10,950	18,073	18,928	17,076	21,331	17,767	17,441
Allowances	7,914	7,331	9,388	10,218	10,439	10,351	10,431
Total contributions and allowances	18,863	25,404	28,317	27,294	31,770	28,118	27,872
Total revenue including election expense rebates and membership fees	33,222*	30,696	34,198	30,350	43,347	29,168	29,000**

*December 7, 2003, through December 31, 2004
** Estimates

THE CAMPAIGN TEAM

In contesting three elections in seven years, Conservatives had built up a substantial institutional capacity including sophisticated polling, fundraising, and DVC capabilities, as well as a wealth of experienced personnel. The party had kept its war room facilities operational since 2007 but ran a leaner operation in 2011, numbering from seventy-five to ninety staffers. The 2011 campaign resembled past efforts with a staff mix of veterans and new operatives who were substituted into positions vacated by former key players. Most significantly, Senator Doug Finley, who had directed the campaigns of 2006 and 2008, was replaced by two former senior PMO staffers: Guy Giorno, who had served as Harper's chief of staff, became the national campaign chair, and Jenni Byrne, previously director of issues management, served as campaign manager. New PMO chief of staff Nigel Wright acted as a senior adviser involved in general decision-making. Many other senior campaign team members came from ministers' offices, the PMO, or were drawn from business consulting and public affairs companies.[10] New in communications was Jason Lietaer. Returning was Ken Boessenkool, who, along with Lietaer and veterans Ryan Sparrow and Alykhan Velshi, held daily conference calls with strategists and media spinners including new senator-spinners Pamela Wallin and Mike Duffy. Mark Spiro returned on a part-time basis to support the target seat management unit. Advertising was coordinated by Dan Robertson, executive director of the Conservative Resource Group.

The leader's tour also took on a traditional look — national in travel and reach — but in tandem with other operations was focused on the media centres that contained the party's targeted, urban growth constituencies. A secondary tour of cabinet ministers campaigning outside their ridings also descended on those regions. Travelling with the Prime Minister and journalists on the main tour was a small and familiar clustering of immediate staff, including the PMO communications director, press secretaries, Harper's principal secretary, and his deputy chief of staff. Trusted confidante Senator Marjory LeBreton again accompanied the PM as senior campaign adviser.[11] For the most part, the tour stayed on message and worked effectively with a war room that excelled in defusing disruptive issues as they occurred.

CONSERVATIVES IN THE THIRTY-NINTH PARLIAMENT

Upon entering the fortieth Parliament, Conservatives envisioned a session similar to those during their first term. It would focus on incrementally moving forward as many of their platform items as possible under the circumstances, while continuing the branding exercise that would support a successful majority bid in an election that could occur anytime. But events immediately following the 2008 election ultimately determined the Conservatives' strategy and ballot question in 2011. The coalition crisis provided an opportunity to advantageously frame the choice they would present voters in 2011: Conservative versus all the rest. The economic crisis presented the opportunity to continue to brand Harper and the government as flexible (and therefore not ideologically doctrinaire), capable economic managers.

COALITION CRISIS

Reacting to the government's economic update in late 2008, ironically the Conservative's most fiscally conservative pronouncement to date, the opposition parties immediately began to organize to replace the government with a Liberal-NDP coalition supported by the Bloc for two years. Despite the growing financial crisis, the economic update contained no massive stimulus program similar to what other national governments were beginning to implement. Rather, it optimistically envisioned fulfilling the government's commitment to keep the budget balanced, a promise made by all the parties during the 2008 campaign. All this was lost, however, in the furor that erupted over the surprise proposal to eliminate per-vote public subsidies to the parties. After initially reacting with some hesitation, Harper, Finance Minister Jim Flaherty, and the rest of the Conservative organization scrambled to first save the government and then establish a new set of fiscal policies that would sustain it through at least one budget cycle. They immediately withdrew the party financing changes and committed to an early budget. None of this was enough for the three opposition leaders, and when they all shook hands before the media at a ceremony to sign their historic coalition deal they presented the Conservatives with the optics they needed to reinforce their 2011 campaign narrative. Amid a growing public backlash against the coalition, the

Conservatives issued communications products for MPs and activists to use in "swamping" talk radio and the Internet with the government's message that the deal was democratically illegitimate because it overturned voters' 2008 decision. This line of attack was instrumental in priming the CPC message in 2011. Although Michael Ignatieff initially balked at the coalition idea, he eventually lent his support, providing the Conservatives with evidence they would use to weaken his credibility when he later issued denials of harbouring similar plans. After managing to delay a series of confidence votes, Harper moved to prorogue Parliament, ensuring the government's survival. But it now had to deliver on the economic crisis.

THE FISCAL RECORD

The Conservatives inherited an enviable fiscal situation from the Liberals in 2006, allowing them to spend lavishly in their first term, build up the public service, maintain healthy increases for health care transfers and generous equalization and HST harmonization transfers, all while implementing a staged 2 percent reduction in the GST, accelerating corporate tax cuts, and providing modest, "boutique" tax cuts as outlined in its 2006 campaign platform. To the chagrin of many fiscal conservatives, program spending increases continued to outpace revenue growth, and the surplus of $14.2 billion in 2006–07 was projected to shrink to only $2.3 billion by 2008–09. The combined effects of the coalition crisis and the deepening recession brought the 2008 CPC election platform plans to a crashing end. After agreeing with other G20 leaders to implement a stimulus plan worth about two percent of each country's GDP, the government complied by offering up a generous package that included bailouts for the North American auto sector, support for Canadian banks, and massive infrastructure spending, all financed by deficits originally predicted to exceed $30 billion per year but that would eventually top $54 billion.[12]

In the face of harsh criticism from normally sympathetic conservative commentators,[13] the party's growth strategy of targeting Ontario meant it was politically unrealistic for it to contemplate sitting on the sidelines while the Ontario and U.S. governments attempted to save the auto industry. Similarly, it would have been difficult if not impossible to avoid joining with the other G20 countries as they engaged in economic stimulus designed to prevent the next Great Depression. Nevertheless, the government shored up its conservative credentials by continuing with its corporate tax rate cuts, and it secured agreement with the provinces to also reduce their business taxes to 10 percent, for a combined Canadian rate of 25 percent. When the Ontario Liberal government released its budget during the first week of the 2011 campaign, it defended the plan as integral to its own growth strategy, severely undercutting the federal Liberal party's position.

As a condition for supporting the Conservatives' first stimulus budget in 2009, new Liberal leader Michael Ignatieff demanded the government issue economic report cards on how the stimulus spending was being rolled out. The Conservatives were only too happy to oblige and took every opportunity to boast about their generosity as well as their competent management. Amid continued grumblings about the ballooning size of the deficit, and opposition attacks that the stimulus spending was proceeding too slowly and being disproportionately distributed to Conservative ridings, the government moved to further advance its public relations efforts by requiring participating municipalities to erect signs, at their cost, advertising the government's Economic Action Plan at each site. When Conservative MPs began showing up in their ridings with oversized novelty cheques emboldened with the party logo and in some cases MPs' signatures, the government quickly admitted that the promotional cheques were partisanship taken a step too far and ordered them stopped. But the signage program would continue. In this sense the government set the tone for its fortieth Parliament government as well as its 2011 campaign: stick to its aggressive messaging plan, backing off only slightly when excesses became counterproductive.

By the time the government prepared to release the 2010 budget, it had survived Ignatieff's declaration that Harper's "time was up" and was also about to further its brinkmanship strategy by packing as much as possible into an omnibus budget bill and daring the opposition to defeat the government, thereby forcing an "unnecessary election." The 2010 budget was a 900-page epistle that included the promised second year of the stimulus plan as well as a wide range of items that were at best only tangentially budget related. Despite various showdowns with the opposition, the budget passed and the government continued to receive enough support to survive until it began preparations for its 2011 edition, which would ultimately become the centrepiece of the Conservatives' 2011 campaign platform. With both the Liberals and NDP providing advance notice that they would defeat the government before its budget could become law, and the Conservatives having accelerated their pre-writ advertising for two months prior to the March budget release, the government clearly had little intention of attempting to purchase a parliamentary truce. Despite containing a few nods to the opposition, particularly the NDP, the Conservatives released a stay-the-course economic blueprint they believed would reinforce a narrative that branded them as the most capable economic managers and force an election.

THE PARLIAMENTARY RECORD

In retrospect, the Harper Conservatives presided over two relatively productive minority parliaments. A total of seventy-three pieces of legislation passed during the fortieth Parliament, similar to the seventy-seven that received royal assent during the thirty-ninth Parliament. While the Economic Action Plan and budgets were signature measures, other parts of the Conservative agenda were also advanced. The government made headway on its crime agenda when it moved to make "citizen's arrests" easier, exploiting the high-profile case of a Toronto grocer who was charged after he took matters into his own hands. They advanced legislation to crack down on gang and drug crimes, and tightened the national sex offender laws. On the international front, the government succeeded in garnering Liberal support for its Afghan agenda, including the winding down of combat operations by the end of 2011. Harper performed well on overseas trips, touting the strength of Canada's financial institutions and its fiscal stability at G8 and G20 meetings and on high-profile trips to China and India, where trade issues were prioritized. Also heavily featured was Harper's presence at many religious and cultural activities that helped reinforce the new-Canadian outreach strategy at home while trumpeting his human rights agenda abroad. His performance was especially strong in front of the foreign media. Harper met with newly elected U.S. president Barack Obama in Ottawa on Obama's first foreign trip in the fall of 2008, where they began crafting plans for integrated border security. Work would also proceed on integrating environmental and energy policy, with the government lobbying the United States to approve pipelines for gas exports.

Energy policy was marginally important during the 2011 campaign, but not because of the Alberta oil sands. Rather, Conservative support for the Labrador power transmission deal caused a brief protest from Quebec Premier Jean Charest. But Conservatives framed the issue as one of regional equality, declaring it would support energy projects in all parts of the country in pursuit of its strategy of making Canada an energy superpower. It provided a similar frame when addressing off-shore tanker traffic on the west coast, ensuring B.C. residents that they would be treated equally as long as tankers were operating off the east coast. For the most part, federal-provincial relations were relatively calm and did not significantly impact the campaign. Health care and equalization deals took those issues off the table, and the government secured Harmonized Sales Tax deals for which the Ontario and B.C. governments were receiving the brunt of criticism rather than the federal Conservatives. The Quebec HST deal remained an irritant, and a promise to conclude that would be included in the party's platform despite its exclusion from the most recent budget. To that end, the premiers either stayed out of the 2011 election campaign altogether or supported it indirectly (as with the Ontario budget) or directly (as when Alberta and Saskatchewan premiers Stelmach and Wall openly advocated a Conservative majority during the later stages of the campaign).

BRANDING, PLATFORM, AND PROMOTIONS

Conservative branding and messaging strategies originated with the coalition crisis and continued with the government's legislative agenda, particularly its stimulus budgets. All efforts were aimed at supporting, for the first time, the bold appeal for a "strong, stable, national, majority Conservative government." By asserting a conceptual framework that lumped all of their opponents together, the Conservatives were able to exploit the most negative elements of each, tarring the rest in the process. They ruthlessly discredited Liberal leader Michael Ignatieff while invoking fear of a national government beholden to separatists, as would have been the case if the 2008 coalition had succeeded. Conservatives aimed to frame the choice as one between rewarding them for their record of economic competence versus fear of the worst elements of all the rest. They invoked a democratic legitimacy theme that played fast and loose with interpretations of parliamentary and constitutional procedure. They tapped into the increasing minority government fatigue and Canadians' frustrations with having a fourth election in seven years by reminding voters that the Conservatives were the only party in a position to form a majority and end the parliamentary instability.[14] Ultimately, their agenda framing proved successful, not only in its conceptualization but also in its ability to adapt to changing campaign dynamics. It also succeeded because it was based on the sound expectation that the Prime Minister would be able to deliver the message consistently on the campaign trail while the party exploited the high levels of trust voters had in him, particularly when considering economic matters.

THE PLATFORM

As was the case in 2008, the 2011 Conservative platform was highly representative of the party's overall campaign strategy: long on extolling the Prime Minister's virtues and the government's record of stable economic stewardship. By necessity, it was short on new initiatives that were not already contained in the 2011 budget. The platform document was visually dominated by Harper, although much less so than in 2008. Again noticeably absent were any illustrations or mentions of cabinet ministers or other members of the Conservative team. Also important were the forty-six sidebar summary statements that appeared throughout the platform, thirty-one of which denigrated the "Ignatieff-led coalition," a message track that was supported by the advertising strategy more than any of the specific Conservative platform planks. The platform contained seven planks that were summarized into five priorities by Harper in his opening message: 1) create jobs; 2) support families; 3) eliminate the deficit; 4) make our streets safe; and 5) stand on guard for Canada — all aimed at substantiating the economic message track and the government's stable and moderately conservative record. In contrast to the Conservatives' three previous campaigns, Harper did not mince words. He boldly began by telling voters, "In this election, Canadians will choose between principled leadership and opportunism; between a stable government and a reckless coalition; between a low-tax plan for jobs and growth and a high-tax agenda that will stall our recovery, kill jobs, and set you and your family back. It's a clear choice, a real choice — and it couldn't be more important." He continued by emphasizing the stable consistency of Conservative policy, which he summarized under the slogan "a low tax plan." He concluded by admonishing Canadian voters that "now is not time for opportunistic experiments" and that only the Conservatives could deliver the stability Canadians were seeking.

The platform was released in its entirety at the end of the second week of the campaign, just prior to the debates and too late to have any significant impact on the overall campaign dynamics. It contained no broadly based "signature" policies such as the 2006 GST cut or child tax credit. Rather, the first three planks[15] supported the preferred economic agenda narrative by offering voters a plethora of micro-level tax and program initiatives. Despite releasing the first of these on the second day of the campaign, and continuing according to the pre-designed strategic plan throughout the writ period, none caught the imagination of voters or sustained enough media attention to significantly alter the course of the election. In an effort at substantiating the fiscal austerity branding, most of the "boutique" benefits being promised would not occur until the deficit was eliminated, at least three years hence, further diminishing their impact. Rather, macro themes dominated, such as the plan to eliminate the deficit and get the job done without raising taxes. This was illustrated by the second plank's focus on the government's record prior to the recession — when surpluses, debt retirement, and tax reductions were the norm — which was summarized as a set of balanced responsible policies that has allowed Canada to fight the global recession from a position of strength.

The remaining planks[16] rounded out the platform by focusing on the government's record in strengthening the military and fighting crime, popular among the base but also an appeal for urban support. The platform committed to continue with the party's democratic reform initiatives, including the government's well-worn commitment to Senate reform, Commons representation adjustments, and the end to per-vote subsidies for the parties. Each item was costed through to the 2015–16 budget year, with new spending of up to $3.1 billion by 2015. The deficit would be eliminated one year earlier than planned through revenue growth and Strategic Operating Review savings that would grow to $4 billion annually by 2014–15. Spending would grow at only 2 percent per year, down substantially from nearly 6 percent annual averages of the past five Conservative budgets.

ADVERTISING AND COMMUNICATIONS

Almost since their inception, the Conservatives have steadily built a sophisticated communications strategy and the organizational capabilities to support it. Aided by their enviable financial position and based on their long-term incremental growth strategy, they purchased ads outside of formal election periods for a variety of purposes, including attempting to sway public opinion during debates over controversial legislation.[17] They famously pummelled Liberal leader Stéphane Dion in three waves of ads almost immediately after he was elected Liberal leader and again to discredit his Green Shift in the lead-up to the 2008 election. They also ran positive ads featuring the Prime Minister, with his team in 2005 and then in a 2008 makeover attempt where he was clad in sweater vests. They ran ads as part of their all-out media blitz against the coalition. And importantly for their 2011 campaign, in the summer of 2009 they launched their "Just Visiting" attack on Ignatieff, variations of which would be used throughout the permanent campaign of the fortieth Parliament and into the election. These included depictions of the Liberal leader as a cosmopolitan intellectual interloper who only came back to Canada after a three-decade absence to satisfy his personal political ambitions. When Ignatieff returned from the summer break in 2009 declaring that Harper's time was up less than a year after the last election, he seemingly substantiated the Conservatives' narrative and the characterization began to stick. When he signalled that he intended to defeat the government no matter what was contained in the 2011 budget, the Conservatives again had the resources and the time to launch a new series of ads based on the same theme, which ran in heavy rotation until the election was called. These were supplemented with ads of Harper, "rising to the challenge," getting the job done as a trustworthy, stable manager working diligently behind his desk on behalf of Canadians while his competitors plotted for power. All of the writ-period paid advertising was national in design and scope except for a small set of ads created specifically to run in Quebec, outside of Montreal. No further province-specific regional advertising was undertaken, although the national ads often ran in heavier rotation in different areas of the country. The Conservatives rounded out their communications and advertising strategy with various web pages, including the party's main pages, a specific Ignatieff's Election page that elevated the attack on the Liberal leader, and a Tory Nation site designed largely to spur on volunteers, recruit more activists, and secure further financial donations. New to the 2011 campaign effort was the addition of Twitter accounts that were used effectively by most of the senior war room and leader's tour staff in ensuring the party's message was prominent in social media circles. After briefly experimenting with a YouTube video of the PM responding to voters' questions about the 2010 Throne Speech, the Conservatives spent little further effort developing social media beyond those elements already established as part of their DVC systems. A limited amount of polling was conducted nightly in key constituencies during the writ period, providing measures of how well the message was being received and how the anti-Ignatieff campaign was resonating, including monitoring any backlash to the negativity.

CAMPAIGN DYNAMICS

The Conservative campaign was able to stick to its overall narrative and execute a classic front-runner's strategy of limiting Harper's exposure to non-choreographed situations to avoid making unscripted mistakes. They planned to stay rigidly on message, making adjustments only when necessary or where circumstances provided opportunities to reinforce the main message, as occurred during the final week of the campaign when the narrative was tweaked to emphasize the "Socialist Dangers" at the expense of the "He Didn't Come Back for You" focus. They planned to capitalize on their reading of the public mood, primarily that Canadians cared more about the economy than ethics, and on Harper's wealth of campaign experience. Knowing that the base was highly motivated they wagered that enough new votes could be found among Canadians who were now sufficiently comfortable with Harper to trust him with a majority. Essentially, they planned five weeks of bland but rigorous reinforcement of their established branding. Or, as veteran Conservative spinner Tim Powers summarized for Postmedia: "actions speak louder than words ... so if you're preaching and asking and talking about stable and steady, you want a campaign that is stable and steady. Almost dull, if you will."[18] And it largely succeeded. Aside from a brief period during the second week when the Liberals appeared to be mounting a challenge, the Conservatives held their lead in all national public opinion polls throughout the campaign while Harper's leadership scores dwarfed those of all his rivals, at least until Layton's late-campaign surge.

This was Harper's and the Conservatives' most aggressive campaign effort yet, both in terms of the bold approach of openly appealing for a majority and in the tone and rhetoric of the messaging. After announcing the election, Harper didn't wait to leave the steps of Rideau Hall before launching into an anti-coalition attack. He continued to hammer at Ignatieff's credibility by insisting that he was not trustworthy because his current denials of coalition plans contradicted his position in 2008. Further, he had a record of changing his position as evidenced by having repeatedly brought the country to the brink of an election, only to back down. But Harper also had to account for some of his own history when the NDP and BQ, both of which had been reinforcing the Conservative messaging by continuing to muse about coalition ideas, began reminiscing about a letter they and Harper sent the Governor General in 2005 in which they sought co-operation. But after the Conservatives' war room effectively counter-spun the issue by releasing statements made at the time by each leader that clearly indicated each had declared their co-operative efforts were not a coalition, Harper remained free to effectively resurrect the issue at crucial junctures, particularly mid-campaign after Ignatieff stumbled badly while musing about post-election minority government scenarios during his one-on-one interview with Peter Mansbridge on the CBC's *The National*. Harper closed the campaign by reminding urban voters in Ontario of the Bob Rae–led NDP provincial government of the 1990s. In doing so, the Conservatives demonstrated that despite their rigid script focused on the endgame, their campaign was nimble enough to adjust to bumps along the road and effectively respond to changing circumstances.

By the second week of the campaign, as other minor events intervened and the national media were clearly tiring of the subject, Harper gradually reduced his coalition references, shifting his rhetoric to the need for the stability that could only be achieved by a Conservative majority in Parliament. He also attempted to emphasize the Conservatives' economic policies by rolling out a family income splitting taxation plan, likening it to the myriad other family tax credits that formed a large part of the government's low-tax record. He announced his intention to extend fitness tax credits and to double the amount eligible for the popular tax-free savings accounts, once the budget was balanced. Conservatives were willing to suffer the critiques associated with the delayed gratification being offered voters not only because it reinforced their low-tax messaging, but also because it provided grounding for their chastising of all of the other parties as reckless spenders. Much of that task fell to Finance Minister Jim Flaherty, who savaged the Liberal platform as unrealistic and irresponsible.

Prior to the debates that marked the traditional mid-point of the campaign, there were bumps along the road. The tight control over the leader's tour came under attack when the national media began substantiating their criticisms about their own restricted access with stories of ordinary citizens being barred or ousted from Harper rallies. After several days of distraction, Harper admitted that staff had taken security measures a step too far, apologized, and moved on, albeit while continuing with the tight security and limited media access. Other minor tempests were dispatched with similar effectiveness before they seriously disrupted the strategic plan. For example, when new concerns about the prior criminal record of a former staffer surfaced during the second week of the campaign, Harper immediately distanced himself by stating that, had he known, he would not have made the hiring decision and that he would check into the process that allowed it to happen. When a damaging draft copy of the Auditor General's report on the G8/G20 spending found its way into journalists' hands, the war room quickly ensured that other drafts were made available, obfuscating the issue while agreeing with the other parties' demands that the report be released during the campaign, knowing all the while that was not going to happen. And finally, in some cases the counter-spin was successful in reinforcing the main message track. When a Saskatoon candidate boasted about his efforts at helping to defund abortion services provided by international aid agencies, Harper reiterated his unyielding assertion that he had no intention of reopening the abortion debate. The war room also ensured that the candidate's commentary about Harper not being onside with his agenda was noted and appropriately framed. In fact, so successfully had the Conservatives distanced themselves from the social conservative agenda that several prominent activists publicly bemoaned their marginalized status within the party and the overall campaign issues matrix, further strengthening the Conservatives' case that they had no extreme right-wing hidden agenda and therefore could now be trusted with majority government power.

By mid-campaign, the Conservatives were happy with their efforts. Media characterization of the overall campaign was not kind to any of the parties, crediting them with producing an election devoid of any meaningful policy debate. As far as Conservatives were concerned, that was just fine. The contempt motion that brought the election about had been forgotten and the ethics issue had been abandoned by the Liberals after it failed to galvanize support. The Liberals had all but conceded the crime agenda when their justice critic stated they would not revoke any of the legislation that had put in place over the past five years; the Conservatives had released their platform in its entirety and were earnestly preparing for the leaders' debates confident that the experienced Harper would perform well.

The evidence about the impact of debates on the outcomes of Canadian federal elections is mixed. Debates are, however, by their nature the most unscripted part of any campaign and therefore carry considerable risks, especially for incumbent frontrunners. The Conservative debate strategy was simple: as frontrunners they did not need to entertain any risks seeking to make significant gains. Quite the contrary. They needed to ensure Harper maintained his composure while appearing calm, controlled, and prime ministerial. They coached him to not overreact to specific attacks, to keep repeating the message, and to deflect criticism until his opponents eventually turned on each other.

The setting and format of the English debate proved advantageous to the Prime Minister. The setting placed Harper on the far left side of viewers' screens, vividly supplying the imaging the campaign was seeking by separating him from the collection (coalition) of other leaders. The format allowed for repeated one-on-one exchanges between the PM and his opponents, as well as them with each other. In his exchanges, Harper looked at the other leaders when they were speaking, but when it was his turn — or when other opportunities were presented — he would turn away from the stage and look directly into the camera, no longer speaking to those in the studio but to the viewers at home, selling the Conservative message. With his opponents focused more on attacking him, or each other, than on explaining their platforms, Harper emerged from the English debate unscathed, credited as the leader most likely to have positively promoted his party's plans and appearing the least negative, thereby effectively providing a counterbalance to the party's ongoing negative advertising campaign. He was not as well received by the French debate audience, but that soon became irrelevant given more dramatic developments in Quebec.

In setting their strategy for the campaign, Conservatives envisioned four potential outcomes they could be facing as the campaign drew to a close: 1) a strong majority that included Quebec; 2) a majority with a reduced Quebec presence; 3) minority government but not more; and 4) a worst-case possibility where the only option was to funnel resources into winnable ridings in a last-ditch attempt at maintaining power. All evidence indicated that the first and fourth scenarios were not in play. What remained to be determined was minority vs. majority. Conservatives knew their situation in Quebec was not good. They had not anticipated the intensity of the collapse of Bloc support, and with it the diminishing effectiveness of their separatist threat message. Having disbanded their NDP opposition research unit they were not operationally prepared to counter Layton's Orange Surge in that province even if they wanted to. But news from Toronto was positive, where it appeared that Conservative candidates were capitalizing on the Liberal meltdown at least as much as were New Democrats. Further, the Conservatives had a response to Layton in Ontario. Amid accusations of reacting slowly, as evidenced by Harper spending a day promoting religious freedoms in foreign countries while the entire media focus shifted to the NDP developments, the Conservatives quickly produced and aired an attack ad targeting Layton's past coalition support. It indicated what would become the thrust of the Conservatives' final offensive as well as demonstrating their ability to be flexible with their message track while maintaining the consistency of the core narrative, placing them in the best strategic position to benefit at the expense of the Liberals in Toronto. They would simply emphasize the socialist threat over the separatist threat while substituting Layton for Ignatieff in the leadership narrative.

During the final week of campaigning the party was determined to stay on message, not get drawn into controversial distractions, stay out of trouble, and generally avoid making any unscripted news. They would rely on their superior organization to mobilize Conservative voters by playing to the fears of an NDP-led coalition, hoping the changing dynamics would allow them to win enough splits to eke out a majority. But with the Liberals continuing to hemorrhage votes, and polls showing a coalition gaining acceptance, Harper was forced to more fully focus on Layton. He ratcheted up his rhetoric by reminding voters that an NDP vote was not a protest vote. It was a vote for an NDP-led government with Jack Layton as prime minister. The move was somewhat risky given Layton's improving leadership ratings, and reminiscent of Harper's final 2008 push where in the last days of that campaign he uttered for the first time the phrase "Prime Minister Stéphane Dion" in an attempt at crystallizing the leadership question. But Conservatives remained convinced that when it came to salient issues, primarily the economy, stability-seeking voters would choose Harper's credentials over Layton's. They also had a week of campaigning left to sell their tweaked narrative. Harper urged conservative-leaning Liberal voters in Ontario to remember how they accidentally elected Bob Rae premier by way of a collective protest vote, and the consequences of that surprise outcome. He brought new Toronto mayor Rob Ford into the Conservative campaign to remind Toronto voters of how they embraced conservatism in the recent municipal elections. On a last day coast-to-coast dash he upped the ante by chastising Layton over his apparent desire to send the country into another constitutional quagmire. Despite receiving the vast majority of endorsements from Canada's newspaper editorial boards, Harper's final pitch was cast in the frame of a late, somewhat desperate, Hail Mary pass by commentators who were generally unimpressed with the Conservative campaign. They were particularly critical of what they perceived to be its lack of focus on expansion, calling it a blown opportunity based on an excessively timid and negative messaging strategy. Most analysts — aided by the plethora of notoriously inaccurate seat projections — predicted a status-quo result and the beginning of the end for Harper's tenure as prime minister. Once again, they underestimated Harper as he and his campaign team proved all doubters wrong.

CONSERVATIVE RESULTS FROM THE
2011 ELECTION CAMPAIGN

The 2011 Conservative campaign succeeded nationally (electing members in every province of the country) and in all regions where its organizational capacity and policy appeal were most prepared and could be efficiently executed. It stumbled in Quebec, the only region where the party did not have the capacity or message track to capitalize on changing voter preferences. Designed to hold the base while seeking gains in targeted ridings and sub-segments of the electorate, the Conservative organization efficiently turned marginal gains in vote share into large seat gains. On less than a 2 percent gain in total support from 2008, and only 3.3 percent better than in 2006, the Conservatives added twenty-two seats to their 2008 total (forty-two more than in 2006), easily achieving a majority. Although somewhat sullied by the one-seat decline in B.C. and the halving of its Quebec caucus to just five members, the Conservatives held or added to their vote and seat totals in every other province and in the territories. Gains in Ontario, concentrated in Toronto, put the Conservatives over the top and demonstrated that majority government is possible without winning substantial support in Quebec.

The Conservatives' hopes to hold their cluster of eleven seats in Quebec, and possibly pick up a few more close wins, were not realized. The party's vote share dropped by more than 5 percent, it was predictably shut out of Montreal, but also lost all its Quebec City seats and three cabinet ministers. While hardly the biggest loser in Quebec, the CPC clearly has considerable work to do in the province if it wants to claim the mantle of a truly national party with strong support in every region — a claim few Canadian governments have been able to make over the past half century but one that is nonetheless often portrayed as a requirement for a dynastic party. But the absence of a large Quebec contingent within the minimum winning electoral base need not substantially detract from its long-term geographical and ideological stability. In fact, it may add to it.[19] Conservative parties have traditionally courted some element of the Quebec electorate in order to obtain power but have also typically found accommodating it problematic. Too often, attempts at recognizing the province's cultural or social differences have fallen short or been jet-tisoned because they conflicted with the expectations of supporters in other parts of the country. If the absence of a significant Quebec presence within its caucus leads Conservatives to expend less effort attempting such accommodations and more time building a small but stable sup-port base in a province that is not naturally conservatively inclined — as they did in formerly hostile Toronto — they have the potential to achieve more respectable, if not exceptional, results.

More important for Conservatives is their successful tapping into the new Ontario-West axis of electoral power,[20] described in much of the immediate post-election analysis as a coalition of the have-provinces. And while the 2011 results certainly lend credence to this analysis — the Conservatives won nearly a majority of the total votes west of the Ottawa River — it is overly dismissive of Conservative successes in the Atlantic region, where they won fourteen of the thirty-two seats, a requirement for achieving the majority and a net gain of five from 2006. It appears that in the Maritimes, particularly New Brunswick (eight of its ten seats went Conservative), there exists a sufficiently strong conservative core based on the red-Tory culture inherited from the legacy of the PC party and nurtured by the likes of that party's last leader, Peter MacKay.

Western Canada, Reform-Alliance's former fiefdom, continued to constitute the bedrock of the Conservative base. This was nowhere more true than in the Prime Minister's home province of Alberta, where the party devoured more than two-thirds of all votes on their way to win-ning all but one of the province's twenty-eight seats. They were almost as strong on the rest of the prairies, capturing more than half of the votes in each of Saskatchewan and Manitoba, winning all but four of those provinces' combined twenty-eight seats. Despite being subjected to considerable local criticism for conducting comparatively little cam-paigning in the region, Conservatives gambled (correctly) that prairie voters would remain loyal while they focused their efforts elsewhere. In British Columbia, the status quo prevailed. They only marginally increased their proportion of the vote and lost a seat in the process. Winning twenty-one of thirty-six B.C. seats was a disappointment, but only from the comparative perspective of the party's prairie performance and its desire to improve in a province where it has consistently won half the seats since the 2003 merger but has never achieved the success of Reform-Alliance, which won nearly four out of every five B.C. seats (twenty-seven of thirty-four) at its apex in 1997. The party also won two of the three territorial seats by holding Nunavut and adding the Yukon. The seventy-four of ninety-five western seats returned as Conservatives constitute 45 percent of the government caucus, including the prime minister and powerful cabinet colleagues, and ensure that westerners are again represented at the centre of Canadian federal politics, possibly more so than at any other time in Canadian political history. Nowhere have Conservative successes been greater than in Ontario. From a base of only two legacy-party seats (both Alliance) won in the 2000 election, Conservatives captured twenty-four seats in 2004, added sixteen to that total in 2006, and eleven more in 2008. In picking up an additional twenty-two Ontario seats in 2011, the Conservatives won more than two-thirds of the total. They swept the "905 region" around Toronto, winning all but one of the twenty-two suburban ridings. Within the city, where no conservative party's candidates had won since 1988, they claimed nine victories, unceremoniously unseating Liberals such as Ken Dryden in York Centre and Joe Volpe in Eglinton-Lawrence. But Toronto was not the only important urban Ontario story for the Conservatives. They held seats first won in 2006 or 2008 and made gains in other, once impregnable Ontario cities. They captured three London ridings, swept Kitchener-Waterloo, and won all but three seats in the Ottawa region.

That the new Ontario base has been built over a series of elections rather than erupting as a sudden event is an indication of the potential long-term stability of the electoral coalition. By adding Ontario urbanites, including many new Canadians, to the existing base of support during a time of considerable economic stress, the Conservatives appear to have carved out for themselves a relatively stable base within the electorate outside of Quebec. Based on its strengths in the fastest growing areas of the country, their electoral support now meets the requirements of a minimum winning majority coalition. As long as division amongst the parties on their left continues, the Conservatives are indeed on the precipice of maintaining power for a generation.

CONCLUSION

The 2011 federal election campaign and the pre-writ campaign that preceded it produced a strong, stable majority Conservative government, the first in twenty-three years. Based on a long-term strategic plan and supported by a formidable political machine, the Conservatives' returns demonstrated that the foundations of a majority government can be achieved primarily from the Ontario and Western electorate without requiring significant wins in Quebec, a novel feature of the new electoral alignment that can only be furthered by the assigning of more Commons seats to Ontario, Alberta, and British Columbia. The party base appears solid primarily because it was built systematically, over time, not on a surge of potentially unstable support that might dissipate when times get tough and enthusiasms cool, a prospect the NDP may yet have to confront. Rather, the bulk of Conservative voters have a habit of remaining relatively loyal from one election to the next, and although Quebec remains a challenge (as it is for all the federal parties), in the rest of the country the Conservatives are organizationally strong, supported by a stable and loyal base, and well poised to press their advantages.

Much of this success is owed to Stephen Harper, who methodically transformed the warring factions of Canadian conservatism into the most formidable political organization in the country. Since its creation in 2003, it has systematically identified its targeted voters, built a narrative that appealed to their interests, and relentlessly pursued them on their way to a first majority. By using some of the most relentless messaging techniques ever employed in Canadian federal politics, Conservatives turned marginal vote gains in the 2011 election into maximum seat gains for the forty-first Parliament. They have successfully inoculated themselves against many of their legacy parties' perceived weaknesses, holding the bulk of their support while incrementally adding new voters by providing Canadians with a competent, flexible, moderately conservative government while in office. Their success in the 2011 election significantly furthers their ambitions to become the dominant federal party of the twenty-first century. The 2011 results also ensure that, going forward, the Conservative Party of Canada is in a better position than any of its rivals to consistently compete for power and may indeed be well be on its way to becoming Canada's next "natural governing party."

NOTES

1. This essay reflects, in part, interviews with a number of people associated with the Conservative Party's campaign. We have committed to not identify our interviewees. We sincerely thank all of those who consented to interviews for their time, insights, and help in making this a more accurate and complete analysis of the campaign.

2. See Sidney Blumenthal, *The Permanent Campaign: Inside the World of Elite Political Operatives* (Boston: Beacon Press, 1980) for the origins of the term; and Norman Ornstein and Thomas Mann, eds., *The Permanent Campaign and its Future* (Washington: American Enterprise Institute and the Brookings Institute, 2000).

3. See Faron Ellis and Peter Woolstencroft, "New Conservatives, Old Realities," in *The Canadian General Election of 2004*, eds. Jon H. Pammett and Christopher Dornan (Toronto: Dundurn Press, 2004), 66–105; and Tom Flanagan, *Harper's Team: Behind the Scenes in the Conservative Rise to Power, 2nd edition* (Montreal and Kingston: McGill-Queen's University Press, 2009).

4. See Tom Flanagan, "Something Blue: Conservative Organization in an Era of Permanent Campaign," paper presented to the CPSA annual meeting, June 2010.

5. David Coletto, Harold J. Jansen, Lisa Young, "Stratarchical Party Organization and Party Finance in Canada," in *Canadian Journal of Political Science*, 44:1 (March 2011): 111–36.

6. Three to date: Montreal in 2005, Winnipeg in 2008, and Ottawa in 2011.

7. Although some disagreement exists as to the extent of the inroads the party made amongst new Canadians, most analysts agree there has been progress. See Stuart Soroka, Fred Cutler, Dietlind Stolle, and Patrick Fournier, "Capturing Change (and Stability) in the 2011 Campaign," in *Policy Options*, June 2011, 70–77.

8. See Tom Flanagan and Harold Jansen, "Election Campaigns under Canada's Party Finance Laws," in *The Canadian Federal Election of 2008*, eds. Jon H. Pammett and Christopher Dornan (Toronto: Dundurn Press, 2009), 194–216.

9. See Elections Canada at *www.elections.ca*.

10. See Kristen Shane, "Tories Running Leaner War Room, Focused on Winning Majority," *The Hill Times*, April 4, 2011.

11. See Marjorie LeBreton, "Thirty-Seven Days 'In the Bubble' with the National Media," in *Policy Options* (June 2011): 78–81 for her reflections on the media and the Conservative leader's tour.

12. Department of Finance, *Budget 2009: Canada's Economic Action Plan*, *www.budget. gc.ca/*.

13. See Faron Ellis, "21st Century Conservatives Can Continue to Succeed," in *Crosscurrents: Contemporary Political Issues, 7th edition*, eds. Paul Barker and Mark Charlton (Toronto: Nelson, forthcoming 2012).

14. See Geoff Norquay, "The 'Ballot Question' in the 2011 Election: Two Wins, Two Losses," in *Policy Options* (June 2011): 47–51.

15. "Here for Jobs and Growth, Here to Eliminate the Deficit and Here for Hard-Working Families."

16. "Here to Stand on Guard for Canada, Here for Law-Abiding Canadians, Here for Communities and Industries, Here for Integrity and Accountability."

17. Tom Flanagan, "Political Communication and the 'Permanent Campaign,'" in *How Canadians Communicate, III*, eds. David Taras, Maria Bakardjieva, and Frits Pannekoek (Calgary: University of Calgary Press, forthcoming 2012).

18. As quoted by Mark Kennedy, Postmedia, in "Teflon Harper's Secret Campaign Weapon: Familiarity," *Vancouver Sun*, April 21, 2011.

19. See Tom Flanagan, "The Emerging Conservative Coalition," in *Policy Options* (June 2011): 101–03.

20. See for example Andrew Coyne, "A New Power Couple: The West is in and Ontario has Joined it in an Unprecedented Realignment of Canadian Politics," in *Maclean's*, May 16, 2011, 60–63.

CHAPTER 3

The Disappearing Liberals: Caught in the Crossfire
Brooke Jeffrey

When Liberal leader Michael Ignatieff introduced a no-confidence motion in the House of Commons on March 23, 2011,
he declared, "We believe that the moment has come for Canadians to
make a choice here between the responsible, progressive, compassionate
choice of the Liberal Party or the irresponsible and undemocratic path
of the Conservative government." Two days later, the federal election
Ignatieff had orchestrated was underway.

If the Liberals had any doubts about the wisdom of their strategy, those
doubts were not obvious in the early days of the campaign. Liberal MPs and
candidates declared themselves ready and eager to take on Prime Minister
Stephen Harper over his lengthy record of obstruction, contempt for
Parliament, and abuse of power, convinced they had successfully defined
the campaign issue. Ignatieff's advisers were publicly optimistic that his
performance during the campaign would surprise and impress Canadians.
Privately, they were also convinced the NDP's dismal polling numbers over
the past several months meant voters would abandon that party in droves
for the Liberals, as the only way to defeat the Conservatives. Moreover, the
party was ready with a solid platform and a well-organized campaign on
the ground. This would not be a repeat of the Liberals' inept performance
in 2008. If winning a majority was out of the question, a minority was certainly within the realm of possibility. At the very least, the party would
improve its standing in the House of Commons and be ready to bring
down the resulting Harper minority when the time was right. Perhaps
equally important, Michael Ignatieff's leadership would be secure.

The speed with which those well-laid plans unravelled and the extent
of the party's collapse were foreseen by no one. In the early days of the

campaign it even appeared the Liberals might have reason to think their strategy was working. Their leader was performing well, exceeding expectations. Their organization seemed solid. Their platform had been released to moderately positive reviews. Yet their standing in the almost daily flood of public opinion polls did not reflect the positive response the Liberals were experiencing on the ground. By the midway point in the campaign, the numbers for the three major parties had barely changed. Many observers described the election as a non-event. When movement finally *did* occur it was in an entirely unanticipated direction, delivering a majority for the Harper Conservatives and official opposition status for the NDP. But this precipitous change in direction was neither as sudden nor as unpredictable as many believed. In fact, the failure of the Liberals to make any headway in the election was the direct result of the party's many sins of omission and commission over the previous two years. Given the extent and significance of the Liberal collapse, a review of these problems is essential to put the party's failure in context. Indeed, it can be argued that the Liberals were defeated before they even reached the starting gate.

EARLY WARNING SIGNS

When Michael Ignatieff was appointed interim leader in December 2008, the Liberals were in turmoil. In the aftermath of Stéphane Dion's failed attempt at forming a coalition with the NDP — a plan thwarted by the Prime Minister's prorogation of Parliament — they believed they could not afford to wait for the party's scheduled May 2009 convention to replace Dion. Nor did they think they could afford another leadership race. As a result, Ignatieff's leadership was merely confirmed at the May meeting, where he was unopposed, Toronto MP Bob Rae and New Brunswick MP Dominic Leblanc having dropped out of the "race" before it got underway. Similarly, Ignatieff's key supporter, Toronto lawyer Alf Apps, was acclaimed as party president.

The challenges facing Ignatieff and the Liberals in the aftermath of the October 2008 election were substantial. As the chapter on the

Liberals in the previous edition of this series noted, "The party's organization, funding and policy problems abound ... the stakes have rarely been higher and the next few years will be critical for the Liberals." The chapter concluded, "[T]here are a number of tremors in the Liberal heartland [Toronto], and in other Liberal strongholds across Ontario, that suggest a tectonic plate movement could be possible if the Liberals are not able to reinvent themselves in time."[1]

Ignatieff and his team were aware of these many challenges. A new order was quickly established in both the parliamentary and extra-parliamentary wings of the party. At party headquarters, Ignatieff organizer Rocco Rossi, a professional fundraiser from Toronto, was appointed National Director in early 2009 with a mandate to improve the party's finances. This was a top priority in light of the reduced public funding the party was receiving due to their decreased share of the popular vote in the 2008 election. A start on improved fundraising had been made after the December 2006 convention, when the party finally established a national membership list. But donations during Dion's leadership had plummeted to a mere $4.3 million in 2007, rising to only $5.9 million in 2008 despite the fact that it was an election year.

Rossi's tenure proved highly productive. In 2009, the party saw a dramatic increase in annual revenue to $9.5 million, and an all-important increase in individual donors to 37,876. However, Rossi abruptly announced his resignation at the end of the year in order to run in the Toronto mayoral race. He was soon replaced with another expert fundraiser, Ian Mackay, but the party's finances once again deteriorated, leading many to speculate that Ignatieff's leadership problems might be playing a role. In 2010, total revenue from fundraising was only $6.6 million. Even more significant, the Conservatives' coffers were full to overflowing at $17.4 million, or more than two and a half times the Liberals' total.

A similar scenario unfolded as Ignatieff attempted to rebuild the party organization for what many considered an imminent election. Having announced that his seventy-seven sitting MPs would be protected from nomination challenges, the new leader then set about appointing provincial chairs and campaign organizers. Nominations in non-held ridings were to be completed by August 2009. In Quebec, where a Liberal revival was considered not just likely but crucial to any hopes the party might have of returning to power, veteran MP Denis Coderre was given the task and soon began delivering candidates for the party across the province.

However, the promising start quickly stalled in light of Coderre's decision to appoint a new face in the former Liberal stronghold of Outremont, against the express wishes of its riding association and the former MP, Chrétien Justice Minister Martin Cauchon. A firestorm of controversy ensued while Ignatieff dithered for more than a week before finally overruling his Quebec lieutenant in favour of Cauchon. That decision, in turn, led to Coderre's resignation at a press conference where he accused Ignatieff of being run by a group of unilingual anglophones from Toronto. Privately, many Liberal MPs agreed with his assessment. One went so far as to exclaim publicly, "We're going to hell in a handbasket. This is like the time just before the 1988 election with John Turner!"[2] Certainly it would have negative consequences for the party in a future election. With the Conservatives out of the running in that province, and the Liberals beginning to make headway as the federalist alternative once more, this was a significant blow.

Ignatieff's efforts at organizational reform on the parliamentary side also produced mixed results. His first target was the Office of the Leader of the Opposition (OLO), which had been hopelessly disorganized under Dion. Senior Ignatieff supporter Ian Davey was appointed Chief of Staff and brought with him Communications Director Jill Fairbrother and Principal Secretary Dan Brock. These appointments restored a measure of professionalism and order to the leader's office, but there were some obvious shortcomings as well. Within months the new team was coming under increasing criticism for its glaring lack of political experience and Toronto-centric perspective.

Things came to a head after the Coderre vs. Cauchon debacle. Caucus unrest forced Ignatieff to take action, and by the end of October Ian Davey and his colleagues were gone. Davey was replaced by former Chrétien adviser Peter Donolo, to the visible relief of veteran Liberals, who believed Donolo's experience would "help revive sagging Liberal fortunes." Even more revealing were the comments of one senior Liberal who noted Donolo was responsible for "transforming the image of Jean Chrétien as yesterday's man," evidently concluding that Ignatieff also was in need of an image makeover.[3]

As for the leader's relations with his caucus, they too had apparently started out well. His appointment of a so-called kitchen cabinet of back-bench MPs to advise him was generally well received. Unlike Paul Martin's overpowering PMO or the solitary rule of Stéphane Dion, the Ignatieff OLO pledged to be consultative and responsive to backbenchers' con-cerns.[4] But the membership of this de facto tactics committee did raise some eyebrows. It was composed predominantly of Ignatieff leadership supporters, and most also had been Martin supporters. Some members with key posts — such as Whip Rodger Cuzner and the committee's chair, Albina Guarnieri — were viewed as lacking the requisite combination of skills and ability for their tasks, while several experienced and better known members of the caucus were conspicuous by their absence.

However, these concerns paled in comparison with the humili-ating defeat of the Liberals' own opposition day motion on maternal health issues, caused by caucus defections. The "own goal" fiasco forced Ignatieff to admit there were "internal issues" the caucus would have to deal with. Others criticized the Whip for his failure to alert the leader and the sponsor of the motion, Bob Rae, that they did not have the num-bers.[5] A similar embarrassment occurred on the vote to eliminate part of the gun registry, a vote that the Liberals opposed but that eight of Ignatieff's backbenchers supported even though the leader had pleaded for caucus solidarity.

Shortly after, Ignatieff was forced to "clarify" his position on medi-care at a meeting of the national caucus, having first appeared to support Quebec Premier Jean Charest's plans to impose user fees. Two months later, Ignatieff was again forced by his caucus to reverse himself, this time over tougher rules for refugee determination. His support for a bipar-tisan deal with the governing Conservatives was not shared by most of his backbenchers. One MP told reporters that Ignatieff "is more conservative than his caucus on external affairs" and that "where we get elected, in the cities, if we tilt to the right on this stuff we're going to lose our base."[6]

Ignatieff's increasingly shaky hold on his caucus was partly due to internal conflict arising from unresolved leadership questions in 2006.

But caucus disunity was also part of a broader issue. As someone who had been deliberately recruited by Apps and Davey to lead the party out of the wilderness after Stéphane Dion's pyrrhic defeat, Ignatieff's *de facto* coronation had not allowed either the caucus or the party rank and file to learn his views on the issues. And, much like Paul Martin, after barely a year as leader Ignatieff was increasingly seen not as a saviour of the party but as an albatross around its neck.

THE LEADERSHIP ISSUE

The question of what Michael Ignatieff — and hence the Liberal Party — stood for was raised innumerable times between his appointment as interim leader and his party's defeat two years later. Whether he was changing his mind on a policy issue or the timing of an election call, the underlying problem inevitably seemed to come down to a lack of conviction, or an inability to communicate that conviction, about what he and the Liberal Party stood for. This problem was reflected in public opinion polls throughout his leadership. In the early days, Ignatieff's lack of political experience provided some explanation for his difficulties. Hence the decision in early February 2009 to support the Conservatives' stimulus budget while placing the government on "probation" by demanding a series of interim progress reports. It was a strategy designed to allow the party time to organize and the leader time to learn the ropes. Their plan now was to force an election in the fall, coinciding with the October economic update and the Conservatives' own fixed election date legislation.

In retrospect, the Liberals may have missed their best opportunity to improve their electoral fortunes by deciding not to launch a June 2009 election. Virtually tied in the polls nationally, the possibility that the party might have made gains during a campaign cannot be ruled out. Throughout April and May, various Ekos and Ipsos Reid polls continued to show the Liberals ahead of the Conservatives in Ontario. Ignatieff's approval rating of 50 percent was also substantially higher than Harper's at 38 percent.

Certainly the delay did not help. Ignatieff made little progress over the summer. His confirmation as leader at the Liberal convention in Vancouver afforded him a golden opportunity to show Canadians who he was and where he wanted to take the country. Instead, his lacklustre acceptance speech kept them guessing. The simultaneous publication of his book, *True Patriot Love*, did nothing to close that gap. Worse still, after the obligatory visit to the Calgary Stampede, Ignatieff essentially disappeared from public view for the summer. His one newsworthy activity — travelling to England to deliver a speech in honour of his academic mentor, Isaiah Berlin — was something the Conservatives eagerly capitalized on to reinforce their message that Ignatieff was "just visiting" Canada.

A Strategic Council poll in early August 2009 revealed Ignatieff's initial boost to the Liberals' fortunes had disappeared. They were now two points behind, and the trend line was down. Even more unsettling, the party was back to the same level of support as in June 2008 under Stéphane Dion. Strategic Council spokesperson Peter Donolo declared the Liberals "have plateaued," and underlined that the party had lost its traditional advantage with women, youth, and urban voters. One of Ignatieff's own advisers admitted "they don't know who this guy is and what he stands for."[7]

Despite these setbacks, many Liberals believed it was essential for them to force an election in the fall. Privately, Bob Rae told colleagues he believed the Liberals would lose all credibility if they did not bring down the government soon. Leaving the Harper Conservatives in power any longer would only reinforce their image as the governing party and allow them to take credit for an eventual recovery. At the same time, it would cause the Liberals to look weak. Many MPs also shared the view of Ignatieff's advisers, who argued when the writ was dropped and the lights came up, the leader would shine. Meanwhile party pollster Michael Marzolini told the caucus that 46 percent of Canadians wanted to see either a Liberal minority or majority government. As a result, Ignatieff announced in late August, "Time's up": the Liberals would no longer prop up the government on confidence votes.

Almost immediately, the Liberals' fortunes began to fade. According to Ipsos Reid, the Conservatives returned to Parliament in September 2009 with the support of 39 percent of decided voters, nine points ahead of the Liberals. In addition, the Ipsos poll revealed that 71 percent of Canadians did not believe an election was necessary at the time, and 54 percent said they would blame Ignatieff if one were called. Luckily for the Liberals, the NDP and the Bloc decided to change their own strategies (the NDP was now at only 12 percent), keeping the government in power through the fall by supporting legislation. Ignatieff was again made to look weak and indecisive as the media mercilessly ridiculed him for his forced retreat. With the party's support continuing to erode, the leader was obliged to replace his initial team of advisers in OLO and bring in Peter Donolo as Chief of Staff in mid-November.

The leader's image was high on the agenda of most of the caucus. Peter Donolo announced his task was to help the leader "sharpen the message" and "toughen up." Pollster Nik Nanos commented shortly after Donolo took up his new duties that the Liberals would have to "remake" Ignatieff, and it would not be an easy task. Nanos argued that Ignatieff needed at a minimum to provide Canadians with his vision, a sentiment echoed by newly minted Quebec lieutenant Marc Garneau, who told reporters the leader needed to communicate a positive message: "We've got to say not only why this is wrong, but what we would do instead."[8]

Ignatieff's approval ratings continued to fall. In February 2010, after hammering away at the Prime Minister's contempt for Parliament during the prorogation, Ignatieff's approval rating was at 10 percent while Harper's stabilized at 25 percent. After the House of Commons returned, the situation deteriorated. By May the Liberals' support had fallen to 25 percent and Ignatieff's leadership was described as being on life-support. Many Liberal MPs and party officials admitted privately that his hold on the leadership would have been threatened if there were any viable alternatives. One commented, "We really want him to succeed because we know we can't change the leader before the next election."[9]

THE LIBERAL EXPRESS AND IGNATIEFF'S SECOND CHANCE

It was in these dire circumstances that the leader's advisers conceived of a cross-country bus tour over the 2010 summer recess. Their objectives were to educate the leader in political campaigning in preparation for an eventual election and, more importantly, to expose "the real Michael Ignatieff" to large numbers of Canadians. On both counts the tour was an unqualified success. Well organized, well received on the ground, and benefiting from almost universally positive media coverage, the Liberal Express was considered a major coup by Liberal advisers, the caucus, and party officials.

Yet in the crucial court of public opinion, the tour did not have an impact. In late July, after nearly a month on the road, and with the government under attack over its scrapping of the long-form census, G20 spending, and security issues, the Liberals had only increased their share of the popular vote by 2 percent, to 29 percent, while the Conservatives held steady at 35 percent.

Although some Liberals concluded not enough Canadians had been paying attention over the summer, others worried they had seen enough and were simply not impressed. "He just doesn't seem able to connect with Canadians," one frustrated adviser commented. One reason for this disconnect was arguably Ignatieff's lack of a broadly defined vision of a Liberal government or a Liberal Canada. Instead of talking about Liberal values, Ignatieff focused on criticizing the Harper government. When asked what he had learned from the tour, he replied, "The Canadians I met are saying, 'We don't trust this government, we don't like this government.'" Then he told reporters, "They want us to hold them to account this fall ... and that's what we're going to do." But pollster Frank Graves of Ekos argued this was only one part of the equation. "They [the Liberals] need to talk about values," he said, and "they need to connect the value differences ... to concrete, costed choices."[10]

This perspective was shared by a number of political pundits and academics whose frustration with the Liberal leader was almost palpable. Political scientist Nelson Wiseman lamented, "Ignatieff excels at glittering generalities."[11] His colleague Denis Smith's thoughtful analysis concluded the Liberal leader was unconvincing because he was acting a part. "The public is uncertain about him because what we see is the actor playing at politics, or the academic thinking about it, not the politician doing it."[12] Columnist Susan Riley put it more bluntly, labelling Ignatieff a dilettante. "What central idea led him to politics? What burning ambition for his country keeps him in a job that is clearly less than appealing? All these [image makeover] launches later, it is still difficult to say ..."[13] As author Ron Graham concluded, "Despite his earlier run for the prize, Ignatieff remained an unknown quantity, a stranger in our midst.... he kept repeating that political leadership was about storytelling without ever telling us a story; he said that Canadian unity needed a narrative but didn't articulate one."[14]

The disheartening lack of progress after the tour continued during the fall sitting of the House. In November 2010, a Harris Decima poll found that 50 percent of Canadians wanted the Conservatives to replace Stephen Harper as their leader, but fully 64 percent wanted the Liberals to replace Michael Ignatieff. Even among Liberal supporters, some 59 percent agreed that they would like a new leader.

The response to these revelations by Ignatieff and his supporters was twofold: first, they argued the negative image was due primarily to the Conservative attack ads; second, they remained convinced that the Liberals and their leader would do better once the writ was dropped and an election campaign began. While the second point could hardly be verified in advance, the role of the Conservative attack ads was undeniable. Yet the Liberals themselves had failed to take the ads seriously enough, soon enough.

THE LIBERALS' RESPONSE TO THE
CONSERVATIVE ATTACK ADS

Given the widespread perception that Conservative attack ads launched against Stéphane Dion had caused considerable damage, the Ignatieff Liberals' failure to respond quickly and decisively to similar ads is more than a little puzzling. In Dion's case, the most frequently offered explanation for Liberal inaction was a lack of money. This was particularly salient since there is no limit on such spending outside of election campaigns. As a result, the Conservatives, with their huge financial advantage, could blanket the media with attack ads as soon as Dion was elected leader.

Yet, fully cognizant of that precedent, the Ignatieff Liberals did little to counter the negative ad blitz launched against him by the Conservatives in early 2009, even though lack of money was apparently not a concern. In fact, one of the earliest comments on the ads came from National Director Rocco Rossi, who claimed he was delighted because they were encouraging infuriated Liberals to give generously to the party. Meanwhile the leader dismissed the ads as a desperation measure by a government unable to handle serious issues. "Is that serious government? Is that serious politics? That's the kind of government we've got," Ignatieff told an audience in Toronto in May 2009 while repeating an earlier threat to force an election over the government's handling of changes to EI legislation.[15]

The Liberals were determined to take the high road, focusing on policy rather than personalities. Certainly the Conservatives' ads contained an unprecedented personal slant, painting Ignatieff as an elitist snob and an opportunist who was out of touch by virtue of having been out of the country for thirty years. Their "just visiting" series was viewed by many advertising experts as particularly effective. Ignatieff's response was less effective. Instead of tackling the accusations head-on and explaining why he had come back to Canada — another golden opportunity to expand on his vision for the country — he relied instead on the lesser argument that many Canadians travel and work abroad. "Does that make them any less Canadian?" he asked rhetorically.

However, behind the scenes there was increasing concern about the potential impact of the ads. Liberal Senator Dennis Dawson tabled a bill in the Senate to limit pre-writ political advertising, and to count any such spending as an election expense in the three-month period before an election. Dawson argued the bill addressed a "real gap" in the Conservatives' fixed election date legislation, since everyone would know when an election would be held. He also noted that former Chief

Electoral Officer Jean-Pierre Kingsley had made the same point in hearings about the Conservatives' legislation in 2006. However, Secretary of State for Democratic Reform Stephen Fletcher dismissed Dawson's proposal as "undemocratic, un-Canadian, unworkable and intellectually corrupt." Fletcher went on to say, "The advertisements are obviously hurting the Liberal Party and this is just an irrational, hypocritical reaction to the information commercials that the Conservatives are running."[16]

When the Liberals finally did respond by producing their own ads, they were bland and impersonal. Each ad ended with the vague slogan "We can do better," which was heavily criticized, but even more criticism was reserved for the setting, which inexplicably featured Ignatieff in casual dress standing in the middle of a forest. The efficacy of the Liberal ads was a moot point, however, since the election did not take place that fall. Instead, drifting steadily downward in the polls, the Liberals made their way through 2010 and did not start to ratchet up the election rhetoric again until January 2011. At that point the Conservatives promptly launched a second round of attack ads, this time painting Ignatieff not only as a self-serving carpetbagger ("Ignatieff, he didn't come back for you") but also warning of his alleged plan to form a coalition with the opposition parties and bring the Conservatives down if they won another minority. "Ignatieff and his ruthless coalition. He did it before," the ads claimed incorrectly, "and he'll do it again."

Ignatieff criticized these ads almost immediately, referring to them as "personal, lowball attacks." He also denied supporting a coalition. But in almost the same breath he went on to urge voters to pay attention to issues the Conservatives were not addressing, and concluded by asking Canadians whether they were better off after five years of Conservative government. In short, he delivered a mixed message that failed to stem the coalition accusations and essentially ignored the question of why he had come back to Canada.

Polling results suggested the Conservative ads had been highly effective. "The negative attack ads launched by the Conservatives did their job," pollster Nik Nanos said. Support for the Liberals had fallen, but, even more significant, Ignatieff's approval rating had dropped sharply. By the end of February 2011 it had fallen to 13.6 percent. This was a particularly significant development since Stephen Harper continued to be disliked by many Canadians. With Harper's unimpressive 34.5 percent rating, Conservative organizers confided they believed it was imperative that the Liberal leader be seen as less attractive.[17]

One month later, the Conservatives released an ad that attacked Ignatieff's family, implying Ignatieff came from a privileged background rather than the immigrant origins he claimed. Incensed, Ignatieff described the ads as "beyond the bounds of decency." They spurred the Liberals to prepare their own version of more personal attack ads, and to develop a theme that they believed would become the election question. The prime minister was accused of being not simply arrogant but undemocratic and an abusive bully with no respect for Parliament or its institutions. "Is this your Canada or Harper's?" the ads asked. One political pundit argued, "This is what the Liberals should have done years ago. It may be too late now."[18]

THE POLICY VACUUM

The Liberal Party of Canada was successful in the past because it was always able to reinvent itself to meet changing circumstances. It did this not by abandoning its traditional values, but by fashioning policies that reflected those values and yet were appropriate to the issues of the day. With Liberal leaders often in place for more than a decade and the party usually in power, the Liberals tended to update their policies at the same time they changed their leader. This pattern of policy and leadership renewal was epitomized by the Pearson/Kent reform process,[19] a period with which Michael Ignatieff — a historian by training and a self-described Pearsonian Liberal — was intimately familiar. The Liberals failed to carry out this policy renewal in the post-Chrétien era. Changing leaders three times in five years, there was virtually no opportunity for serious policy development.

Equally significant, the new leader and his advisers, as well as much of the caucus, appeared to have learned the wrong lessons from the 2008 election debacle. Despite considerable evidence to the contrary, they were convinced that Stéphane Dion's Green Shift and the Liberal platform were responsible for their defeat, instead of the many other crucial factors such as Dion's poor image and lack of leadership skills, the ineptness of the Liberal campaign, or the lack of money for advertising. Convinced that Dion had steered the party too far to the left, the Liberals were determined to avoid being seen as left-leaning, despite expert advice that this was precisely the direction they should be heading in order to succeed. Similarly, having concluded Dion's Green Shift was too far ahead of public opinion, the Liberals seemed afraid to discuss anything related to the environment, to the point that Ignatieff himself spoke in defence of the oil sands on several occasions.

In much the same fashion, the Liberals appeared to be virtually paralyzed by the Conservative narrative concerning taxes and deficits. They were not prepared to take the bold step of declaring that eventually taxes would have to go up. Nor were they ready to argue that on occasion a deficit might be the better alternative. In September 2009, still anticipating a fall election, Michael Ignatieff announced his platform for the "economy of tomorrow," which he confidently declared would involve eliminating the $50-billion deficit *without raising taxes*. When asked by reporters how this could be done he said they would have to wait and see, an approach that earned him ridicule.[20] By the spring of 2011, the only elaboration on this pledge was to declare he would not proceed with the Conservatives' scheduled tax cut for corporations.

This self-imposed set of restrictions — ruling out in advance any increase in taxes, emphasis on sustainable development, or policies that might appear left-wing — left the Liberals with a greatly reduced field of policy options. It also left them unable to address some of the most important issues of the day, on which Canadians were repeatedly telling pollsters they wanted to see action.

Then there were traditional "liberal" issues on which the Liberals were strangely silent. The Liberals were not willing to oppose the government's increasingly draconian law and order agenda, lest they be labelled soft on crime. Their apparently deliberate avoidance of any discussion of Quebec, national unity, or federalism was even more astonishing, given their traditional advantage over the Conservatives and the NDP on those issues. Last but hardly least, the Liberals were increasingly inclined to avoid discussion of many foreign policy issues, having found themselves embroiled in internal conflict over Israel and the Middle East, and then Afghanistan, in the early days of Ignatieff's leadership.

This is not to suggest that the Liberal leader was not making any policy statements at all. On the contrary, during 2009 he had identified several issues of concern. From proposed EI reforms and the promotion of high-speed rail to the need for a national childcare plan, a national industrial strategy, and a national policy on postsecondary education, Ignatieff covered a raft of policy areas, but only in generalities. Perhaps more importantly, he did not seem *committed* to any of them. And he once again failed to place the various proposals in a broader context or relate them to fundamental Liberal values.

By September 2010, with the Liberals low in the polls once again, even supporters of Ignatieff's leadership were complaining about a lack of a concrete policy agenda. "He has put absolutely nothing on the table, it's just empty rhetoric," one senior Liberal stated, while another argued some planks had been released but "we need to do more to get our message across." Still another criticized the apparent lack of focus. "We can't be all things to all people," he said. All of these points were supported by statements from pollsters, who agreed the Liberals should be concerned but stressed that it was not too late. According to Frank Graves of Ekos, the solution was simple. "He has to convey his ideas through a Dick and Jane version of his platform. And he needs to narrow it down. Here's the five or six things I want you to know that will be different in Canada tomorrow if you pick me as opposed to my opponent."[21]

THE THINKERS' CONFERENCE

When the fall 2009 election did not materialize, the Liberals announced they would hold an old-fashioned, Pearson/Kent Kingston-style conference. "Canada at 150: Rising to the Challenge" was described by the leader as having two objectives: deciding what Canada should look like in 2017, and mapping how to get there.[22]

Initial reaction to the conference announcement was positive. But enthusiasm among Liberals soon dwindled when it was learned that no advance work would be done, no papers would be prepared for discussion, and, most extraordinarily, no Liberals would be asked to participate. In fact, Liberal MPs and Senators were expressly *not* invited. Instead, they were encouraged to hold town hall sessions in their ridings during the prorogation, on the understanding that the results of those meetings would somehow "feed in" to the conference. Moreover, since this was not a party event there would be no resolutions, and no need for any commitments regarding any of the policies suggested. Yet the press release for the conference indicated the outcome of the conference — and not a party policy process — would help to determine the shape of the Liberal platform for the next election.

The date of the so-called Thinkers' Conference was pushed back several times when it became painfully obvious that few big thinkers wanted to attend, especially when they discovered they would have to pay a registration fee of $695. In the end the conference was held in late March. It assembled an impressive list of speakers on a wide range of topics. Many significant issues were raised, and presenters did in fact come from across the political spectrum. In some cases, as with former ambassador Robert Fowler and former Bank of Canada Governor David Dodge, pointed criticism was levelled at the Liberals for their failure to tackle some of the tough questions of the day or to criticize the Harper government adequately on some of its policy choices. Fowler went further when he stated, "I believe to a significant extent the Liberal Party has lost its way, at least in policy terms — and is in danger of losing its soul."[23]

When the conference wrapped up, it was unclear what if anything would be done as follow-up. "Smart people talked," a columnist wrote, "but were the Liberals listening?"[24] Michael Ignatieff's closing remarks suggested the answer was a qualified yes. On the one hand, he outlined an ambitious agenda of investments in health care and education, pension reform and protection of the environment. On the other hand, ignoring the message from David Dodge and others, it appeared he expected the agenda to be funded by cancelling the government's corporate tax cuts. Innovation and competitiveness, which several panelists had argued were essential to pay for enhanced social programs, were largely ignored.

Over the summer, as Ignatieff toured the country on his Liberal Express, little was added to this message. During the fall 2010 session of Parliament, the Liberals again raised "Are you better off?" as the potential election question, only to reject it in favour of a declaration that the Liberal agenda was based on hope, not fear. With the tabling of the budget the Liberals moved on to promote their so-called family pack of social policies as the alternative to the Conservatives' "jets and jails." Then, with the Speaker's historic rulings that the government was in contempt of Parliament, the election question became Harper and his antidemocratic, authoritarian approach to governing. Nevertheless, when the writ was dropped on May 23 it was the Conservatives who defined the election.

THE CAMPAIGN AND THE COALITION CONUNDRUM

After precipitating the election, the Liberals were eager and optimistic in public. Privately, they were cautiously hopeful. They knew a majority was out of the question, but many still had hopes for a minority and at the very least they expected to improve their showing at the expense of the NDP, whom they believed to be in decline. Meanwhile the government was in trouble over a growing number of scandals and the timing could hardly have been better for the Liberals, since the scandals reinforced the narrative the Liberals had finally decided upon for the election, namely that Canadians needed to get rid of an out-of-control, undemocratic, authoritarian and possibly corrupt government.

In his media scrum after the government's defeat in the House of Commons, Ignatieff stressed the theme of ethics and accountability. He also introduced one of the Liberals' campaign slogans, "Can you trust the Harper government?" Then came the predictable question about Ignatieff's views on a coalition government. The Conservatives had raised the spectre of an opposition party coalition regularly over the previous two years. When the prospect of a fall election loomed in 2009, the Conservatives' plan to call for a "stable majority" was widely reported.[25]

Ignatieff was ready for the question, in the sense that he had a reply available immediately. "There's a blue door and a red door in this election," he said, apparently thinking this settled the matter. It was an answer designed to marginalize the NDP, by maintaining there were only two parties that could form a government. However, this answer failed to satisfy the reporter, who pursued the issue. Ignatieff demurred. The situation deteriorated as others took up the cry to answer the question and the leader left, leaving the issue hanging for two days.

Ignatieff's failure to give a clear answer, and more importantly his reluctance to categorically rule out a coalition, were mystifying. He had often stated that he did not approve of Stéphane Dion's plan in 2008. According to him, he had only reluctantly agreed not to oppose the idea at the time, and had been the very last MP to sign on to the deal. He also knew that a coalition was both politically unappealing to Canadians and unnecessary. He could have answered that he would not form a coalition under any circumstances, but he would form a minority government which other parties supported, just as Stephen Harper had done for the past five years. This position could have appealed both to NDP supporters and to "red tories."

Michael Ignatieff finally issued a statement in which he emphatically ruled out the option of forming a coalition government with the NDP. However, the damage had been done. As one journalist concluded, "The coalition is on the table now and the Conservatives will use it to their utmost advantage."[26]

THE HIGH PERFORMANCE LEADER
AND THE LIBERAL CAMPAIGN

After this early campaign stumble Michael Ignatieff recovered to perform far above expectations for the duration of the campaign. He was clearly energized, and evidently relieved to be moving out from the wings onto the main stage. In contrast with Stephen Harper, who was being kept in a tightly scripted bubble, Ignatieff appeared relaxed and genuine as he took questions and spoke with strangers at an unusually high number of campaign events each day. Virtually everyone agreed that he appeared to be enjoying himself, and media coverage of the leader's tour was almost universally positive.[27]

One result of the leader's high-octane performance was a welcome display of party unity. As one observer put it, "Ignatieff's confidence on the road appears to have put an end to the endless sniping from fellow Liberals ... The rank-and-file show signs of being motivated to work for a leader they believe is now an asset rather than a liability."[28] This was certainly true among Liberals in the Greater Toronto Area, who only months earlier had been privately expressing concerns about their fate. The unrest had forced Ontario co-chair Jeff Kehoe to recruit former Chrétien minister Elinor Caplan as a special adviser and to declare publicly, "There are no cracks in our armour."

Although they could never hope to match the more extensive and well-financed organizational efforts of the Conservatives, the Liberal campaign was clearly competent. Given the shambles of the 2008 campaign, this alone was seen as a major achievement. Another positive side effect of the leader's fine performance was the number of volunteers coming forward to work on the Liberal campaign. In addition, as even Conservative organizers admitted, the Liberals possessed many highly competent and experienced election organizers. Their war room was still the envy of the other parties. With Peter Donolo and Gordon Ashworth involved in the day-to-day campaign activities, no one expected any major gaffes or crises this time around.

Nor did anyone anticipate the initial missteps of the Prime Minister. Apart from his problems on the coalition proposal from 2004, Harper ran into further difficulty over the structure and timing of the leader's debates. With attention focused on the issue of the Green Party leader's participation, Harper indicated he was open to "any number of possibilities." Then he went on to state, "We could also have a debate between Mr. Ignatieff and myself, since, after all, the real choice in this election is between a Conservative government or an Ignatieff-led government that all of these other parties will support.[29] Ignatieff replied promptly through his Twitter account: "A one-on-one debate? Any time, any place."

This, of course, was hardly what Harper's handlers had in mind, and they promptly began a careful retreat. Ignatieff took advantage of Harper's apparent reluctance by staging events with debate props — a chair for a moderator and an empty chair for the absent Harper. Media coverage emphasized the image of the Prime Minister as the experienced campaigner, suddenly afraid to take any risks against the novice challenger who had nothing to lose. Although one poll released shortly after the writ was dropped had indicated that voters were not seized of the ethics and accountability issue, the Liberals were convinced it was only a matter of time before their campaign question took hold.

The Liberals also had a clear and coherent targeting strategy. They had identified a cluster of ridings, primarily in Ontario, that they believed they could take back from the Conservatives. Many had only been lost by narrow margins in 2008, while others, such as Oakville, had seen a larger margin of victory but were considered vulnerable because of weak candidates or specific local issues that favoured the Liberals. It was in Oakville that Michael Ignatieff released the first plank of the Liberal platform, speaking to a crowd of students at Sheridan College.

POLICY AND THE LIBERAL PLATFORM

For several days in a row the Liberals followed the example of the Conservative strategy of 2008, releasing a plank a day and hoping to garner positive media coverage and public attention. At first the plan seemed to work. The release of the Liberals' first plank, on education, was widely reported in a positive light. The "Learning Passport" was designed specifically to assist lower-income students and their families by providing assistance for them to attend postsecondary institutions.

In addition to outlining how the plank would provide an incentive to support life-long learning, the measure was widely described by the media as only one element in the Liberals' "family pack," which was exactly the coverage the Liberals had hoped for.

Their plan was to demonstrate the significant differences in approach to families between their party and the Conservatives, whose main commitment had been an income-splitting measure for families with children. The Harper announcement greatly aided the Liberals in their message that they were the party that understood the challenges facing modern Canadian families, since the Conservatives' measure would only apply to a minority of families and would benefit wealthy Canadians the most. Furthermore, it would not be introduced until the deficit had been eliminated, sometime in the future.

Having already unveiled a plan in the fall that would provide assistance to so-called sandwich generation families obliged to care for aging parents and/or ill family members, the Liberals proceeded over the next few days to unveil platform planks on childcare, increases to the Guaranteed Income Supplement, and increased contributions to the Canada Pension Plan, all of which also received prominent and positive coverage.

Then on April 3 the leader unveiled the entire Liberal platform. Entitled "Your Family, Your Future, Your Canada," the document was a testament to the influence of Peter Donolo and others in moving the Liberals to the left. A traditional Liberal approach to issues was evident in virtually every section of the platform, from jobs and the economy to social justice and foreign policy. One section on democratic renewal played to the campaign theme of Harper's contempt for Parliament, promising to enhance the power of committees and to introduce the concept of a People's Question Period. At the same time the platform reflected a Chrétien-esque fondness for pragmatism and balance, demonstrated through the fiscal responsibility emphasized in plans for reducing the deficit. Even more importantly, the platform finally offered a rationale for the Liberal platform in the form of "Equality of Opportunity," the theme stressed by Michael Ignatieff in his introduction to the platform and one that had been identified by policy icon Tom Kent in an opinion piece several months earlier.[30]

The Liberal platform was widely reported and generally well received by the media. CTV reporter Craig Oliver, for example, declared that "the document will serve as a template, a touchstone they can use as a reference points in coming weeks on every campaign issue that comes at them from every direction." Oliver also argued the document served another purpose: "It is a statement of principle." And for Michael Ignatieff, whom Oliver described as giving a "bravura performance" in explaining the planks, "it means an end to the time during which critics could ask 'What does he stand for.'"[31]

Some Liberals questioned the wisdom of releasing the entire document so early, noting that Stephen Harper had waited until virtually the end of the 2008 campaign to release the Conservative platform, thereby avoiding potential criticism and at the same time continuing to receive daily coverage of his individual planks. In fact, after a few days of coverage the Liberal platform did disappear from the media's radar screen. But a primary reason was the leader's failure to follow through on anything that Craig Oliver had expected. Although the document had been described by several journalists as a Red Book–like platform, it was not widely seen by Canadians. In 1993, Jean Chrétien and his candidates had used the Red Book as a constant campaign prop. In 2011, although it was accessible in full on the web, there were no ubiquitous copies of the platform in the hands of all Liberal candidates, nor did the leader use it regularly as a campaign prop. Even more surprising, he rarely referred to the overarching theme of equality of opportunity, and when he made reference to platform planks, it was in the micro-policy terms that once again gave the impression there was no underlying set of values.

Another reason for the platform's lack of prominence may have been its lack of big ideas. Determined to demonstrate they were fiscally prudent, rather than the reckless tax-and-spend Liberals painted by the Prime Minister, they had wrestled with the reality of the Conservatives' $56-billion deficit and produced the least ambitious Liberal platform in many years. As one insider complained, it was fine to have limited commitments when they were the government, but as the challenger it was necessary to take risks and think big.

The platform release came only a day after a major poll indicated that fully 54 percent of Canadians would prefer a Liberal/NDP coalition to a Harper majority, and an even more surprising 50 percent would even support a coalition including the Bloc. The Liberals therefore had every expectation that their campaign strategy was working, and Stephen Harper's relentless attacks on a "reckless coalition" were backfiring. They also believed the release of their entire platform, fully costed, would enhance their credibility with voters as a government in waiting. Indeed, approaching the mid-point of the campaign and the leaders' debates, they were convinced they were on the right track. However, another poll released on April 9, just before the leaders' debates, suggested that they were actually not making any progress. The Liberals had only increased their support from 24 percent to 26 percent since March 26, while the Tories had declined from 43 percent to 41 percent and the NDP had gained three percentage points to sit at 19 percent. The response of senior advisers and many candidates, at least publicly, was to question the validity of the polls. "That's not what it feels like on the ground," one Toronto candidate declared. "There is so much enthusiasm, and a positive vibe unlike anything we experienced in the last few campaigns." Many remained convinced that they only needed a strong performance from their leader in the debates to successfully execute their strategy.

THE LEADERS' DEBATES: TOO LITTLE, TOO LATE

The leaders' debates dedicated significant chunks of time to one-on-one exchanges among the four leaders. The Liberals believed this could play to their leader's strengths, especially as they hoped to provoke Stephen Harper into straying from his strictly scripted path. Although Michael Ignatieff was the only newcomer to the debates, he did have significant debate experience and they felt confident he could do well in such a situation.

Unfortunately for the Liberals, the Prime Minister maintained a calm, almost disengaged demeanour throughout both the French and English debates and could not be drawn into a serious disagreement with anyone. Meanwhile Ignatieff, while competent, did not dazzle. Although he delivered a few good lines, particularly when discussing Harper's contempt for Parliament, there were no knockout punches. Perhaps more importantly, he missed several excellent opportunities to move from the negative to the positive and outline the Liberal vision. Entirely absent in the April 12 English-language debate, the Liberal platform made a brief appearance in the French debate on April 14, but once again it was the micro version that Ignatieff highlighted, referring for example to his "Learning Passport," a reference which clearly was not understood by the vast majority of the audience.

Even more puzzling was Ignatieff's failure to take advantage of an opportunity presented by Bloc leader Gilles Duceppe, who told Harper that Quebecers did not like Conservative values. Then he went on to say that he personally had not seen a federal politician whose values he shared since Lester Pearson. With Ignatieff scheduled to speak next, viewers might have expected the Liberal leader to build on that unexpected statement to highlight Liberal values, his own values, and the values reflected in the Liberal platform. Instead, Ignatieff returned to the theme of trust and lack of confidence in the Harper government.

In this context it was NDP leader Jack Layton who took up the slack. Appearing calm and relaxed in both languages, the smiling leader disarmed many viewers with his combination of confidence and humour. And it was Layton who delivered the only serious blow to Ignatieff, accusing him of being absent from the House of Commons much of the time. "If you want the job you have to show up for work," Layton declared. Since the issue of Ignatieff's poor attendance record had been highlighted on the NDP website for some time, his inability to respond was mystifying.

CAUGHT IN THE CROSSFIRE: THE LIBERAL COLLAPSE

Within days of the debates, almost everything about the 2011 election changed and changed for the worse for the Liberals. From a non-event that was drifting towards the finish line, the election became a seriously contested race. From a contest between the two "major" parties, the Liberals and the Conservatives, it quickly became a three-horse race in which the NDP appeared to be moving up fast on the outside. The

Liberals now found themselves caught in the crossfire, forced to fend off threats from both the left and the right. With Stephen Harper pounding home his argument for a majority government, and Jack Layton appealing personally to voters much more than Michael Ignatieff, there seemed to be little the Liberals could do. Instead of strategically voting for the Liberals, it was becoming possible for voters to consider strategically voting for the NDP.

By April 17, polls consistently showed Stephen Harper and Jack Layton gaining momentum, while the campaigns of Michael Ignatieff and Gilles Duceppe were having no impact. Ignatieff responded to this news by arguing there was still time to turn the sinking Liberal ship around. Then he referred to the "scandal" of the Conservatives having no platform, and stated, "I really think the Liberal platform speaks to Canadian families at this time." Unfortunately, this defence of the Liberals' Red Book was too little and far too late. Those comments were followed by the "Rise Up" speech, which Ignatieff delivered in Sudbury the next day, building on the theme of a Bruce Springsteen song. The speech began by admitting, "We're in a funny place." It went on to outline a litany of Conservative misdemeanours from prorogation to the contempt of Parliament charges, reinforcing the Liberals' campaign question, "Who do you trust?"

For the Liberals, the depth of their difficulties became clear a few days later when an April 25 poll revealed that Canadians had indeed focused on the question of trust and accountability but had come up with the wrong answer. Instead of the Liberals, it was the Conservatives who were viewed as most trustworthy. Canadians already had serious reservations about Ignatieff's leadership, and his mishandling of the coalition question, in addition to the Conservatives' relentless assault on his questionable commitment to Canada, had apparently made up their minds.

From there the bottom fell out of the Liberal campaign. Large swaths of Ontario, and even metropolitan Toronto, were beginning to appear vulnerable. One senior adviser privately confided they were lucky the campaign was not longer. Yet the Liberals continued to execute the strategy they had devised before the campaign began. In the last week, Michael Ignatieff spent most of his time in Ontario, and much of that time was spent in NDP and Conservative-held ridings which the party still believed they could take back. In an interview with the *Globe and Mail* on April 25, deputy leader Bob Rae insisted the Liberals would hold their traditional ridings and argued that polls should always be taken with a grain of salt, particularly since the Liberal experience on the ground was still positive.

When the dust settled on May 2, the full extent of the Liberal collapse was painfully obvious. The once mighty party was reduced to a mere shell. From their already embarrassing pre-election total of seventy-seven seats they now held only thirty-four, most from the Atlantic. They had lost seats in every region, and in particular had lost strongholds in Quebec and Ontario that no one could have anticipated. Michael Ignatieff, having been defeated in his own Toronto riding, announced the following day that he would be resigning immediately as Liberal leader, and the post-mortem began.

REASONS FOR THE LIBERAL COLLAPSE

It is an understatement to say the campaign did not unfold as the Liberals had hoped. The first question to be asked is whether the Liberals' initial expectations were realistic. On the one hand, the NDP was in poor shape at the beginning of the campaign; the Liberals were not unrealistic in their expectation that they might be able to benefit from strategic voting at the expense of the NDP, especially in Ontario. Similarly, no one predicted the extent of the Bloc collapse in Quebec. In fact, the solid base of the Bloc was the one thing almost all commentators had agreed on in advance of the election.

On the other hand, the polling numbers for the Liberals over the previous two years, and especially in the months leading up to their fateful decision to force the election, lend credence to the argument that they had no hope of winning and were, in fact, defeated before they began. In his presentation to the annual meeting of the Canadian Political Science Association in Waterloo in mid-May, Ipsos principal Darrell

Bricker posed the question "What were they thinking?" As his analysis made clear, on virtually every possible indicator the Liberals had been behind, and badly so, *before the writ was dropped.* For example, some 57 percent of Canadians indicated they thought Canada was "on the right track" and 45 percent believed Stephen Harper deserved to be re-elected. Health care and the economy were viewed as the most important issues facing the country, while the issue of trust in government, the Liberals' campaign issue, was located a distant fifth. Nevertheless, on that issue of trust, some 39 percent of Canadians picked Harper, while 34 percent picked Jack Layton and only 19 percent selected Michael Ignatieff. On the question of who could best manage the economy the Conservatives led by 47 percent to 23 percent over the Liberals. Perhaps most revealing, when asked which one of the party leaders they would like to be prime minister if an opposition coalition replaced the Conservatives, fully 59 percent selected Jack Layton as opposed to 27 percent for Michael Ignatieff. As Bricker concluded, this election more than any over the past decades was about leadership. In that regard, the Liberal disadvantage going into the campaign was likely impossible to overcome.

There were other reasons why the party's showing was so unexpectedly poor. Among them are the ones identified earlier in this chapter that have dogged the party for several years, including organization, financing, the lack of serious policy development, and the inability to articulate Liberal values. As president Alf Apps admitted, the party had lost the "ground war" of voter mobilization, especially in Ontario. In Quebec, where nomination battles had already cost them any momentum before the writ was dropped, the absence of local organization had opened up a vacuum in which the NDP could make progress *faute de mieux.* Meanwhile, the defeat of the Liberals in Toronto would suggest another important factor, namely their failure to maintain and reinforce their support among new Canadians. All of this, of course, is in addition to the party's long-standing problem of regional representation from the West.

THE FUTURE OF THE LIBERALS

As the Liberals confront the very real problems they will face in the next few years, it is important to note that many dire scenarios were painted almost immediately after the stunning defeat of the Turner Liberals in 1984. Yet only nine years later the party had returned to power with the first of three solid majorities and many observers began speaking of a Liberal dynasty.

However, in 1984, the party remained the official opposition, and the NDP found themselves in even worse shape than the Liberals. In some respects, then, the current situation of the Liberal Party is worse than 1984. In Parliament they are no longer the official opposition, an unprecedented development that will have significant financial costs for the leader's office and the Liberal Research Bureau. Their allotted time in the House of Commons during Question Period will also be much less, as will their representation on parliamentary committees. It is unclear how much this will matter in the long run. Good performances in Question Period do not win elections. Moreover, good performances by the third party leader and his or her critics will often receive good media coverage, as they did for Jack Layton and the NDP. With a high-profile interim leader in Bob Rae, and good bench strength in their critics, the Liberals may well be able to achieve a substantial amount of media coverage. And, as the Turner opposition era demonstrated, credible support for the caucus and the party could be maintained on shoestring budgets thanks to committed staff and volunteers.

The national party's financial situation may or may not be worse in the coming four years. The Liberals currently are not deeply in debt, as the Turner Liberals were throughout their time in opposition, and they have improved their fundraising skills. But the impending elimination of the public per-vote subsidies available to them since 2004 (with no concomitant return to higher levels of personal contributions), will be a very serious blow. Numerous commentators, including such unlikely sources as former Harper colleagues Gerry Nicholls and Tom Flanagan, have publicly criticized Harper's plans, arguing that they will destroy the opposition parties and, even more telling, that the prime minister's motive is personal animus rather than philosophical commitment.[32] One analyst has calculated that only 18 percent of the revenue used by the Liberals per vote in their 2011 campaign came from private sources.[33] Indeed, with only three years to improve their contributions from individuals before the subsidies are eliminated entirely, the funding problem could be the most significant one the party will face in the immediate future.

Still there are a number of reasons for optimism. As countless surveys have demonstrated, Canadians have not moved to the right. There is still a solid base for a party of the centre reflecting traditional liberal values. Nor has there been a shift to the left. Many analysts have emphasized the importance of Jack Layton's leadership, rather than the NDP philosophy or platform, in the so-called Orange Crush that swept over Quebec and parts of Ontario (see Chapter 4). In Quebec, the collapse of the Bloc Québécois and the tenuous support for the NDP may well offer the Liberals an opportunity to reinvent themselves as the dominant federalist party in that province. In addition, as a variety of analysts have demonstrated, the Liberal losses in Ontario were not as significant in terms of voter support as the results might have suggested and their chances of reclaiming that support are reasonably good.

Perhaps most important, the Liberal brand remains strong and the party has an enviably competent and experienced membership on which to build. With the recent decisions to delay the holding of another leadership convention until late 2012 or early 2013, the party has given itself time to begin the serious work of organization, fundraising, and policy development that are long overdue. And, with another election unlikely before 2015, there is considerable time for grassroots input and consultation. Meanwhile, the selection of Bob Rae as interim leader ensures that the party will have some visibility and experience in the House of Commons, to take advantage of the inevitable mistakes of the large contingent of novice NDP MPs.

Whether the party will be able to address these problems remains to be seen. Certainly the experience of the last three election campaigns has demonstrated the futility of shortcuts based on leadership change alone, or on any rush to regain power. The Liberal Party should not be counted out on the basis of this election, but nor should its recovery and eventual return to power be taken for granted. Much will depend on the

willingness of the Liberal membership to come together and contribute
to the party's rebuilding, and on the party's ability to return to basics and
define essential Liberal values in the context of the twenty-first century.

NOTES

1. Brooke Jeffrey, "Missed Opportunity: The Invisible Liberals," in *The Canadian Federal Election of 2008*, eds. Jon H. Pammett and Christopher Dornan (Toronto: Dundurn Press, 2009), 94.
2. Harris Macleod and Abbas Rana, "Grit Battle Over Outremont Could Impact Liberal Candidates Nationally," *The Hill Times*, October 5, 2009, 1.
3. David Akin, "Grits Upbeat After Staff Change," *Ottawa Citizen*, October 29, 2009, C8.
4. Although described by Ignatieff's office and the press as a new format for back-benchers' input to enhance their role, the structure closely resembled the traditional Tactics Committee that previous Liberal leaders had employed in opposition. In fact, under Turner the input of the Rat Pack was not only heeded but also often controversial, with other Liberals calling for more OLO restraint on the committee's decision-making.
5. Andrew Mayeda and David Akin, "Liberals Have Internal Issues: Ignatieff," *Ottawa Citizen*, March 25, 2010, A4.
6. Campbell Clark, "MPs Force Ignatieff's Hand" *Globe and Mail*, June 5, 2010, A12.
7. Campbell Clark, "Ignatieff Earns Same Rating as Dion Pre-Election," *Globe and Mail*, August 12, 2009, A5.
8. Harris Macleod, "Ignatieff's To Do List," *The Hill Times*, November 16, 2009, 4.
9. Angelo Perischili, "Liberals in Chaos from Liberal Leadership Point of View," *The Hill Times*, May 24, 2010, 6.
10. Jane Taber, "Handshake By Handshake, The Liberals Refine Their Strategy," *Globe and Mail*, September 1, A8.
11. Nelson Wiseman, "Ignatieff Excels at Glittering Generalities," *The Hill Times*, June 1, 2009, 10.
12. Denis Smith, "Michael Ignatieff: Is He Just Acting?" *Globe and Mail*, September 14, 2009, A13.
13. Susan Riley, "Another Makeover for Michael," *Ottawa Citizen*, July 16,2010, A14.
14. Ron Graham. "Lost Leader: Why Michael Ignatieff Hasn't Knocked our Socks Off," *The Walrus*, January 2010, 36.
15. Mike Funston and Bruce Campion-Smith, "Ignatieff Strikes Back at Attack Ads," *Toronto Star*, May 15, 2009.
16. Bea Vongdouangchanh, "Liberals Want to Limit Pre-Writ Political Advertising," *The Hill Times*, June 1, 2009, 32.

17. John Ibbitson, "Tory Attack Ads Pack a Punch that Leaves Liberals Reeling," *Globe and Mail*, February 21, 2011, A4.

18. Lawrence Martin, "Grit Game Plan: Goodbye High Road," *Globe and Mail*, March 21, 2011, A21.

19. In opposition, the Liberals under Pearson engaged in a lengthy and productive renewal process started by a grassroots group that came to be known as Cell 13 and included such prominent future party organizers as Richard Stanbury, Keith Davey, and Jim Coutts. The culmination of their efforts was the Kingston Conference, shepherded by policy guru Tom Kent, at which much of the Liberals' platform, including social programs, was adopted.

20. James Travers, "Baffling Liberal Reluctance to Extend Economic Narrative to its Logical Conclusion," *Toronto Star*, September 24, 2009.

21. Abbas Rana, "Ignatieff Has Put Nothing on the Table," *The Hill Times*, September 21, 2009, 7.

22. Conference Program, "Canada at 150," 4.

23. Kevin Carmichael and John Ibbitson, "Liberal Party in Danger of Losing its Soul," *Globe and Mail*, March 29, 2010, A8.

24. Jeffrey Simpson, "Smart People Talked but were the Liberals Listening?", *Globe and Mail*, March 29, 2010, A19.

25. Daniel Leblanc and Campbell Clark. "Tories Changing Election Tune to Stress Majority", *Globe and Mail,* August 20, 2009, A4.

26. Adrian Macnair, "Ignatieff's Stance on Coalitions Clear, But Came too Late," *National Post*, March 29, 2011.

27. Adam Radwanski, "Ignatieff's Unexpected Sparkle Brightens Liberal Hopes," *Globe and Mail*, April 2, 2011, A4.

28. Radwanski, "Ignatieff's Unexpected Sparkle."

29. Bruce Campion-Smith and Les Whittington, "Harper Challenges Ignatieff to a Debate," *Toronto Star*, March 30, 2011.

30. Tom Kent, "First, a Few Questions for Ignatieff and the Liberals," *Globe and Mail*, July 2, 2010, A13.

31. Craig Oliver, "Liberal Platform a Statement of Principle," *Craig's Take, www.ctv.ca*, April 3, 2011.

32. Gerry Nicholls, "Kill the Subsidy, Not the Liberal Party," *Ottawa Citizen*, May 24, 2011, A12.

33. Eric Grenier, "How Much Will Killing Per-Vote Subsidy Stack Odds in *Tory* Favour?", *Globe and Mail*, June 13, 2011.

CHAPTER 4

Political Marketing and the
NDP's Historic Breakthrough
David McGrane

In his book to introduce the NDP to Canadians in 1961, Stanley
Knowles argued that the Conservatives and Liberals were "alike as two
peas in a pod" and that there were signals that Canada would follow the
lead of the United Kingdom and move to a two-party system of social
democrats versus conservatives.[1] Almost exactly fifty years later, the
NDP finally made a historic electoral breakthrough towards the type of
two-party system envisioned by Knowles. For the first time in the history
of the NDP or its predecessor, the CCF, the party won more seats and a
higher popular vote than the Liberals and formed the official opposition
in the House of Commons. Indeed, the Liberal returns in the 2011 election (18.9 percent of the popular vote and thirty-four seats) looked like a
result typically associated with the NDP in federal elections over the past
five decades. Further, while the CCF/NDP had only ever won a total of
three seats in Quebec and the Liberals had swept the province on several
occasions, in 2011 the NDP won fifty-nine out of seventy-five seats in
Quebec. Simply put, the historical positions of the NDP and the Liberals
were switched after the election. The Liberals were relegated to a rump
third party in the House of Commons with few seats in Quebec while
the NDP became the government-in-waiting and the principal voice of
Quebec in Ottawa.

This chapter argues that the NDP's historic breakthrough in the 2011
election should be partly attributed to its political marketing. As a sub-
field of political science, political marketing initially emphasized political communication (e.g. political advertisements). However, its scope
has considerably broadened.[2] This chapter conceives the political marketing of a party to be a constant process involving gathering market

intelligence through informal and formal means, developing party policies and a party brand, mobilizing party members, building relationships with stakeholders, positioning in relation to competing parties, targeting certain segments of voters, allocating scarce resources, and communicating a party's policy offerings through paid advertising and the management of news media.

The chapter begins by discussing the several changes that the federal NDP made to its political marketing after Jack Layton became leader in terms of professionalization, centralization of party structures, embracing presidential-style politics, moving to a moderate third-way version of social democracy, expanding outside of its traditional regional strongholds, and restructuring its relationship with the labour movement. Using Computer Assisted Qualitative Data Analysis Software (CAQDAS) to assess NDP commercials and press releases as well as interviews with party operatives and local activists, the chapter then turns to an analysis of the 2011 campaign. It shows that the NDP was primarily a competitor-oriented "market follower" in English Canada and a voter-oriented "market challenger" in Quebec. As such, the party's strategy in English Canada was focused on winning over so-called Layton Liberals by using the leader's popularity to introduce these voters to the party's moderate and practical social democratic policies, which were close to Liberal policies but slightly distinctive. In Quebec, the NDP decided not to attack other parties but to focus on voters' frustration with the dysfunctional nature of Canada's Parliament and to use Layton's popularity to suggest that the NDP could be trusted to achieve change in Ottawa. The party's choice to follow a political marketing strategy that was both voter-oriented and competitor-oriented necessitated the centralization and professionalization of its campaign machine.

The final section argues that 2011 could be seen as a critical election that has, at least temporarily, realigned the Canadian electorate. It is suggested that the roots of this potential realignment lay primarily in the emergence of the new Conservative Party of Canada (which has polarized Canadian politics), the string of minority Parliaments that raised the profile of the NDP and its leader, and a growing cynicism within the Canadian electorate. Particularly in Quebec, the NDP's political marketing (both prior to and during the 2011 election) put it into a position to take advantage of these structural shifts within Canadian politics.

PREPARING THE GROUND:
LEADERSHIP AND POLITICAL MARKETING

In his work on political marketing in Canada, Alex Marland sees the NDP as traditionally being hesitant to adopt political marketing techniques and follow the lead of its professional party operatives due to strong ideological commitments to certain policy positions and decentralized party structures.[3] However, after the NDP's poor showing in the 2000 election, Jack Layton became leader and proceeded to gradually develop the party's political marketing prowess. Layton and his team embarked on the professionalization of the party's campaigns and a centralization of party structures over the three federal elections in 2004, 2006, and 2008.[4] Further, Layton's team increased the sophistication of the federal party's fundraising machine, which combined with new public subsidies to place the NDP on a more equal financial footing with the Liberals (and to a lesser extent the Conservatives) than in the past.[5] New party financing rules banning union and corporate donations also engendered certain changes in the party's structure and image. While Jansen and Young have documented how the NDP has continued to benefit from indirect support from unions,[6] the alterations of party financing rules liberated the NDP from the old charge that the party was in the back pocket of labour and gave party professionals more independence from the oversight of union representatives. At the same time, since new rules stated that any organizational aid that a provincial NDP party gave to the federal party qualified as an in-kind corporate donation, the federal party became less dependent on provincial parties for local organization and began to have its own staff in each province reporting directly to party headquarters in Ottawa. With its new organizational structure and financing, the Layton-led NDP made a concentrated effort to expand outside of its traditional regional bases, particularly in Newfoundland,

Alberta, and Quebec. The NDP also came to embrace "presidential politics" as the party concentrated increasingly on Layton and his own personal story as opposed to its partnerships with stakeholders outside of the party or the NDP team (other MPs).

The concept of Third-Way social democracy emerged in the late 1990s in connection with Tony Blair's New Labour and the work of Anthony Giddens.[7] While the NDP's 1999 convention had firmly stated its rejection of the Third Way, which it associated with deregulation and unfettered global capitalism[8], Layton nonetheless moved the party's policy positions slowly in that direction. The party strategists interviewed for this chapter were uncomfortable with the suggestion that the NDP had drifted to the centre in order to steal Liberal voters, as this implied that the NDP had somehow became Liberals in orange livery. Rather, strategists argued that the NDP had became more pragmatic under Layton's leadership and moved to an ideological position similar to provincial NDP governments in Saskatchewan and Manitoba. Third Way social democracy in these provinces entails the rejection of neo-liberalism's indifference to inequality and its call for limited government, as well as jettisoning the more statist elements of traditional postwar social democracy such as the creation of a growing number of universal social programs and increased public ownership.[9] The free market is seen as the primary wealth generator of society and must be encouraged through strategic interventions by the state, such as direct subsidies to business and low personal income taxes, while the welfare state is expanded slowly through targeted initiatives in the context of balanced budgets. Under Layton's leadership, more traditional social democratic positions, such as increased taxation of wealthy individuals (i.e. an inheritance tax), the acceptance of deficit spending, the rapid creation of new universal social programs, and references to expanding public ownership were gradually eliminated from the party's discourse. While Layton or party officials never forthrightly said that they were moving to the centre, the strategy for replacing Liberals in this manner was explicitly laid out in a book by Jamey Heath, Layton's former communications director, in 2007.[10]

For a party known for internal ideological conflict, what was remarkable about these changes was that they took place with little public party infighting and the party's parliamentary caucus remained united around its leader (with the notable exceptions of splits over gun control and same-sex marriage). The lack of internal conflict coupled with the party's move towards Third Way politics undoubtedly increased its credibility in the eyes of Canadian voters.

LEADERSHIP AND PRACTICAL SOCIAL DEMOCRACY: PLATFORM AND TELEVISION ADVERTISING

Despite the strengths of the party's political marketing noted above, many pundits predicted that the NDP would lose seats as the 2011 election began. They believed that the NDP made an error in deciding to join the other opposition parties to defeat a popular budget, and there was a strong possibility that fear over a Conservative majority could shift soft NDP voters towards the Liberals.[11] Most importantly, there were large questions about Layton's health as he was on crutches due to a fractured hip and was continuing his fight with prostate cancer. Public opinion polling from the first three months of 2011 seemed to confirm this conclusion, showing the NDP falling somewhere between 13 percent and 18 percent of the national popular vote.[12]

In English Canada, the NDP did not aim its strategy at the roughly 18 percent of Canadians that its polling found to be committed New Democrat voters but focused its gathering of market intelligence on the 5 percent of potential NDP supporters that the party dubbed "Layton Liberals." These voters were generally thirty-five to forty-five years old, upper and middle income earners, had the Liberals as their first choice and the NDP as their second choice, and were unsure of Ignatieff but trusted Layton. They were susceptible to Liberal arguments that voting NDP was a wasted vote. It was surmised that these soft Liberal voters could be won over by an emphasis on both Layton's leadership and Third Way social democratic policies. Party strategists believed that Layton's popularity and trustworthiness could be used as a conduit through which these voters could be introduced to the NDP's practical version of social democracy.

To use Butler and Collins's terminology, the NDP was a "market follower" which did not try to appeal to a large cross-section of the English Canadian political market. Rather, the party attempted to make incremental gains by targeting Layton Liberals through a market following strategy called "copying,"[13] which entails replicating other products on the market with just enough differentiation to make a company's brand distinctive. Similar to the Liberals in previous campaigns, the NDP platform presented the party as the realistic centre-left alternative to the Conservatives. The theme of the NDP platform was simply that Ottawa is broken and Jack Layton has a practical plan to fix it. Since Alexa McDonough released a relatively detailed platform entitled *A Framework for Canada's Future* during the 1997 campaign, NDP platforms have became increasingly less visionary and more pragmatic. Instead of new universal programs established over several years of spending, the 2011 platform was broken down into five modest pledges of "hire more doctors and nurses, strengthen your pension, kick-start job creation, help out your family budget, and fix Ottawa for good."

The policy differences between the Liberal and NDP platforms were present but slight. Both parties were in favour of a cap and trade system of pollution credits for industry, balancing the budget, keeping personal taxes stable, spending more on childcare spaces, reducing the cost of post-secondary education, rehabilitative criminal justice, limiting prime ministerial power, tax credits for energy-efficient home renovations, a higher guaranteed income supplement for seniors, increasing federal funding for affordable housing, more funding for municipal infrastructure, and reviewing the Conservatives' purchase of new F-35 jet fighters. On other issues, the Liberals and the NDP took similar positions, with the NDP positioning themselves just slightly to the left of the Liberals. For example, the Liberals pledged to return the corporate tax rate to 18 percent while the NDP wanted to bump it up to 19.5 percent. The Liberals promised a "gradual increase of the defined benefits" of the Canadian Pension Plan (CPP) while the NDP committed to the "eventual goal" of doubling CPP benefits. On health care, the platform reflected the NDP's move to the centre. It did not advocate expanding health care into previously uncovered areas, or creating a new national and universal pharmacare program as it did in 2008. Rather, similar to the Liberals[14], the platform asserted that the NDP would simply hire more doctors and nurses, make prescription drugs affordable, and spend more on homecare. The NDP promised tax credits for all new hires by small business, whereas the Liberals pledged a holiday on EI premiums for small businesses that hired young workers. The NDP's pledge to reduce the small business tax rate from 11 percent to 9 percent very much followed the lead of NDP governments in Saskatchewan and Manitoba. The NDP platform was able, however, to stake out distinctive ground on the issue of affordability. The NDP's promises to cap credit card fees at prime plus 5 percent, take the federal sales tax off home heating, and unlock cellular phones to allow customers to change providers without changing phones had no parallel in the Liberal platform.

Previous NDP campaigns had targeted soft Liberal voters by emphasizing how the Liberal government had betrayed its own values and how the NDP, as Canada's "social conscience," needed seats in the House of Commons to keep the Liberal government honest. As such, New Democrats could make a difference even though they did not form government. Echoing language about his prime ministerial ambitions that he had first used during the 2008 election, Layton introduced the party's 2011 platform by promising, "As Prime Minister, I will work with others to get Ottawa working for you. And I will deliver results in the first 100 days. You can hold me to it." Such a message was copying the Liberals in its implication that the NDP was now the centre-left party that should be considered the real alternative to the Harper Conservatives. In presenting itself as a possible governing party and Layton as the potential prime minister, the NDP was attempting to undermine Liberal arguments for strategic voting. Strategists saw the early presentation of the NDP as a governing party (a possibility that seemed quite plausible with all of the media attention on a potential minority Parliament and coalition governments) setting up messages later in the campaign about voters having a choice, as opposed to Ignatieff's arguments that voting Liberal was necessary to prevent a Harper majority.

Figure 1.

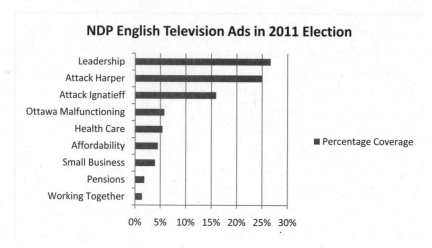

The analysis in Figure 1 was performed through the transcription of the NDP's English television advertisements into text and the inductive coding of those transcripts using a CAQDAS program called Nvivo 9 that calculates "percentage coverage" based on the number of characters coded into a particular theme.[15] The figure illustrates what Robert Ormrod calls competitor orientation in political marketing.[16] For Ormrod, the political marketing of a party is unevenly oriented in four directions. First, political marketing is obviously oriented towards discovering and satisfying needs and wants of a party's targeted voters determined primarily through internal polling and focus groups. Beyond voter orientation, Ormrod argues that the political marketing of a party encompasses an internal orientation towards marshalling the financial and volunteer support of party members, involving members in policy development, adhering to members' conception of the party's ideology, and using members as source of informal market intelligence to discern what targeted voters desire. The political marketing of a party also has an external orientation to powerful stakeholders in society such as churches, businesses, unions, and social movements by using their research to develop policy, adopt policy positions that would garner their public approval, and enter into formal or informal alliances. In terms of competitor orientation, strategy is shaped in light of the nature of political competition and the possibilities of future co-operation or conflict with other parties. Depending on their unique circumstances, parties will emphasize certain orientations and de-emphasize others in their political marketing.

Competitor orientation structured the primary theme of the NDP's English advertising: negative attacks on Harper and Ignatieff contrasted with positive messages about Layton's leadership. The party's initial advertisements were negative but were not meant to scare voters: rather, they were framed around the light-hearted theme "Not so great Canadian moments," showing Harper and Ignatieff as cartoonish stick men. The final two English NDP television advertisements of the campaign (released on days twenty-seven and thirty-two) focused exclusively on positive attributes of Layton's leadership: his determination, empathy, trustworthiness, and role as a representative of change in Ottawa. The commercial in heavy rotation in the final week of the campaign showed Layton standing in front of a large Canadian flag and delivering the tag line "You know that I am a fighter." It emphasized his ability to deliver practical results and made the NDP leader seem prime ministerial. With the election only days away, party strategists wanted the ballot box question to be: which leader do you trust to get things done for you and your family? While it was not consciously planned by party strategists, Layton's cane (which at times he waved in the air at NDP rallies) became a symbol of his determination to fight for the average voter instead of his ailing health. If anything, Layton's health problems made him seem more human compared to the aloof personas of Harper and Ignatieff.[17]

Using marketing intelligence, NDP strategists knew voters were much more attracted to the "Layton brand" than the "NDP brand," and they also knew that the "Ignatieff brand" was much less popular than the "Liberal brand." Consequently, none of the English television commercials during the campaign verbally mentioned the acronym "NDP" or the words "New Democrats." The NDP logo appeared at the end of advertisements, but even then "Jack Layton" was in much larger font than "NDP." The emphasis on Layton is a perfect example of voter orientation and competitor orientation within party branding. The idea was to target soft Liberal voters who disliked Ignatieff and were attracted to Layton but had reservations about the NDP.

As a "market follower," the NDP's English advertisements showed evidence of copying in that the policy issues emphasized were ones where the NDP's position was similar, yet slightly more generous, than the Liberals. In particular, the issue of aiding small business was meant to establish the Third Way credentials of the party in the eyes of the Layton Liberals. The focus on small business was also meant to build a contrast between the neo-liberal corporate tax cuts of Stephen Harper and the more sensible, Third Way approach of helping small business. On health care, the NDP's emphasis on its practical plan to hire more doctors assuaged any fears of Layton Liberals about the party's fiscal irresponsibility. Party strategists knew that the party could not compete with the Conservatives on the issue of macro-economic stability but believed that NDP messages on the economy could resonate with voters if they concentrated on micro-economic "pocketbook" issues. As such, the mentions of affordability were meant to particularly resonate with British Columbia and Ontario voters concerned with the HST, as well as Layton Liberals and traditional NDP voters who were feeling financially insecure after the global economic recession of 2008–2010. Pensions were the most important issue for the labour movement in the 2011 election, and the mention of pensions may be seen as a particular appeal to the NDP's most important stakeholder. However, party strategists also saw messages around pensions being targeted at Layton Liberals in their forties who were concerned about their financial security once they reached retirement age.

A final message in the party's English television commercials was that the NDP would fix Ottawa by working together, instead of relentlessly engaging in partisanship and political gamesmanship. Again, this message was competitor-oriented as a contrast to the Conservatives and the Liberals who rejected working together. Considering the controversy over a coalition government as a possible outcome of the election (especially if it included the Bloc Québécois), the ads were intentionally unclear on what the NDP meant by "working together." Nonetheless, the implication was that the NDP was open to co-operating with other parties (particularly the Liberals) in a minority situation. Indeed, the NDP platform stated that "New Democrats are committed to making

Parliament work better. If the mandate we receive justifies it, we will work with other federalist parties, through informal or appropriate stable arrangements."[18] Party strategists also noted that not explicitly defining the theme of "working together" allowed it take on other meanings by the end of the campaign depending on the voter: Quebec and English Canada working together, new and old NDP voters working together, or Layton and average Canadians working together.

In Quebec, the NDP played the role of "market challenger" who aimed at stealing votes from the market leader (the Bloc Québécois) who controlled a large cross-section of the political market. The NDP decided that Bloc Québécois votes could be dislodged by assuring soft Bloc voters that the NDP had a social agenda in line with Quebec values and that it could enact practical changes to get Ottawa properly functioning. Political marketing authors Butler and Collins label this market challenging approach as "high-payoff, but high risk"[19] because supporters of the market leader could simply ignore the appeals of the challenger due to their long-term loyalty to the market leading party. A lower risk and lower reward approach for a market challenger would be to concentrate on stealing market share from smaller or similarly sized competitors.

Figure 2.

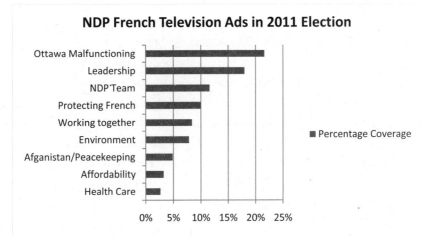

NDP French Television Ads in 2011 Election

Figure 2 illustrates how the NDP's campaign in Quebec adopted a market challenger strategic posture. The first notable element of the NDP's Quebec campaign was that its television advertisements never mentioned any of the other parties or their leaders. Party strategists calculated that an attack on the Bloc would be seen as an attack on Quebec. In this sense, the NDP's political marketing in Quebec was much more voter oriented as opposed to competitor oriented. The main message of the advertising was how the leadership of Jack Layton could remedy the malfunctioning of Canada's Parliament. The first Quebec television advertisements were released on Day 6 and featured a hamster running on a wheel for approximately seven seconds until the text appeared in the corner of screen: "La politique fait du surplace à Ottawa. Il est temps que ça change. [Politics is going round and round in Ottawa. It's time that changes.]" Four other French advertisements followed that featured Layton and Quebec NDP MP Thomas Mulcair speaking about issues (protecting the French language and Québécois culture, pacifism, and the environment) where the NDP felt that its positions were close to the dominant values of Quebec. The pair also mentioned two issues, health care and the high cost of living, that strategists thought would resonate with voters.

The message of the NDP representing change and working together illustrated the party's market challenger strategic posture. As opposed to the Bloc, Layton and his team would work together with Quebecers and other parties to get Parliament working for the values that Quebecers hold dear. The contrast was obvious. The Bloc was interested in the same old debates about sovereignty, and its defensive posture in the House of Commons could never enact the change that was needed. Due to its nature as a regional and sovereignist party, the Bloc was severely limited in delivering results to Quebecers. On other hand, because of its pan-Canadian and federalist nature, the NDP could work with other opposition parties in the House of Commons in a minority government situation to effect real change and the party could even receive cabinet seats in the event of a coalition.

MOVING INTO SECOND PLACE:
LEADERSHIP TOUR AND LEADERS' DEBATES

Considering the importance of "presidential politics" to the NDP, the leader's tour was the primary vehicle to relay both national and local messages to voters. The NDP begin a leadership tour by visiting primarily Conservative-held ridings to cement its credibility as a "Harper fighter." It generally maintained this type of schedule, but did visit some Liberal-held ridings in the Greater Toronto Area and Bloc-held ridings outside of Montreal. In the thirty-four days of the active campaign (the days of the debates excluded), Layton's tour was structured in the following fashion: Ontario (32 percent), Quebec (22 percent), British Columbia (18 percent), Saskatchewan (7 percent), Nova Scotia (6 percent), Manitoba (4 percent), Alberta (3 percent), Newfoundland (3 percent), New Brunswick (1 percent), PEI (1 percent), and NWT (1 percent).[20] This geographical breakdown basically conforms to the provinces that party had targeted as part of its strategy to grow its seat total.

Using Nvivo 9, an inductive coding analysis was performed to assess the press releases issued by the NDP during the campaign. Table 1 depicts the themes of the NDP campaign as they evolved through the campaign and the leader's tour.

Since Jack Layton spent almost 80 percent of the campaign outside of Quebec, this table should be taken as primarily representative of the NDP's English Canada campaign. While we are able to see some of what the party had identified as "Quebec" issues (environment, peacekeeping, and protecting French) peeking through, "Quebec" issues never dominated the party's discourse at any time during any week of the campaign. The table confirms the NDP's competitor orientation but shows how the party's attacks on Harper and Ignatieff were unevenly distributed during the campaign. NDP strategists decided to attack Harper during the first three weeks of the campaign to establish the NDP as a viable alternative to the Conservatives. Then the party ramped up the attacks on Ignatieff in week four to discredit the NDP's potential rival for voters opposed to the Conservatives. When it became obvious during the final week of the campaign that the Liberals were floundering, the NDP then

Table 1. Percentage Coverage of Themes in Federal NDP Press Releases by Week

Week 1 (March 26–April 1)	Week 2 (April 2–April 8)	Week 3 (April 9–April 15)	Week 4 (April 16–April 22)	Week 5 (April 23–May 1)
Attack Harper: 37%	Health care: 24%	Attack Harper: 33%	Attack Ignatieff: 16%	Leadership: 34%
Social media: 13%	Attack Harper: 16%	Leadership: 16%	Leadership: 16%	Attack Harper: 16%
Leadership: 8%	Seniors: 12%	Social media: 13%	MP Absenteeism: 12%	Momentum: 8%
Affordability: 8%	Increase military spending: 12%	Infrastructure and cities: 11%	Agriculture: 10%	HST: 6%
Small business: 7%	Crime: 9%	Momentum: 10%	Affordability: 10%	Childcare: 6%
NDP team: 5%	Veterans: 9%	Women candidates: 9%	Infrastructure and cities: 10%	Work safety laws: 6%
Ottawa broken: 4%	Leadership: 8%	Attack Ignatieff: 7%	Seniors: 9%	NDP Team: 5%
Environment: 4%	Pensions: 6%	Affordability: 6%	Attack Harper: 8%	Women Candidates: 4%
Health care: 3%	NDP Team: 5%	Health care: 4%	Environment: 8%	Only NDP can defeat Harper: 3%
Only NDP can defeat Harper: 2%	Affordability: 2%	Small business: 2%	Momentum in polls: 6%	Region taken for granted: 2%
HST: 2%	Parental leave: 1%	Only NDP can defeat Harper: 2%	Work together: 4%	Work together: 2%
Work together: 1%	Ottawa broken: 1%	Pensions: 1%	Small Business: 3%	Attack Ignatieff: 2%
Attack Ignatieff: 0.5%	Attack Ignatieff: 1%	HST: 0.4%	NDP Team: 3%	Health Care: 2%
	Afghanistan/ Peacekeeping : 0.5%	Ottawa Broken: 0.3%	Region taken for granted: 2%	Affordability: 2%
			Health care: 1%	Women's equality: 1%
			Protect French: 0.5%	Environment: 1%
			Afghanistan / Peacekeeping: 0.2%	Pensions: 1%
			Pensions: 0.2%	Small Business: 1%
				Ottawa broken: 1%
				Afghanistan / Peacekeeping: 0.4%

* Note that percentages may total more than 100 percent because some passages were coded twice if they implied two different themes.

attacked Harper again to cement its credibility as the true alternative to the Conservatives and to win over voters who might be enticed by the prospect of a minority NDP government rather than a Harper majority.

The table also shows how the party tried to establish its Third Way credentials early in the campaign by focusing on issues not usually associated with the NDP: small business, helping veterans, increasing military spending on building naval ships (to respond to disasters, protect Canada's shoreline, and support peacekeeping), and fighting crime through hiring more police officers, preventing gang recruitment, and issuing tougher sentences on home invasions and carjacking. Strategists felt that it was important to focus on these traditionally non-NDP issues because Canadians expected a potential governing party to have a well-rounded set of policies. While the middle weeks of the NDP campaign concentrated on defining the party's practical policies to fix Ottawa, the last week focused more on getting out NDP supporters by emphasizing Layton's leadership. As such, in the last week Layton tried to inspire NDP voters by hammering home the themes of voters having a choice in this election (against the strategic voting argument of the Liberals) and voting for a change to fix Ottawa.

Since the strategy of the campaign was to keep the spotlight on Layton, Table 1 illustrates that NDP did not have a strong orientation toward external groups during this campaign. There was a nod to the labour movement as the NDP consistently mentioned pensions and Layton observed the National Day of Mourning for workers killed and injured on the job. However, despite having detailed commitments in the NDP platform aimed at Aboriginals, students, New Canadians, and low-income people, organizations that represented these groups were not mentioned in the press releases nor was there a day on the campaign trail exclusively devoted to their concerns.[21]

A major turning point of the NDP's campaign appeared to be the Leaders' Debates. For a party running a competitor-oriented campaign in English Canada, the debates obviously provided a critical opportunity. In the English language debate, the strategy was to create a three-way Liberal/NDP/Conservative dynamic that would illustrate that Layton was a more trusted and practical alternative to Harper than Ignatieff. In his attacks on Harper, Layton succeeded in hammering home his primary message that "Ottawa's broken and we're gonna fix it."[22] At the same time, he was able to raise doubts about Ignatieff's ability to be an effective opposition leader by criticizing his attendance record in the House of Commons, characterizing him as a supporter of Harper's policies and the Prime Minister's "best friend." As a market follower, Layton was offering voters similar policies to the Liberals but more effective leadership and a sharper contrast to Harper.

In the French-language debate, Layton followed a more voter-oriented and market challenger strategy in appealing directly to soft nationalist voters to abandon the Bloc Québécois and support the NDP. Strategists wanted Layton to go toe to toe with Duceppe and felt that every time that Duceppe attacked Layton it increased the NDP's credibility in Quebec. His main message was outlining to voters how the NDP's policies on the environment, health care, and Afghanistan were in line with the progressive values of Quebecers and emphasizing his soft nationalist positions such as the application of Bill 101 in federal jurisdiction, asymmetrical federalism that respects provincial jurisdiction by allowing the opting out of federal programs with compensation, and requiring future Supreme Court appointments to be bilingual. He likened the Bloc to a hockey team made up of defencemen who, unlike the NDP, could never be part of a government in Ottawa.

Flash polls taken immediately after the French and English leaders' debates illustrated that voters' opinions of Layton had dramatically improved and he was seen as having the best ideas on health care and the environment.[23] Francophone voters even indicated that Layton had the "overall" best ideas and policies ahead of Gilles Duceppe. An Angus Reid poll released five days after leaders' debate indicated that the NDP's strategy had worked.[24] The Liberals were losing ground to the NDP and the two parties were tied at 25 percent of the national popular vote, while Bloc support was slipping and the NDP had firmly established itself as the most popular federalist party in Quebec.

CENTRALIZATION WITH A HINT OF LOCAL FLEXIBILITY: CAMPAIGN ORGANIZATION

While researchers agree that the CCF/NDP began as a mass party, there is considerable disagreement on the extent to which it has moved to becoming a cadre (elitist) party since its founding.[25] In terms of its campaign organization in the 2011 election, the NDP's choice to follow political marketing that was primarily voter-oriented and competitor-oriented necessitated the centralization and professionalization typically associated with cadre parties. Both a voter and competitor orientation generally puts power into the hands of professional party operatives who shape the party's communications using formal market intelligence and an assessment of the party's position within the political market. In the 2011 federal election, this type of political marketing required a surgical precision to choose the issues that appealed to targeted voters and frame these issues within the complex context of multi-party competition, minority Parliaments, and strategic voting. On the other hand, an internal orientation within political marketing would have entailed involving members in policy development, using members as a source of informal market intelligence, and supporting local input in devising national strategy. Similarly, an external orientation would have sought the public approval of stakeholders and the incorporation of their organization into campaign structures.

Interviews with party strategists in Ottawa and local activists in Saskatchewan confirm that the NDP's 2011 campaign was very centralized and professional. Whereas the Election Planning Committee (EPC) for previous campaigns had been made up of members of the party's Federal Council and Executive, the NDP Federal Council passed a motion in 2010 to simply designate the Party Executive as the EPC for the next election. While the Party Executive set the overarching goals, the real strategizing to achieve these goals was done by a much smaller group of party operatives referred to as the senior campaign team that met weekly from end of the 2008 election until the writ was dropped for the 2011 election. This state of "permanent campaign" was different from past NDP campaigns when the national campaign manager would be appointed only weeks before the writ was dropped. The senior campaign team was a small, informal entity made up of members of the Leader's Office and top campaign officials from party headquarters that did not report to the caucus or any body within the party's organization. This team was responsible for assessing campaign readiness, devising the overall strategy of the upcoming campaign (which could happen at any moment due to the minority Parliament), and coordinating the NDP's legislative agenda and House of Commons strategy with emerging campaign themes. The NDP platform was devised by officials in the policy department at party headquarters after consulting with the Party Executive, Federal Council, caucus, and the Manitoba and Nova Scotia NDP provincial governments. The platform was presented to Layton, who retained the power of final approval. There was no effort to involve party members in determining the five priorities that the NDP emphasized or which ideas from existing NDP policies made it into the platform and which were left out.

Once the campaign began, a campaign headquarters with a large staff of full-time professional workers was set up at the party's central office in Ottawa under the direction of the national campaign director, Brad Levigne. Through interviews with party strategists in Ottawa, it was confirmed that the functions of the party's campaign scored 100 percent on Stromback's Professionalized Campaign index.[26] The central campaign decided on the approximately seventy targeted seats (including the thirty-six incumbents) and worked closely with a campaign manager for each province to ensure that these ridings got the resources they needed. Market intelligence was shared with provincial campaign managers, but the provincial campaigns conducted no formal polling or focus groups of their own. Further, all of the federal ridings had been geo-mapped to overlay Census data onto the polls of the every riding. As such, the central campaign could micro-target polls in certain ridings with campaign literature aimed at a specific demographic group that was prominent in that neighbourhood. Interestingly, the Quebec campaign was not structured much differently from any other province, and its campaign director reported directly to the central campaign and received all of the market intelligence from Ottawa.

In English Canada, candidates were not an important part of the NDP's political marketing, which was centred on its leader and its competitors.

English Canadian incumbent NDP MPs played a role as spokespersons in local media but were nearly invisible in the national campaign. The concept of the star candidates and the NDP team was more important to the party's political marketing in Quebec, where the party felt that it had a less established presence. Thomas Mulcair was featured in French television advertisements and served as the party's main spokesperson in Quebec. Françoise Boivin (former Liberal MP), Nycole Turmel (first female President of the Public Service Alliance of Canada), Roméo Saganash (Quebec's first Innu lawyer), Tyron Benskin (Vice-President of the Alliance of Canadian Cinema, Television and Radio Artists), Claude Patry (former union president), and Raymond Côté (community activist) were also identified by the party as star candidates who formed the core of the NDP's Quebec team. These star candidates became the NDP's spokespeople in their respective regional Quebec media markets.

As opposed to the 2008 election, when four NDP candidates had to resign because of inappropriate behaviour in their past, no allegations dogged the NDP during this campaign with the exception of stories about a 1996 visit by Layton to a massage parlour where illegal activities had taken place. The lack of allegations of past inappropriate behaviour by candidates may have been the result of a new process that centrally vetted all candidates in each nomination contest and of the large role that the candidate search person in Ottawa played in finding local candidates. The central party office also worked to ensure that the party had a diverse slate of candidates. The NDP has a long-standing policy that nominations in non-incumbent ridings must have one or more affirmative action candidates or the central party office must be satisfied that an adequate search for such candidates had taken place. This policy seemed to work well as the party recruited ten Aboriginal candidates (compared to five for the Conservatives and eight for the Liberals) and ten openly gay candidates (compared to zero for the Conservatives and three for the Liberals). The largest success story was the NDP's having 125 female candidates, nearly 41 percent of all its candidates, which was the highest percentage fielded by a political party in Canada's history. This success in attracting women candidates can be partly attributed to a new program run by the central party office that assigned established female politicians and party activists as mentors to women running for an NDP nomination. The NDP went on to elect forty of its female candidates to the House of Commons, which represents 39 percent of their parliamentary caucus. The NDP's new Quebec caucus is a source of considerable diversity with a large number of women, visible minorities, and youth as well as two Aboriginals and two gay men.

Despite the overall centralization of the campaign, there were some interesting elements of decentralization that could be seen as vestiges of the NDP's past as a mass party. While "messages of the day" were sent daily to all candidates from the central office, there was no formal embargo on what local candidates could say or the media outlets that they could talk to. Despite candidates being allowed to deviate from the party's message as they saw fit, there were few controversial comments from NDP candidates. Further, local campaigns were allowed the flexibility to structure their campaigns and messages in ways that they felt suited local circumstances. However, few local campaigns availed themselves of this opportunity due to the lack of local financial resources, little sharing of the central campaign's market intelligence with local campaigns, and the fact the central campaign had already sent them a variety of campaign materials that been tested in their city or region. Another element of decentralization was the creation of a new mechanism to send information from local campaigns to the central campaign in Ottawa. The NDP used the NationalField software package,[27] which worked like an internal Facebook for campaign workers where they could post the experiences they were having in their local campaigns. The central office then used this informal market intelligence to alter messages targeted to that part of the country.

It should also be noted that the NDP did make a concerted effort to mobilize member participation during the campaign through social media and the Internet. This effort not only reached out to NDP members but also to what Heidar and Saglie call "registered sympathisers" who were willing to be identified as supporters but did not want to commit to buying a membership.[28] Through an aggressive Internet advertising campaign, the party built an extensive database of e-mail addresses of supporters and members to which it sent invitations to participate in

Layton's events through live streaming video, directions on how to participate in the NDP's online campaigns, and fundraising appeals.

As a recent article illustrates, most of the federal NDP's funds are raised by the party's central office, which enjoys a dominant financial position over local riding associations.[29] While the NDP's central campaign spent the maximum allowable limit during the 2008 campaign, the 308 local NDP candidates only spent a quarter of their maximum allowable limit. Recognizing low candidate spending as a problem, the central party ran a program to match fifty cents of every dollar fundraised by local associations in March and April of 2010. Though final numbers from the 2011 campaign are not yet available, party officials confirmed that local candidates spent more of their maximum allowable limits than in 2008. For its part, the central campaign aimed to spend its maximum allowable amount of $21 million during the 2011 campaign, like the Liberals and Conservatives. The latter parties, however, were able to gain a financial advantage in pre-writ spending.[30]

One of the major alterations to NDP campaigns caused by the changes to party financing laws was that unionists previously seconded to local national campaigns were considered in-kind contributions, and prohibited. The result has been that, during federal elections, the Canadian Labour Congress (CLC) has begun to run a political action campaign that is completely independent of the NDP. Since 2004, the CLC has run its "Better Choices" campaign, whose underlying message was that the NDP was a better choice, but members were not explicitly urged to vote NDP. In tandem with the Better Choices campaign, the CLC introduced a new addition to its political action during the federal election in 2011. Expanding on a pilot project attempted during the 2008 election, it created a Labour Outreach Committee composed of partisan unions[31] affiliated with the NDP. This committee set up offices in forty-eight targeted ridings in English Canada where the NDP could gain a seat or where the NDP incumbent was in a tough fight. Union staff in these offices organized union members to volunteer for the NDP, directly communicated with local union members outlining reasons that they should vote for the NDP, and organized meet-and-greet sessions between union members and the NDP candidate. As such, these union staff aided the NDP without being an official part of its campaign. The NDP ended up winning thirty-eight out of the forty-eight seats that the committee had targeted. It should be noted that the Quebec labour centrals did not support the NDP, preferring to openly endorse the Bloc Québécois or call on their members to vote for the party with the best chance to beat a Conservative in their riding.

This examination of the 2011 campaign organization illustrates that the NDP's political marketing was not very oriented to its members or its external stakeholders. However, there was almost no public criticism of the party from unions, local party members, or candidates; party strategists found local activists and union leaders to be privately much happier with how the campaign was run than previous campaigns. Perhaps this contentment signals a shift in the culture of the NDP. The leadership of the party paid attention to keeping party members informed and mobilized through the Internet during the campaign and allowed a considerable margin of local flexibility. The result of these efforts may have been that party members were more willing to accept the necessity for the party's professional corps to craft a campaign strategy without their involvement. For its part, the labour movement has become more independent of the NDP, and sees itself as an autonomous actor in the political arena. While it remains organically connected to the NDP, it wants to run its own lobbying campaigns as opposed to depending on the NDP caucus in the House of Commons, and it is now forced by party financing rules to run arm's-length activities during an election campaign. The result is that the NDP is free to professionalize itself and emphasize the issues that its strategists believe are to its advantage with less ideological and strategic control from the labour movement.

ANALYSIS OF THE RESULTS: THE "CRITICAL ELECTION" OF 2011?

In his seminal article written in 1955, V.O. Key argued that groups of voters are "aligned" to certain political parties along religious, regional, class, or ethnic lines.[32] Realignment theory, which flowed from Key's article, argues that periods of electoral realignment begin with a "critical election" where voter behaviour changes in response to the advent of new social or economic forces, extraordinary political events, or the emergence of new issues and parties.[33] An examination of the NDP's gains in popular vote in Table 2 provides evidence that the 2011 federal election demonstrated a pattern of vote shifts which could be consistent with a realignment of the Canadian electorate.

Table 2. NDP Results by Province and Territory in the 2008 and 2011 Canadian Federal Elections

Province	2008 Vote	2008 Seats	2011 Vote	Vote Gain	2011 Seats	Seat Gain
NL	33.7%	1	32.6%	-1.1%	2	1
PEI	9.8%	0	15.4%	5.6%	0	0
NS	28.9%	2	30.3%	1.4%	3	1
NB	21.9%	1	29.8%	7.9%	1	0
QC	12.1%	1	42.9%	30.8%	59	58
ON	18.2%	17	25.6%	7.4%	22	5
MB	24.0%	4	25.8%	1.8%	2	-2
SK	25.5%	0	32.3%	6.8%	0	0
AB	12.7%	1	16.8%	4.1%	1	0
BC	26.1%	9	32.5%	6.4%	12	3
NWT	41.4%	1	45.8%	4.4%	1	0
NU	27.6%	0	19.4%	-8.2%	0	0
YK	8.7%	0	14.4%	5.7%	0	0
National	18.2%	37	30.6%	12.4%	103	66

The case of Quebec jumps out as an example of a shift in voter alignment where thousands of voters choose to support the NDP for the first time in areas where the CCF/NDP had no history of electoral success. While the shift is not so dramatic, there is evidence of realignment in favour of the NDP in English Canada as well. In Atlantic Canada, the NDP reached historic heights: they beat the Liberals in popular vote in Nova Scotia for only the second time its history and in New Brunswick for the first time. In Ontario, the NDP also reached a historical high point in its popular support and beat the Liberals both in terms of seats and popular vote for the first time in that province's electoral history. In Western Canada, the NDP had replaced the Liberals as the main left-of-centre party since the 1970s. Yet, even in these provinces, the NDP achieved popular vote totals that had only been seen for the party during the 1980s. Due to the first-past-the-post system, the NDP was overly compensated for its increased popular vote in Quebec seats and undercompensated for its rise in popular vote in English Canada, achieving only an eight-seat gain outside of Quebec. However, the fact that the NDP beat the Liberals in popular vote in every province except Newfoundland and Prince Edward Island, and that the NDP's total vote in English Canada increased from 2.07 million in 2008 to 2.88 million in 2011, alerts us to the possibility that this federal election may have been a critical election that could trigger a realignment of Canadian politics towards a two-party system.

The results of the 2011 election indicate that the creation of the Conservative Party of Canada in the early 2000s ultimately proved beneficial for the NDP. As Duverger's Law states, a first-past-the-post system generally encourages the creation of a two-party system because votes for third parties seem wasted.[34] In English Canada, the new Conservative party hastened the decline of the Liberals by providing a single choice for voters previously split between the Progressive Conservatives and Reform/Canadian Alliance and winning over segments of the electorate that traditionally voted Liberal. At the same time, the new Conservative party's style of governing and some of its policies polarized the electorate into stricter right/left ideological camps. As the Liberals' viability as a governing party diminished, many of its remaining supporters in English Canada (dubbed Layton Liberals by NDP strategists) became susceptible to appeals from a third party. The effect of Duverger's Law, which had worked against the NDP for its entire history, became mitigated. As the Liberals struggled in opposition with two ineffective leaders, an unclear ideology, and on-again, off-again support of the Conservative government, the NDP was able to market itself to Layton Liberals as a viable alternative to Stephen Harper by emphasizing its Third Way social democratic ideas and trusted leader, and by signalling to voters that they had a choice.

The election of Jack Layton as leader of the NDP coincided with a string of minority Parliaments that had made the party a major political player in Ottawa. The party's political marketing used the NDP's increased clout in Ottawa to build up Layton's image. Since the party negotiated what it called a "Better Balanced Budget" with the Martin government in 2005, the NDP had consciously attempted to portray Layton as an honest broker in the House of Commons who could be trusted to co-operate with other parties to bring about tangible results for ordinary Canadians. As Layton negotiated budgets with Harper and Martin and brokered coalition deals with the other opposition parties, he seemed increasingly prime ministerial. Whereas the NDP under McDonough had always struggled to define its relevance to national politics since it seemed so far removed from political power, voters could now imagine the NDP as a potential governing party.

As declining public trust and rising discontent with governing institutions has been found to be related to voting for third parties,[35] it is possible that the NDP's pledge to "fix Ottawa" resonated with Layton Liberals who had grown cynical about the political games and extreme partisanship in consecutive minority Parliaments. Cynical about the ability of old-line parties to bring about change and put aside partisanship to work with others, these Layton Liberals may have been enticed by the possibility of a NDP-led minority government willing to cooperate with other parties as a replacement for the Harper minority government. A Nanos poll taken late in the campaign confirmed that an NDP-led minority government was favoured by nearly one-third of voters in Atlantic Canada and one-quarter of voters in Ontario.[36] Given the closeness of the NDP's and Liberals' policy positions and the fact that all three of the opposition parties had entered into a coalition agreement two years earlier, there was little reason to believe that an NDP minority government could not co-operate with the other parties in the House of Commons to get practical results for Canadians. In short, the NDP's pledge to work together to fix Ottawa was made believable to Layton Liberals through the relatively extraordinary events of the minority Parliaments of the last seven years that had changed their perception of the NDP and its leader.

In Quebec, the emergence of the Conservative Party was also beneficial for the NDP. While there is a *bleu* tradition in Quebec going back to before Confederation, the Conservative Party of Canada was formed out of two political parties that had less than 12 percent combined support in Quebec in the 2000 federal election. Quebec has a deeply ingrained strain of social democracy in its political culture that has its roots in the social Catholic thought of the first half of the twentieth century.[37] The touchstones of this social democratic political culture are collectivism, acceptance of state intervention in the economy, and the accomplishment of greater societal equality through the welfare state. In McGrane's analysis, social democracy and sovereignty-association became intractably linked during the 1960s and remained mutually reinforcing concepts through the two periods of Parti Québécois (PQ) governments.[38] Indeed, he finds a number of striking similarities between the Third Way policies of the Saskatchewan NDP government under Romanow and the policies of the PQ governments under Parizeau, Bouchard, and Landry.

Due to the nature of Quebec's political culture, the Harper Conservatives never succeeded in appealing to a wide cross-section of Quebec voters despite their embracing of soft nationalist positions such as allowing Quebec a seat at UNESCO and supporting a motion in the House of Commons to declare Quebec a nation within Canada. On issues of social justice, foreign policy, and the environment, the Conservatives were consistently on opposite sides of the majority of Quebecers. By voting NDP, Quebecers were protesting the fact that the Harper government did not respect their social democratic political culture or what they thought of as Quebec values. The political marketing of the NDP in 2011 that emphasized moderate social democratic policies, respect for Quebec values of pacifism and protecting the environment, and soft Québécois nationalist positions created an attractive alternative to the Harper Conservatives that was in line with province's political culture.

Further, with Layton's Quebec roots and the recruitment of candidates like Mulcair and Boivin, the NDP presented itself as more than simply the English Canadian party it had been in the past.

However, social democratic voters could have easily have continued to vote for Bloc Québécois to voice their displeasure with the Harper Conservatives. Indeed, the Bloc Québécois designed its campaign around the premise that only a vote for the Bloc could prevent a Harper majority government. What was not evident prior to the election was that the NDP's rising profile in minority Parliaments and the extraordinary events surrounding the potential of a coalition government in 2008 had changed the dynamics of federal politics in Quebec. It should be noted that the prospect of a coalition government was very popular in Quebec during the prorogation crisis of 2008 and the same Nanos poll referred to above showed that 43 percent of Quebecers were hoping that the outcome of the 2011 election was a minority NDP government. Possibly, the events surrounding the prorogation in 2008 made Quebecers realize that the Bloc Québécois would never be accepted in a coalition government and their inability to work together with other parties severely limited their capacity to achieve tangible results.

The potential of an NDP-led minority government and the possibility of a Harper majority government openly hostile to Quebec values put the national question into a different light. The Bloc Québécois had been making essentially the same appeal since 1993: vote for the Bloc because only the Bloc can protect the interests of the Québécois nation in Ottawa while waiting for the dream of sovereignty to be realized. However, after five elections, the Bloc's nationalism appeared insular, defensive, and ineffective. Chapter 5 by Éric Bélanger and Richard Nadeau outlines how the gradual decline in the prominence of the issue of sovereignty combined with the lack of a burning federal scandal or linguistic issue to diminish the need for a sovereignist party in Ottawa to defend Quebec's interests. As such, they argue that both short-term and long-term conditions had never been so disadvantageous for the BQ.

The Bloc's appeal to its soft voters was further weakened as the new political dynamics of minority Parliaments and the new Conservative Party combined with a heightened sense of voter cynicism among the

Quebec electorate. A recent spate of high-profile political scandals in their province[39] and the hyper-partisanship of the House of Commons seemed to have created an anti-incumbent feeling among Quebec voters. Indeed, a Léger Marketing poll cited in Chapter 5 found that almost half of NDP voters in Quebec stated that they voted NDP because "I've had enough of other parties and I wanted change." NDP strategists realized that the NDP "owned" the change issue in Quebec because the Bloc had been re-elected in many ridings for five consecutive elections, the Conservatives were in government, and the Liberals were in government in Quebec City and had previously formed a federal government that had been tarred by the sponsorship scandal. The NDP was the only party with a clean slate in Quebec, and its message about Ottawa malfunctioning and the need for parties to work together connected well with a Quebec electorate looking for a party representing change but still in line with their values. Having rejected the Bloc and lacking suitable alternatives, a significant group of Quebec voters, in all regions of the province, decided to vote for a social democratic federalist party instead of a social democratic sovereignist party for the first time in the province's history. As such, they did not change values but changed parties.

CONCLUSION: THE NDP WITHOUT JACK LAYTON

An important implication of the argument of this chapter is that agency matters in politics. Agents within the NDP devised political marketing that was ultimately successful in taking advantage of the opportunities provided during the 2011 election campaign. Therefore, the historical breakthrough of the NDP in 2011 may be partly attributed to its political marketing, which might have successfully orchestrated the shift towards a two-party system in Canadian politics.

Unfortunately, the agent at the forefront of the NDP's historic victory is now gone. The untimely death of Jack Layton only four months after the federal election has engendered considerable uncertainty concerning the future of the NDP. Observers have asked how much of the party's success was dependent upon Layton and if a post-Layton NDP is doomed to wither? Layton was a critical component of the party's success, and his presence at the helm of the party will be sorely missed. However, it is important to realize that the foundation of the NDP's success, which was built by Layton and his team, is still there. As shown in this chapter, the NDP is a vastly more credible, centrist, and national party than when Layton took over. For the first time in its history, it is the official Opposition and will play a prominent role in the House of Commons as the government in waiting. The Liberals and the Bloc Québécois, the NDP's rivals for left-of-centre votes, are struggling to define themselves in the new political landscape.

Still, any new NDP leader faces significant challenges. The role of being a bridge between Quebec and the rest of Canada and a vehicle for Quebecers' new engagement with federalism has been thrust on the NDP. As an Anglo-Quebecer, Layton was able to straddle Canada's two solitudes and provide a rallying point for both English Canadian and Quebec voters who were opposed to the Harper Conservatives. The new leader of the NDP must broker compromises from both the Quebec and English-Canadian MPs in the NDP's caucus to prevent open disagreement on divisive issues. The new leader will also have to find ways to avoid internal friction between the moderate and radical factions of the party. Whoever takes over from Layton will have to craft a left-of-centre ideological position that is both acceptable to party members and seen as realistic by Canadian voters. Finally, the new leader must also prevent an exodus of the professional political talent in Ottawa — people such as national director Brad Lavigne and strategic communications director Kathleen Monk — that the party attracted during the Layton years. These professionals have valuable experience that is needed as the party tackles its new job as official Opposition, particularly with the bevy of new, inexperienced MPs coming from Quebec.

The 2011 federal election transformed Jack Layton into a political legend. He overcame his health problems to run an astoundingly successful campaign that inspired many Canadians who had never voted for the NDP to take a chance on the party. While it is impossible to replace a legend, the NDP now has the political marketing prowess to build upon Layton's legacy. Despite the fact that Quebec voters have been occasionally fickle, as the case of the Diefenbaker and Mulroney Progressive Conservatives illustrate, they were quite loyal to the Liberal Party throughout the twentieth century and were faithful to the Bloc Québécois for five elections. With the visibility gained as official opposition, the NDP could continue to eat away at the Liberal popular vote in English Canada and maintain its strength in Quebec. The result could be a continued move towards a two-party system with the Conservatives as the party of the centre-right and the NDP as the party of the centre-left. If so, such a two-party system would have its origins in the critical election of 2011 and the NDP's political marketing success during that campaign.

NOTES

The information contained in several sections of this chapter was obtained by telephone interviews with NDP candidates and officials done May 17–19, 2011. An agreement was made with informants to publish their names but not to attribute any exact quotations or information to a particular person. The following NDP activists and party officials graciously agreed to be interviewed: Brad Levigne (National Campaign Director), Nathan Rothman (National Director of Organization), Karl Bélanger (Press Secretary to Jack Layton), Drew Anderson (National Director of Communications), Kathleen Monk (War Room Media Director and National Media Spokesperson), Danny Mallett (Director of Political Action for the Canadian Labour Congress), John Tzupa (Regional Campaign Manager for Saskatchewan), Erica Spracklin (Campaign Manager for the non-targeted riding of Saskatoon–Wanuskewin), John Parry (candidate for the non-targeted riding of Saskatoon–Wanuskewin), and Nettie Wiebe (candidate for the targeted riding of Saskatoon–Rosetown–Biggar). The author would also like to thank his research assistant, Sarah Shoker, for her help in gathering media stories on the NDP campaign, as well as Alan Whitehorn and Alex Marland for their comments on an earlier draft.

1.   Stanley Knowles, *The New Party* (Toronto: McClelland and Stewart, 1961), 96–97.
2.   See Jennifer Lees-Marshment, *Political Marketing: Principles and Applications* (Abingdon: Routledge, 2009).
3.   Alex Marland, "Canadian Political Parties' Strategic and Tactical Marketing: The 1993 and 2006 Canadian Federal Elections" in *Political Marketing in Canada*, eds. Alex Marland, Thierry Giasson, and Jennifer Lees-Marshment (Vancouver: UBC Press, forthcoming); and Alex Marland, "Canadian Political Parties: Market-Orientated or Ideological Slagbrains," in *Political Marketing in Comparative Perspective*, eds.

Darren Lilleker and Jennifer Lees-Marshment (Manchester: Manchester University Press, 2005).

4. See Alan Whitehorn, "Jack Layton and the NDP: Gains But No Breakthrough," in *The Canadian General Election of 2004*, eds. Jon H. Pammett and Christopher Dornan (Toronto: Dundurn, 2004); Alan Whitehorn, "The NDP and the Enigma of Strategic Voting," in *The Canadian Federal Election of 2006*, eds. Jon H. Pammett and Christopher Dornan (Toronto: Dundurn, 2006); and Lynda Erickson and David Laycock, "Modernization, Incremental Progress, and the Challenge of Relevance," in *The Canadian Federal Election of 2008*, eds. Jon H. Pammett and Christopher Dornan (Toronto: Dundurn, 2008), 109.

5. See Harold Jensen and Lisa Young, "Cartels, Syndicates, and Coalitions: Canada's Political Parties after the 2004 Reforms" in *Money, Politics, and Democracy*, eds. Harold Jansen and Lisa Young (Vancouver: UBC Press, 2011).

6. Harold Jansen and Lisa Young, "Solidarity Forever? The NDP, Organized Labour, and the Changing Face of Party Finance in Canada," *Canadian Journal of Political Science* 42, no 3 (September 2009): 657–678.

7. See Anthony Giddens, *The Third Way: The Renewal of Social Democracy* (Cambridge: Polity Press, 1998).

8. See Paul Adams, "The NDP Still Veers to the Left," *Globe and Mail*, August 30, 1999, A1.

9. For a description of the ideas and policies of the Third Way in Saskatchewan and Manitoba see David McGrane, "Which Third Way? A Comparison of the Romanow and Calvert NDP Governments from 1991 to 2007," in *Saskatchewan Politics: Crowding the Centre*, ed. Howard Leeson (Regina: Canadian Plains Research Center, 2008); and Jared Wesley, *Campaigns and Cultures on the Canadian Prairies* (Vancouver: UBC Press, 2011).

10. Jamey Heath, *Dead Centre: Hope, Possibility, and Unity for Canadian Progressives* (Mississauga: John Wiley and Sons, 2007).

11. John Ibbiston, "Why a Defeated Budget Helps Harper's Hunt for a Majority," *Globe and Mail*, March 23, 2011; Jeffrey Simpson, "One Adroit Budget, One More Conservative Government," *Globe and Mail*, March 23, 2011; and Barbara Yaffe, "Has Harper Duped Opposition into Election?", *Vancouver Sun*, March 24, 2011.

12. Laurier Institute for the Study of Public Opinion and Policy, "Federal Party Support Table: January 2007–April 2011," accessed April 26, 2011, *www.wlu.ca/lispop/fed-supporttable.html*.

13. Patrick Butler and Neil Collins, "Strategic Analysis in Political Markets," *European Journal of Marketing* 30, no. 10/11 (1996): 30.

14. The Liberals' platform offered to hire more doctors and nurses in rural areas, create a "coast to coast to coast" plan to increase catastrophic drug coverage and lower the cost of prescription drugs, and provide EI benefits and tax credits for Canadians who provide homecare family members. Liberal Party of Canada, *Your Family, Your Future, Your Canada, Election Platform for the 2011 Canadian Federal Election*, 30, 37, and 38.

15. QSR International, *Nvivo 9 Basics*, Doncaster, Australia: QSR International, 2010, 54.
16. See Robert Ormrod, "A Conceptual Model of Political Market Orientation," *Journal of Nonprofit & Public Sector Marketing* 14, no. 1/2 (2005): 47–64.
17. Chris Cobb, "Cane-Wielding Layton Strikes 'Emotional Chord,'" *Postnews Media*, April 29, 2011.
18. NDP, *Giving Your Family a Break*, 2011, 23.
19. Butler and Collins, "Strategic Analysis in Political Markets," 30.
20. Note that days when Layton visited two provinces, each province was assigned half of a day.
21. The press releases refer in passing to Aboriginals in the context of increasing child-care spaces and refer to poverty only in the context of senior citizens.
22. Staff, "A Leaders' Debate Scorecard," *Toronto Star*, April 12, 2011.
23. Ipsos-Reid, *Federal Election Pre/post Debate Flash Poll Results*, April 12, 2011; and Ipsos-Reid, *French Language Federal Election Pre/post Debate Flash Poll Results*, April 13, 2011.
24. Angus Reid, "Tories Ahead in Canada, But NDP Ties Liberals as Layton Connects with Voters," April 18, 2011.
25. Young and Zakuta have both argued that the CCF moved to the cadre party model while Whitehorn and Sayers hold that the party tried to maintain mass party attributes. See Alan Whitehorn, *Canadian Socialism: Essays on the CCF-NDP* (Don Mills: Oxford University Press, 1992); Walter Young, *Anatomy of a Party: The National CCF 1932–1961* (Toronto: University of Toronto Press, 1969); Anthony Sayers, *Parties, Candidates, and Constituency Campaigns in Canadian Elections* (Vancouver: University of British Columbia Press, 1999); and Leo Zakuta, *A Protest Movement Becalmed: A Study of Change in the CCF* (Toronto: University of Toronto Press, 1964).
26. Jesper Stromback, "Political Marketing and Professionalized Campaigning," *Journal of Political Marketing* 6: 49–67.
27. This software package was successfully used in Obama's 2008 presidential campaign. See *www.nationalfield.org*.
28. Knut Heidar and Jo Saglie, "Predestined Parties? Organizational Change in Norwegian Political Parties," *Party Politics* 9, no. 2 (2003): 219–239.
29. David Coletto, Harold J. Jansen, and Lisa Young, "Stratarchical Party Organization and Party Finance in Canada," *Canadian Journal of Political Science* 44, no. 1 (2011): 111–136.
30. While financial statements from 2010 were not available at the time of writing, financial statements indicate that the NDP spent $7.9 million, compared to $17 million for the Liberals and $27 million for the Conservatives in 2009.
31. The following partisan unions were represented on the Labour Outreach Committee: PSAC, CUPE, IMA, Steelworkers, CEP, UFCW, CAW, and COPE. It is interesting to note that the CAW, which decided once again to support Liberals in some ridings and the NDP in other ridings, was a part of this committee but did not provide any comparable support to the Liberals.

32. V.O. Key, "A Theory of Critical Elections," *Journal of Politics* 17 (1955): 3–18.

33. See Theodore Rosenof, *Realignment: The Theory that Changed the Way We Think about American Politics* (Lanham: Rowman and Littlefield, 2003).

34. Maurice Duverger, *Political Parties: Their Organization and Activity in the Modern State* (New York: Wiley, 1963), 217.

35. Éric Bélanger and Richard Nadeau, "Political Trust and the Vote in Multiparty Elections: The Canadian Case," *European Journal of Political Research* 44, no. 1 (2005): 121–146.

36. Nanos Research, "West of Ottawa River Canadians want Tory minority, Quebec NDP minority," May 1, 2011.

37. See David McGrane, *From Traditional to Third Way Social Democracy: The Emergence and Evolution of Social Democratic Ideas and Policies in Saskatchewan and Quebec in the 20th Century* (PhD diss., Department of Political Science, Carleton University, June 2007).

38. *Ibid.*

39. Both the Montreal municipal government and the provincial government in Quebec had been rocked by scandals relating to government contracts and the construction industry.

CHAPTER 5

The Bloc Québécois: Capsized by the Orange Wave

Éric Bélanger | Richard Nadeau

The 2011 federal election turned out to be an historic one for the Bloc Québécois, but in a very negative way. After experiencing some major breakthroughs in the election that followed the Meech Lake and Charlottetown Constitutional Accords (1993) and the election held around the time that the federal sponsorship scandal erupted (2004), the Bloc this time has been reduced to only four seats in the House of Commons, its worst result since it won thirty-eight seats in the 2000 election. Even Gilles Duceppe, the party's leader since 1997 and one of the most popular politicians in Quebec, was not re-elected in his riding of Laurier–Sainte-Marie. The Bloc Québécois managed to finish second in the province in terms of vote share, with nearly one Quebec voter in four still supporting the party. Nonetheless, the New Democratic Party's "orange wave" in Quebec all but sank the Bloc in 2011.

Back in September 2008, during the previous federal election campaign, former Parti Québécois minister Jacques Brassard made a splash by telling *La Presse* that he thought the Bloc had become a clone of the NDP ever since leaving the issue of Quebec sovereignty more or less on the sidelines.[1] With the nationalist debate not being salient at all in the 2011 election, it seems that a large number of *Bloquistes* came to agree with Brassard, and decided to support the "real" social-democratic party, rather than its copy.[2] In this campaign, the central question that gradually came to face voters in Quebec was not simply which party could prevent a Conservative majority, but which one could prevent a Conservative government at all. Contrary to the limited possibilities for the Bloc, the NDP could actually aspire to replace — at least in the medium term — this right-wing government that was so decried by Gilles Duceppe and his team of candidates.

Even though a large number of Bloc voters appear to have flocked to the NDP in this election, support for Jack Layton's party also came in good part from previous Liberal and Conservative voters. According to preliminary results from the 2011 Canadian Election Study's campaign survey, in Quebec both "federalists and sovereignists came over to the NDP. In the second half of the campaign in Quebec, the Liberals were holding just over half of their 2008 voters, and the Conservatives and Bloc Québécois only two-thirds of theirs. The NDP was the beneficiary, taking about three-quarters of those leaving the three other main parties."[3]

Thus, in 2011 the Bloc Québécois seems to have been hit by a perfect storm. For the first time in that party's twenty-year history, a peculiar combination of factors struck them all at once. Support for sovereignty was relatively low, there was no Quebec-centric issue that made it urgent or crucial for Quebecers to support — at least tactically — a separatist option, and the campaign dynamics clearly favoured a rival party that had slowly been gaining ground in Quebec ever since the 2004 federal election. Before discussing in more detail the factors that may have led to the Bloc Québécois's setback, we first sum up the past three years of the BQ in Parliament, then provide an account of the party's 2011 campaign message and the five weeks of campaigning led by Gilles Duceppe and his troops.

THE BLOC IN THE FORTIETH PARLIAMENT: BUSINESS AS USUAL

The weeks that followed the October 2008 federal election in Canada proved to be tumultuous to say the least. Parliament was plunged into an unprecedented crisis due to the opposition parties' signed agreement to form a Liberal-NDP coalition to replace the newly installed minority Conservative government. The crisis was ignited by the Conservatives' proposal to put an end to the regime of public party financing as part of their new economic recovery plan.[4] Gilles Duceppe signed onto Stéphane

Dion and Jack Layton's agreement, thereby guaranteeing that the Bloc Québécois would support a Liberal-NDP coalition government at least until summer 2010. Even though the coalition project was found to be popular in Quebec opinion polls, more so than in the rest of the country, there were many within the sovereignist movement who were very much ill at ease with the idea of Duceppe allowing Dion — a long-time enemy of Quebec separatists — to become prime minister of Canada. The crisis ended in early December with the prorogation of Parliament.

In the first weeks of January 2009 Gilles Duceppe toured Quebec's regions. He stated that during his tour he had been able to witness Quebecers' deep disillusionment with Stephen Harper's discourse and actions during the parliamentary crisis. He claimed that the BQ was ready for either a new election in the spring or a new coalition agreement, in the eventuality that the upcoming federal budget were to be voted down.[5] However, a few days later, newly appointed Liberal leader Michael Ignatieff announced that his party would not enter into any new coalition talks.

Once Ignatieff put an end to the whole coalition drama, it was business as usual for the Bloc. In February the party held a general meeting in Saint-Hyacinthe during which Gilles Duceppe received the confidence of 94.8 percent of the delegates. In his concluding speech he strongly criticized Ignatieff, accusing him of having let Quebecers down by abandoning the coalition project.[6] The Bloc's attacks on the new Liberal leader continued throughout the spring, as a number of CROP and Léger Marketing vote intention polls showed that the Liberal Party was on the rise in Quebec and even slightly ahead of the Bloc. Indeed, in a few partisan speeches made in Montreal, Ignatieff called upon Quebec nationalist voters by saying that Quebecers' place in Ottawa ought to be in government — they did not deserve to remain in opposition permanently.[7]

In spring 2009, the Bloc was proactive in Parliament. Disappointed with the Conservative government's economic recovery plan, Gilles Duceppe's party proposed its own $32-billion plan, which emphasized the need for subsidizing forest industries and the manufacturing sector, as well as the necessity for reducing the amount of time before a worker could receive employment insurance.[8] The Bloc Québécois's position against Bill C-268, which proposed a minimum sentence of five years for offences involving child trafficking, led to some controversy. Bloc MP Serge Ménard defended his party's position by arguing that the Parliament should let judges do their job and decide the appropriate sentence on a case-by-case basis.[9] Later that year, all Bloc MPs also voted against Bill C-391, which aimed to repeal the long-gun registry.

In September the BQ decided to support a government Ways and Means motion, thereby avoiding a fall election. Gilles Duceppe justified his party's support saying that the motion did not include anything detrimental to Quebec's interests. However, a week later the Bloc MPs supported the Liberal Party's motion of no-confidence (although an election was again avoided because the NDP decided to abstain). Despite the government's survival, the Bloc launched an important negative publicity campaign against both the Conservative and Liberal leaders. Published in most major newspapers across Quebec, a large ad put half of Harper's face side by side with half of Ignatieff's. Above the picture, the message "*Deux partis, un regard*" ("Two parties, one single view") was written in large print, with further explanation underneath claiming that both leaders shared the same restrictive view of the Québécois nation and voted the same way on all Quebec-related issues in the House. At the bottom of the ad was the mention that only the BQ is standing up to defend Quebec's interests. Furthering the point, Gilles Duceppe highlighted to the press that Michael Ignatieff, like Stephen Harper, was in favour of oil extraction in the Alberta tar sands and of the creation of a pan-Canadian securities commission, and was opposed to the application of Bill 101's provisions to federal institutions.[10]

Earlier in the year, Bloc MPs Réal Ménard and Paul Crête had vacated their seats to run as candidates in municipal and provincial elections, respectively. Two federal by-elections were thus held in Quebec on November 9, 2009. The Bloc Québécois kept its Hochelaga seat with Daniel Paillé succeeding Ménard. Although Paillé's victory was relatively easy, it was the NDP candidate who finished in second place with nearly 20 percent of votes cast. In the district of Montmagny–L'Islet–Kamouraska–Rivière-du-Loup, Conservative candidate Bernard Généreux managed to take the seat from the BQ with a margin of five percentage points. The Bloc had held this seat ever since 1993. Both of these by-elections raised warning signs that should probably have been heeded by the Bloc leadership. Instead, Gilles Duceppe declared that from now on, except in cases of *force majeure* he would not allow his MPs to resign mid-mandate like Ménard and Crête, as he concluded that voter discontent with Crête's early resignation was the main reason why his party had lost that seat to the Conservatives.[11]

With Michael Ignatieff's Liberals now on the decline in Quebec vote intention polls, the Bloc Québécois started focusing again on the Conservatives.[12] Bloc MPs talked "green" and emphasized environmental issues in the wake of the December 2009 Copenhagen international conference on climate change. One key argument was the importance of reducing by half the province of Quebec's reliance on oil over the next ten years. The Bloc also strongly condemned the Conservative government's support of the tar sands oil extraction industry as well as its lack of a serious plan for reducing greenhouse gases in Canada. Another one of the BQ's important lines of attack was Prime Minister Harper's foreign policy, saying that in general it was out of touch with Quebecers' values and with Canada's past actions on the international scene, and that because of that Canada was "unworthy" of obtaining a seat in the United Nations' Security Council. According to the Bloc, further evidence of the Conservative government being "dangerous" for Quebecers was Bill C-12, which aimed at revising Canada's electoral map by adding thirty seats to the House of Commons but with no new seats for Quebec, something that would in effect reduce Quebec's political weight in Ottawa. The BQ tabled a motion that would guarantee that Quebec's current proportion of seats in the House (24.3 percent) be maintained permanently. Although supported by the NDP, the Bloc's motion was defeated in April 2010 (but in the end Bill C-12 was not adopted either).

In 2010 the sovereignist movement wished to celebrate a number of symbolic anniversaries: thirty years since the first referendum on Quebec independence, fifteen years since the second referendum, as well as twenty years since the failure of the Meech Lake Accord and the creation of the Bloc Québécois. Gilles Duceppe himself celebrated twenty years of his career as a Bloc MP in Ottawa in August, with close to eight hundred guests.[13] The BQ and its leader thus believed that 2010 was a perfect year to try to boost support for their constitutional option. Duceppe declared that it was their duty to demonstrate to Quebec federalist voters that the Canadian federation could never be reformed to Quebec's satisfaction; according to him, the fruit of reform will never be ripe because the tree itself is rotten.[14] On a more controversial note, the Bloc leader let it slip that his party's core mission was to "resist" the Canadian regime until Quebec was "freed," an unfortunate choice of words that many federal politicians were quick to associate with Second World War vocabulary.[15]

In April 2010, Gilles Duceppe toured six Canadian cities in order to explain the reasons for the existence of a sovereignty movement and why the idea of an independent Quebec remained relevant today. The following fall, the BQ leader went on tour in the United States and Europe. In Washington, D.C., Duceppe warned some think tank representatives that it was only a matter of time before the sovereignists would be back in power in Quebec and would eventually hold another referendum. He argued that it would then be in the United States' best interest not to intervene in the debate and, if the referendum's outcome were to be positive, to recognize quickly the independence of Quebec so as to help prevent the political conflict from dragging on.[16] On his European tour, Duceppe visited Vimy, Strasbourg, Paris, Barcelona, Edinburgh, and London. On top of giving a few public talks about Quebec politics and secession, the goal was also to firm up the links between the Bloc Québécois and other separatist movements, including the Scottish National Party, as well as try to rebuild the bridges between Quebec sovereignists and the political party of French President Nicolas Sarkozy (the latter had been highly critical of the movement in 2008).[17] In retrospect, one can observe that sovereignty support in Quebec did not react much to all this activity and has remained stable in the low 40 percent range ever since the beginning of 2010.[18] In addition, these BQ tours were ridiculed by most media commentators outside Quebec as being somewhat pointless,[19] while in Quebec they went almost unnoticed.

At the end of January 2011, Gilles Duceppe announced that his party's support for the upcoming federal budget would be conditional on the province of Quebec obtaining about $5 billion in various commitments. He requested among other things that the $2.2-billion sales tax harmonization dispute with the government of Quebec be settled in the budget, that $1.5 billion be provided to Quebec as compensation for past reforms in the equalization transfer payments, and that $175 million of federal funding be contributed to the construction of a new arena in Quebec City.[20] Certainly, the BQ's support of the arena project was partly strategic. The Harper government had already announced that it would not contribute financially to the project, and the Bloc was hoping to benefit from this refusal and recapture several Conservative-held seats in the Quebec City region in the upcoming election. Since September 2010, Duceppe himself visited this area about once a week.[21] In any case, it seems clear that all these demands were not acceded to by the Conservatives to ensure that the BQ would not support the budget, and that they would get their election. That being said, all signs suggest that the Bloc had the same goal of triggering an election by making these demands.

The BQ members formally adopted their party's electoral platform in a general meeting held in mid-February 2011. In a rather bold move, they included in their platform a statement that, in case of no parliamentary majority, the Bloc kept open the possibility of supporting a coalition of political parties as long as this coalition were deemed to respect the Quebec population's interests and values.[22] During the meeting the strength of Gilles Duceppe's leadership over his party was confirmed yet again as he received a confidence vote of 95.3 percent.

On March 24, independent Senator Jean-Claude Rivest gave a much-commented-upon interview to *Le Devoir* in which he expressed deep concern over what he found to be the absence of Quebec in the political discourse heard in the rest of the country. According to him, Canadians outside Quebec had now ceased to care about Quebec. He claimed that the three federalist parties no longer seemed interested in representing and defending Quebec's realities and distinctiveness. Senator Rivest finally stated that if the Bloc Québécois existed it was simply because the other federalist parties were "lousy."[23] The next day the Conservative minority government was brought down via a motion of no-confidence and a new federal election was called for May 2.

THE BLOC PLATFORM AND PUBLICITY

Mirroring somehow Senator Rivest's concerns, the Bloc Québécois's new slogan was "*Parlons Qc*" ("Let's talk about Qc"). The slogan was meant to imply that the BQ was the only federal party actually talking about Quebec issues and concerns. At the same time, it might be said that this slogan was perhaps more parochial than usual, and less effective. Saying let's talk about Quebec implies one doesn't want to talk about anything else, which may have come across as narrow-mindedness in the eyes of some voters. Finally, one can guess that the "Qc" was seen by the Bloc as a hip way of reaching out to the young generation of voters, many of whom are fond of using abbreviations in their online social networking.

The party's election platform was also titled "*Parlons Qc*." The document's 190 pages addressed five main themes. The first had to do with the Québécois nation. The Bloc stated that Quebec's culture, language, and political rights ought to be respected. More precisely, the party asked that the distinctiveness of Quebec's economy be recognized in any federal economic policies, and that provincial language laws be applied everywhere in Quebec including in federal jurisdictions. The party also asked for more transparency on the part of the federal government, especially in all matters dealing with lobbying and access to information.

The second theme dealt with issues of justice, immigration, and welfare. No new statements were made in this section of the platform; these were all ideas already proposed in the past by the Bloc, including its regular pledge for a vast reform of the Employment Insurance program. The third theme concerned the economy. The BQ emphasized sustainable development as its preferred economic strategy, and argued that the province of Quebec ought to become less reliant on fossil fuels for its energy consumption. The party also brought back memories of the Conservative government's abandon of the Kyoto Protocol, saying that this change in policy went against Quebec's environmental positions and preferences. The sales tax harmonization dispute was also front and centre in this section of the platform.

The fourth theme involved regional development. Again, most of the party's positions here were not new. Recurring topics like a high-speed rail connection between Windsor and Quebec City or the supply of broadband Internet access across the province were emphasized. The same could be said of the platform's fifth and final theme about Quebec's place in the world. The Bloc again stated that Canada should end its military intervention in Afghanistan as soon as possible and replace it with humanitarian aid efforts. The party also criticized the increase in Canada's military spending and argued that international aid should prioritize African countries. It was finally asked that more powers be transferred to the Quebec provincial government for representing itself on the international scene.

One overarching theme in the Bloc Québécois's 2011 platform was the constant criticism of the Harper government, as well as the recurring idea that the Conservatives and Michael Ignatieff's Liberals were one and the same when it comes to Quebec issues and interests. Right at the beginning of the document, on page 10, there is a blank page with a single sentence in the middle: "*Au Québec, le seul parti capable de barrer la route aux Conservateurs, c'est le Bloc Québécois.*" Finally, we can notice the absence of any reference to the NDP in the whole document, evidence that Jack Layton's party was never seen as a real competitor by the *Bloquistes* in this campaign.

The BQ's television advertisements were closely tied to the platform's themes, with one ad for each of the five following themes: *Parlons Québec, Parlons vérité, Parlons culture, Parlons régions, Parlons solidarité* (Let's talk about Quebec, the truth, culture, regions, solidarity). The ads underlined the Bloc's themes of the Conservative government's lack of honesty, its disrespect for democratic values and women's rights, and its preference for defending the interests of both the oil and car industries rather than those of Quebec's families. All the ads invariably showed leader Gilles Duceppe sitting at a large table in a bright white room and surrounded by his team of candidates, who were seen having lively discussions. In the final television ad of the campaign, Duceppe was seen travelling across the province in his campaign bus. In voice-over he said that he wishes to change things and to work for Quebec's progress. He asked Quebecers to go out and vote, saying that with 8 million voices "*ils vont nous entendre parler Québec jusqu'au Canada*" (they will hear us talk about Quebec all the way to Canada).

In the 2011 campaign the Bloc Québécois made some efforts in using the new social networks available. In addition to the party's standard webpage, a blog was created (*le Blogue Québécois*) on which Gilles Duceppe and others posted a number of messages and announcements. A Facebook page and a Twitter account were also created, but they were not really used actively by the BQ during the campaign; in fact, only Rosemont–La Petite-Patrie MP Bernard Bigras had an active Facebook page in the weeks preceding the election campaign.[24] The most active Bloc candidates on Twitter during the campaign were Meili Faille, Thierry St-Cyr, Richard Nadeau, Yvon Lévesque, and Félix Grenier.[25] Most of their tweets were about campaign activity announcements in their ridings as well as quick comments on various daily news, including criticizing the other candidates.

THE BLOC'S CAMPAIGN

The trends in Quebec vote intentions during the 2011 federal election campaign are presented in Figure 1 based on weekly averages of poll results. The figure indicates that the Bloc's decline was gradual and started early in the campaign, but accelerated during the last week. As for NDP support, it increased significantly during the first two weeks before going through the roof in the last week. Vote intentions for the other two main parties, Conservatives and Liberals, experienced a slight but gradual decline over the course of the campaign.

Figure 1. Vote Intentions in Quebec During the 2011 Campaign (in %)

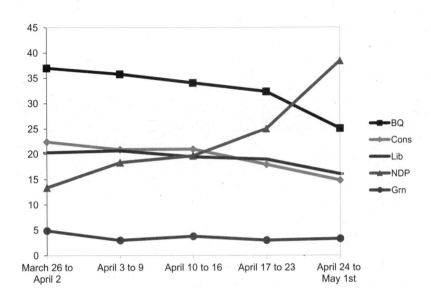

Source: 67 polls from Nanos Research (32), Ekos (14), Angus-Reid (5), Léger Marketing (4), Harris-Decima (4), Ipsos (1), Abacus Data (2), Compass (1), Segma (1), Forum Research (1), Innovative Research (1), and CROP (1); sample sizes vary from poll to poll.

The first few days of the Bloc's campaign were mainly aimed at rejecting Stephen Harper's arguments against a possible Liberal-NDP coalition government that would be supported by the Bloc. Gilles Duceppe issued a letter written in 2004 by Harper himself, then official opposition leader, and co-signed by Jack Layton and Duceppe, in which it was implicitly suggested to the Governor General to consider asking the opposition parties to form a ruling coalition in case Paul Martin's minority government were to lose the confidence of the House of Commons.[26] Duceppe's interpretation of the letter's content was quickly corroborated by Layton. The Bloc leader argued that a government coalition formed by opposition parties — and supported by a separatist party — had thus been seen as legitimate by Harper back then and so there was no reason for this idea to be viewed as illegitimate seven years later. This line of attack allowed Duceppe to criticize the Prime Minister for his lack of honesty and integrity. Liberal leader Michael Ignatieff then officially rejected any plans of forming a ruling coalition with the NDP, thus putting this issue more or less to rest for the remainder of the campaign (see Chapter 3).

On March 28, the Bloc Québécois unveiled its electoral platform.[27] The other leaders quickly made a mockery of the separatist party's slogan "*Parlons Qc*," saying that it reflected plainly the fact that the Bloc could do nothing in Ottawa other than simply "talk, talk, talk." Some also criticized the Bloc's platform by saying that Quebec's sovereignty was not one of the party's five main campaign themes. Gilles Duceppe replied by arguing that sovereignty was actually at the core of every one of those themes. This particular criticism would come back frequently in the media over the next couple of weeks. In fact, in this campaign the Bloc came under attack from well-known Quebec-based specialists and pundits, some of them (like Éric Bédard, Mathieu Bock-Côté, and former Bloc leader Michel Gauthier) openly nationalists.[28] Most of them accused Duceppe and his party of repeating the same old mantra and myths, and they claimed that the Bloc's argument of being the only party able to defend Quebec's values and interests had lost a good deal of its appeal and credibility after twenty years.

The next week was spent targeting the Conservative Party. The Bloc leader strongly criticized Stephen Harper's promise of a loan guarantee to the Churchill Falls hydroelectric project in Newfoundland and Labrador. He said that this promise was a "slap in the face" of Quebec because it meant that Ottawa would help fund a large competitor to Hydro-Québec in the New England electricity market.[29] Duceppe also attacked the Conservatives' French language slogan ("*Notre région au pouvoir*"). He argued that the Tories would never defend the interests of the Quebec region because that party was more concerned about defending those of the West, Ontario, and Newfoundland and Labrador instead.[30] Gilles Duceppe also dismissed the Conservatives' promise to settle the $2.2-billion sales tax harmonization dispute with Quebec as "a sweet dream."[31] Seeing as this issue had been a long-standing demand, the fact that it had now been officially settled by the Tories meant that the Bloc had just lost another one of its soap boxes. Duceppe barely spoke about Michael Ignatieff and the Liberals, and when he mentioned the NDP and its leader he usually did so in a dismissive manner, always referring to Layton as "*mon ami Jack*" as if to portray him as a nice and largely inoffensive adversary.[32]

A few days before the leaders debates of April 12–13, Angus Reid was the first polling firm to report that the NDP was in second place in Quebec vote intentions (with 24 percent support versus 34 percent for the Bloc). Two Ekos polls confirmed that trend soon after. Still, Gilles Duceppe continued to pay little attention to Jack Layton. During the two debates he mostly attacked Stephen Harper and kept arguing that the Bloc Québécois's main objective in this election was to block the road to a Conservative majority, as it had in 2008 — to which Layton responded: "Mr. Harper is still there!"[33] The Bloc leader repeated that his party supports any federal policy "as long as it is good for Quebec." In the French debate he proved to be more aggressive towards Jack Layton, for instance saying that his "friend Jack" had no more chance than him of becoming prime minister of Canada. At one point, however, he was caught off guard by Layton, who asked him about some anti-Aboriginal comments made by Yvon Lévesque, Bloc MP for Abitibi–Baie-James–Nunavik–Eeyou.[34] Duceppe was largely considered as having won the French debate if only because of his experience and his easiness with the language. Yet many underlined that his fighting style this time came across more as arrogance or even anger towards his adversaries, perhaps owing to the fact that he appeared tired of campaigning after so many years of minority governments and frequent elections.

Probably sensing that a strong Quebec-centric issue was still lacking in this campaign, the Bloc leader raised the topic of the constitution in the wake of the debates.[35] Duceppe reminded Quebecers that the constitutional debate had yet to be resolved, and he challenged the other party leaders to clarify their position on this. Stephen Harper and Michael Ignatieff remained cautious in their respective replies, both saying that while it was unfortunate that Quebec still had not signed the 1982 Canadian constitution it was not time yet to reopen any constitutional talks. Jack Layton proved more willing to address the issue. He stated that he wanted to "create the winning conditions for Canada in Quebec." This could be achieved, for instance, by following his party's 2005 Sherbrooke Declaration, in which the NDP pledged to respect provincial jurisdictions, and by agreeing to let some of Bill 101's provisions regarding the use of the French language in the workplace be applied to federal institutions based in Quebec.

On the weekend of April 16–17, the Parti Québécois held in Montreal its first general meeting in six years. Gilles Duceppe had been invited to the meeting. He gave a speech in which he claimed, "With a Bloc strong in Ottawa, and the PQ [eventually] back into power in Quebec City, everything will be possible again," because the sovereignist movement will then have reunited the key conditions for holding a new referendum on Quebec independence.[36] Stephen Harper was quick to note Duceppe's threat of a third referendum, arguing that Quebecers and Canadians preferred to have a stable majority government that would take care of the economy instead of delving back into old quarrels over national unity.[37]

In the week that followed the leaders' debates, national polls were showing a slight but steady surge in NDP voting intentions. The NDP rise was felt more in Quebec, and in reaction to this the Bloc Québécois was now starting to target the party. Gilles Duceppe stated that Quebecers should not let themselves be distracted by Jack Layton's good-humoured image and that they should be wary of the fact that Layton supported many policies that went against Quebec's interests, such as Harper's Churchill Falls loan guarantee.[38] On a more candid note, he declared in a radio interview that an NDP vote had no more value than a vote cast for the Natural Law Party; he also reiterated that Jack Layton would never be prime minister of Canada.[39] Despite these efforts at ridicule, a new CROP poll published on April 21 reported that for the first time ever the NDP had now become the first choice of a plurality of Quebecers with 36 percent of support (versus 31 percent going to the Bloc).[40] In addition, strong criticisms continued to be heard in the media, with some saying that this was the Bloc's worst campaign since 1997.[41]

Panic became immediately noticeable within the Bloc camp. A major change in direction was needed in order to stop this apparent hemorrhage of support. Gilles Duceppe and his political advisers took the following weekend to totally rethink the party's strategy. A new message would now dominate the last week of the Bloc's campaign: this federal election is not primarily about preventing a Conservative majority government, but rather a struggle between federalists and sovereignists. In other words, Duceppe now wished to remind Quebecers (but especially *Bloquistes*) tempted to support the NDP that they were about to vote for a federalist party, not just a social-democratic one. Sovereignists, be they from the left, right, or centre, should vote for the Bloc because it is the only sovereignist party competing in this election. Duceppe claimed that Quebec's sovereignty and liberty was the real issue at stake in this campaign, a more important one than simply stopping a Harper majority. The Bloc was thus seeking to reframe the campaign around the one dimension of competition on which it was standing alone at one of the polarizing poles (one sovereignist party "putting Quebec first" versus three federalist ones "putting Canada first").[42]

To help reinforce this new message, the Bloc brought some well-known separatist figures to the fore. On April 25, former Quebec Premier Jacques Parizeau gave a public talk in which he said that the Bloc's adversaries were trying to pull the wool over Quebecers' eyes and he warned the population to resist any temptation to support them.[43] Two days later, former union leader Gérald Larose took the stage in turn. However, his own talk proved highly controversial and an embarrassment to Gilles Duceppe. Larose described Jack Layton as "*un imposteur crapuleux*" ("a villainous fraud") because the latter was not clarifying his constitutional position; he went as far as qualifying all federal politicians as "professional hustlers." Larose later withdrew his words.[44] On April 30, PQ leader Pauline Marois toured alongside Duceppe in five vulnerable Bloc strongholds in the Montérégie and Quebec City areas in a further attempt to remobilize the core sovereignist base.[45]

The Bloc leader also spent these final few days of the campaign trying to discredit the NDP's team of candidates in Quebec. He claimed that many of them who were running in francophone ridings were actually unilingual anglophones, which in his eyes was something both anomalous and disrespectful of Quebecers.[46] He also highlighted the NDP team's lack of political experience. But Duceppe's message got lost among news that all the final campaign polls were projecting an "orange wave" across the province and that two former staff members of the Bloc had publicly stated they would support the NDP in this election, saying that the Bloc had reached its limit and that it was time for Quebecers to move on.[47] In an interview given to *Le Devoir* near the end of the campaign, Gilles Duceppe confessed to having never seen the NDP coming in his rearview mirror.[48]

Although on election night most everyone was expecting a significant setback for the Bloc Québécois, the extent of the party's collapse was truly astonishing. The Bloc managed to only hold on to four seats, a net loss of forty-four (see Table 1). Even Gilles Duceppe lost his Laurier–Sainte-Marie seat by a margin of nearly 5,400 votes. The outcome immediately led Duceppe to announce his resignation as party leader. The four Bloc survivors were Maria Mourani (Ahuntsic), Louis Plamondon (Bas-Richelieu–Nicolet–Bécancour), Jean-François Fortin (Haute-Gaspésie–La Mitis–Matane–Matapédia), and André Bellavance (Richmond–Arthabaska). All of the Bloc's lost seats went to the NDP, although it should be noted that the Bloc finished second in all of these ridings save for three. The Bloc Québécois's share of the vote decreased to 23 percent, by far the lowest level of support the party had received since its creation. The vote share going to Jack Layton's party in Quebec reached an all-time high of 43 percent. In addition to the forty-four seats stolen from the Bloc, the NDP was able to gain fourteen other seats in the province from the Liberals, the Conservatives, and independent MP André Arthur. Three Conservative cabinet members from Quebec — Josée Verner, Lawrence Cannon, and Pierre Blackburn — lost their seats to NDP candidates. Perhaps surprising given these major shifts in support, voter turnout in Quebec was 62 percent, only slightly above the national average.

Table 1. Federal Election Results in Quebec Since the Bloc's Creation

	1993	1997	2000	2004	2006	2008	2011
Bloc Québécois	49.3%	37.9%	39.9%	48.8%	42.1%	38.1%	23.4%
	(54)	(44)	(38)	(54)	(51)	(49)	(4)
New Democratic Party	1.5%	2.0%	1.8%	4.6%	7.5%	12.2%	42.9%
						(1)	(59)
Liberal Party	33.0%	36.7%	44.2%	33.9%	20.7%	23.7%	14.2%
	(19)	(26)	(36)	(21)	(13)	(14)	(7)
Conservative Party				8.8%	24.6%	21.7%	16.5%
					(10)	(10)	(5)
Progressive Conservative Party	13.5%	22.2%	5.6%				
	(1)	(5)	(1)				
Reform Party / Canadian Alliance		0.3%	6.2%				
Green Party	0.1%	0.1%	0.6%	3.2%	4.0%	3.5%	2.1%

Source: *Elections Canada*. The table indicates the percentage point share of the Quebec vote, with the number of seats in parentheses below.

THE BLOC CAPSIZED BY THE ORANGE WAVE

There are many ways to explain the rise of the NDP, to the detriment of the Bloc Québécois, in this past election. These explanations bring forth both long-term factors, such as declining support for sovereignty across Quebec, as well as more timely factors, such as the quality of the electoral campaigns of each party. Let us examine more closely these different explanations.

First, it seems tempting to hypothesize that the Bloc's setback was attributable to a sharp decline in sovereignist fervour in Quebec. In the past, it is true that the Bloc has been at its most successful during times of constitutional crisis, such as in 1993 with the failure of the Meech Lake Accord and in 2004 with the sponsorship scandal (of which the effects could still be felt in the 2006 election; see Table 1). It is also true that the less spectacular results of this same party in 1997, 2000, and 2008 occurred during elections where the national question was not so much at the forefront. This explanation is not entirely satisfying. Certainly, support for sovereignty at the time of the 2011 election did not reach 1993 or 2004 levels, when a majority of Quebecers were in favour of it. That being said, the proportion of Quebecers supporting sovereignty according to a February 2011 Léger Marketing survey was 42 percent — more or less the same percentage as in the 1997, 2000, and 2008 elections.

In 1993 and 2004 support for sovereignty bordered on 55 percent and support for the Bloc reached 49 percent (and the party elected fifty-four MPs in both elections). During the other four elections where support for sovereignty was slightly over 40 percent (i.e., in 1997, 2000, 2006, and 2008) the Bloc received on average 40 percent of the vote. The conclusion is clear. Over the course of the first six elections in its history, the Bloc Québécois has always obtained an electoral score that is slightly less than that of support for sovereignty. The most recent election breaks this trend of the past twenty years. In this case, the gap between support for Quebec sovereignty (42 percent) and support for the BQ (23 percent) was a historic 19 percentage points. How can we explain this unforeseen lag between Quebecers' constitutional preferences and their electoral choices during the last campaign? Asked differently, why is it that a substantial number of Bloc supporters, still sovereignists, chose to defect and support the NDP in 2011?

The above questions call for looking more closely at a second series of factors that can explain the Bloc's defeat, more specifically at the short-term dynamics of electoral campaigns, in particular leader image and the issues debated. A brief overview of past BQ campaigns is interesting in this respect. It is without a doubt possible to say that this party, well-served by political circumstances and led by popular leaders, has dominated its adversaries during the electoral campaigns of 1993, 2004, 2006, and 2008. As an exception, Gilles Duceppe's first campaign in 1997 turned out to be advantageous for Jean Charest's Conservatives in Quebec.[49] The situation is also more nuanced for the 2000 election, where observers have generally concluded that there was a tie between Gilles Duceppe's Bloc Québécois and Jean Chrétien's Liberal Party.

This brief reminder of the first six campaigns of the Bloc Québécois is revealing. The BQ has sometimes benefited from fundamental factors, such as the rise in support for sovereignty, and sometimes benefited from short-term factors, such as leader popularity (as seen in 1993 and 2004). In other circumstances the Bloc has also enjoyed a favourable context without necessarily coinciding with a rise in sovereignist support. In this regard, the 2008 campaign is particularly interesting. At that time the sovereignist movement seemed to be slowing down and the Bloc appeared short on ideas. At the start of the campaign observers were expecting important gains for the Conservative Party to the detriment of the BQ. However, a few faux pas on the part of the Conservatives, notably with regard to financing of cultural programs and young offenders, changed the campaign's dynamics[50] and allowed the Bloc, in the end, to collect 38 percent of the votes and to elect about fifty MPs. The 2006 campaign saw the beginning of the Bloc's decline, but the positive effects for the BQ from the sponsorship scandal were still being felt. With regard to the worst electoral campaign the Bloc had known until 2011 (i.e., Gilles Duceppe's first in 1997), the campaign unfurled in a context where the close result of the last referendum and the presence of Lucien Bouchard as head of the Quebec government contributed to igniting nationalist sentiment in Quebec. Thus, the need to support the BQ in the 1997 election had a strategic importance, even in the short run, which is something that was absent in the 2011 election.

The BQ's difficult campaign in the most recent election contributed to reuniting for the first time in twenty years a set of losing conditions for the party. The 2011 campaign was the first one that the Bloc led in a context where support for sovereignty was relatively weak, where the tactical importance of supporting a sovereignist party in Ottawa did not seem so urgent, and where the campaign dynamics clearly favoured a rival party, the NDP (on some of the reasons for the latter, see Chapter 4). Never have the long- and short-term factors been more disadvantageous for the BQ than in the 2011 federal campaign.

This unexpected turn of events provides most of the explanation for the BQ's setback in the 2011 election. However, this particular mix of factors does not explain everything, since a fundamental piece of data is necessary to complete the analysis. We must investigate the relationship between Quebecers and the NDP. Certainly, support for this party has always been modest in Quebec, albeit on the rise in the previous three elections (see Table 1). That being said, some New Democratic leaders, such as Ed Broadbent in the 1980s and Jack Layton since becoming head of the party, have benefited from a wave of sympathy in Quebec. What is more, the NDP has never been in power and thus could not be associated with policies unfavourable to Quebec (despite that party's support for the Clarity Act and the unilateral repatriation of the Constitution in 1982, although one can assume that these events happened long enough ago to reduce their importance to most of the nationalist voters).

The openness of Quebec to the NDP also contrasts with Quebecers' reservations towards the two traditional federalist parties on the electoral scene. Quebecers have held strong reservations towards the Liberal Party of Canada since the unilateral repatriation of the Constitution and the sponsorship scandal. The reservations towards the Conservative Party are better explained through the failure of the Meech Lake Accord and by the reformist current now found in this party, seen as being hostile to Quebec's interests and to its more left-leaning values. Without a doubt this lack of sympathy explains why the BQ could maintain its grasp for so long in Quebec. The absence of real change among the main federalist parties has long allowed the Bloc to enjoy support by default.[51] In other words, the choice to support the Bloc Québécois has long seemed in the eyes of some voters as the best tactical choice.

Quebecers' sympathy towards Jack Layton and their lack of deep reservations about the NDP were necessary conditions that led a large number of BQ supporters to defect (see also Chapter 4). In this sense, one cannot talk about the rise of the NDP in Quebec without thinking of the rise of the *Action démocratique du Québec* (although a right-wing organization) in the 2007 provincial election. At the time, Quebecers were disappointed with the incumbent Liberal government and unenthusiastic about the PQ's decision to select André Boisclair as the party's leader. The ADQ's position on the issue of "reasonable accommodations," the unpopularity of André Boisclair, and the very positive image of ADQ leader Mario Dumont produced a bundle of factors that led a significant segment of the electorate to desert the PQ.[52] A similar configuration of factors seems to have produced the "orange wave" of May 2011.

A Léger Marketing survey[53] carried out just after the May 2 election is particularly useful for understanding what might have motivated Quebec voters, notably those of the BQ and NDP as well as those who decided to leave the BQ ranks for the NDP. In this opinion poll, a certain number of explanations that may justify a person's vote were given to respondents, who could choose up to three that seemed to explain their vote choice. The main reasons given by respondents who voted for the NDP are enlightening. The first, given by almost half of the respondents (45 percent), was as follows: "I've had enough of the other parties and I wanted a change." The same desire for change was expressed by 33 percent of respondents in the following form: "After twenty years of domination by the Bloc Québécois, it was time to move on to something else." Even more revealing is the fact that 34 percent explained their vote choice as a way to block the Conservative Party. The NDP thus seems to have stolen the BQ's main argument, which in 2008 called for Quebecers to support them for that same reason. Finally, 24 percent of NDP voters explained their vote choice by choosing the statement "Jack Layton is the best leader." The fact that only 10 percent of the voters who remained loyal to the Bloc Québécois justified their vote using the same motif highlights just how much the NDP leader dominated his BQ counterpart during this campaign.

The motivations of BQ voters who defected to the NDP are no less revealing. Half of them (50 percent) explained their decision to support the NDP by taking up the central argument of the BQ, which was to stop the election of a Conservative majority government ("I wanted to stop a Conservative majority and the NDP seemed like the best choice for stopping them"). The same desire for change is evident amongst these former BQ supporters, as 41 percent of them chose the statement "I've had enough of the other parties and I wanted a change" to justify their vote. Even more surprising is perhaps the fact that 33 percent of former Bloc supporters selected the most radical expression of a desire for change by choosing the statement "After 20 years of domination by the Bloc Québécois, it was time to move on to something else." The absence of reservations towards the NDP is also clear. More than 30 percent of the BQ transfers recognized that the similarities in the values of both parties made their choice easier ("For me, the NDP is a good alternative to the Bloc Québécois because their values are similar"). The fact that around 20 percent of new NDP recruits from the BQ chose to vote for this party because of Jack Layton's personality once again highlights the domination of the NDP leader during the campaign.

The motivations of voters who stayed loyal to the Bloc show the limits of the party's campaign in 2011. These motivations rest primarily on long-term considerations: 55 percent of Bloc supporters say that they voted for the party because it is "the best for defending Quebec's interests"; 36 percent because it was the only possible choice for a sovereignist voter; 33 percent because the Bloc is "the party that best understands the needs of Quebecers"; and 20 percent because this party is "the only one that understands the importance of the French language in Quebec." It is surprising to note that none of these motivations had a direct link to the Bloc's messages during the campaign. The fact that all these reasons could have been given before the start of the campaign suggests that the Bloc was unable in its campaign message to "upgrade" the fundamental reasons to support the party. By failing to do so, the BQ projected the image of a party that had difficulty in renewing itself and therefore opened the door to the expression of a desire for change among a large number of its own supporters. The fact that only 20 percent of Bloc voters justified their choice as wanting to block the Conservative Party and only 10 percent) supported the Bloc because they said that Gilles Duceppe was the best leader is indicative of how unconvincing the party's message had been during the 2011 election.

CONCLUSION: THE END OF THE BLOC QUÉBÉCOIS?

The resounding defeat of the Bloc Québécois in the 2011 election raises two questions. The first is whether this election marks the end, at least for the near future, of the substantial presence of a sovereignist political party in the federal Parliament. The second concerns the longevity of the NDP's success in Quebec. Can we say that 2011 was a realigning election and that the NDP will from now on be the main political force in Quebec on the federal scene, or is it more appropriate to see the breakthrough success of the NDP as ephemeral?

The disposition of Quebec voters to massively switch allegiances from one election to another calls for prudence in any sort of response to these questions. In 1980 Quebecers supported Pierre Trudeau's Liberal Party (with 68 percent of the vote and seventy-four MPs in Ottawa). Four years later, half of Quebec fell into the Conservative camp (50 percent of support and fifty-eight MPs). In 1993 the Bloc Québécois came into the picture, and after approximately fifteen years of dominance by this party (partially due to effects from the electoral system and the splitting of the federalist vote in Quebec) it is now the NDP's turn to enjoy the support of huge numbers of Quebecers.

Such variations in the voting behaviour of Quebecers may seem erratic, at least upon first glance. However, key elements explain this volatility, which has over time remained tied to the status of Quebec within Canada and more particularly to the best way of representing the province's interests in Ottawa. The massive Liberal victory in 1980 is the last time that Quebecers largely opted for this party to defend their province's interests and the interests of French-Canadians. The unilateral repatriation of the Constitution in 1982 shattered the historic link between Quebec and the Liberal Party of Canada. Faced with this situation, Quebecers opted for the Progressive Conservative Party of Brian Mulroney in 1984 by pouring their hopes into the party's expressed desire to reintegrate Quebec into the Canadian Constitution "with honour and enthusiasm." The failure of the Meech Lake Accord at the hands of the Conservative government pushed Quebecers to rally behind the Bloc Québécois and to stay loyal to this party during a tumultuous period marked by the 1995 referendum on Quebec sovereignty and by the federal sponsorship scandal.

A particular configuration of factors led Quebec voters to transfer their support to the NDP during the last election. Weariness over the constitutional debate, the decline in support for sovereignty, an uninspired Bloc campaign, and the emergence of an attractive federalist option combined to produce a stunning result on May 2 in Quebec. However, it is unsure if the NDP's success will last. The death of Jack Layton, an underperformance of the party's new MPs, tensions between the Quebec and non-Quebec members of the caucus, the articulation of unpopular "pan-Canadian" positions in Quebec, and the possible election of the Parti Québécois in the next provincial election will be factors that could easily drive a certain number of NDP voters back to the BQ fold. Since May 2, some NDP voters have even felt sorry for the Bloc's massive crumbling. There is no doubt that the sovereignist movement will look to capitalize on this sentiment in the coming years. If the NDP proves to be disappointing and the election of a PQ government brings the national question back onto the agenda, the Bloc could see better days. However, for that, the party must renew its platform and offer Quebec voters a rejuvenated discourse that will provide strong reasons justifying the presence of a sovereignist party in Ottawa.

For now, the party remains barely afloat. The Bloc will see the public source of its funding disappear gradually due to the party's greatly reduced share of the vote as well as Prime Minister Harper's intention of abolishing Canada's public regime of party financing before the next election.[54] The BQ will also lose its official party status in the House of Commons as well as most of its public relations, research, and advisory staffs.[55] A week after his party's defeat (and his own personal one) Gilles Duceppe was still visibly shaken by the outcome when he addressed the media. Re-elected MP Louis Plamondon is acting as interim leader until a successor to Duceppe is formally selected. But the next four years will prove to be difficult for whoever becomes the next BQ leader. As former Bloc MP Daniel Paillé bluntly said after the campaign, "Before choosing a new driver we need to ask ourselves what kind of car we wish to drive."[56] Indeed, the question of the Bloc Québécois's identity has never imposed itself so acutely as it has since the orange wave swept the province in the May 2011 election.

Over the past thirty years, Quebecers have massively supported four different political parties — the Liberal Party, the Progressive Conservative Party, the Bloc Québécois, and now the NDP — to make their interests known in Ottawa. However, the party that has achieved the most durable success during this period has been the Bloc. For this reason alone, one must be cautious before making any predictions of its disappearance. Depending on the context and on the strength of the federalist alternatives, perhaps the Bloc Québécois may one day have the wind back in its sails.

NOTES

We thank Mireille Petitclerc and Chris Chhim for their helpful assistance in preparing this chapter.

1. Quoted in Tristan Péloquin, "'Le Bloc n'est pas un clone du NPD,'" *La Presse*, September 12, 2008, A2.
2. Éric Bédard, "La fin du consensus libéral?", *Policy Options*, June–July 2011, 127.
3. Stuart Soroka, Fred Cutler, Dietlind Stolle, and Patrick Fournier, "Capturing Change (and Stability) in the 2011 Campaign," *Policy Options*, June–July 2011, 73.
4. For a complete summary of the 2008 parliamentary crisis, see Christopher Dornan, "Introduction: The Outcome in Retrospect," in *The Canadian Federal Election of 2008*, eds. Jon H. Pammett and Christopher Dornan (Toronto: Dundurn Press, 2009), 7–15.
5. Karim Benessaieh, "La coalition est toujours vivante," *La Presse*, January 21, 2009, A22.
6. Martin Croteau, "Duceppe fustige Ignatieff," *La Presse*, February 1, 2009, A4.
7. E.g., Joël-Denis Bellavance, "'La place des Québécois est au pouvoir,'" *La Presse*, March 23, 2009, A6.
8. Malorie Beauchemin, "Le Bloc propose un nouveau 'plan d'aide' de 32 milliards," *La Presse*, May 1, 2009, A10.
9. Alec Castonguay, "Un feuillet controversé attaque le Bloc québécois," *Le Devoir*, June 29, 2009, online edition.
10. Denis Lessard, "Ignatieff et Harper: même 'regard,'" *La Presse*, September 9, 2009, A13.
11. Malorie Beauchemin, "'Nous avons tiré des leçons' dit Duceppe," *La Presse*, December 14, 2009, A8.
12. Joël-Denis Bellavance, "Des libéraux en quête d'appuis, des bloquistes bien en selle," *La Presse*, June 18, 2010, A3.
13. Catherine Handfield, "Hommage souverainiste à Gilles Duceppe," *La Presse*, August 16, 2010, A4.
14. Hugo De Grandpré, "Gilles Duceppe durcit le ton en faveur de la souveraineté," *La Presse*, February 4, 2010, A14.
15. Hugo De Grandpré, "Gilles Duceppe sur la défensive," *La Presse*, March 23, 2010, A14.
16. Joël-Denis Bellavance, "Duceppe fait l'apologie de la souveraineté à Washington," *La Presse*, October 16, 2010, A32.
17. Michel Dolbec, "Duceppe tisse des liens avec la droite française," *La Presse*, November 11, 2010, A17.
18. E.g., CROP, *Évolution du climat politique au Québec*, May 2011, 20–21.
19. Malorie Beauchemin, "Démystifier la souveraineté hors Québec," *La Presse*, April 17, 2010, A11.
20. Denis Lessard, "5 milliards pour le Québec," *La Presse*, January 27, 2011, A15.
21 Malorie Beauchemin, "Le Bloc cible la région de Québec," *La Presse*, January 13, 2011, A18.

22. Joël-Denis Bellavance, "Le Bloc relance l'idée d'une coalition," *La Presse*, February 15, 2011, A12.

23. Robert Dutrisac, "Le Québec n'intéresse plus les partis fédéraux," *Le Devoir*, March 24, 2011, online edition.

24. Jean-Marie Villeneuve, "Plusieurs candidats étaient mal préparés pour la première campagne web," *Le Soleil*, April 10, 2011, online edition.

25. According to Politwitter, last consulted June 10, 2011. *http://politwitter.ca/federal/bloc.*

26. Paul Journet, "Duceppe attaque l'intégrité du premier ministre," *La Presse*, March 28, 2011, A9; Vincent Marissal, "Exit la coalition," *La Presse*, March 28, 2011, A7.

27. Paul Journet, "Parlons Québec (et souveraineté)," *La Presse*, March 29, 2011, A8.

28. Here is a sample from op-eds published in *La Presse*: Éric Bédard, "Je lâche le Bloc," March 30, 2011, A25; Jean-Yves Lajoie, "Les cinq mythes du Bloc," April 1, 2011, A23; Mathieu Bock-Côté, "La mystique des valeurs québécoises," April 5, 2011, A19; Paul Journet, "Une campagne 'aseptisée,' dit Gauthier," April 9–10, 2011, A10; Michel Pruneau, "Le Bloc doit disparaître," April 16, 2011, A35; Jean-Herman Guay, "Le Bloc s'effrite," April 23, 2011, A33; Abdel Kader Khali, "Pourquoi j'appuie Jack," April 26, 2011, A21; Marc Simard, "Les contrevérités du Bloc," April 27, 2011, A29; Pierre Rivard, "Débloquer l'avenir," April 28, 2011, A21.

29. Joël-Denis Bellavance, "Le Bloc et Charest coincés entre l'arbre et l'écorce," *La Presse*, April 2, 2011, A10.

30. "En campagne — Jour 9," *Le Devoir*, April 4, 2011, online edition.

31. Hugo De Grandpré, "Un budget équilibré d'ici 2014–2015," *La Presse*, April 9–10, 2011, A9.

32. Paul Journet, "Duceppe n'a qu'un ennemi: Harper," *La Presse*, March 30, 2011, A10.

33. Vincent Marissal, "Layton et Duceppe volent le show," *La Presse*, April 14, 2011, A3.

34. Marissal, "Layton et Duceppe volent le show."

35. Malorie Beauchemin, Hugo De Grandpré, and Paul Journet, "Revoilà la Constitution," *La Presse*, April 15, 2011, A7.

36. Anabelle Nicoud, "Avec les souverainistes unis, tout redevient possible, croit Duceppe," *La Presse*, April 17, 2011, online edition.

37. Malorie Beauchemin, "Harper brandit la menace d'un troisième référendum," *La Presse*, April 19, 2011, A6.

38. La Presse Canadienne, "Duceppe lance un appel à ses troupes pour contrer la montée des appuis au NPD," *Le Devoir*, April 18, 2011, online edition.

39. La Presse Canadienne, "Gilles Duceppe tourne en dérision les prétentions au pouvoir du NPD," *Le Devoir*, April 19, 2011, online edition; Anabelle Nicoud, "Le NPD dans la ligne de mire du BQ," *La Presse*, April 20, 2011, A14.

40. Joël-Denis Bellavance, "Le NPD prend la tête au Québec," *La Presse*, April 21, 2011, A2.

41. E.g., Vincent Marissal, "Sérieux, ce bon Jack!", *La Presse*, April 21, 2011, A3.

42. Anabelle Nicoud, "La souveraineté ramenée à l'avant par le Bloc," *La Presse*, April 26, 2011, A10; Joël-Denis Bellavance, "L'option d'une coalition refroidie par Duceppe," *La Presse*, April 26, 2011, A10.

43. Nicoud, "La souveraineté ramenée à l'avant par le Bloc,"
44. Vincent Brousseau-Pouliot and Martin Croteau, "Mea-culpa pour Gérald Larose," *La Presse*, April 28, 2011, A6.
45. Vincent Brousseau-Pouliot, "Duceppe fait appel à Marois," *La Presse*, April 30, 2011, A15.
46. Vincent Brousseau-Pouliot, "Un manque de respect, dit Duceppe," *La Presse*, April 29, 2011, A7.
47. Joël-Denis Bellavance, "Des souverainistes passent dans le camp du NPD," *La Presse*, April 29, 2011, A3.
48. Guillaume Bourgault-Côté, "Duceppe n'avait pas vu venir le NPD," *Le Devoir*, April 27, 2011, online edition.
49. See Neil Nevitte, André Blais, Elisabeth Gidengil, and Richard Nadeau, "Why Did the Bloc Québécois Lose Ground?" in *Unsteady State: The 1997 Canadian Federal Election* (Don Mills: Oxford University Press, 2000), 117–26.
50. See Éric Bélanger and Richard Nadeau, "The Bloc Québécois: Victory by Default," in *The Canadian Federal Election of 2008*, eds. Jon H. Pammett and Christopher Dornan (Toronto: Dundurn Press, 2009), 136–61.
51. Bélanger and Nadeau, "The Bloc Québécois: Victory by Default."
52. See Éric Bélanger and Richard Nadeau, *Le comportement électoral des Québécois* (Montréal: Presses de l'Université de Montréal, 2009).
53. Guillaume Bourgault-Côté, "Layton jugé le mieux placé pour bloquer Harper," *Le Devoir*, May 7, 2011, online edition.
54. Joël-Denis Bellavance, "Des lendemains difficiles en vue pour les bloquistes et les libéraux," *La Presse*, May 5, 2011, A12.
55. Malorie Beauchemin, "Réorganisation douloureuse pour le Bloc," *La Presse*, May 28, 2011, A6.
56. Joël-Denis Bellavance, "Bloc: Paillé appelle à la réflexion," *La Presse*, May 11, 2011, A14.

CHAPTER 6

Party of One:
Elizabeth May's Campaign Breakthrough
Susan Harada

One day before she will take her place in the back corner of the House of Commons — and two days after her swearing-in as the new Member of Parliament for Saanich–Gulf Islands (SGI) — Elizabeth May still does not have a Parliamentary office. Given the number of new and departing members engaged in the legislative equivalent of musical chairs, and given her place in the pecking order, she faces a bit of a wait. So for now, the Green Party of Canada's offices in downtown Ottawa are the closest May will get to Parliament Hill when she needs a desk and computer. But that does not seem to have fazed her in the slightest as she arrives at party headquarters, fresh from speaking at a protest against a military trade show at Ottawa's Lansdowne Park and en route to a quick lunch meeting a few blocks away with some other MPs. It is simply one more of the myriad details she must deal with in her transition to sitting MP.

There is no party protocol to guide her. The Green Party is also grappling with the happy dilemma of sorting out how best to proceed with its first-ever MP, one who also happens to be its leader. For example, now that May will draw an MP's salary of $157,000, should the Greens still pay her $70,000 leader's salary, especially given that party funding is about to be squeezed? If yes, should she get the full amount, or should she simply get a percentage, given that much of her time will be spent as an MP on constituency and parliamentary business rather than as a party leader on party business? And on that subject, how should she divide her time between her duties as MP and her duties as leader?

"Federal Council asked me in our first meeting after the election, and I said I just need to be very clear that my primary responsibility is to the voters of Saanich–Gulf Islands," she said. "Because I believe that that's endemic in what's wrong with how other parliamentarians behave. They think their primary responsibility is to their party bosses. Now, I'm my own party leader so I don't have that problem. But ... the Green belief in grassroots democracy is one of our founding core Green values globally ... so of course that means as a Member of Parliament elected by the voters of Saanich–Gulf Islands, that's job one. Being leader of the Green Party comes second. And I told Council, and nobody said, 'Hang on, you can't say that, we got you there.' Nope. Everybody said, 'No, no, right, quite right.' So ... I don't think there's going to be any conflict around my primary responsibility."[1]

It happens that the Greens enhanced their Code of Conduct shortly before the election, focusing on the notion of fiduciary responsibility vested in those in decision-making positions, such as members of the party's governing Federal Council. According to council chair John Streicker, "By fiduciary responsibility what I mean is that we have a higher obligation to our members to uphold the interests of the party as a whole."[2] The Code of Conduct is based on the Greens' guiding principles. And that fits with how May will approach her duty as a voting MP. "I believe in representative democracy," she said. "I don't think Members of Parliament should vote based on a referendum." She plans to vote in ways consistent with Green Party policies and principles, which she says are in turn consistent with the values of Saanich–Gulf Islands residents: "My own conscience is my decision-maker. I don't decide issues by referendum, of the Green Party *or* of constituents. I mean, they've elected me as a person, knowing who I am and how I think and what I value. So I think that will work."

Her confident assertion of the values held by Saanich–Gulf Islands residents is hard won. It comes after waging a relentless ground campaign that officially began in the fall of 2009. It culminated in a decisive victory: May won 46.3 percent of the popular vote (31,890), more than ten points ahead of Conservative Gary Lunn, the incumbent cabinet minister who had held the riding through five elections since 1997. Lunn finished with 35.7 percent (24,544). What's more, in all the years he represented the riding, he never attracted May's level of support. New Democrat Edith Loring-Kuhanga was well behind, with 11.9 percent (8,185), and Liberal

Renée Hetherington, a climate scientist initially viewed as a potential threat to May, stood at 6.1 percent (4,208).

As it turned out, May's achievement was one among many other, more monumental, election results. The national media were largely preoccupied with the Conservative majority, and the Quebec- and Ontario-based implosion of the traditional Canadian political order. She was left to celebrate her victory unchallenged, for the most part. Still, interspersed with the neutral and positive headlines — "Green Party makes history"[3]; "May: new voice for the centre?"[4]; "Third try's a charm for Elizabeth May"[5] — were the other inevitable observations. "Perhaps the term historic was meant as a verbal ointment to soothe over how badly the Green party did everywhere else," according to *National Post* columnist Rex Murphy.[6] "She'll be spending most of her time out of sight, if not out of mind, at least as far as formal parliamentary proceedings," wrote the CBC's Kady O'Malley.[7]

In fact, all of those headlines and views have a claim on being right. May's win as the first elected Green Party member is indeed historic, tempered though it is by the reality that she will have to fight hard for a parliamentary profile. On the other hand, no other Green candidates even came close to emulating her feat. The party was deserted by almost a third of its previous supporters. In the end, the Greens stood at 3.9 percent nationally (576,221). It is a significant drop from the 6.8 percent (937,613) of 2008, and is even below the 4.3 percent (582,247) they won during their initial breakthrough election in 2004. It is also a financial blow. It means an immediate cut of nearly three-quarters of a million dollars to the Greens' annual per-vote subsidy, on top of the overall phase-out slated to start in 2012.

The extent to which the Greens bled support becomes clear when looking beyond the collapse of its national vote to specific local results. In key Ontario ridings such as Bruce–Grey–Owen Sound and Guelph, for example, where the Greens finished second and third respectively in 2008, support evaporated.[8] Only one Green pushed into second place (albeit some 45 percentage points behind the first-place Conservative), compared to the five second-place Green candidates in 2008. Only one Green, council chair John Streicker in the Yukon, saw a significant increase, growing to 18.9 percent from 12.8 in 2008. Most critical from a local party-building perspective, only seven Green candidates won enough votes to qualify for federal funding to offset their campaign expenses. That is an enormous drop from the party's record high of forty-one in 2008. And the feat that put the Greens on the electoral map in 2004 — running 308 candidates — was not replicated in 2011. They were five candidates short of a full slate. So of their five campaign goals — elect the leader; run 308 candidates; increase the popular vote; grow the vote in targeted ridings; and hold/increase the number of ridings with 10 percent of the popular vote[9] — only one was fully met.

Unsurprisingly then, the days following the election left what the Greens' executive director Johan Hamels described as a "mixed feeling" within the party.[10] In Ottawa Centre, where the Greens had toiled for years to build a presence, candidate Jen Hunter's support got chopped in half, and she was left stranded between elation and disappointment. "It's exciting that the Greens have elected our first MP," she said. Still, a price was paid. "We lost about half of our national support, I think intentionally, as we invested all our resources into getting Elizabeth elected, so on a personal level it was quite disappointing … As I said to my team, we ran a great campaign, and all we can say is that we know that every single one of those votes, we got, because there was no national campaign to support us."[11]

Curtailing the national campaign was, in fact, part of a deliberate "Saanich strategy" adopted following the party's mixed results in the previous election. Given the arc of the Green Party's growth — claiming national party status in 2004 with a full slate of candidates, solidifying core support in 2006 with slight growth in popular vote — the next substantive marker of political relevance was electoral victory. When that proved elusive again in 2008 — even under a dynamic and articulate new leader — it became clear that the Greens as a national player, and May as head of the party, likely had only one more federal campaign in which to prove themselves.

By that measure, the Green Party can consider the 2011 election a resounding triumph. With support spread across the country rather than concentrated regionally, the Greens' chances of success in a federal election under Canada's first-past-the-post system had always been rated as dismal at best. However, this time May did what she had to do on behalf of her party: she won her seat, and she won it by dint of smart strategy, focused resources, organization, and the sheer force of her outsized personality. In the military parlance of political discourse, she established the crucial beachhead in Saanich–Gulf Islands. But for what, and for whom, and to what end? Those are key questions, and the answers will be shaped by how May and the Greens choose to deploy behind that beachhead in the coming years. Their next moves will be just as critical to the party's future as was the decision to pour almost all of their resources into getting their leader into the House of Commons.

THE ROAD TO SAANICH–GULF ISLANDS

The Saanich strategy took shape in the post-mortem days of the October 2008 election. It had been a rocky campaign for May — her second campaign,[12] but her first as a federal party leader heading a national effort. There was what became known as "The Deal" with Liberal leader Stéphane Dion, which saw both leaders pledge not to run candidates in each other's ridings. Green Party members saw it as an alliance with the Liberals that undercut their bid to be recognized as a political force in their own right. There was the strategic voting controversy, which erupted over May's confusing messaging around the necessity of blocking Conservative leader Steven Harper at all costs. And finally there were the election results, which left the Greens shut out of Parliament.

The grumbling grew during the troubled latter half of the campaign, and deepened in the wake of the election. In the minds of some Greens, the leader had cost them votes.[13] In May's view, party priorities and media coverage had cost her a victory in her riding of Central Nova. Neither she nor the Greens made her own campaign a priority, she said, nor did the media acknowledge she had a chance of winning.[14] She wrote a blunt confidential post-mortem memo to Federal Council. Among the problems she identified were the double demands she carried, as a candidate vying for a first-time seat and as a party leader tasked to front a cross-country campaign. How could she win "when I am out of the riding more than half the time. The push and pull is tough," she wrote. "Can we have any kind of decision that the Leader winning her seat is a top priority? (*the* Top Priority?) If I had been in Central Nova the whole time (except for national debates), I would have won."[15]

Whether she would have defeated incumbent Conservative cabinet minister Peter MacKay had she spent more time in the riding was no certainty. On the other hand, her plea for a focused strategy to win her seat resonated. Within the context of the Greens' long-running "political party versus a movement" conflict, it spoke to those who maintained their effectiveness was blunted without a political power base. The debate, up to that point, largely focused on whether building a strong central party, seeking "star" candidates, and pouring resources into a few potentially winnable ridings would be a betrayal of their grassroots principles. Identifying the leader's riding as the priority carried the potential to push them even further from the grassroots; it could radically tilt the traditional horizontal power structure originally constructed to absorb the leader rather than set her/him at the apex as anything more than party spokesperson.

However, the Greens had publicly staked their electoral expectations on the high-profile former activist. The fact that she remained seatless dealt their credibility a blow. According to May, they received an influx of emails from Canadians critical of the fact that the party could not get her elected.[16] In the end, the same pragmatism that propelled the Greens into choosing May in 2006 over a lesser known but long-time party member propelled them into opting for a more traditional political approach. By spring 2009, they had a fully fleshed out campaign plan; electing their leader was at the top of the list. "Now the party is convinced that our number one goal is to elect me to the House of Commons," May announced in June 2009. "So that changes quite a lot of things."[17]

The key issue then became where she should run. In the east, they looked at Central Nova, Halifax, and Cumberland–Colchester–Musquodoboit Valley. In Ontario it was Guelph and Bruce–Grey–Owen Sound. And on the west coast it was Saanich–Gulf Islands, where the Greens started gaining popular vote during the 2004 campaign. Their polling probed support levels for May specifically, as well as for the

Green Party generally. In the end, May said, SGI was "leaps and bounds more potentially Green than anyplace else we looked." Opting for that riding would involve a cross-country move that would pit her against yet another incumbent Conservative cabinet minister. Not everyone was convinced it was the right choice. Nevertheless, the decision was made, and she viewed it as being a significant turning point in the life of the party: "To say 'We're going to strategically decide as a party that it's harder than we thought to elect that first Green, and we're not going to just rely on doing better everywhere and hoping someone makes the break-through.' This is all very, very, indicative of the fact that it's a political party … it's still a movement, but we're operating as a political party."[18]

The Green membership has often been riven by fundamental dis-agreements over how the party should insert itself into Canadian poli-tics, so it was not surprising that the new leader-focused strategy did not go uncontested from within. A long-time environmental activist named Stuart Hertzog, who opposed what he characterized as the Greens' increasing "tendency towards anti-democratic centralization," challenged May's nomination.[19] May ultimately won the nomination contest, but not before Hertzog complained to Elections Canada about a national party funding transfer to the Electoral District Association (EDA) in Saanich–Gulf Islands, which he believed gave May an unfair advantage.[20] Both May and the Greens dismissed the claims; in the end, Elections Canada did not find "sufficient grounds" to further investigate.[21] Still, the intra-party conflict underscored the fact that the Greens were still struggling with the fundamental shifts in party culture brought on by their attempts to capi-talize on their increasingly meaningful electoral outcomes. Significantly, the majority on Federal Council supported not only the focus on May but also the selection of SGI and the financing of her campaign.

"There may have been feelings among some members or council that, is that the right choice or whatever? But it was a decision made and voted on by council, so to me there was no dispute about the fact that that's what we were going to do," said then executive director of the Greens Maureen Murphy. "We were going to absolutely funnel financial resources into Saanich, human resources as much as possible through volunteers, and make that a focus so that we could get Elizabeth May elected ... I'm not saying that there aren't people out there who thought maybe something else should have been our priority but that is the one we agreed on and voted on."[22]

Speculation of an election call in the fall of 2009 necessitated a near-constant state of campaign-readiness. In late summer, John Fryer, a long-time labour activist and public policy expert who joined the party after May was elected leader, became the SGI campaign manager on a volunteer basis. The party transferred approximately $50,000 to SGI, and Fryer began recruiting staff and set up a storefront campaign office on the main street in Sidney. Near the beginning of 2010, he chose a "much grittier part of the riding" on the edge of Victoria's suburbs for a second office. As he put it, it was a "more densely populated part of the riding where working people live. And the Greens don't do too well at getting working people's votes. They're very much a sort of middle- and upper-middle class kind of party in terms of the people that [they] attract ... And my tradition comes from [thinking] there's more workers than anybody else so why don't we go for their votes."[23]

To that end, he set what he called his "old-fashioned" strategy in motion. He aimed to knock on every door in the riding three times. There was huge resistance among his young staff, he admitted later, but at one point, he did have some forty volunteers a week assigned to the door-to-door canvassing. Fryer also convinced Federal Council he needed more money. In total in 2009, the party transferred nearly $67,000 into SGI, and May's previous EDA of Central Nova transferred in approximately $25,000.[24] The party also committed another $30,000 a month for the first five months of 2010. As election talk shifted to a spring date, they decided they could reassess the SGI financing at the end of May. But by then, the Greens' landscape had shifted in a number of significant ways.

STREAMLINING THE PARTY STRUCTURE

The delayed election call worked to May's advantage. It gave her some breathing room, time to establish herself in SGI. But her work to build for the longer term was often overshadowed in the short term by bursts of bad news that affected morale and reignited simmering internal party discord. Membership was at approximately nine thousand — down from the record twelve thousand attracted during the 2008 campaign. The Greens did poorly in the four by-elections called for November 2009 in Nova Scotia, Quebec, and B.C. Results were dismal: popular vote ranged from 1.7 to 4.3 percent. In the Nova Scotia riding, the party squeaked ahead of the Christian Heritage Party of Canada by a mere 0.1 percent.

With respect to finances, the remaining debt from the party's $3.4 million campaign in 2008 was on track to be paid off by July 2010. But the pre-writ effort in SGI was an expensive proposition by Green standards, and the party was wary of going into a new campaign while still paying off the last one. Party-building positions — in organizing, volunteer coordinating, and fundraising — were cut. The position of political director was eliminated less than a year after it was created. The executive director quit. The head of Federal Council resigned.[25] In March 2010, Fryer stepped down from his post as May's campaign manager, saying that he had done what he had set out to do in Saanich–Gulf Islands. In June 2010, the party's deputy leader defected to the Bloc Québécois, after only seven months on the job.

With climate change issues seemingly pushed aside in the public's mind in the wake of the failed 2009 Copenhagen conference,[26] and with May largely consumed by her ongoing SGI campaign, the only headlines the Greens seemed to earn had to do with their own troubles.[27] As a lifelong activist, May's environmental credentials and intellectual abilities were never in question. But as the leader of a grassroots party still in the throes of focusing its political goals and forming its political identity, she was often a polarizing figure. Conflicting views about her leadership came to a head as the party turned its attention to the Biennial General Meeting (BGM) to be held in Toronto in the summer of 2010.

The Greens' by-laws entrenched a fixed four-year term for the leader, followed by a leadership contest should there be more than one contender for the position. May's term was set to expire at the time of the BGM, and speculation about possible challengers grew.[28] Mindful that a leadership contest could leave the party vulnerable should a federal election be called in mid-stream, Federal Council moved to resolve the dilemma. In doing so, it brought to a head the discord that had been brewing. There were those who supported May and those who did not, but beyond the personality-based politics were conflicting strands of Green Party thinking over issues of transparency, grassroots democracy, and political pragmatism.

The differing approaches within the membership were apparent in the various strategically crafted directives and amendments that were proposed before the BGM. A group of Greens, which included deputy leader Adriane Carr and the now-executive director Johan Hamels, put forward a directive endorsing May's leadership. In addition, Federal Council proposed an amendment that would cancel the fixed term. Instead, a leadership review would be held within six months of a federal general election; if the leader received support from less than 60 percent of the membership, a leadership contest would be triggered.

An opposing amendment was put forward by a group that included the member who had resigned as council chair; it proposed instead that the fixed term be extended for one time only, with a leadership contest to start within eight weeks of the next election. And a further opposing directive came from Green Party member Sylvie Lemieux, the nominated candidate for Glengarry-Prescott-Russell: it would retain the fixed term and commit the party to a leadership race at some point between fall 2010 and spring 2011, unless a federal election were to be called. Lemieux posted an appeal to party members on her blog. "I have put forward a motion for a leadership contest to be held this year, 2010, as the GPC Constitution stipulates because I believe it is a necessary activity for the Green Party to engage in," she wrote. "Even if you are hesitant about holding a Leadership Contest before the next federal election, I encourage you to view a motion for a leadership contest as an opportunity for growth, to raise awareness, to bring in new members and to openly talk about where the Party is heading. A Leadership Review on the other hand is an internal process that will limit our expansion and will not likely be a shared experience with Canadians at large."[29]

Further complicating matters were the additional competing proposals that would affect the leader's power: one amendment called for the creation of a small Executive Council under the auspices of the larger

Federal Council, which would include the leader as a voting member; the other called for a general restructuring of Council that would strip the leader of a vote.

An online and mail-in ballot vote of the proposals was held prior to the convention. Midway through the process, May circulated an email to Green Party members. She called on them to get involved and vote, and added, "Some resolutions would cause an immediate leadership race, forcing me to resign — even before the next election ... We have some excellent resolutions to expand council to include a francophone có-chair, more youth and more women. We also have other resolutions which erode the leadership. Resolution G10-c01 would change council's structure and place the leader in more of a staff position, with no vote. I ask for your support that the Leader may continue to have a vote on council."[30]

The email set off a furious debate over the equity of May using party lists in order to circulate a message airing her views on the resolutions, while those who sponsored opposing resolutions — namely Lemieux — could not do the same.[31] It did not end there. Lemieux announced in July 2010 that she would seek the party's leadership at the earliest opportunity, in order to "rejuvenate" the organization.[32] Significantly, she chose to make her announcement in Guelph, where the strategic voting controversy during the 2008 campaign left many members unhappy with May's leadership.[33]

Lemieux's declaration had the effect of concretizing the leadership discussion, and may have done much to mobilize May's support. As it turned out, 85 percent of the 995 members who voted on the directive endorsing her leadership supported her. Approximately 74 percent of the 914 who voted on Federal Council's proposal for a leadership review in lieu of a fixed term were in favour. The results were released a week before the BGM was set to begin,[34] and they dampened any sense that a potentially polarizing floor fight was in the offing. When it came time to actually put the proposed amendments to the approximately four hundred members in attendance at the BGM, the ones that supported May, a looser leadership term, and her ability to retain a vote on Federal Council carried the day.[35]

Although only one-tenth of the party's approximately nine-thousand-strong membership participated in the pre-BGM ballot, including the vote on the directive endorsing her leadership, in May's view, that was enough. "Every member across the country had the opportunity to vote. You'd assume the people who were most committed to getting rid of me as leader were the ones most likely to vote, and the ones who really think I'm a great leader wouldn't bother voting," she said nearly a year later. Her confidence is underscored by the fact that only 113 members voted directly against her: "I'm not too worried. I'm not operating as an MP or leader of the Green Party with actually a moment's concern about people who don't like what I'm doing within the Green Party. We have a Federal Council, it's duly elected. You know, I pay attention to concerns and complaints if they want to contact me. But I'm not looking over my shoulder."[36]

The very public debate had been a somewhat messy exercise, but it ultimately enabled May and the Greens to emerge with some crucial issues — including party factionalism and confidence in her leadership — resolved. The membership chose an open leadership term, albeit with a mandated review process, which moved the Greens closer to the more leader-centric framework of traditional political parties. At the same time, the majority rejected the opposing arguments that forgoing a regular leadership contest ran counter to Green values of grassroots, participatory democracy.

Most significantly on the organizational front, they opted to streamline and in effect centralize. Federal Council would retain its role as the overall governing body, but its seven "councillors at large" would be dropped in favour of a six-member Executive Council. This smaller group would allow for more nimble decision-making, and would include the leader (as a voting member) and executive director (as a non-voting member). "This is very much part of the growth of the Green Party," May said at the time. "We are ... recognizing that we are not solely a movement or a group of activists who enjoy getting together to debate policy as an academic exercise. We are serious about playing an important role on the Canadian political scene, we are serious about being useful as Parliamentarians," she told journalists. "And as a federal political party on the verge of electing its first MPs, we need to make sure that our internal systems are up to the challenge."[37]

THE SAANICH CAMPAIGN

"Diverse" and "sprawling" are the words most often used to describe the Saanich–Gulf Islands riding. Its boundaries capture the Gulf Islands, a big chunk of Saanich, and a portion of the Capital Regional District; its topography ranges from farmland to coastline, suburbs to reserves. Approximately one-fifth of the residents are immigrants; approximately one-fifth are sixty-five years or older.[38] Residents in the Gulf Islands, centred on Saltspring Island, were viewed as being a natural Green constituency; elsewhere there was a mix of the wealthy retired, mainly from Alberta or Ontario, and the working population.

With Fryer's departure in 2009, Jonathan Dickie, who had first worked with May on her Central Nova campaign, was moved into the post of SGI campaign manager. In the early days, the campaign strategy was traditional and straightforward — to introduce May to as many people as possible. Dickie organized the political equivalent of a pyramid scheme, recruiting supporters to invite over neighbours — particularly those not planning to vote Green — for a coffee and a chance to meet May. The hope was that those people would leave the coffee party, if not converted, than at least impressed enough to talk about her with others, who would in turn pay more attention to her candidacy. May attended as many community events as she could. She stood on street corners and waved at passing cars.

Figuring that a package of sunflower seeds would be left lying around a constituent's home longer than a regular campaign brochure, Dickie ordered specially designed packets printed with campaign information, and volunteers stuffed them with sunflower seeds. It became their main canvassing tool.[39] In Ottawa, the central party launched a national phone canvass, recruiting volunteers from across the country to phone into the riding to help identify potential support.[40] According to Dickie, there was a noticeable shift about eight months into the pre-writ campaign. May, too, said there was no mistaking the groundswell. "I really wasn't in any fundamental doubt about winning in that riding," she said. "Not for a year and a half."[41]

Their feelings were somewhat borne out by polls. A Harris-Decima poll commissioned by the party in 2009 prior to May choosing SGI showed her with the same support level as Lunn, at 33 percent.[42] A McAllister Opinion Research poll commissioned a little more than a year later found that of decided voters who planned to vote, her support was at 32 percent, while Lunn was at 34 percent.[43] That poll showed her support was holding, but did not capture the movement that May and her team were feeling on the ground. Nevertheless, with the August BGM behind her and her leadership assured, May continued the strategy of connecting with constituents, one small group at a time.

By the end of 2010, the federal party had put approximately $240,000 into SGI, on top of the previously noted $92,000 transferred in by the party and Central Nova EDA in 2009. In the first three months of 2011 until the election was called, another $90,000 flowed in from national coffers.[44] The SGI spending limit for the election was set by Elections Canada at $95,460,[45] and according to Dickie they went through close to that amount during the five-week campaign on staffing, standard campaign materials such as lawn signs and bumper stickers, as well as travel and events throughout the large riding.

Given May's heavy pre-writ campaigning over some eighteen months, by the time she launched the official campaign on March 26, Dickie felt they were in a very strong position indeed. "As we entered the writ period we realized we had done our job very well. Our polling was showing that we had decreased the support for Liberals and New Democrats in this riding to very low levels, to such low levels that we had to refocus on starting to pull away some harder Conservative support," he said.[46]

There are deep conservative roots in that area. Expectations are for political representation that works from the bottom up, not the other way around. That is language the Green Party understands and speaks, so the May campaign was comfortable setting its sights on constituents it had not targeted to that point. "We focused on a strategy of talking about democracy," Dickie said. "The Reform Party, when they first gained strength, they were talking about things like abolishing the Senate, democracy, better representation by their MPs. And that was kind of the feedback we were getting from people in this community who tended to vote Conservative in the past, was that they were not feeling represented, that their MP was representing Ottawa to them instead of representing them in Ottawa."

According to Dickie, they also reached across party lines to appeal to a wider base by branding the campaign more heavily on May than on the Green Party. Her message about the need to approach politics differently — about introducing civility to political behavior and discourse — resonated in SGI, where claims of unethical tactics in 2008 dogged the Conservative victory.[47] Ironically, the Liberal candidate charged Green supporters were harassing her to drop out of the race, something May denied.[48] With a little under two weeks left before election day, her campaign had a poll in hand that showed her with a healthy lead over Lunn. Her support level among decided voters was at 45 percent; his was at 38 percent. The NDP and Liberal candidates were at 9 percent each. But there were still some wild cards to consider: the 16 percent of undecided constituents identified by the poll[49] and the ability of May's team to translate declarations of support into actual votes on election day.

THE NATIONAL CAMPAIGN

Wary of becoming mired in debt again, and mindful that the vote subsidy could be cut after the election, the Greens set a tight budget for their national effort — approximately $2 million, compared to the $3.4 million sunk into the 2008 campaign. They financed a little more than half through a bank loan; the rest ($770,000) came from fundraising efforts during the writ period. The bulk of the money ($1 million) went toward media/advertising, and another large chunk ($400,000) enabled the Greens to staff a national campaign team based in Ottawa nearly four-dozen strong. As was the case in 2008, the party beefed up its communications team and set up an information centre to field inquiries from the public.

It was a scaled-back version of the 2008 campaign, sharply focused around the need to accommodate the fact that May would be tied to her own election effort for most of the five-week period. She launched the national campaign out of SGI, a shift from the previous campaign, when she was nowhere near her own riding on day one of the campaign. And rather than meandering across the country by train for huge chunks of time, as was the case in 2008, she only emerged from SGI for two short tours. The first five-day trip began in Toronto and took her to Montreal and Halifax before looping back through southern Ontario. She spent another few days on a western trip to Edmonton and Calgary. The Greens were counting on the media to help drive their national campaign. The hope was that between the platform launch in Toronto, a continual series of policy-related announcements, and the leaders' debates, the party could maintain a national profile commensurate with the exposure they received in 2008, despite the fact that May remained largely hunkered down in SGI.

However, earned media is never a sure thing, especially for the "fifth" political party. In May's view, it was a frustrating reversal from the previous election. "In 2008, time outside my constituency hurt me locally, but we got great national coverage. In 2011, time outside my riding was as if I just vaulted into an altered plane of reality where no one knew where I was. I might as well have been on Mars."[50]

A number of factors likely played into the difference. For one, in 2008 there had been numerous stories about May and the strategic voting controversy. It earned them headlines, just not the kind they wanted. In 2011, but for the stories about the Green candidate for Fleetwood-Port Kells, who resigned over a remark about rape on his Facebook page,[51] the campaign unfolded remarkably smoothly. Secondly, the Greens went into the campaign with popular support ranging between 4 to 8 percent in national polls, and never really lifted above that. Contrast that to 2008, when they were often polling at 12 to 13 percent, creating a sense of momentum.[52] Their 2011 dip in the polls was matched by a dip in public anxiety about the environment relative to other matters. The environment consistently ranked well below health care and the economy as a national issue of concern.[53] This, too, was a change from 2008, when concern about climate change featured prominently on the political agenda until recession fears pushed the economy to the forefront.

The Greens were also hampered by May's exclusion from the leaders' debates. The news that she would be barred from participating, along with the party's subsequent court challenge of the broadcast consortium's decision, received national attention. However, they did not benefit from a long-lasting bump in attention as they had during the previous campaign, when May waged her ultimately successful public opinion war to be let in. That can be partially attributed to the fact that, having learned their lesson in 2008, the other party leaders did not oppose her participation. They thus deprived journalists and the public of a political target. And unlike in 2008, when an independent MP joined the Greens just prior to the election call, the party did not have what the consortium claimed was a basic requirement for inclusion — a sitting MP.[54] Ultimately denied a spot, May was excised from the 2011 narratives. She did not fit within standard journalistic debate storylines — preparation, performance, post-debate public opinion — so once it was clear the consortium's decision would stand, there was simply no opportunity for her to insert herself into the national coverage. More important, she was denied the legitimacy that debate participation bestows. It sent a clear message that the Greens were still viewed as being on the outside of the political mainstream, looking in.

And finally, the impact of May's SGI-based campaign is not to be underestimated. Without the broader narrative framework provided by a leader's tour, the Greens found it difficult to sustain national media interest on a daily basis. The party did try other ways of garnering media attention and connecting to the public. Green Party deputy leader Georges Laraque, a former professional hockey player, was sent out on the campaign trail in Quebec and western Canada. Out in SGI, May was shadowed by a party videographer. Footage of announcements and rallies were transmitted to national headquarters, where an editor would polish them and post them online. This dovetailed with the party's push to utilize social media more often. In fact, the Greens' first national ad in 2011, an "attack ad on attack ads" released before the writ period, had its strongest boost through social media. Limited ad time was bought on mainstream television networks, but Greens were urged to help it go viral through Twitter and Facebook accounts. The party posted it on its YouTube site, where it attracted more than fifty thousand views over two days.[55]

These efforts helped mitigate the impact of the May's minimal national presence. But the importance of party leaders on vote choice and the halo effect created when a leader visits local ridings during an election campaign have been well documented.[56] The curtailment of May's leader's tour, coupled with the pullback of resources in order to focus on SGI and, to a lesser extent, a select group of other targeted ridings, also contributed to the drop in the Greens' popular vote.

The loss of support cannot be attributed to the party's platform. It was largely consistent with policies set out in 2008, and contained no surprises. Organized around three main themes — the economy, communities, and democracy — the cornerstone remained the revenue neutral "green tax shift" based on a $50 per tonne carbon tax set to rise to $60 per tonne within three years. The other planks built on previous efforts to broaden Green appeal, to demonstrate that it was not a single-issue party, and to prove it was fiscally responsible. As such, it would introduce income splitting, lower EI and CPP contributions, and reduce the deficit by some $10 billion over three years. It proposed a $15.6-billion investment on such things as a national pharmacare program, municipal superfunds, and a national affordable housing program. It put forward policies to legalize and tax marijuana, roll back corporate tax cuts, and cut military spending and shift priorities toward peacekeeping. Overall, the set of policies kept the Greens largely left of centre. It received top grades in some quarters for its solid environmental base, and mixed reviews in others mainly with respect to its proposed budget.[57]

GETTING OUT THE VOTE

Election day in Saanich–Gulf Islands dawned cool and rainy. Even so, with polling stations set to open at 7:00 a.m. PDT, May was up early and out on the street, waving at cars. Her five-hundred-strong core group of volunteers, who had already canvassed 80 percent of the riding on foot over the course of the campaign, knocked on doors one last time. Everyone on the party's list was called twice. It was a national effort, according to Dickie. The party pulled together to make approximately thirty thousand phone calls into SGI that day. In spite of the positive April poll, he worried that May's support would prove soft, that it would be eclipsed by the hardcore Conservative constituency and a Lunn team that was much more experienced at getting out its vote.

The first results put May in the lead right away, but members of the campaign team weren't ready to celebrate. With pockets of solid Green support dwarfed by areas of the riding that were traditionally Conservative, they weren't confident the lead would hold. "I was terrified early on," the Greens' deputy director of communications, Camille Labchuk, recalled. "It can be really difficult to trust what you're seeing on TV and the computer when you don't know which polls are reporting yet."[58] But as the numbers kept coming in, May's margin kept getting wider. Just after 8:00 p.m., Labchuk's phone rang. It was Lunn's campaign manager, wanting to arrange a call between Lunn and May. "That was really surprising, it was so early for him to be conceding," Labchuk said. In fact, one of the first things May asked Lunn was whether he was "sure," she added. "What we found out later was that the polls that had come in were the polls that were in areas that were supposed to be good for him. And I think that's when he knew that he had lost it."

Shortly after she hung up the phone, May took her victory walk through the crowd, a phalanx of cameras preceding her, to the podium. "I stand here as the first elected Green Member of Parliament in Canadian history," she announced. Her smile could not have been bigger. Her supporters could not have been louder. "We have to prove to all of Canada," she went on, "that one MP for the Green Party, one MP with a different approach, one MP not squashed by partisanship and entangled in cynicism, can actually make a big difference."[59]

She carried that theme into her post-election interviews. Faced with questions about how effective she could realistically be, sitting as the lone Green MP in a Conservative majority Parliament, she acknowledged the difficulties ahead. Nevertheless, she said, her priorities were to end heckling during Question Period in the House of Commons, and to break down party barriers. "Even though it's a majority government I want to find ways to get MPs from all sides of the House to set aside partisanship and work together," she said.[60]

In May's view, the desire for civility in politics is the main reason she won SGI. One hundred percent of her support came from people who want fundamental change in the way politics is conducted, she said. Eighty percent sprung from local environmental concerns, such as fish farms and coastline protection from oil tankers. And as she sees it, a smaller chunk of support came from people who simply felt the first-past-the-post system was unfairly shutting the Greens out of the House of Commons, and who wanted to do something about it. Given her analysis of how her vote breaks down, she is under no illusions that SGI constituents have suddenly become big-g Greens. "It would be wrong to interpret it as a lot of Liberals and NDP and Conservatives who've decided that they are forever now Green Party, and they've changed their affiliations. That's not the case," she said. She believes a lot of her vote will go back to the other parties at the provincial level, and that in terms of some of her support, crucial democratic values were uppermost. "It was personal," she said. "But it wasn't absent the very large reality that voters in Saanich–Gulf Islands would be making history, and getting the Green Party leader into the House of Commons."[61]

CONCLUSION

Leading up to election day, for the first time in the life of their party, the Canadian Greens were in a position to envision a future that included a Green MP. They tried on various scenarios. How would it work if May were elected? Even better, what if it were May and one other? What they did not anticipate was a majority Conservative government. Notions of possessing the ability to influence politics and policy as a member of a formal or informal coalition were, as May put it, "all blown apart" on election night when she realized it would not be a hung Parliament. Nor, unsurprisingly, would she have the rights granted to parties with official status, which requires twelve elected members, such as a regular voice in Question Period and committee membership.

She has since rethought her strategy, and will work within the system from the bottom up, by focusing on the rules of procedure and process. This will include, she hopes, the eventual deployment of a small cadre of interns to monitor committees on her behalf, so she can use her time and her presence strategically. It will also include inserting herself into the process in ways that she maintains will be respectful and confident. She will not be "desperate" to be heard, as she says some would believe. And she will certainly not be a "joke," as she says others have maintained. "There's a kind of a construct that would want to see me as an outsider," she said. "But I'm very comfortable in Parliament. And I'm not going to be an outsider on the inside. I know the rules. I know what my rights are. I'm not going to ask for things that are unreasonable."

As for the party, it has some decisions to make as it faces down the next four years. Clearly its plans will be circumscribed by money. Qualifying for the vote subsidy breathed life into the Greens in 2004. It has relied heavily on that public funding ever since. Only one-third of its current annual $3-million operating budget comes from fundraising. If it is to survive the phase-out of the subsidy, it will need to streamline operations and concentrate remaining resources on bringing in more money from Canadians. Those efforts will divert them from a singular party-building focus in the wake of May's election. And it carries two implications: the Greens will need to mobilize a core volunteer base now more than ever if they hope to maintain relevance as a national party, and they will have to depend heavily on their leader — more heavily, perhaps, than they had ever imagined.

The party's organized presence across the country has shrunk. From the approximately 240 Electoral District Associations or official riding organizations it had registered in 2009, it was down to 195 in 2011. Whether it can afford to now spend money and time attempting to estab-lish 308 EDAs is one question. Whether it even wants to is another. The Greens may very well opt to apply their Saanich strategy to a few select ridings in preparation for the next election rather than spreading their capital too thinly in areas that are unlikely to deliver votes. And if that is the road they choose, the challenge becomes persuading the rest of the membership to continue travelling with them. In all likelihood they would still aim for a full slate of candidates for the next campaign. But even with a leader sitting in the House of Commons, it might be difficult to attract significant volunteer support in ridings not organized by regis-tered EDAs or singled out for extra campaign resources.

Speaking in his capacity as the Green's 2011 Yukon candidate, John Streicker says it is crucial to find a way to encourage the grassroots while still focusing their electoral effort. "The issue comes down to making sure that how we concentrate that effort still adheres to our principles," he said. "A lot of people come to the Green Party because we sense that there is an ethic around it, that the power of politics isn't the purpose. So if we sell that principle just for the power of politics then I think we will split apart at the seams."[62]

A weakened organized grassroots presence could also have the consequence — perhaps unintended — of further concentrating the Greens' decision-making. Already, power over candidate selection has been transferred to the leader. In a reversal of the previous bottom-up process, in which the leader would approve candidates after they were selected by EDAs, candidate hopefuls for election 2011 applied directly to the central party. The EDAs held candidate nomination contests only after the leader approved the applicants.[63] It professionalizes the process and brings the Greens in line with the traditional political parties, but in handing more discretionary power to the leader it is a major shift for the grassroots party.

The Greens are aware that it will be difficult to find the right balance between building directly behind May's beachhead and spreading out some resources in the interests of broadening the bulwark. "As a result of the internal realities of having such a strong leader, and the external realities that aren't always within our control, right now the face of the Green Party is Elizabeth May," Streicker said. "What I think has been missed by the broad public is that we have a lot of depth. So what we need to do is to start to show the public that depth. We need to create an understanding that the Green Party isn't an individual."[64]

For now, much depends on whether that individual can deliver on her assertion that one person can indeed make a big difference in Parliament. May's success would attract more strong Green candidates and support. It would also largely dictate the party's strategy going into the next election. In the meantime, the Greens will press ahead with their post-election process, which includes its first mandated leadership review, as well as elections for Executive Council. They took seven years to capitalize on their 2004 breakthrough, to grow from being a political group on the fringes to being a political party with a sitting MP. Their next challenges will be greater still, as they set out to maximize the benefits of having their leader in the House of Commons, craft strategies to shore up their fundraising and membership, and develop ways of participating in the country's political life that will convince Canadians they are more than just a party of one.

NOTES

My sincere thanks to all Green Party members and staff, past and present, who took the time to share their experiences and knowledge of the party and its operations with respect to Election 2011.

1. Elizabeth May, Green Party leader, interview with author, June 1, 2011.
2. John Streicker, Green Party federal council chair, interview with author, May 6, 2011.
3. CTV.ca News Staff, "Green Party Makes History: Élizabeth May Wins Seat," last modified May 3, 2011. *http://m.ctv.ca/topstories/20110502/elizabeth-may-wins-riding-green-110502.html.*
4. A. Bruce, "May: New Voice for the Centre?," last modified May 5, 2011. *http:// timestranscript.canadaeast.com/opinion/article/1403772.*
5. P. Fong, "Third Try's a Charm for Elizabeth May," last modified May 3, 2011. *www.the star.com/news/canada/politics/article/984576--third-try-s-a-charm-for-elizabeth-may.*
6. R. Murphy, "Once Green Seat Out of 308 Is Not 'Historic,'" May 14, 2011. *http:// fullcomment.nationalpost.com/2011/05/14/rex-murphy-one-green-seat-out-of-308-is-not-historic.*
7. K. O'Malley, #Parl41Watch: Welcome to Parliament, Ms. May. The Back Bench Is That Way. *Inside Politics*, accessed May 16, 2011. *www.cbc.ca/news/politics/inside-politics-blog/2011/05/parl41watch-welcome-to-parliament-ms-may-the-back-bench-is-that-way.html.*
8. In Bruce–Grey–Owen Sound, the Greens went from 27.2 percent of the vote in 2008 to 10 percent in 2011. In Guelph, they went from 21.1 to 6.1 percent.
9. Green Party of Canada, 2009. Campaign Plan 2009 for the 41st General Election: summary for EDAs and candidates.
10. Johan Hamels, Green Party executive director, interview with author, May 11, 2011.
11. Jen Hunter, Green Party candidate for Ottawa Centre, interview with author, May 17, 2011.
12. May's first campaign as Green leader was during a November 2006 federal by-election, when she ran in London North Centre. She had a surprisingly strong showing, finishing second to the Liberal candidate. For more details, see the Elections Canada website at *www.elections.ca/content.aspx?section=res&dir=rep/ off/ovr_2006&document=index&lang=e&textonly=false.*

13. For more, see S. Harada, "The Promise of May: The Green Party of Canada's Campaign 2008," in *The Canadian Federal Election of 2008*, eds. Jon H. Pammett and Christopher Dornan (Toronto: Dundurn Press), 162–93.

14. *Ibid.*

15. E. May, "Leader's Report on the 2008 Election," Elizabeth May's blog, last modified November 5, 2008. *http://greenparty.ca/en/node/8515.*

16. Elizabeth May, Green Party leader, telephone interview with author, September 26, 2009.

17. S. Delacourt, "Greens' Fall Thoughts Turn to May: Election Planning Shifts to Getting Seat for Leader," *Toronto Star*, June 26, 2009, A15.

18. Elizabeth May, Green Party leader, telephone interview with author, September 26, 2009.

19. S. Hertzog, "Why I am Standing as a Nomination Candidate," accessed May 27, 2011. *http://blogs.stuzog.com/greenpolitics/2009/08/why-i-am-standing-as-a-nomination-candidate/.*

20. S. Hertzog, "My Complaint to Elections Canada," accessed May 27, 2011. *http://blogs.stuzog.com/greenpolitics/2009/09/my-complaint-to-elections-canada/.*

21. K. Derosa, "Complaint Against Greens Nixed," *Times Colonist*, December 2, 2009, A8. See also, Green Party of Canada, "SGI Complaints Groundless, Elections Canada," accessed May 27, 2011. *www.elizabethmay.ca/?s=sgi+complaint+groundles s&submit=.*

22. Maureen Murphy, former Green Party executive director, interview with author, May 7, 2010.

23. John Fryer, former SGI campaign manager, telephone interview with author, June 9, 2010.

24. Elections Canada, "Return Details — Statement of Transfers Received (Part 2d)," accessed May 30, 2011. *www.elections.ca/scripts/webpep/fin2/detail_report.aspx.*

25. Maureen Murphy, former Green Party executive director, interview with author, May 7, 2010.

26. See, for example, S.N. Furtuna, "The EU and the Curious Case of the Copenhagen Accord." CES Working Papers Online, II, accessed May 31, 2011. *www.cse.uaic. ro/WorkingPapers/articles/CESWP2010_I2_FUR.pdf,* and Green Party of Canada, "Climate Betrayal in Copenhagen," accessed May 31, 2011. *http://greenparty.ca/ media-release/2009-12-18/climate-betrayal-copenhagen.*

27. See, for example, D. Akin, "Top Greens Put Pressure on Party Leader May," *Canwest News Service*, January 24, 2010; M. De Souza, "May Shocked as Green Deputy Defects to Bloc," *Canwest News Service*, June 15, 2010; and L. Martin, "It's a Tough Climate for Elizabeth May and the Greens," *Globe and Mail*, March 18, 2010, A19.

28. See, for example, M. Day, "An Open Letter [to] the Green Party of Canada," accessed May 31, 2011. *http://greencanada.wordpress.com/2010/02/21/an-open-letter-the-green-party-of-canada-federal-council.*

29. S. Lemieux, "Growing the Green Party is Our #1 Priority," accessed June 2, 2011. *www.sylvielemieux.ca/blog/growing-green-party-our-1-priority.*

30. E. May, "RE: A Note from Elizabeth May. To: Green Party Members."

31. See, for example, R. Routledge, R. 2010. "Leadership Issues and the 2010 BGM," accessed May 31, 2011. *http://webcache.googleusercontent.com/search?q=cache: Ktb4yC14G6sJ:greenparty.ca/blogs/1912/2010-06-30/leadership-issues-and-2010-bgm+g10-c10+green+party+johansson&cd=6&hl=en&ct=clnk&client=safari&sour ce=www.google.com*; and Blogbot "Let Sylvie Lemieux Email All Members about Motion G10-d11," accessed May 31, 2011. *www.bloggingcanadians.ca/GreenBlogs/ let-sylvie-lemieux-email-all-members-about-motion-g10-d11/.*

32. N. Greenaway, "Surprise Declaration Stirs Green Party Leadership Pot," *Postmedia News*, July 21, 2010, and S. Tracey, "Race to Challenge Green Leader Launched in Guelph," *GuelphMercury.com*, July 19, 2010.

33. For more, see S. Harada, "The Promise of May."

34. Green Party of Canada, "Green Party Members Vote Overwhelmingly in Support of Elizabeth," accessed June 2, 2011. *http://greenparty.ca/media-release/2010-08-11/ green-party-members-vote-overwhelmingly-support-elizabeth-may.*

35. Lemieux offered what was publicly recognized as an olive branch at the BGM, proposing to amend her directive to delay a leadership contest to within six months of the next federal election, unless the leader won her seat. She urged members to vote against her original motion should the amendment not be accepted. Ninety-one percent of the members present voted down the motion.

36. Elizabeth May, Green Party leader, interview with author, June 1, 2011.

37. Elizabeth May, Green Party leader, news conference at the Green Party of Canada Biennial General Meeting, August 21, 2010.

38. Statistics Canada, "Federal Electoral District Profile of Saanich–Gulf Islands, British Columbia (2003 Representation Order), 2006 Census," accessed May 30, 2011. *http://www12.statcan.ca/census-recensement/2006/dp-pd/prof/92-595/P2C.cfm? TPL=RETR&LANG=E&GC=59024.* See also C.E. Harnett, "Saanich–Gulf Islands: A Tight-Race Battleground," *Times Colonist*, D6.

39. Jonathan Dickie, Green Party campaign manager, Saanich–Gulf Islands, telephone interview with author, May 9, 2011.

40. Catharine Johannsen, then Green Party political director, interview with author, October 2, 2009.

41. Elizabeth May, Green Party leader, interview with author, June 1, 2011.

42. A. Macleod, "Can Elizabeth May Win a Seat in BC?," accessed June 3, 2011. *www. greenpartystrategy.com/articles/can-elizabeth-may-win-seat-bc*; and D. Travis, "The Bad News: Mixed Messages," *www.greenpartystrategy.com/articles/bad-news-mixed-messages.*

43. The McAllister Opinion Research poll was a random survey of 402 adults between August 21–25, 2010, with a +/-4.8 percent margin of error, nineteen times out of twenty. See Green Party of Canada, "Greens have Momentum in SGI," accessed June 3, 2011. *http://greenparty.ca/media-release/2010-09-03/greens-have-momentum-sgi*; and K. Westad, "Green Party's May Gaining Ground on Lunn in Saanich–Gulf Islands, Poll Suggests," accessed June 3, 2011. *www.elizabethmay.ca/*

in-the-news/green-partys-may-gaining-ground-on-lunn-in-saanich-gulf-islands-poll-suggests/.

44. Johan Hamels, Green Party executive director, interview with author, June 1, 2011.
45. Elections Canada, "Final Candidate Election Expenses Limits," accessed June 3, 2011. *www.elections.ca/content.aspx?section=ele&document=index&dir=41ge/limcan&lang=e.*
46. Jonathan Dickie, Green Party campaign manager, Saanich–Gulf Islands, telephone interview with author, May 9, 2011.
47. In 2008, voters were reportedly phoned on election day and prompted to support the NDP candidate, who had publicly dropped out of the race, but too late to have his name removed from the ballot. He received 3,667 votes, while Lunn defeated the Liberal candidate by 2,261 votes. For details, see C. Plecash, C. "Elections Canada Investigating, Results Marred by Claims of Phone-Based Voter Suppression Campaign," *The Hill Times*, May 16, 2011; and Victoria *Times Colonist*, October 30, 2008, "Saanich–Gulf Islands Election Tactics under Microscope," accessed June 3, 2011. *www.canada.com/victoriatimescolonist/news/comment/story.html?id=f70f8ede-0da9-45ea-a06c-c47817864d55.*
48. CBC News (26 April 2011). "Green Party Leader Denies Targeting Liberal Rival," last modified April 26, 2011. *www.cbc.ca/news/politics/story/2011/04/26/bc-saanich-gulf-island-may-hetherington.html?ref=rss.*
49. Three-hundred-and-eighty-nine people were interviewed between April 18–19, 2011. The margin of error is +/-4.9 percent, nineteen times out of twenty. See Oracle Poll Research, "Saanich Gulf Island Riding Report," accessed June 3, 2011. *http://greenparty.ca/files/attachments/poll_-_saanich_gulf_islands_april_20th_2011.pdf.*
50. Elizabeth May, Green Party leader, interview with author, June 1, 2011.
51. See, for example, S. Dhillon, "Green Candidate in B.C. Riding Resigns over Comments on Rape," *Globe and Mail*, April 13, 2011; and Green Party of Canada, "Statement by the Green Party concerning Alan Saldanha," accessed June 5, 2011. *http://greenparty.ca/media-release/2011-04-13/statement-green-party-concerning-alan-saldanha.*
52. Laurier Institute for the Study of Public Opinion and Policy. "Federal Party Support Table: January 2007–May 2011," accessed June 4, 2011. *www.wlu.ca/lispop/fedsupporttable.html#questions.*
53. See, for example, Nanos Research, "Healthcare Top Issue of Concern," accessed June 4, 2011. *www.nanosresearch.com/library/polls/POLNAT-W11-T461E.pdf*; C. Chai, C., "Health Care Top Issue for Canadians: Election Poll." *The Vancouver Sun*, March 28, 2011; and H. Loney, "Standard of Living Number One Election Issue for Canada's Youth," accessed June 4, 2011. *www.globalnews.ca/decisioncanada/story.html?id=4684548.*
54. S. Harada, "The Promise of May."
55. Kieran Green, Green Party director of communications, telephone interview with author, April 18, 2011. See Green Party of Canada, "Change the Channel on Attack Ads," accessed June 4, 2011. *www.youtube.com/user/canadiangreenparty#p/u/6/j-GekKKNUTU.*

56. See, for example, P. Bélanger, R.K. Carty, and M. Eagles, "The Geography of Canadian Parties' Electoral Campaigns: Leaders' Tours and Constituency Election Results," *Political Geography* 22 (2003): 439–45; and E. Gidengil, A. Blais, R. Nadeau, and N. Nevitte, "Are Party Leaders Becoming More Important To Vote Choice in Canada?" American Political Science Association, Washington, D.C., 2000.

57. The Pembina Institute, "Pembina Reacts to the Green Party Platform," accessed June 5, 2011. *www.pembina.org/media-release/2199*; "Sierra Club Canada Releases its 2011 Federal Election Environmental Report Card," accessed June 5, 2011. *www.sierraclub.ca/en/climate-change/media/release/sierra-club-canada-releases-its-2011-federal-election-environmental-rep*; and M. McDiarmid, "Green Party Unveils Platform," *The National*, CBC Television, April 7, 2011.

58. Camille Labchuk, Green Party deputy director of communications, telephone interview with author, May 10, 2011.

59. Green Party of Canada, "Elizabeth's Speech — Election Night 2011," accessed May 16, 2011. *http://greenparty.ca/video/2011-05-04/elizabeths-speech-election-night-2011*.

60. CBC News, "Green Leader Elected," accessed May 16, 2011. *www.cbc.ca/news/politics/canadavotes2011/story/2011/05/02/cv-election-greens.html*.

61. Elizabeth May, Green Party leader, interview with author, June 1, 2011.

62. John Streicker, Green Party candidate for Yukon, interview with author, May 24, 2011.

63. Sharon Labchuk, Green Party director of organizing, interview with author, April 12, 2011.

64. John Streicker, Green Party candidate for Yukon, interview with author, May 6, 2011.

CHAPTER 7

Constituency Campaigning in the 2011 Canadian Federal Election
Alex Marland

Campaigning in electoral districts used to be included in general election summaries like this one. But then interest in local dynamics diminished as television increased the importance of party leaders and as research indicated that what happens in electoral districts matters only in close races. It was also exceptionally difficult to monitor the many hundreds of races held simultaneously across the country, and so post-election reviews tended to profile single electoral districts or offer provincial summaries.[1] The Internet and 24-7 media have brought changes. In a shortened news cycle, local races have become interesting diversions from the party leaders' daily photo-ops and scripted remarks. It is also now much easier to document how journalists present constituency campaigning in the 308 electoral districts across Canada.[2]

RULES FOR CONSTITUENCY CAMPAIGNING IN 2011

The boundaries of Canada's 308 electoral districts were set according to the *Electoral Boundaries Readjustment Act*, and campaigning is governed by the *Canada Elections Act*. This stipulates rules for candidate nominations, election communication, staffing, fundraising, and spending (see Table 1). The rules deal with financial matters, from dissuading nuisance candidates by requiring a $1,000 nomination deposit to both subsidizing and limiting contributions and expenditures.

Table 1. Rules for Constituency Campaigning in 2011

	Key Features
Candidate Nomination	• signatures of 100+ residents (min. 50 in physically vast ridings) • $1,000 deposit required • if a party candidate: written endorsement from the party leader
Communication	• candidates must be able to canvass in public places and multiple-residence buildings • candidates receive copies of Elections Canada's list of electors for communicating and fundraising (incumbents receive the updated list annually)
Staff	• need an official agent and auditor • may designate two representatives to scrutinize voting at a polling station and who receive "bingo cards" identifying who has voted
Fundraising	• maximum of $1,100 contributed per elector per candidate • tax-deductible receipts issued for donations of $20+ • the national party, its district associations, and its candidates may transfer money between one another during the campaign
Spending	• nomination campaign spending capped at 20% of the election limit • candidates' spending capped at a mean of $91,703 (ranging from $69,635 in Malpeque, P.E.I. to $134,352 in Oak Ridges–Markham, Ontario) • a third party (e.g., advocacy group) may not spend more than $3,765 for or against a candidate in a district
Post-election	• $1,000 deposit returned if a summary of fundraising and spending filed with Elections Canada • candidates with at least 10% of the vote refunded 60% of their spending

Source: *Canada Elections Act* and *Elections Canada* backgrounders

In 2011, securing at least 10 percent of the vote in the riding was thus a minimum objective because it would bring a 60 percent refund of expenses. As well, legislation stipulated that qualifying parties would receive $2 annually for each vote received, meaning that political organiza-tions were motivated to pull votes even in seats that were unlikely to change hands. "Bringing the vote up in every riding is important because of elec-tion financing. Everything that we do helps through the campaign and the bottom line in the end," said the Liberals' campaign co-chair in Alberta.[3] The NDP manager there added that the vote subsidy "falls into the equa-tion for a lot of people who vote NDP in ridings where our odds are long."[4] The Conservatives pledged that with a majority government they would phase out such subsidies, but with such an outcome in doubt the existing financial structure would remain an incentive to get out the vote.

RETIREMENTS AND SEATS TO WATCH

Throughout the Fortieth Parliament, opinion polls indicated that another minority government outcome was likely.[5] Members of Parliament (MPs), aware that an election was pending, were in permanent campaign mode. Many incumbents and challengers had spent the past year knocking on doors, meeting with opinion leaders, and hosting roundtables and community forums. For instance, rookie Liberal MP Siobhan Coady (St. John's South–Mount Pearl), who had won her seat by less than 3 percent in 2008 after being the runner-up in 2004 and 2006, regularly advertised public meetings, hosted visiting Liberal MPs, addressed local events, and maintained an active online presence. Likewise, some challengers who had won their party's nomination months before had put their lives on hold to campaign without knowing when the election would be called.

On March 25, 2011, all MPs except one pending retiree were in Ottawa to vote along party lines on the Liberals' motion of non-confidence against the Conservative government. NDP MP Megan Leslie (Dartmouth–Cole Harbour) reflected on members quickly travelling to their districts to begin campaigning: "It was funny. I was on a plane with every other Nova Scotia incumbent. We were all on the same plane together, all heading back to our home communities."[6] For an elected official, getting to go home for a long period could be a welcome change. "The good thing is you don't have to go to Ottawa every week, so you're not on a plane all the time. And you get to sleep in your own bed," said Liberal Geoff Regan (Halifax West).[7] However, a handful of incumbents do not spend much time in their riding during a campaign: the party leaders, obviously, but also popular incumbents who were tapped to assist in other ridings. Jason Kenney, the Minister of Citizenship, Immigration and Multiculturalism, who was in charge of the Tories' ethnic outreach strategy, delayed returning to Calgary Southeast so that he could visit other ridings; meanwhile, Conservative supporters in Calgary began phoning electors elsewhere in Canada.

Incumbents have a range of advantages over challengers, including human and financial resources.[8] Long-time MPs not seeking re-election in British Columbia included four Conservatives: Minister Chuck Strahl (Chilliwack–Fraser Canyon); Minister Stockwell Day (Okanagan Coquihalla), who had led the Canadian Alliance Party in the 2000 campaign; Jim Abbott (Kootenay–Columbia); and John Cummins (Delta–Richmond East). Liberals not running again included Speaker of the House Peter Milliken (Kingston and the Islands), Albina Guarnieri (Mississauga East–Cooksville), Raymonde Folco (Laval–Les Iles), and Keith Martin (Esquimalt–Juan De Fuca). Several Bloc Québécois MPs did not seek re-election, including Serge Ménard (Marc-Aurèle-Fortin); nor did Bill Siksay of the NDP (Burnaby-Douglas). Due to this exodus of incumbents in British Columbia, there would be more seats in play in an already competitive region, including Saanich–Gulf Islands, where Green Party leader Elizabeth May was seeking to defeat Conservative Minister Gary Lunn.

These opportunities contributed to each party's seat triage: the identification of safe seats that it expects to retain with little effort, seats where a competitive race will demand resources, and seats that are largely ignored because the party is likely to be defeated.[9] National support in the form of money, workers, communications, and leader's visits is directed at marginal ridings, at competitive races, and in support of star candidates. Triage can lead to broad areas of the country being showered with attention while other areas go ignored. The Tories were said to be targeting forty-five battleground ridings based on voting data, wedge issues, candidate recruitment, and elector profiles including ethnicity, especially seats in southern Ontario's 905 area code.[10]

CANDIDATES

The process of sorting out who should represent a political party in a riding is usually orderly and routine.[11] There are inevitable complaints about a party's nomination rules for signing up members, about outsiders being "parachuted" into the riding, and whether a leader should have the final say over candidate selection. The leadership circle worries about party representatives going off message with the national campaign or, worse, boxing the leader into such damage control that a candidate has to be dismissed. National strategists are acutely aware that their opponents maintain databases of public statements and seek to turn any indiscretion into a national controversy. This is why political parties subject prospective candidates to rigorous background reviews including lengthy questionnaires and criminal record checks. Even so, candidate controversies constantly emerge.

All told, 1,587 people were candidates in 2011. The Bloc Québécois (75 in Quebec), Liberal (308), and NDP (308) fielded full slates, though one Liberal who was dismissed remained on the ballot. The Conservatives had 307, because they did not challenge Independent Conservative André Arthur in Portneuf–Jaques-Cartier, whom Tories campaigned with. The Greens had 304 candidates due to problems in a handful of districts. Thirteen other parties were represented, ranging from seventy candidates for the Marxist-Leninists to the lone representative of the National Party of Canada. There were also fifty-five independents and six "no affiliation" contestants.

Anthony Sayers's categorizations of Canadian election candidates as high profile, local notable, party insider, or stopgap[12] was applicable in 2011. Across the country, a number of former MPs, provincial legislators (including cabinet ministers), and municipal politicians ran for office. Rookies with a positive public image included union leaders, law enforcers, and community activists, but few of them could be considered stars. The Conservatives hoped that Chris Alexander (Ajax–Pickering), a former representative of the United Nations in Afghanistan, and Senator Larry Smith (Lac-Saint-Louis), past commissioner of the Canadian Football League, would defeat Liberal incumbents. The Liberals attracted former premiers of the Northwest Territories and Nunavut in Joe Handley and Paul Okalik, respectively. Romeo Saganash, a representative of the Grand Council of Crees, ran under the NDP banner in Abitibi–Baie-James–Nunavik–Eeyou, as did former Nova Scotia NDP leader Robert Chisholm in Dartmouth–Cole Harbour. Other notable races included Durham, given that Minister Bev Oda had been held in contempt for misleading Parliament; Edmonton-Strathcona, where the NDP's Linda Duncan hoped to retain the only Alberta riding not held by the Tories; Simcoe-Grey, where former Conservative Minister Helena Guergis would be running as an Independent Conservative; and Outremont, where NDP MP Thomas Mulcair would attempt to hold his party's only Quebec seat; and the forty-two ridings that were won by margins of 5 percent or less in 2008, including Papineau, where the Bloc would try to defeat Liberal Justin Trudeau.

There were also numerous stopgaps in hopeless seats with little support. The media reported many such NDP contestants. In Northumberland–Quinte West, a student was replaced with a man who was away in Kenya. The party fielded Edmontonians in two Calgary ridings. Three weeks into the election, NDP candidates in Ottawa-Orléans and in Vaughn were nowhere to be found, and its Ajax–Pickering designee was vacationing in the Dominican Republic. Attention to NDP "ghost" candidates who were little more than names on a ballot increased sharply as the party's support rose in the polls. The Bloc Québécois candidate in Mégantic–L'Érable became alarmed that the New Democrats had parachuted in an anglophone. On April 23, a Liberal Party ad warned electors that the NDP had "incredibly inexperienced candidates" and "no real team." On April 26, a top *Globe and Mail* story was about the NDP candidate in Berthier–Maskinongé, Ruth Ellen Brosseau, an employee at a campus pub in Ottawa who was vacationing in Las Vegas. The *Globe* also disclosed that contact information for most of the NDP's Quebec contestants was not listed on the party's website; that some were students who had never visited their riding; and that one's Twitter posts were about "hockey, comic books and computer games."[13] Moreover, a Scarborough NDP candidate was moonlighting as a campaign manager in a neighbouring riding; the one in Richmond–Arthabaska left for three weeks in France; and reporters could offer little more than a guess at a candidate's age in some Ontario and Quebec districts. On April 29, alone among the parties, the NDP replaced "meet your candidate" with "where to vote" on its website homepage.

A sizeable proportion of Greens were also stopgaps. For instance, in Skeena–Bulkley Valley a Green proclaimed that he had no money whatsoever for travel, for an office, or even for Internet access. And yet in some ridings there was evidence of the Green Party national organization's efforts to build district associations. "It's terrific. I can concentrate on what I'm supposed to do — be a candidate and know the issues. It makes my life a lot easier," the Edmonton Centre Green candidate said about the local base of volunteers.[14]

What motivates the many people who do not run with the mainstream parties and are all but destined to lose? Some independents were upset with partisan acrimony, some had failed to win their party nomination, and, in Peterborough, a Second World War veteran in his early nineties ran. Members of fringe parties saw the election as an opportunity to raise issues that would otherwise be ignored. The leader of the Pirate Party, who ran in Edmonton Centre, knocked on doors and distributed leaflets to advocate for more relaxed copyright laws; in Chilliwack, a Western Block Party candidate promoted Western separatism. "It's a pretty rough go. You get a lot of ridicule," said a Canadian Action Party hopeful.[15] Conversely, some did not campaign at all: "The only thing we're really doing is getting our name on the ballot. We're not really doing any campaigning," said a Christian Heritage candidate.[16] Others were pragmatic: "It's not likely that we are going to be elected. See, I'm not a skilled politician. A skilled politician would have a spin to put on that," said a Libertarian.[17]

CONSTITUENCY CAMPAIGNING

Constituency campaigns are a microcosm of the national contest and are the parties' local sales force. A "kitchen cabinet" — often friends and family and/or members of the Electoral District Association — discusses strategy and tactics with a campaign manager through whom decisions are filtered. Campaign workers are tasked with "baking homemade cookies for the troops every day, sweeping the floor, staking lawn signs, answering phones or canvassing supporters ... photocopying and making up foot canvassing kits for the people who go door-to-door," as a reporter in Edmonton observed.[18]

The first few days of a campaign are especially hectic. Volunteers are identified and fundraising letters initiated. Office space must be rented and furnished; larger ridings may need multiple satellite offices. Fundraising letters are initiated and nomination signatures coordinated for Elections Canada. Rallies are held at busy street intersections or on train platforms. Due to the high-profile nature of the confidence vote, candidates initially reported observing higher public awareness of the election, while others sensed voter fatigue given that this was the fourth federal election in seven years.

Canadian elections tend not to be held in the winter due to the logistical difficulties.[19] There was chilly weather in late March and into mid-April in many places. Reporters across Canada observed that signage did not appear very quickly. "We've been pounding in lawn signs — trying to with the frozen soil — and getting out on the doorsteps, making sure I have an extra pair of socks so I don't freeze," said the NDP candidate in Palliser on the first day of the campaign.[20] A month later a challenger in Montreal attributed his cold to distributing signs on a frigid April evening, while in Sudbury a debate moderator periodically relayed playoff hockey updates. In contrast, amidst Vancouver's balmy weather an NDP candidate sought media attention by skydiving.

Putting up signs and billboards on prime public real estate is an immediate local priority. Inevitably concerns emerged about placement on public spaces — deemed unsightly, a traffic hazard, and/or against municipal bylaws — which led to some being removed. In Toronto the transit commission introduced a ban on election advertising on subway platforms. Hec Clouthier, an independent in Renfrew–Nipissing–Pembroke, opted for mobile billboards. Four trucks were driven around the riding with large signs featuring his image and the slogan "Give 'em Hec!"[21]

Publicizing the opening of a local headquarters signifies the launch of the party's constituency campaign. Supporters are invited to listen to a speech, to mingle, to munch, and sometimes to sing or dance to theme music. For Justin Trudeau, a political celebrity, 350 supporters packed his headquarters, including area MPs, senators, and community leaders. But for most it was a more routine celebration marked by friends, family, and partisans, if they had a public headquarters at all. Later, some Liberals hosted a "platform party" at their headquarters to coincide with the release of the national Liberal platform, during which attendees interacted with the party's leader via video conference, a technology that Elizabeth May also used to connect one-on-one with various ridings.

A mainstay of constituency campaigning is canvassing, mostly knocking on doors at electors' homes, but also visiting retirement homes, restaurants, and shopping malls. This involves a combination of saying hello, identifying potential supporters, and dropping off campaign literature. "There's no magic formula, it's old-style campaigning. It's doorstep to doorstep, house to house, street to street," said Liberal MP Ujjal Dosanjh (Vancouver South).[22] "Pretty much 90 percent of my time is get up and knock on doors. You've got to get out and meet people. There really isn't any other way," added the NDP candidate in Essex.[23] For some there was a methodical approach to door knocking. "I have a set schedule where I'll be canvassing two polls every day for thirty-six days starting on Monday. So basically you're talking about trying to visit five hundred people every day for the next thirty-six days," said the NDP aspirant in Kingston.[24] "Don't ever miss a house," panted Conservative incumbent Laurie Hawn in between residences in Edmonton Centre.[25] Towards the end of the campaign, the NDP candidate in Langley complained of blisters on his feet from so much walking, while in Thornhill the Liberal campaign had a registered massage therapist available to give foot rubs.

Many campaigners said that they liked talking with people on doorsteps. "Of all the things I do, I like knocking on doors the best. At events you don't always have time to have the kinds of in-depth conversations you can have with people when you go door-to-door," remarked the Liberal candidate in Leeds-Grenville.[26] In Northumberland–Quinte West the Liberal contestant was careful to write a message on her brochure before dropping it off when nobody answered the door. "We do this so people understand that Canada Post didn't deliver these. We were here and wanted to talk to them," she explained.[27] Yet for others canvassing was a chore. As Liberal incumbent Glen Pearson (London North Centre), put it: "I hate election time … How would you feel knocking on five thousand doors, saying, 'Please like me?'"[28]

After the initial rush, candidates settled into a routine of canvassing, media interviews, and attending events such as party breakfasts, football banquets, charitable dinners, library openings, and garden shows. "It's the personal contact that's important. You try to get to every tea, dinner, and barbecue that you can," explained Bev Oda.[29] They also toured with municipal leaders to discuss local infrastructure such as a decaying roadway or a water treatment plant. Issuing news releases advocating for government resources or regulations to support local jobs was a common practice.

Securing testimonials from opinion leaders is another long-standing technique. Sometimes this briefly attracted national media coverage, such as support for Conservative MP Julian Fantino (Vaughan) from his former Liberal opponent, but most endorsements were routine, such as from a former university president, a senator, a union, or an environmentalist. Campaigning with high-profile federal and provincial parliamentarians and with municipal politicians remained a favourite technique. Bloc Québécois representatives were publicly endorsed by Parti Québécois MNAs; Stockwell Day stumped with various Tories; former Liberal Prime Minister Paul Martin campaigned in Vancouver and Edmonton; and Justin Trudeau visited ridings in Toronto and Vancouver. The recipients of such support signalled that they had inside connections and were in a competitive race. Visiting distant ridings was not without risk to the opinion leader: in Trudeau's case the Bloc linked his absence to a local narrative that he was a "député fantôme."[30]

The most significant endorsements came with a visit from the party leader, who was introduced by the candidate to local supporters. Prime

Minister Stephen Harper (Calgary Southwest) began with rallies in Quebec City and Toronto suburbs, Michael Ignatieff (Etobicoke–Lakeshore) in Ottawa and Montreal, and Jack Layton (Toronto–Danforth) in Edmonton and Surrey. As further evidence of triage, none of them bothered to visit Calgary except Harper, who sought re-election as a Calgary MP and arrived for the last day of the campaign. One of the benefits of heading a regional protest party was that when the Bloc Québécois released its platform in Montreal, leader Gilles Duceppe (Laurier–Sainte Marie) campaigned 250 kilometres away with a local challenger, leaving the publicity to two Bloc candidates, one of whom was running against Trudeau.

In electoral districts the tone of discourse varied. In Kootenay–Columbia, the Conservative and NDP candidates said that they got along and would enjoy campaigning against each other. In Halton, the four main contestants were women, which was thought to have contributed to a civilized tone of discussion; as the Green candidate remarked, "I'm seeing some really lovely co-operation."[31] By comparison, in Haliburton–Kawartha Lakes–Brock the Conservative boycotted a newspaper managed by his Liberal opponent and the federal Tories removed it from their news release distribution list. In response, the publisher wrote a scathing editorial suggesting the Conservatives' goal was to put the paper out of business.

Local debates and "meet the candidates" events are traditionally hosted by chambers of commerce, universities and schools, municipal councils, and other community organizations, including local radio stations and cable TV. In 2011, local views were expressed on national-level issues such as health care, jobs, taxes, childcare, poverty, the environment, the gun registry, and the Harper government's record. Specific economic concerns ran the gamut: securing a third energy cable from PEI to the mainland; replacing Montreal's Champlain Bridge; removing radioactive waste in Cobourg; developing a harbour in Sault Ste. Marie; stopping the mining of asbestos in Sarnia; building an airport tunnel in Calgary. One televised debate, in Newton–North Delta, between the Conservative, Liberal, and NDP candidates, was held entirely in Punjabi. Media reports painted these as rancorous affairs full of one-upmanship and a partisan audience applauding, heckling, and booing.

Candidates from all parties, especially incumbents, sometimes avoid being the target of such discontent by refusing to participate in debates. In 2011, a recurring theme was of Conservative absences, such as the Toronto candidate who cited a scheduling conflict to explain his decision not to attend a debate held at a "queer" community centre where his predecessor had been booed in 2008. News of such absences was so consistent in English media that a CBC staffer maintained an online list which on April 28 identified sixty-six Conservatives who had missed at least one debate, compared with five Bloc, eight Liberals, and eight NDP.[32] Perhaps the governing party was behaving rationally given that in Canada people running with opposition parties, especially those who do not win, benefit the most from constituency campaigning.[33] How to explain this publicly? "Often, you attract a few dozen people, all of whom are hardcore partisans," said Jason Kenney. "They're often not debates so much as serial monologues."[34] Spokespeople in his party's headquarters repeated that messaging: "The national war room's advice to Conservative candidates is to do what's best for their local campaigns. Many of our candidates feel their time is better spent door-knocking or doing other things [rather] than attending debate after debate. Some find debates to be packed with partisans who've already made up their minds on how to vote."[35]

This desire to avoid controversy was relayed to constituency campaigns, and, in the case of Conservative Jim Hillyer (Lethbridge), was communicated to local media: "[T]he campaign team has determined that rather than having Jim spend his time engaged in partisan bickering, the best way for him to reach out to constituents is to spend his time out in the various communities, knocking on doors and speaking with people on a more personal level. In order to maximize the time he has to do this, Jim will not be attending any further forums during the campaign. There will be no further comment on this matter."[36]

The local Bloc campaign relayed a similar message in Roberval–Lac-Saint-Jean, except it emphasized needing to prepare for the party leader's visit. There were also reports of candidates from all parties, but especially Conservatives, declining or not acknowledging interview requests. As the Conservative campaign manager in Winnipeg North explained,

"We're trying to focus on meeting with voters, and door knocking, instead of doing media interviews."[37]

Some experiments with non-confrontational formats seemed more successful. In New Westminster a casual meet-and-greet at a restaurant was well attended by candidates from two area ridings and apparently enjoyed by attendees. In some Edmonton ridings a speed dating format was used. In one such case electors sat in four circles, each with its own moderator, and candidates rotated amongst the groups every ten minutes. These formats appear to have enabled more electors to ask questions while reducing partisan conflict, and the availability of food and alcohol seemed to encourage an informal atmosphere, though there were some complaints about noise and frustration that speakers still toed the party line. In St. John's, a forum on the fishery featured a panel of party candidates from different ridings who were given questions in advance, and the organizers set the tone as a working group so well that the media reported a spirit of co-operation. These successes contrasted with the elector in Northumberland–Quinte West who walked out of a traditional debate saying, "I'm sick of the bickering and tired of the same old answers."[38]

FUNDRAISING

Within a political party, money gets transferred between the national party and electoral districts. This allows the party to spend strategically as funds raised in safe ridings are redistributed to targeted seats. Tory fundraising in Calgary, for instance, was redirected to the lone Edmonton seat that the Conservatives did not hold. However, the news media did not report much about candidates seeking donations from supporters. There were occasional mentions of workers organizing fundraising events and selling tickets to listen to notable Parliamentarians giving a speech, such as the $20 fee to hear Conservative Senator Pamela Wallin in Moose Jaw, or $100 for a luncheon with former Ontario Premier Bill Davis in Guelph. A variation in Timmins–James Bay saw the Liberals bring in a

$100 fundraising dinner. Money was raised in other rid-
barbecues, by hiring musicians, or by singing in a choir.
arms owners, "Operation: Turf Mark Holland" (turfmhol-
land.ca), ently raised $10,000 to support Chris Alexander's bid to
defeat Liberal Public Safety critic Mark Holland in Ajax–Pickering. Such
a lack of emphasis on money matters stands in sharp contrast to the
importance of fundraising south of the border.

NEW MEDIA

Notwithstanding its unrealized potential for raising money, the Internet
was a major electioneering tool in 2011. In the days after the government fell, most of the parties' websites still presented information
about a riding, rather than about a person, even in the case of incumbents. The exception was the Liberals, whose homepage on March 27
featured a large scrolling banner inviting visitors to "Find your Liberal
candidate and learn how to get involved this election"; users could
click through to a grid of 225 candidates with links to local websites,
Facebook, and Twitter accounts. By March 29 the Bloc's site added an
"Équipe" tab, and it was redesigned on March 31 with a tab for candidates. In early April the NDP's site added a splash page that included
an option to insert a postal code to "get information on your candidate."
On April 3, the Conservative Web site changed its "find my riding" tab
into "find my candidate"; likewise, on April 6 the Greens morphed the
"join now" tab to "find your candidate." Over time, these main sites integrated basic templates that provided biographical details and local contact information, including candidate headquarter addresses, Facebook
links, and sometimes mobile phone numbers.

Initially, some incumbents' sites offered a choice of clicking through
to a parliamentary site or to a re-election site. In other cases, such as the
finance minister's jimflaherty.com site, a message appeared that it was
"under construction," whereas other MPs' sites were stagnant. This delay
may be attributed to the fact that websites created before the official

election period and used during the campaign must be reported as an election expense. When campaign sites were launched they featured prominent buttons for visitors to donate, volunteer, request a sign, or receive an electronic newsletter. They were updated with information about rallies, party messages, videos, or in some instances the addition of an iPhone app or Twitter microblog scrolls.

From the outset many Liberal and NDP candidates' sites had a similar party look and feel. A week into the campaign, some Conservatives' nameplates were rebranded to include a "Here for Canada" slogan, and some Bloc pages featured candidates with the party's "Qc" speech balloon (re: "parlons Québec"). A common way of attracting Web traffic was purchasing banner advertising on community news sites and inserting Web addresses on promotional materials such as brochures, signs, and newspaper ads, which occasionally also featured a quick response barcode so that camera phones could be used to download information.

Portable communications devices such as BlackBerrys and then iPhones have allowed candidates to stay in touch with workers and to respond to email messages. In 2011, with many of them including incumbents setting up their first Facebook pages and Twitter accounts, these devices increased candidates' interactivity and ability to monitor developments. Charlie Angus, the NDP MP who was first elected in Timmins–James Bay in 2004, remarked, "I've been noticing how dramatically different it is with all the social networking tools available now. It's been a much more interactive campaign, with a lot more personal contact."[39] Social networking was seen as a way to counteract the problem of people not answering their doors and the challenge of reaching them by phone. Some responded to messages during pauses in a canvass and updated online followers about what part of the riding they were in. "I can do it, literally, while I'm walking between doors," said the NDP candidate in Essex,[40] though often staffers wrote the updates, posted photographs, or monitored opponents. Social media was also an efficient way to issue a media advisory; while online video was used, as a constituency campaign tactic it was largely an experiment.

Some contestants engaged in live two-hour interactive video discussions with electors. The Bloc challenger in Honoré Mercier held occasional online "happy hour" video chats that were billed on his website as "des 5 @ 7 virtuels où vous pourrez discutez avec Martin Laroche en temps reel."[41] Occasionally YouTube videos received local media attention, such as in Chilliwack–Fraser Canyon, where Liberal Diane Janzen poked fun at a columnist's remark that "cows don't vote Liberal" by posting a video of her interviewing a farmer whose cows sported Liberal signs.[42] Sometimes the media reported on video intended to embarrass a candidate, such as footage of Chris Alexander saying that according to World Bank standards Canada did not have poverty. But videos had a small audience and were not even necessarily viewed in the riding. Janzen's video received 300 views; a testimonial from Paul Martin endorsing Liberal MP Irwin Cotler (Mount Royal) attracted 150. Even the *Edmonton Journal*'s efforts to promote seven tasteful videos of the four major candidates in Edmonton-Centre, which were uploaded on April 16, resulted in an average of just 184 views two weeks later.

Not everyone was sold on social media. Some opted against using it, and many local activists still preferred personal interaction. Many reporters counted candidates' Twitter followers in the single, double, or low triple digits. Conservative incumbent Gord Brown (Leeds-Grenville) observed, "I don't think social media is playing a major role locally. I don't sense that it's playing a significant part, yet."[43] It also presents a risk. Facebook and Twitter, like Google in 2008, provided a wealth of data mining content for journalists looking for an easy story and for parties seeking desperately to discredit an opponent. Moreover, the ease of making and uploading photo, audio, and video files means that parties are becoming risk-averse to their local representatives participating in public events because a wayward remark will likely be distributed online within hours.

A safer political use for technology is electronic town halls, which seem to be replacing in-person debates. Many campaigns issued automated phone messages ("robocalls") to inform recipients about a nomination meeting or a rally, to circulate a message from an endorser such as Toronto Mayor Rob Ford, or to remind supporters to vote. Teleconferencing invited recipients to stay on the line and listen to a live local discussion. Buttons could be pressed to be put in a queue to ask a question or to participate in an instant poll. In one case, a Conservative MP avoided attending a debate about agriculture by scheduling a tele–town hall with the agriculture minister. The experience of the Conservative candidate in Brant indicates that the telephone was much more popular than Internet technology, given that his telephone forum attracted 3,800 participants, compared with 200 for a video discussion.[44]

SUSTAINABLE CAMPAIGNING

Even though climate change was hardly at the tops of voters' minds as it had been in the 2008 campaign, some local candidates expressed concern about their carbon footprint. Michel Guimond, the Bloc incumbent in Montmorency–Charlevoix–Haute-Côte-Nord, pledged to run a carbon-neutral campaign by giving money to local environmental groups to offset greenhouse gases generated by his sticker-adorned car. Elizabeth May drove around her riding in a hybrid electric vehicle. The Green contestant in Kamloops-Thompson-Cariboo convinced his NDP opponent to car pool and ride bikes while vowing to endorse the candidate whose campaign emitted the fewest carbon emissions. The team of an NDP incumbent in Halifax transported her signs in a trailer towed by a bicycle. Some Greens in BC and Ontario rode the bus all day with a party sign while chatting with electors.

Across Canada signs were reused: duct tape was placed over "elect" to change it to "re-elect"; former MPs reclaimed their old "re-elect" signs; and, in the case of Helena Guergis, the word "independent" was inserted above "Conservative." A number of Greens across Canada pledged to reduce the number of signs, to reuse them in future campaigns, and to recycle them afterwards. Greens often said that they used social networking for environmental reasons, but likely also for financial and practical ones. Some campaigners engaged in environment-themed events, such as coordinating a park cleanup or raising money for related causes, while the Liberal candidate in Edmonton–Mill Woods–Beaumont planned to donate money that would have been spent on lawn signs to a food bank.

CONTROVERSIES

In 308 simultaneous contests, there are bound to be controversies. People get excited as they promote competing ideas, priorities, and loyalties. Reporters and bloggers have an appetite for election hullabaloo that war rooms gleefully feed, exploiting local indiscretions by opponents' candidates. In 2011, party news releases citing controversial quotes and YouTube video concerning a candidate were noticeably timed to destabilize an opposing leader's visit to an electoral district, or used as evidence for a broader narrative against that leader.

Internal party problems were rarely displayed publicly. Conservatives who did not get the nomination in Okanagan Coquihalla complained that the selection process was "rigged" because they were given insufficient notice to file documents and did not have access to the list of local members.[45] When the *Vancouver Sun* revealed that the Conservative nominee in Delta–Richmond East had a history of financial problems the party phoned him to say that that he would be replaced. "I chose not to resign," he said, "and then I was told that I was not going to be running."[46] In the first week of the campaign there was so much news of party switching (such as the NDP candidate in Elgin-Middlesex-London resigning to support the Liberals) that the CBC maintained a blog, "Riding Roster Roulette," to list party switches by candidates, staffers, and endorsers. Towards the end of the campaign Environment Minister Peter Kent (Thornhill) complained that his party had not sufficiently vetted its candidates when news broke that the Conservative challenger in Scarborough-Southwest was a supporter of the Tamil Tigers.

Journalists routinely reported on rancorous local debates or repeated "he said, she said" minutiae. They also bought into partisan hyperbole about the significance of a candidate's indiscretion, and sometimes this attracted national attention. To put the notoriety of such perceived local blunders in perspective, on April 7 the *National Post* itemized eighteen "scandals" to that point, of which thirteen involved constituency campaigns.[47] Wherever possible, a leader's tour attempted to distance itself from such diversions. Just days into the campaign, on March 30 Conservative spokesman Dimitri Soudas said that the party would no longer answer questions about local campaigns, though such a firewall did not hold.

There are too many cases to list here, but examples of constituency controversies can be broadly categorized as "inside baseball," a gaffe, or a political problem. A number of publicized controversies were likely quickly forgotten by all but insiders. Some examples of such inside baseball include:

- the Tory incumbent in Saint-Boniface was denounced for being ageist for stating that the Liberal incumbent in a neighbouring riding had "passed her expiry date";[48]
- the Liberal Party announced that when scrutinizing the Facebook account of the Conservative candidate in Vancouver South they discovered that she had issued a promotional calendar with a photo of the Chinese president airbrushed out; and,
- the Liberal contestant in South Surrey–White Rock–Cloverdale questioned whether taxpayers subsidized the Conservative incumbent's "re-elect Russ Hiebert" brochure that was distributed prior to the election call.[49] Similar complaints were voiced in other ridings when MPs' 10 percenters and householders were received well after the government fell.

Some blunders were noticed nationally by the attentive public. Some examples of such gaffes:

- Conservative MP Cheryl Gallant (Renfrew–Nipissing–Pembroke) referred to Michael Ignatieff as "Igaffi" on Twitter in a reference to Libyan dictator Moammar Gadhafi, for which she also apologized by Twitter, and which prompted Trudeau to tweet that Gallant was a "twit." Gallant did not use Twitter again during the campaign;[50]
- the Liberals defended their representative in Pitt Meadows–Maple Ridge–Mission, who they felt had moved on from a drunken driving conviction; and,

- the Bloc candidate in Abitibi–Baie-James–Nunavik–Eeyou invited charges of racism for claiming that his NDP opponent was unelectable because he is Aboriginal.

Some local controversies destabilized the national party campaign. Notable examples of these political problems:

- the Conservatives distributed transcripts and audio clips of the Liberal candidate in Wild Rose wherein he said that some sexual offenders should not be jailed;
- the Liberals charged that the Conservative challenger to MP Ruby Dhalla in Brampton–Springdale exerted influence in granting immigration visas and had joined the Canadian immigration minister in meetings in India;
- the Greens rejected their Fleetwood–Port Kells candidate when it was revealed that he had written, "If rape is inevitable, lie back and enjoy it!" on his Facebook page;[51]
- a leaked email from a Tory staffer in Toronto invited ethnic voters wearing "national folklore costumes" to participate in a "great TV photo op" by sitting behind Harper at a rally. The volunteer had to be dismissed;[52]
- the Liberals said they would drop their candidate in Manicouagan when the NDP exposed remarks he had made about Aboriginals. However, he did not consent to being removed from the ballot and his Liberal campaign signs stayed up;
- Harper had to address the anti-abortion remarks of Conservative incumbent Brad Trost (Saskatoon-Humboldt) after the Liberals released a recording of a recent speech. Soudas distanced the leader's tour by dismissing Trost as "a backbencher";[53] and,
- the PM defended the Tory candidate in Vancouver South who had been endorsed by a man who was acquitted in the Air India bombing.

There were also media reports of a number of dirty tricks in constituencies. Buying opponents' .ca and .com domain names occurs; in Kitchener-Conestoga, a Conservative redirected online searches for the local Liberal to an anti-Ignatieff site. In Nepean-Carleton, about one hundred large Liberal signs were spray painted with crosshairs, while in Brampton West police charged a Liberal worker for having Conservative signs in his truck. A trick that receives little attention is canvassers removing an opponent's flyers from mailboxes, but in 2011 a Green canvasser photographed a Liberal doing just that in Eglinton–Lawrence, and then attracted news coverage with her photo essay on the file-sharing site Picasa, forcing MP Joe Volpe to dismiss the worker.

Another timeworn trick is to phone opponents in the night, which is what eleven Liberal MPs complained about towards the end of the campaign, with a new variation being the "spoofing" of the Liberal party's telemarketing firm by using a fake caller ID name. As election day neared, in some ridings there were claims of fear mongering and smear campaigns, such as of opponents promoting rumours, phoning electors with false information, circulating untruthful emails, and posting negative YouTube videos. The Toronto police investigated the evening vandalism of cars parked outside of homes with Liberal signs in St. Paul's and in nearby Trinity–Spadina. In response, the campaign of St. Paul's incumbent Carolyn Bennett issued a warning robocall to their sign takers, after which she wrote on Twitter: "Just got a call from a brilliant supporter who is going to take her sign out every evening & put it back every am."[54]

ELECTION DAY

In the final week, newspapers started publishing their endorsements of local candidates. Constituency campaigns intensified their efforts, prepared GOTV operations, and planned election night parties. "All campaigns are ramping up to maximum speed. Any opportunity I have I am knocking on doors and focusing on those people who are still undecided," said Conservative MP Phil McColeman (Brant).[55] Conservative incumbent Ron Cann (Kelowna–Lake Country), whose margin of victory in 2008 had exceeded 40 percent, remarked, "We're not taking anything for granted. We're running our campaign like we're down by two votes."[56]

On election day, volunteers across Canada sought to mobilize supporters by contacting them and offering rides to the polls. There was speculation that, in light of its lack of constituency infrastructure in Quebec, the NDP would have difficulty converting newfound support to action at the ballot box. By contrast, in Windsor NDP canvassers consulted their lists of identified supporters, to whom they distributed vote reminder leaflets in the morning and later checked to ensure they had voted. In several ridings there were reports of spoofed Elections Canada phone messages that falsely stated that the recipient's polling centre had been moved due to high turnout.

While the national party standings draw much of the public's attention on election day, it is the riding level where individual successes and failures are registered. The 2011 campaign produced memorable results given that two party leaders (Ignatieff and Duceppe) were defeated as MPs, another leader (May) won her party's first ever seat, and Bloc Québécois candidates were replaced en masse by New Democrats, including in ridings that at the beginning of the campaign had been considered impenetrable. Many other incumbents were re-elected, including most of the Conservative cabinet, the Liberals' Trudeau, and the NDP's Duncan and Mulcair. Among the MPs who were defeated were Conservative Ministers Lawrence Cannon (Pontiac) and Gary Lunn; the two independents (Arthur and Guergis); Liberals Coady, Dhalla, Dosanjh, Holland, and Pearson; and more than half of the 2006 Liberal party leadership race contestants: Ken Dryden (York-Centre), Martha Hall Findlay (Willowdale), Gerard Kennedy (Parkdale–High Park), Ignatieff, and Volpe. Consequently, many new faces would be seen in the House of Commons, including "star" candidates Chisholm and Saganash, and Conservatives such as Alexander, who benefited from that party's southern Ontario breakthrough.

As the results became known, victors often reasoned that their local team had worked hard and that their leader was an asset, while losers blamed circumstances beyond their control. All thanked their workers and their family. Some reflected on a positive experience: "I made great friends, I met great people at the doors," said the runner-up in Kootenay–Columbia.[57] Others tasted sour grapes. The runner-up in Humber–St. Barbe–Baie Verte complained that the incumbent had done nothing for the riding and that electors merely "like the fact he hugs people and gets on open line [radio] and shoots off his mouth."[58]

The biggest changeover was seen in Quebec. Bloc Québécois candidates were left scratching their heads, confident in the vitality of their constituency campaigns, but stunned by the NDP wave. "I do not understand, especially since the NDP candidate did not campaign. She is a complete unknown," said Diane Bourgeois (Terrebonne-Blainville), a four-time Bloc MP.[59] "This is not because we had a bad campaign. We worked hard on the ground. I don't think it was possible to do better," remarked the Bloc candidate in Marc-Aurèle-Fortin.[60] Added defeated three-time Bloc MP Paule Brunelle (Trois-Rivières), "It's a total surprise. This is not a wave, it's a tsunami. We met people today and it seemed fine, even better than the other campaigns … I do not understand how people voted for someone who does not know the riding."[61]

The media reported on the many New Democrats elected in Quebec, including some of the party's aforementioned stopgap candidates. Most notorious among them was Brosseau, the anglophone who defeated a three-time incumbent by nearly six thousand votes in a francophone riding she had never visited, and who was dubbed "Vegas girl" by the media in recognition of her mid-campaign vacation. Brosseau came to symbolize the irrelevance of local campaigning in Quebec and the election of NDP placeholder candidates and political neophytes, including four McGill University students such as Matthew Dubé (Chambly-Borduas), who had tweeted about comic books, and nineteen-year-old Pierre-Luc Dusseault (Sherbrooke), who did campaign and became the youngest person ever elected to the House of Commons. The NDP instructed these new elected officials not to speak with the media, instead designating Mulcair as their spokesperson, and sought to delay the opening of Parliament so that they could train their new members.

CONCLUSION

With varying enthusiasm, candidates in the 2011 Canadian federal election acted as local salespeople of the national party, and seemed to recognize the democratic engagement function of interacting with electors.
The short duration of a minority Parliament contributed to early candidate nominations, considerable pre-campaigning, and a lack of star candidates. Given that the media is prone to reporting on inside baseball,
gaffes, and political problems, parties would be wise to further inten-
sify their background checks and training of candidates, especially if the
leader's tour is likely to visit a candidate's riding. Those seeking to feed
journalists with such information should consider that every day of the
national media chasing a forgettable local blunder is a lost opportunity
to develop public interest in substantive issues and policy alternatives.

One of the most fascinating aspects of the results of the 2011
Canadian general election was the success of NDP candidates, especially
in Quebec, who at the outset of the campaign nobody dreamed might
win. Entire local campaigns were rendered irrelevant by voter disen-
chantment with one party (the Bloc) and infatuation with another (the
NDP). Many electors prioritized macro factors of leadership, party labels,
and broad issues, and paid no heed to local representation. If incumbents
who campaigned vigorously were defeated by candidates who did not
even show up in the riding, what impact can lawn signs, door knocking,
local debates, or a candidate's social networking possibly have? What
was the point of exerting effort in the twenty-one seats, sixteen of which
were Alberta ridings won by Conservatives, where the margin of victory
was more than 50 percent of the vote? In such a context the rationality
of investing resources in constituency campaigning must be questioned,
and there is validation for the preeminence of a national strategy that
must not be distracted by local matters. Even so, in the fifty-one ridings
where the margin of victory was less than 5 percent, including the five
seats won by less than a hundred votes, a well-run ground game was
likely an important complement to the air war. As the 2011 case illustrates, the challenge for parties and candidates is that predicting ridings
where local campaigning will matter is a gamble.

Reporters are fascinated about reporting on what's new, and so some of them dubbed 2011 the 'Twitter campaign." This is an overstatement, and yet the role of communications technology is unquestionably growing. There was some indication that social networking contributed to sustainable campaigning, that it led to a more engaged electorate, and that it helps candidates get messages. Conversely, video conferencing and YouTube videos were hardly worth the effort, though the former was an efficient way for a party leader to communicate with local partisans. The ability for politicians to control such communications means that they are placing less importance on traditional all-candidate debates, and even shunning media interviews, which will increase the onus on community leaders to organize non-confrontational meet-and-greets. Telephone technology seems to have been a better use of resources, whether this was for robocall messages or tele–town halls; however, there is concern that it can be used for dirty tricks. The Harper administration's elimination of the vote subsidy will increase the role of all such technology as candidates face pressure to fundraise more aggressively than they did in 2011.

It remains to be seen to what extent pre-campaign strategies and tactics will change in a majority government that has a fixed date election scheduled. During the 41st Parliament, the ability of New Democrat MPs to represent and serve their constituents will be a subject of interest. In the next campaign, we can anticipate continued media attention to candidates' electioneering (particularly in Quebec), their use of technology, local controversies, and money matters.

NOTES

1. Such as *Papers on the 1962 Election*, ed. John Meisel (Toronto: University of Toronto Press, 1964).
2. Information was gleaned through monitoring of a rotating sample of more than seventy national and local news media websites across Canada. This was supplemented by searching for further information online, by periodic monitoring of the major political parties' websites, and by consulting a sample of candidates' websites. More than 750 media stories were reviewed by the author, who has archived the news

articles, website screenshots, and URLs, which are available upon request. This was possible due to the daily media monitoring support of Memorial University research assistant Michael Penney.

3.   Jason Fekete, "Why Parties Gladly Fight 'Losing Cause' in Alberta," *Calgary Herald*, April 10, 2011.

4.   Richard Cuthbertson and Laura Stone, "NDP Candidates in Calgary Highlight 'Lost Cause' Conundrum," *Edmonton Journal*, April 17, 2011.

5.   For an overview of constituency campaigning in the 2008 Canadian federal election, see Munroe Eagles and Annika Hagley, "Constituency Campaigning in Canada," in *Election*, ed. Heather MacIvor (Toronto: Emond Montgomery Publications, 2009), 109–34.

6.   Bill Spurr and Davene Jeffrey, "MPs Jump Back into Campaign Mode," *The Chronicle Herald* (Halifax), March 28, 2011.

7.   Spurr and Jeffrey, "MPs Jump Back."

8.   Andrea Lawlor, "An Uphill Battle: The Effect of a Competitive Campaign on Incumbency Support in Canada" (paper prepared for the annual conference of the European Consortium of Political Research, Dublin, Ireland, August 30–September 1, 2010).

9.   Thomas Flanagan, "Campaign Strategy: Triage and the Concentration of Resources," in *Election*, ed. Heather MacIvor (Toronto: Emond Montgomery Publications, 2009), 155–72.

10. Bea Vongdouahgchanh, "Conservatives Target 45 Vulnerable Ridings in Effort to Win Majority Next Time," *The Hill Times*, January 20, 2011.

11. For more on candidate nominations, see William Cross, "Candidate Nomination in Canada's Political Parties," in *The Canadian Federal Election of 2006*, eds. Jon H. Pammett and Christopher Dornan (Toronto: Dundurn Press, 2006), 171–95.

12. Anthony M. Sayers, *Parties, Candidates, and Constituency Campaigns in Canadian Elections* (Vancouver: UBC Press, 1999).

13. Bill Curry, "NDP Candidate Takes Mid-Campaign Vacation in Vegas," *Globe and Mail*, April 26, 2011.

14. Elise Stolte, "New Riding Associations Bolster Edmonton's Green Party Candidates," *Edmonton Journal*, April 7, 2011.

15. Janet French, "Candidates Find it Lonely on the Fringe," *The Saskatoon StarPhoenix*, April 25, 2011.

16. Jen Gerson, "Profile: Hopefuls Face 'Tough Sell' in True-Blue Crowfoot Riding," *Calgary Herald*, April 27, 2011.

17. Drew Halfnight, "Fringe Candidates Target Guelph Seat in Next Election," *Guelph Mercury*, March 28, 2011.

18. Kenyon Wallace, "Tory MP Denies Accusation After 'Expiry Date' Comments," *Toronto Star*, March 29, 2011.

19. Alex J. Marland, "Promotional and Other Spending by Party Candidates in the 2006 Canadian Federal Election Campaign," *Canadian Journal of Media Studies*, 3(1) (2008): 57–88.

20. Scott McLean, "Regina Incumbents Come Out Firing," Global News (Saskatoon), March 26, 2011.

21. Steve Newman, "Billboard Approach for Clouthier," *Renfrew Mercury*, April 7, 2011.

22. Ian Austin, "Dosanjh Battles for Political Life," *The Province* (Vancouver), April 8, 2011.

23. Brian Cross, "Office Seekers Tweet and Greet," *The Windsor Star*, April 9, 2011.

24. Tori Stafford, "Candidates Are Off and Running," *Kingston Whig-Standard*, March 28, 2011.

25. Josh Wingrove, "Conservatives Find it Harder to Rope in Alberta Vote," *Globe and Mail*, April 26, 2011.

26. Steve Pettibone, "Loveys Aims for Success with New-Style Politics," *Brockville Recorder and Times*, April 23, 2011.

27. Jeff Gard, "Rudd Takes Her Message Door to Door," *Northumberland Today*, April 15, 2011.

28. Jennifer O'Brien, "Election Fever in London," *London Free Press*, March 26, 2011.

29. Carola Vyhnak, "Foes Await Fallout over Oda Fib Flap," *Toronto Star*, April 13, 2011.

30. Marco Fortier, "Justin Trudeau n'est pas un liberal comme les autres," *Rue Frontenac* (Montreal), April 22, 2011.

31. Katie Daubs, "Halton Riding: For Once, Gender Imbalance Is a Welcome Sign," *Toronto Star*, April 17, 2011.

32. Janyce McGregor, "All-Candidate No-Shows: More Examples for Our List," CBC News online (politics blog), April 28, 2011.

33. R. Kenneth Carty and Munroe Eagles, "Do Local Campaigns Matter? Campaign Spending, the Local Canvas and Party Support in Canada," *Electoral Studies*, 18 (1999): 69–87.

34. John Ibbitson and Daniel Leblanc, "Cone of Silence Tightens on Tories," *Globe and Mail*, April 7, 2011.

35. Sarah Boesveld, "All-Candidates' Debates: Relics of the Past?" *National Post*, April 28, 2011.

36. Dori Modney, "Conservative Candidate Jim Hillyer Deletes Forums from His Campaigning," Country 95 News (Lethbridge), April 20, 2011.

37. Mychaylo Prystupa, "Libs, NDP Battle for Winnipeg North," CBC News (Manitoba), April 19, 2011.

38. Ernst Kuglin, "Race Is Heating Up," *The Trentonian*, April 21, 2011.

39. Kate McLaren, "Off and Running," *Timmins Press*, March 28, 2011.

40. Brian Cross, "Office Seekers Tweet and Greet," *The Windsor Star*, April 9, 2011.

41. Martin Laroche, Honoré-Mercier. *http://parlonsmartinlaroche.org/*. April 30, 2011.

42. Paul Henderson, "Janzen Has Beef with Cow Comment," *Chilliwack Times*, April 8, 2011.

43. Steve Pettibone, "Politicians Begin to Embrace Social Media," *The Recorder & Times*, April 6, 2011.

44. Sean Allen, "Brant Campaign Goes Online," *Brant News*, April 14, 2011.

45. Doug Ward, "Race to Replace Stockwell Day was 'Rigged': Party Members," *Vancouver Sun*, March 24, 2011.

46. Rod Mickleburg, "Nominated on Monday, Tory Candidate Booted on Thursday," *Globe and Mail*, March 24, 2011.

47. "Scandals and Gaffes: A Look at 18 Scandals on the Campaign Trail," *National Post*, April 7, 2011.

48. "Manitoba Candidates."

49. Alex Browne, "MP's Conservative Campaign Literature 'Jumped the Gun,'" *Peace Arch News* (White Rock), March 29, 2011.

50. Kelly Roche, "Tory MP Apologizes for 'Igaffi' Tweet," *Toronto Sun*, April 1, 2011.

51. "Campaign Notes," *Ottawa Citizen*, April 15, 2011.

52. Joe Friesen, "Seeking Ethnic Dress for Photo Op 'Unacceptable,' Tories Tell Riding," *Globe and Mail*, April 13, 2011.

53. Cassandra Kyle and Jeremy Warren, "Conservative MP Brad Trost 'Proud' of Helping 'Defund' Abortion Provider," *The StarPhoenix* (Saskatoon), April 22, 2011.

54. Carolyn Bennett, "@Carolyn_Bennett." *http://twitter.com/#!/Carolyn_Bennett*. April 23, 2011.

55. Sean Allen, "Candidates Launch Final Push," *Brant News*, April 28, 2011.

56. Julia Wong, "Last Minute Campaigning." CHBC Global News (Okanagan), May 1, 2011.

57. Kerstin Renner, "David Wilks Will Become New MP for Kootenay–Columbia," *Kootenay News Advertiser*, May 2, 2011.

58. Gary Kean, "Byrne Baby Byrne," *The Western Star* (Corner Brook), May 3, 2011.

59. Translated from Valérie Gonther, "(MAJ) Diane Bourgeois, défaite dans Terrebonne-Blainville," *Le Trait d'Union* (Terrebonne), May 2, 2011.

60. Translated from Caroline d'Astous, "Défaite crève-cœur pour le Bloc québécois," *Nord Info et Voix des Mille-Iles* (Sainte-Thérèse), May 3, 2011.

61. Translated from Marie-Ève Bourgoing-Alarie, "La forteresse cede," *L'Hebdo Journal* (Trois-Rivières), May 2, 2011.

CHAPTER 8

Polls: Seeing Through the Glass Darkly

André Turcotte

On April 21, just ten days before the end of what had been up till then a generally banal election campaign, a CROP poll was released showing the NDP surging into the lead in the province of Quebec. Specifically, CROP showed the NDP at 36 percent in the province, ahead of the Bloc at 31 percent, with the Conservatives and Liberals far behind at 17 and 13 percent, respectively.[1] The poll surprised most observers, and the results were immediately questioned. CROP itself contributed to the controversy by breaking with the usual practice associated with the release of survey results in that it did not include a margin of error, citing the non-randomness of the sample. No prior polls had the Bloc trailing its opponents, and it would take four more days for another poll to confirm the NDP gains in Quebec. Thus, for at least a week, polls generated more excitement than events on the campaign trail.

With hindsight, it is easy to argue that the controversy over the CROP poll was unwarranted. In fact, the five-point NDP lead in that poll was a quarter of the twenty-point difference in popular vote between the NDP and the Bloc that registered on voting day. But to dismiss the controversy in hindsight is to miss the opportunity to reflect on the role of public opinion polls in politics in general and in the 2011 federal election in particular.

Looking at the election is instructive, because much of what is good and bad with polling became evident both in the run-up to it and during the campaign. There was an abundance — if not an overabundance — of findings: wild variations in results, contradictions, short-sighted reporting, emerging trends, doubts, interesting insights, and, in the end, partial redemption for most. As well, very little was learned from the poll-fueled analyses so dominant in the period between election campaigns. Accordingly, to provide a more complete picture, this chapter will go beyond the analysis of the polls published during the writ period. Specifically, the analysis will be divided into three parts: the first will examine polls published between November 2008 and March 2011, from the previous election until the beginning of the 2011 writ period. The second will concentrate on the period between March 25, 2011, and the release of the CROP poll. The chapter will conclude with an analysis of the polls published during the last ten days of the campaign, and reflections on the potential lessons learned.

THE FIRST PERIOD: NOVEMBER 2008–MARCH 2011

A total of 239 nationwide polls on federal voting intentions were published between the 2008 election and when the writ was dropped in 2011.[2] This represents an average of one poll published every three days or so. Considering this profusion of data, it is somewhat surprising to realize that polls were published at a slower pace than in the previous election cycle. A total of 184 such polls made their way into the media coverage between the 2006 and 2008 elections: an average of one poll every other day. The fascination with polls in Canada has built over time and has to some extent mirrored their increasing prominence in the United States. As Ladd and Benson have noted, between 1976 and 1988 there was an exponential increase in media polls in American politics,[3] and this surge has continued ever since. Polls are also an increasingly important part of European election coverage.[4] What was once an interesting novelty has become a permanent and prevalent fixture in the coverage of politics in Canada as well as in most other democratic countries. With this status has come praise and criticism.

In their 1940 book *The Pulse of Democracy,* George Gallup and Saul Rae made the case in support of public opinion polling as a safeguard of democracy. They asserted: "Shall the common people be free to express their basic needs and purposes, or shall they be dominated by a small ruling clique."[5] Gallup and Rae railed against the prevailing intellectual climate and perceived thinkers such as Walter Lippmann as having very little faith in the wisdom of public opinion. For Gallup, Rae, and the proponents of public opinion polling since, the health of democracy depended on "building a machinery for directly approaching the mass of the people and hearing what they have to say."[6] Today, as Susan Herbst has argued, "The modern public opinion poll, or 'sample survey' is now an essential part of politics. Those who compete for political office, the journalists who report on their campaigns, and the voters who must choose among aspirants, all pay close attention to numbers that supposedly describe public opinion."[7] Polls are not simply a way to ensure that people are heard. Their prevalence contributes to framing political discourse and shaping the nature of media coverage. We will return to those themes later.

The development of public opinion polling in Canada goes back to the 1930s, with the founding of Canadian Facts in 1932.[8] The Gallup Organization set up a Canadian affiliate — the Canadian Institute of Public Opinion (CIPO) — in the 1940s. Prime Minister Mackenzie King secretly commissioned CIPO to conduct a poll before the 1942 plebiscite on wartime conscription, and with that "political polling was born in Canada."[9] By 1945, *The Gallup Poll* began to be published regularly in Canadian newspapers, and the media release of polling results has grown considerably ever since. While Gallup is no longer active in Canada, it has been replaced by firms such as IPSOS-Reid, EKOS Research, Nanos Research, and Harris-Decima, to name only the most prominent.

Critics are quick to point out the very public examples of the limitations of polling and have been doing so for decades. In the aftermath of the 1948 U.S. presidential election when pollsters incorrectly predicted that Thomas Dewey would beat Harry S Truman, Archibald Crossley — one of the founding fathers of polling — declared: "Polling may need a shot in the arm, but it certainly does not need a shot in the back. The snipers on all sides are having a field day."[10] As Donsbach and Traugott recently mentioned, "Almost every modern democracy has seen its Waterloo involving public pollsters in the last few years."[11] For as long as polls have claimed to predict the outcomes of elections, there have been instances of them getting the results completely wrong. But criticism of polling is not confined to methodological lapses or failures. Many have begun to decry the over-reliance on polling results in the coverage of politics. For instance, Patterson disparages the presence of "polls by the hundreds" and believes that pre-election polls are one of the factors contributing to the poor quality of campaigns and elections in the United States. One of his arguments is that polls are almost exclusively used to promote horse-race coverage, and journalists often misinterpret actual change from one poll to the next. This leads to inaccurate reporting of what may actually be happening in the campaigns.[12] Another long-standing criticism questions the ability of polls or any other instrument to "measure" public opinion or to quantify the voice of people. It is beyond the scope of this chapter to address and resolve these controversies. It is the general view of this author that while it is easy to find faults with polls, we must also recognize the important role they play in the current practice of democracy. According to Donsbach and Traugott, "Two technologies have changed our modern political systems more than anything else: television and public opinion research."[13] However, as we will see below, pollsters may have exaggerated the degree to which they can accurately measure public opinion by downplaying the impact of statistical significance and margins of error in return for greater public profile. More importantly, the media repeatedly misrepresent actual change in opinion as expressed in polls. In the end, one may have to agree with Humphrey Taylor, former chair of Louis Harris & Associates, when he said that "polls are the worst way of measuring public opinion and public behaviour, or predicting elections — except for all the others."[14] But general support for polls does not preclude serious reflection on some of the problems plaguing current practices with a view to seeking improvement. In this section, we will turn our attention to three specific issues related to the plethora of polls in the 2011 federal election. First, we will look at some unexplainable contradictions in pre-writ polls. Then we will look at the uses and misuses of pre-election polls. And finally, we will consider what those polls are actually measuring and what insights, if any, these "polls by the hundreds" shed upon the actual campaign outcome.

Pollsters are always quick to answer their critics by pointing to their relative success in accurately predicting the vote on election day, and the media are as quick to accept that argument. If this was the case, polling

would be possibly the only profession in which being right once in a
while is a sufficient measure of success. As mentioned above, a total of
239 polls were released between the 2008 election and the 2011 writ
period. As Table 1 indicates, we can isolate seventeen instances over that
period of time — involving fifty-two different polls from eleven different
firms — where the data reported paint a contradictory picture of the
voting landscape to an extent that cannot be simply explained away by
methodological differences.

Table 1. Contradictions 2008–2011

Firms	Dates	Conservatives	Liberals	NDP	Bloc	Green
First						
Praxicus Public Strategies	December 4, 2008	47	24	14	8	8
COMPAS	December 4, 2008	51	20	10	8	6
Ekos Research	December 4, 2008	42.2	23.6	15.0	10.2	9.0
Second						
Angus Reid Strategies	December 12, 2008	42	22	18	10	7
IPSOS Reid	December 11, 2008	47	24	14	8	8
Third						
IPSOS Reid	January 8, 2009	39	28	15	9	9
Nanos Research	January 7, 2009	33	34	19	7	7
Fourth						
Strategic Counsel	February 8, 2009	32	33	17	5	13
Harris-Decima	February 8, 2009	33	31	15	10	10
IPSOS-Reid	February 7, 2009	37	31	14	10	7

Fifth						
Angus Reid Strategies	March 11, 2009	35	31	16	10	7
Harris-Decima	March 8, 2009	32	33	14	9	10
Strategic Counsel	March 8, 2009	35	31	16	9	10
Sixth						
EKOS Research	July 7, 2009	31.8	32.2	16.0	9.3	10.7
Angus Reid Strategies	July 3, 2009	36	30	16	10	7
Seventh						
Angus Reid Strategies	August 26, 2009	34	30	18	8	9
EKOS Research	August 25, 2009	32.6	30.9	15.7	9.5	11.3
Harris-Decima	August 24, 2009	31	32	16	9	11
IPSOS-Reid	August 24, 2009	39	28	14	8	10
Eighth						
EKOS Research	September 15, 2009	35.1	29.9	16.5	9.6	9.0
Angus Reid Strategies	September 13, 2009	36	29	17	10	7
Harris-Decima	September 13, 2009	34	30	15	9	10
IPSOS-Reid	September 13, 2009	39	30	12	9	8
Ninth						
Angus Reid Strategies	October 14, 2009	41	27	16	8	6
EKOS Research	October 13, 2009	40.7	25.5	14.3	9.1	10.5
Harris-Decima	October 12, 2009	35	28	15	10	10

Tenth					
Environics	February 9, 2010	33	37	13	8	9
EKOS Research	February 9, 2010	31.0	29.0	15.5	10.3	11.3
Eleventh					
Environics	February 24, 2010	31	30	16	9	13
EKOS Research	February 23, 2010	33.4	30.3	15.8	8.2	10.4
IPSOS-Reid	February 22, 2010	37	29	16	9	7
Twelfth					
EKOS Research	May 4, 2010	33.1	26.1	16	10.2	11.5
Nanos Research	May 3, 2010	37.2	33.2	16.2	9.6	3.8
Thirteenth					
Leger Marketing	May 27, 2010	37	25	17	11	8
Angus Reid Public Opinion	May 27, 2010	35	27	19	9	8
Environics	May 26, 2010	36	30	15	10	7
Fourteenth					
IPSOS-Reid	December 9, 2010	39	29	12	10	9
Angus Reid Public Opinion	December 7, 2010	38	26	18	10	7
EKOS Research	December 7, 2010	33.7	29.2	14.4	9.8	10.4
Abacus Data	December 6, 2010	35	24	20	10	10
Nanos Research	December 5, 2010	38.1	31.2	17,2	10.2	3.2

Fifteenth					
Harris-Decima	February 27, 2011	36	28	15	9	9
IPSOS-Reid	February 27, 2011	43	27	13	10	5
Sixteenth					
Leger Marketing	March 10, 2011	36	23	18	10	10
IPSOS-Reid	March 9, 2011	40	27	16	11	5
Angus Reid Public Opinion	March 9, 2011	39	23	17	9	9
EKOS Research	March 8, 2011	35.2	27.8	14.9	8.8	10.1
Seventeenth					
Angus Reid Public Opinion	March 24, 2011	39	25	19	10	7
Leger Marketing	March 24, 2011	39	23	19	9	7
EKOS Research	March 24, 2011	35.3	28.1	14.2	9.7	10.6
IPSOS Reid	March 23, 2011	43	24	16	10	6
Harris-Decima	March 20, 2011	34	28	17	10	9

Source: Adapted from *www.electionsalmanach.com* and *www.sfu/ca/~aheard/election/polls*

Less than two months after the October 14, 2008, election, three polls were released on the same day (December 4, 2008): depending on the polling firm, the voting public was informed that the actual 5.5 percentage point vote difference between the Conservatives and the Liberals on election day had expanded to 31 points (Conservatives at 51 percent and Liberals at 20 percent), 23 points (Conservatives at 47 percent and Liberals at 24 percent), or 18.6 points (Conservatives at 42.2 percent and Liberals at 23.6 percent). One week later, the Conservative lead was either 20 points or 23 points. Combined, these five separate polls had

Tory support ranging between 51 percent and 42 percent. Liberal support was more stable, ranging between 24 percent and 20 percent, while NDP support was anywhere between 10 percent and 18 percent. None of the polls reported a margin of error greater than 3.1 percentage points.

In the first three months of 2009, polling firms could not agree on whether the Liberals or Conservatives were in the lead. In January, one firm put the Conservatives ahead with an eleven-point lead over the Liberals, while another poll put the Liberals one point ahead of the Conservatives. In February, one poll showed the Liberals with a one-point lead, another gave a two-point lead to the Conservatives, while a third put the Conservatives ahead with a relatively comfortable six-point lead. More congruence could be found in March, but nevertheless one firm had the Liberals in the lead while the Conservatives remained ahead according to two polling organizations.

If we turn our attention to February 2010, five polls were released by three different firms within a two-week period. During that time, Conservative support ranged between 37 percent and 31 percent and Liberal support between 37 percent and 29 percent. While NDP and Bloc support varied within acceptable margins, Green support ranged between 7 percent and 13 percent. Moreover, the Harper Conservatives enjoyed either an eight-point or a one-point lead, and one firm had the Liberals leading by four percentage points.

The reader can peruse the findings in Table 1 and find several other strange and contradictory stories. In most instances, the main difference rests in the wide range in support between the Conservatives and the Liberals. This is significant because if one wanted to evaluate the political situation in Ottawa — especially in a minority government situation — it made a difference whether the governing Tories had a comfortable lead over the Liberals and therefore found reason to be confident in pushing their policy agenda, or if the two parties were in a statistical dead heat, or if the opposition enjoyed a slight lead and was therefore well positioned to topple the government and force an election.

Finding an answer to such discrepancies is difficult. The usual culprits are methodological errors, different methodologies, margins of error, and question wording.[15] Between elections, very little information is provided about the methodologies used to measure voting preferences, and there are no benchmarks against which to measure accuracy. The contradictions presented in Table 1 suggest that, at least some of the times, polls provide an inconsistent picture of voting preferences. The media do not report background information about the nature of the polls, the context within which they are conducted, or their sponsors. The details provided are limited to interview dates, sample size, and the margin of error on the overall sample. The media very rarely commission their own studies and rely on polling firms to provide data for free. Without the financial support of a media sponsor, polling firms are not in a position to conduct studies solely dedicated to understanding the political environment and tend to include questions about voting intentions as part of omnibus surveys to minimize costs. This practice is particularly susceptible to the threat to validity typically referred to as question order. Several studies have examined the impact of question order on validity,[16] and the general conclusion is that for "attitude or opinion questions, related prior questions can affect responses to questions about little known topics or to questions about which the respondent has mixed feelings."[17] Despite these limitations, data are readily shared with the media in return for exposure and publicity for the polling firm.

While all these factors play a role in influencing polling results, the uses and misuses of polling and the nature of public opinion itself also provide insights into the limitations of public opinion research as it is currently conducted, especially outside of the writ period. Michael Traugott identified three main issues affecting the reporting of polling results: first, journalists must be aware of interest groups wanting to promote their positions with poll data; second, the media have difficulties distinguishing between meaningful change and change falling within the margin of error; third, most journalists simply do not have the necessary knowledge about methodology to make sense of conflicting reports of public opinion.[18] Patterson made similar claims but focused more squarely on the media fascination with polls. For him, "the use of polls spurs horse-race reporting or the tendency to treat elections as if they were sporting events ... and this tends to overshadow all else."[19] Consequently, journalists tend to exaggerate change from one poll to the next since "stability is poorly suited to journalists' need to say something new each day."[20] Journalists have become increasingly reliant on polling information to structure their reporting. Moreover, the availability of polling data at little or no cost is difficult to resist for financially strapped media organizations. Frank Brettschneider is particularly critical of this situation. He laments "the changing relationship between pollsters on the one side and journalists as well as news organizations on the other: from competition and conflict at the beginning to a symbiotic relationship nowadays."[21] In the end, the comfortable and mutually beneficial relationship between media and pollsters, combined with a dearth of methodological knowledge, has created a situation in which a critical evaluation of polling by the media is unlikely to happen.

Another important question deals with what, if anything, is measured by pre-writ horse-race polls. Several decades ago, Philip Converse described the electorate as largely devoid of meaningful beliefs, even on topics that have been the basis of intense elite political controversy for long periods of time.[22] Converse's general picture of the voting public has been corroborated and refined over the years, especially in John Zaller's *The Nature and Origins of Mass Opinion*[23] and by Sniderman and Theriault, who concluded that "citizens' judgments are impulsive, oversimplified, intemperate, ill-considered and ill-informed."[24] In a low-knowledge and low-interest environment, one must wonder if polls have simply become media content,[25] more likely to entertain than provide any insights about public opinion dynamics and political realities. Looking at Table 1 once again, few insights were provided by the last five polls released before the writ was dropped. First, Conservative and Liberal support continued to vary greatly depending on the polling firm. Specifically, polling firms positioned Conservative support anywhere between 43 percent and 34 percent. Moreover, the Harper Conservatives enjoyed a lead over the second-place Liberals oscillating between 19 and 6 points. And there was no sign of the upcoming NDP surge or of the Bloc collapse. In fact, as we turn to the election period, media polls missed most of what was interesting about the 2011 campaign.

THE SECOND PERIOD: MARCH 25 TO APRIL 20, 2011

A "mere" 76 nationwide election polls were released during the writ period in 2011, significantly fewer than in 2008 when 113 polls were published during the campaign. A total of twelve polling firms released data in 2011, up from seven firms in 2008. Combined with the 239 pre-writ polls, the voting intentions of Canadians were probed a total of 315 times between the 2008 and 2011 elections.

In general, media coverage of polling results becomes more substantive during election campaigns. From time to time, the coverage moves beyond party standings and looks at key determinants of vote choice. Journalists are more likely to write in-depth analyses and rely on polls to gauge the public mood and the perceptions of parties and leaders. For example, the *Toronto Star* provided an in-depth analysis of voting intentions in its March 26 edition. The analysis looked beyond horse race numbers and examined important elements such as Leaders' approval ratings, stability of vote choice, and the most important issues.[26] However, Richard Brennan — the *Star*'s national affairs writer — could not resist making typical sweeping statements barely supported by the data. The most troubling aspect of his analysis was the repeated emphasis on the battle between the Conservatives and the Liberals in the Greater Toronto Area, despite the fact that the margin of error for that region was +/- 5 percentage points based on an unspecified sample size.[27]

A consensus emerged from the first series of polls published at the onset of the campaign. Every poll put the Tories ahead of the Liberals, with the NDP not too far behind. The Bloc had a solid lead in the province of Quebec, while the Greens received single-digit support across the country. There remained some variations in support depending on which data one was using, but all pointed in the same general direction. There was even stronger consensus at the end of the campaign. By that time, most polls gave a solid lead to the Conservatives and suggested that the NDP had moved past the Liberals to take second place. There was a clear sense that Bloc support had collapsed, but most remained unsure of the extent of the damage.

The main focus of this section is to examine what happened between those two points in time. If we look at data from three of the most prominent polling firms[28] during the campaign (see Figure 1), we see that while the firms successfully identified the winner of the election, they do not agree on how the Harper Conservatives got there. There were also some discrepancies in describing the evolution of both the Liberal and NDP campaigns. Moreover, IPSOS-Reid consistently reported Conservative and NDP support higher than its two competitors while showing Liberal support lower than both EKOS and Nanos Research. We will look at the support for each of the three main parties in turn.

The Conservative Support

According to most observers, the Conservatives began the campaign within striking distance of a majority[29] and gained momentum on their way to a comfortable win.[30] Polling data tell a different story. For instance, if one looks at the evolution of Conservative support as charted by IPSOS-Reid, the Conservatives had a terrible campaign. They began the election contest with support in the mid-40s and steadily lost ground in the first few days. They regained most of that support in the middle of the campaign only to experience a serious decline as election day approached. The IPSOS-Reid storyline suggests a Conservative Party limping over the finish line.

Both Nanos Research and EKOS Research offer a different narrative. According to both firms, the Conservatives gained support in the opening weeks of the campaign. For Nanos Research, Conservative support peaked early — around April 3 — and, as IPSOS-Reid also suggested, then went into an almost constant decline. For EKOS Research, Conservative support peaked much later in the campaign — on April 17 — and remained more or less stable as the campaign waned.

Figure 1. Campaign Narratives

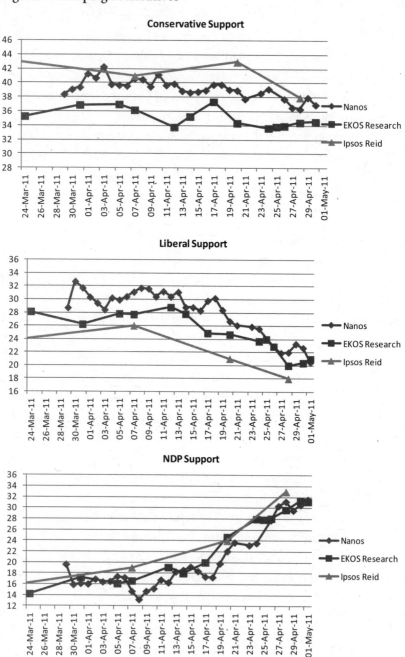

Source: Adapted from *www.electionsalmanach.com.*

The Liberal Support

There are similarities and differences in the way polling firms told the story of the Liberal campaign in the 2011 election. First, the data from both Nanos Research and IPSOS-Reid suggested that the Liberals had a strong launch of their campaign. In contrast, EKOS Research saw a decline in Liberal support during the same period of time. For Nanos Research, the upsurge in Liberal support was short-lived since within days the Liberals experienced their first collapse in support. Both EKOS Research and IPSOS-Reid painted the opposite picture with the troops led by Ignatieff steadily gaining in support during the first two weeks or so. After that initial collapse detected only by Nanos Research, the three firms agreed that the Liberal campaign was gaining ground. For EKOS Research, things took a turn for the worse for the Liberals around April 13 and never really recovered. Nanos Research saw things improving for the Liberals until April 19 — almost a week longer than EKOS Research. After that date, all three firms captured the collapse of Liberals, most dramatically documented by IPSOS-Reid.

The NDP Support

There was more congruence between the three firms in documenting the rise of the NDP. With the exception of Nanos Research, which suggested that the NDP suffered a significant loss in support at the beginning of the campaign and then again around April 5, the data showed NDP support relatively steady in the first few days after the writ was dropped. Then, in the second part of the campaign, NDP support began to climb. Nanos Research once again showed a decline between April 15 and 17, but things began to change for the NDP around April 21. This date is significant since it was when the CROP poll showed the NDP in the lead in Quebec. From that point on, the NDP was on the rise, culminating with its historic showing on May 2, 2011. We will return to the potential significance of the CROP poll in the next section.

To add to the confusion, we saw a proliferation of websites translating polling data into seat projections. This practice was popularized in the late 1980s by Barry Kay and others at the Laurier Institute for the Study of Public Opinion and Policy.[31] Kay and his colleagues have continued the practice, and their website allows anyone to make their own seat projections for any upcoming elections for which polling data is available. In 2011, others joined the fray, most notably democraticSPACE[32] and ThreeHundredEight.[33] All seat projection methodologies are generally based on a proportional swing vote model. As one can read on ThreeHundredEight's website, the general approach is as follows: "The projections are based on the popular vote projections that are made for each province and region. Those projections are based on an aggregate of all publically available polling data, weighted by the age of the poll, the size of the sample, and the track record of each pollster. Past election results and corrections for past error rates are also taken into account."[34]

Each website has different weighting approaches, but the general methodology is similar. The principal attraction of the seat projection websites is the ability to see the potential impact of change in electoral support on seat distribution in the legislature. The accuracy of the predictions depends on the reliability of the data provided by polling firms. Adding to the difficulty of the task is the reliance of the projection models on regional and provincial data, which yield substantial margins of error. While the websites generated substantial attention, they were unable to correctly predict the outcome in 2011. ThreeHundredEight predicted a Conservative minority government. For their part, democraticSPACE hedged its bets and offered a wide range of potential scenarios but still missed the mark for both the Liberals and the Bloc.

The apparent discrepancies between polls convinced the media to spend some time reflecting on the conduct of public opinion research.[35] The emphasis was placed on the methodologies used by the different pollsters, especially with regards to data collection. In the 2011 campaign, EKOS relied on a technology generally referred to as a "robocall," which is an automated system that calls random numbers and asks respondents to punch in their answers using the telephone keypad. Nanos Research conducted telephone surveys while IPSOS-Reid collected data through an online panel. Telephone surveys have many advantages. Most importantly, this data collection method provides the best opportunities for quality control over the entire data collection process.[36] However, low response rates have plagued the polling industry to the extent that most firms have turned to the Internet as a more reliable way to collect data. Internet surveys also have many advantages. They are generally cheaper, and online surveys can be completed very rapidly and in a timely fashion. While response rates vary from study to study, they are higher than for most telephone surveys. However, since participation depends on self-selection, it is difficult to conduct online surveys based on probability sampling. But as the polling industry is recognizing the obsolescence of telephone surveys, serious efforts are being made to ensure the reliability of Internet surveys.[37]

Undoubtedly, methodological differences have an impact on the results, but they provide only part of the explanation. Looking back to Figure 1, it is important to note that the discrepancies between polls almost disappeared in the latter part of the campaign. Without changing data collection methods, Nanos Research, IPSOS-Reid, and EKOS Research arrived at similar results as election day neared.

THE THIRD PERIOD: THE LAST TEN DAYS

Of the seventy-six polls published during the campaign, twenty-seven were released in the last ten days. Of particular interest was the NDP surge, particularly in Quebec, and the extent to which it would translate into a record number of seats for the New Democrats. This focus on one province exposed another limitation of the media coverage of polling.

Typically, the sample size for nationwide polls varies between one and two thousand respondents. While this yields findings that are accurate within a margin of error of +/- 3 percentage points, the margin of error increases substantially for regional results. Even for a province as large as Quebec, the margin of error would typically be more than +/- 6 percentage points. Accordingly, any discussion of Quebec findings gleaned from national surveys would be directional at best. The same can be said for analysis dealing with other parts of the country. But such caution is largely ignored in the media, and regional margin of errors are rarely mentioned.[38] Regional findings are reported with the same level of certainty as overall findings.

The other issue stemming from the release of the CROP poll and the ensuing media focus on the NDP has to do with the impact of polling on public opinion. Much has been written about the potential bandwagon or underdog effects of published polls. In very simple terms, a bandwagon effect occurs when voters change their vote choice in order to support the party or leader who is seemingly in the lead. In contrast, voters can rally behind the underdog — the party or leader who appears to be trailing — either as a show of support or in the hope of orchestrating a come-from-behind victory. In a meta-analysis of the effects of published polls on citizens, first conducted by Hardmeier and Roth (2000) and later adapted by Hardmeier (2008), the authors concluded that the bandwagon effect is significant but small, and somewhat larger than the underdog effect.[39] There is also a largely theoretical body of research inspired by Elisabeth Noelle-Neumann's *The Spiral of Silence*,[40] which suggests that people will seek information in order to adjust their behaviour to majority trends out of fear of isolation. The empirical evidence for the existence of a spiral of silence is sparse and generally mixed.[41] But for those who have been directly involved in election campaigns, the impact of polls on campaign strategy and on media coverage is undeniable. After the release of the CROP poll, any balance in coverage evaporated. The Liberal and Green camps at the national level — and to some extent the Bloc campaign in Quebec — were forced into an uphill and somewhat futile battle to change the storyline and regain the spotlight. The new story was about Jack Layton, and the NDP surge dominated the news to the detriment of the other opposition parties. As Liberal pollster Michael Marzolini pointed out, while the Liberal campaign tried to recover and counter the surge, nothing connected.[42]

One cannot look at published polls during an election campaign without addressing the issue of accuracy. This chapter went to great pains to point out some instances where contradictions in polling data simply could not be explained away by methodological rationalizations. As noted above, when faced with apparent contradictions, pollsters point out that the most important test of their accuracy comes on election day. Accordingly, Table 2 reviews the pollsters' performance in the 2011 Canadian election.

Table 2. The Pollsters' Report Card

Firms	Dates	Conservatives	Liberals	NDP	Bloc	Greens	Difference
Election		39.6	18.9	30.6	6	3.7	
Nanos Research	May 1, 2011	37.1	20.5	31.6	5.7	3.8	5.5
Harris-Decima	May 1, 2011	36	19	30	6	6	6.6
EKOS Research	May 1, 2011	33.9	21	31.2	6.4	6	11.1
Angus Reid	April 29, 2011	37	19	33	6	4	5.4
COMPAS	April 29, 2011	46	17	26	7	4	14.2
IPSOS-Reid	April 28, 2011	38	18	33	7	4	6.2

Source: Adapted from *www.electionsalmanach.com* and *www.sfu.ca/~aheard/election/polls*

Two firms — Nanos Research and Angus Reid — did particularly well. They both underestimated Conservative and overestimated Liberal and NDP support, but the discrepancies were small and well within the margin of error. Both IPSOS-Reid and Harris-Decima also performed adequately. Once again, both firms underestimated Conservative support, particularly Harris-Decima. EKOS Research performed generally well but was negatively affected by underreporting Conservative support to an extent well outside of the margin of error. EKOS was more accurate in predicting support for the other four parties. COMPAS missed the mark.

Considering the fact that several inconsistencies were isolated in the publications of polling results in the pre-writ period and the fact that inconsistencies continued in the first few weeks of the campaign, how can we explain the partial redemption for most polling firms in the last ten days of the campaign? As mentioned in the previous section, firms did not change their data collection approaches in the closing days of the campaign therefore weakening the relevance of methodological argument. It would seem that polls are much better at measuring vote choice and attitudes among an attentive public. Looking at the U.S., David Moore pointed out that polls are particularly inaccurate during the presidential primaries simply because they are measuring the opinions of what he called a "fictitious national primary electorate."[43] His insights can be applied to the Canadian context. Polls published between elections reflect the voting intentions of a largely fictitious electorate, too disinterested and disengaged to reflect seriously about which political party would be likely to get their support. Building on Converse's work, it would appear that only when people are engaged in the election do horse-race numbers actually reflect the mood of the voting public.

POST-MORTEM

As Sibylle Hardmeier has observed: "Modern political opinion polls are accompanied by two constants: the debate about their quality on the one hand and the debate about their alleged effects in the run-up to elections and voting behaviour on the other."[44] This chapter was an attempt to reflect on both constants with the 2011 Canadian federal election as the backdrop, A third constant in most analyses of election polls is a call for reform and a more rigorous reporting of the methodology of polling.

Elaborate guidelines to regulate the publication of polls have 'been advocated since the late 1960s. In1969, the American Association for Public Opinion Research developed a list of "Standards for Minimal Disclosure."[45] In Canada, efforts to standardize the publication of polls began in the 1970s, first by the *Comité des sondages du Regroupement québécois des sciences sociales* and later by Guy Lachapelle in his report to the Royal Commission on Electoral Reform and Party Financing in 1991. The recommendations aim at ensuring that the public gets in-depth information about the conduct of polls and their findings. Accordingly, the publication of survey results should include the following:

1. The name of the sponsor of the poll
2. The name of the polling institute
3. The interview period
4. The data collection method used
5. The size of the original sample
6. The number of non-eligible respondents
7. The rejection and response rates
8. The number of respondents
9. The margin of error
10. The sampling method
11. The wording of the questions[46]

These basic details would be a step in the right direction since "numerous studies in various countries have shown that most media neglect to provide readers or viewers with the necessary parameters with which it is possible to assess the quality or validity of the results."[47] With this information, citizens would have the opportunity to judge, if not the accuracy, at least the legitimacy of the information they are being presented with. But after decades of calling for such reforms with no success, it is unlikely that changes will occur in the near future, unless the polling industry demands them. Moreover, disclosure of methodological details would remedy only part of the current situation.

While pollsters should make their work more transparent and comprehensible, journalists should improve their knowledge of empirical research. Pollsters should remain in charge of the data they are providing and not entrust journalists to write analyses that too often go beyond the poll results. Pollsters should collaborate with the media to ensure that poll data are correctly interpreted. Another positive step would be to aim less for quantity and more for quality. There is no legitimate need for more than three hundred media polls within an electoral cycle. As this chapter has shown, this abundance of data obfuscates rather than illuminates the political landscape. A focus on more depth would show the benefits of polling and highlight its potential. It would show the public the reasons parties and corporations have become so reliant on public opinion data. Such a change would be beneficial to the polling industry, whose credibility is being tarnished by current media coverage. While horse-race polls have a place in the coverage of politics, there is more to be learned from polling. If this instrument is to reclaim its role as the mechanism to ensure that the people are heard, they should be given an opportunity to tell us more than simply who is ahead.

NOTES

1. Joël-Denis Bellavance, "Le NDP prend la tête au Québec," last modified April 21, 2011, *cyberpresse.ca*.
2. Adapted from *www.electionsalmanach.com* and *www.sfu.ca/~aheard/election/polls*.
3. See E. C. Ladd and John Benson, "The Growth of News Polls in American Politics," in *Media Polls in American Politics*, eds. Thomas E. Mann and Gary R. Orren (Washington DC: Brookings Institute Press, 1992).
4. Wolfgang Donsbach, "Who's Afraid of Election Polls" (paper presented at the ESOMAR Conference, Amsterdam, 2001).
5. George Gallup and Saul Rae, *The Pulse of Democracy: The Public-Opinion Poll and How It Works* (New York: Simon and Schuster, 1940), 6.
6. Gallup and Rae, *The Pulse of Democracy*, 13.
7. Susan Herbst, *Numbered Voices: How Opinion Polling Has Shaped American Politics* (Chicago: The University of Chicago Press, 1993), 1.
8. Peter Butler, *Polling and Public Opinion: A Canadian Perspective* (Toronto: University of Toronto Press, 2007), 40.
9. André Turcotte, "Polling as Modern Alchemy: Measuring Public Opinion in Canadian Elections," in *Elections*, ed. Heather McIvor (Toronto: Edmond Montgomery Publications Limited, 2010), 207.
10. Norman C. Meier and Harold W. Saunders, eds., *The Polls and Public Opinion* (New York: Henry Holt and Co., 1949), 160.
11. Wolfgang Donsbach and Michael W. Traugott, eds. *The SAGE Handbook of Public Opinion Research* (Los Angeles: SAGE Publications, 2008), 4.
12. Thomas E. Patterson, "Of Polls, Mountains," *Public Opinion Quarterly*, 69 (2005): 716–24.
13. Donsbach and Traugott, eds., *The SAGE Handbook of Public Opinion Research*, 3.
14. Kenneth F. Warren, *In Defense of Public Opinion Polling* (Boulder, Colorado: Westview Press, 2002), 45.

15. Several books and articles have been written about the methodological pitfalls associated with polling. For a more in-depth discussion, see W.A. Belson, *The Design and Understanding of Survey Questions* (Aldershot: Gower, 1981); or H.F. Weisberg, *The Total Survey Error Approach: A Guide to the New Science of Survey Research* (Chicago: University of Chicago Press, 2005).
16. See, for example, R. Tourangeau et al., "Carryover Effects in Attitude Surveys," *Public Opinion Quarterly*, 53(1989): 495–524.
17. K.A. Rasinski, "Designing Reliable and Valid Questionnaires," in *The SAGE Handbook of Public Opinion Research*, eds. Donsbach and Traugott, 370.
18. Michael W. Traugott, "The Uses and Misuses of Polls," in *The SAGE Handbook of Public Opinion Research*, eds. Donsbach and Traugott, 232–39.
19. Patterson, "Of Polls, Mountains," 718.
20. *Ibid.*, 721.
21. Frank Brettschneider, "The News Media's Use of Opinion Polls," in *The SAGE Handbook of Public Opinion Research*, eds. Donsbach and Traugott, 479.
22. Philip Converse, "The Nature of Belief System in Mass Publics," in *Ideology and Discontent*, ed. D. Apter. (New York: The Free Press 1964), 245.
23. John Zaller, *The Nature and Origins of Mass Opinion* (Cambridge: Cambridge University Press, 1992).
24. P.M. Sniderman and S.M. Theriault, "The Structure of Political Argument and Logic of Issue Framing" in *Studies in Public Opinion: Attitudes, Nonattitudes, Measurement Error and Change*, eds. W.E. Saris and P.M. Sniderman (Princeton: Princeton University Press, 2004), 134.
25. Brettschneider, "The News Media's Use of Opinion Polls," 482.
26. Richard J. Brennan, "Tories in Majority Territory," *The Toronto Star*, March 26, 2011, A1.
27. *Ibid.*
28. Nanos Research, EKOS Research, and IPSOS-Reid were chosen for this analysis for a combination of reasons. Nanos Research and EKOS Research were the most consistent in tracking vote choice during the campaign. IPSOS-Reid was less active but is the most prominent polling firm in Canada.
29. Mark Kennedy, "Tories in Majority Territory: Poll," *Ottawa Citizen*, A1.
30. Patrick Brethour, "With Gains Across Ontario, Tories Find Stability," *Globe and Mail*, A1.
31. See *www.wlu.ca/lispop*.
32. *www.democraticspace.com*. This website made some predictions in the 2008 election but, like the others, became more prominent in 2011.
33. *www.threehundredeight.com*.
34. See *www.threehundredeight.com* for a fuller description.
35. Steve Ladurantaye, "When Polls Differ, Pollsters Worry," *Globe and Mail*, A7.
36. Paul J. Lavrakas, "Surveys by Telephone," in *The SAGE Handbook of Public Opinion Research*, eds. Donsbach and Traugott, 250.
37. For a full discussion of some of the steps taken to improve the quality of Internet surveys, see Vasja Vehovar et al., "Internet Surveys" in *The SAGE Handbook of Public Opinion Research*, eds. Donsbach and Traugott, 271–83.

38. See for examples, Les Perreaux, "Quebec's Jackomania Makes NDP Target" or Patrick Brethour, "Will NDP's West Coast Surge Pay Off for Tories," *Globe and Mail*, April 22, 2011, A4.

39. See Sibylle Hardmeier, "The Effects of Published Polls on Citizens," in *The SAGE Handbook of Public Opinion Research*, eds. Donsbach and Traugott, 505.

40. Elisabeth Noelle-Neumann, *The Spiral of Silence*, 2nd edition (Chicago: The University of Chicago Press, 1993).

41. Dietram A. Scheufele, "Spiral of Silence Theory" in *The SAGE Handbook of Public Opinion Research*, eds. Donsbach and Traugott, 175–83.

42. Jane Taber, "The Two-Day NDP Surge that Sank the Liberals," *Globe and Mail*, May 7, 2011, A18.

43. David W. Moore, *The Opinion Makers*, 150.

44. Hardmeier, "The Effects of Published Polls on Citizens," 504.

45. Brettschneider, "The News Media's Use of Opinion Polls," 482.

46. Guy Lachapelle, *Polls and the Media in Canadian Elections* (Ottawa: Supply and Services Canada, 1991), 114.

47. Donsbach, "Who's Afraid of Election Polls," 14.

CHAPTER 9

The Campaign in the Digital Media
Mary Francoli | Josh Greenberg | Christopher Waddell

In the four elections since Canada began a period of minority government in 2004, the news media have changed dramatically, first with the rise of blogs and citizen journalism and more recently with the growth of social networking sites. During this time, mainstream news organizations have undergone an economic crisis, become less concentrated in ownership, and wrestled with integrating new technologies into their operations while trying to decide what information to post immediately on their websites and what to hold for their traditional products (newspapers and newscasts). Audiences are fragmenting, and while some see this as a crisis for traditional media, others are optimistic that if they can adapt to the new mediascape they have an opportunity to thrive. In short, the role of legacy news organizations, the function of their digital offspring and new social media, and their impact on the political life of the nation are very much in flux.

Changes in communication technology are both shaping and being shaped by new forms of social organization. Daily followers of Canadian politics and election campaigns now regularly use websites primarily of mainstream news media to stay on top of campaign developments. Traditional media outlets such as newspapers and broadcast media continue to play a central role in democracy by informing citizens and shaping the focus of public conversations, but newspapers are becoming less newsy, pushing time-sensitive material to the web. However, the "top-down dissemination technologies that supported them are being supplanted by an open, many-to-many networked media environment."[1] This presents a challenge for assessing how the media covered the election. A conventional content analysis of major newspapers — the *Globe and Mail*, the *National Post*, and the *Toronto Star* — would miss the shift to news online. Moreover, some believe that the framing of campaign issues and perceptions of how political parties are faring is slowly shifting to social media through platforms such as Twitter and Facebook. Although there have always been opportunities for journalists to correspond with readers, or for voters to communicate with elected officials and with those seeking office, these have traditionally been structured and formalized by institutional settings and contexts that, in a social media era, become porous and less stable. Despite the clear shifts that are occurring to newspapers and in the realm of social media, what is changing less dramatically in both format and content are the main television newscasts — *The National* on CBC, *CTV National News*, and *Global National*. Despite prognostications about the "death of mass media,"[2] those television newscasts each still attract nightly audiences of between 500,000 and more than 1 million viewers. Elections are prime fodder for all-news cable channels, but their content changes hourly, while audiences are small and drift in one minute and out the next. Nightly newscasts continue to be the way most Canadians get a concise end-of-day summary of what has happened on the campaign trail. For these reasons, this assessment of how the media covered the campaign will focus primarily on those nightly newscasts. Yet it also examines how the main parties utilized social media, along with how the media framed the role of social networking sites and their putative influence on the campaign.

THE CAMPAIGN ON TELEVISION

Several conclusions are immediately apparent from viewing thirty-six days of the three newscasts. The most obvious is that television campaign coverage hasn't changed very much since the 1970s. Stephen Harper, Michael Ignatieff, and Jack Layton were mentioned every night on the three national newscasts, although not always with full stories. Sometimes it was just a brief report read by the anchor, on occasion accompanied by a clip from the leader. The networks covered Green

Party leader Elizabeth May only rarely: on the campaign's opening day, upon release of the party's platform, and then when the networks refused to include her in the two televised leaders' debates. The CBC gave infrequent coverage to the Bloc Québécois while the other two networks paid little attention to the Quebec campaign altogether, until it became clear that the NDP was gaining in the province at the expense of the Bloc. CTV and Global run thirty-minute newscasts, which have about twenty-two minutes for news, while CBC has an hour a night (about forty-five minutes excluding commercials) for a traditional newscast and longer treatment of selected issues. During the campaign a lot of that nightly CBC time went to the election, except in the final week when all the networks increasingly focused on the lead-up to the April 29 royal wedding of Prince William — three days before Canadians voted.

Campaign events and coverage of those events are formulaic and dysfunctional for voters who hope or expect the media to examine the most important issues and to report on how the parties differ in their approaches to each. The parties and the television networks are linked in a mutually dependent relationship. The parties stage events that provide pictures and form the basis of the network nightly campaign stories as well as providing access to campaign materials and key spokespeople. In exchange, the networks take those carefully designed party backdrops and images and distribute them to voters through their stories, regardless of whether the images match the story being told that night by the reporter. For instance, a significant part of the visual background to nightly stories will be of a party's leader's daily rally or staged event, even if the content of the story is about an issue, such as a candidate's faux pas, that has nothing to do with that day's pictures. Campaign success for a party comes from constructing events and images that the media use that visually tell the story the party wants voters to see and understand, regardless of what the reporter is saying in his or her script.

In this campaign, the Conservatives, Liberals, and New Democrats all chose to place their leaders before similar in-the-round audiences, walking and talking daily like television game show hosts. Equally, there was a mind-numbing sameness and lack of imagination in coverage of the leaders' tours. No matter the network, story length was almost always in the 1:45- to 2:00-minute range, running a bit longer on week-ends where there is less competition for airtime. Almost every story on all three networks opened with a throw from an anchor to a reporter on camera with a rally or tour bus backdrop. It concluded with the reporter reciting an on-camera closing, frequently almost yelling at viewers with campaign rally noise in the background, occasionally followed by a quick question and answer between the reporter and anchor. The cost of cam-paign coverage (approximately $45,000 a seat on each leader's plane for each reporter, producer, and camera/sound/editor plus the cost of hotels, meals, overtime, etc.) meant the five major networks (CBC, CTV, Global, RadioCanada, and TVA) pooled their visual coverage with one camera team on each leader's tour supplying the same pictures and clips to all networks (as they have done in every campaign since 1997). That com-monality drove home the interchangeability of the leaders' tour coverage.

There was also a sharp divergence between the interests of voters, their choices on election day, and the coverage of the leaders' tours. Largely inconsequential incidents or events dominated the daily tour coverage on all three networks, and these were often reprises of issues that had not demonstrated any ability to galvanize widespread or lasting public sentiment during the life of the previous Parliament. Stephen Harper suc-ceeded on the campaign's opening day in framing the election as being a choice between a "power-hungry coalition" of opposition parties and a "stable majority" Conservative government. That issue dominated all tele-vision coverage in the campaign's early days and was the focus of almost every media question of both Harper and Liberal leader Michael Ignatieff as they launched their campaigns (NDP leader Jack Layton didn't allow any media questions March 26 as the campaign kicked off).

Over the following five weeks, stories on a series of unrelated events and issues supplemented the coalition theme; but, due in no small part to the Conservative Party's communication strategy, the spectre of a coalition was always lurking in the background. In succession, the other issues that received nightly attention included questions about the activities of a Conservative campaign worker in Edmonton; the tightly scripted nature of the Harper campaign with reporters getting only five questions a day (four for the reporters on the leader's tour and one local question); people being evicted from Conservative rallies due to possible links to other parties; previous fraud convictions of a senior adviser to Harper; the Liberals removing Quebec candidate André Forbes for allegedly expressing white supremacist views while not removing an Edmonton candidate who had questioned sentences in sexual assault cases; the Auditor General's leaked tentative assessment of uncontrolled spending on the 2010 G8/G20 summits; a Conservative email inviting people to come to a rally dressed in ethnic costumes; the fate of a report about documents pertaining to the treatment of Afghan detainees; and the plight of Helena Guergis, a once-obscure junior cabinet minister fired by Harper who was now running as an independent and seeking redemption for her alleged mistreatment. That collection of unrelated stories, mixed with occasional mentions of policy announcements, dominated newscast election coverage until about April 20, when journalists and pundits began to take notice of trends in opinion poll data that confirmed gathering NDP strength in Quebec at the expense of the Bloc. That support and questions of how broadly it would extend across the country, accompanied by discussion of the extent of the collapse of the Liberals, dominated television news in the campaign's last week.

While most television coverage was little different from past campaigns, it was encouraging to see a few examples of networks acknowledging the degree to which they have become dependent on political parties for news material. All three networks noted the NDP was the source of the comments given to reporters that led Ignatieff to dump his Quebec candidate Forbes; yet all three networks reported it, only Global acknowledged it was the Conservatives who circulated comments to the media from Liberal candidate and former judge John Reilly regarding sexual assaults, strategically timed to match a Harper "tough on crime" visit to the Toronto-area riding of cabinet minister and former police chief Julian Fantino. It was CTV that noted on April 25 that it was the Liberals who were shopping to the media a five-hundred-page binder of supposedly damaging Harper quotes from his career in politics they claimed was compiled by Conservatives.

Most of the issues raised in leaders' tour coverage until the last week involved Conservative actions and opposition responses and was usually negative, as the governing party is the focus of attacks from all the other parties. Yet that appears to have barely registered with voters. The Conservatives won a surprisingly strong majority with 166 seats — 23 more than in 2008 — as the party's vote share rose to 39.2 percent from 37.7 percent three years earlier. In Ontario, Conservative support grew a remarkable five percentage points to 44.4 percent from 39.2 percent in 2008.

One explanation is that the content of leaders' tour coverage had nothing to do with the interests of key blocs of voters. Canadians' concerns emerged in the stories done far away from the tours. Most of this additional coverage came from the CBC thanks to having an hour every night (except Saturdays) on *The National*. Longer stories (in the three- to four-minute range) done by reporter Saša Petricic — reporting from New Hazleton, B.C., on March 30; Standard, Alberta, on April 11; Welland, Ontario, on April 17; and St. John's, Newfoundland, on April 29 — focused on the views of voters off the beaten track. A consistent theme from voters here is concern about the state of the economy, jobs, rising prices, and inflation. A similar April 17 story by the CBC's Ian Hanomansing from Squamish, B.C., highlights voter concern about few jobs for young people and the squeeze between raising prices to cover costs and consumers' unwillingness to pay more, which was a growing threat to viability for owners of small businesses such as restaurants. The economy also popped up on occasion in a cross-Canada series from a camper by Global's Mike Armstrong; however, his stories focused more on communities and less on issues.

The dominant impression in all those CBC stories was voter unease about their economic futures. Importantly, this subject virtually never surfaced in the reporter scripts and stand-ups of nightly coverage devoted to leaders' tours, yet it was a constant presence in the visual images viewers saw every night. One sequence of sound and images appeared night after night in stories about the Conservative leader's tour — Stephen Harper being applauded by party supporters appearing to be the ordinary voting public. Sometimes he entered a room to applause, but most often all three TV networks used his daily campaign pitch for "a strong stable majority Conservative government" followed by enthusiastic cheers from the bleachers. As he told the CBC's Peter Mansbridge in an April 21 interview,

"The key issue for us is the economy and I think that's what voters are focused on, should be focused on. I think we have the record there and I think the country needs a strong stable government to move the economy forward ..." That message appeared time after time in news stories on all three networks. No matter what the content of that day's newscast story (and many were not flattering to the Conservatives), the overpowering visual image was of Harper being applauded for his key message that only a Conservative majority government can protect and grow jobs and the economy. Although it is true the Conservatives carefully screened attendees to ensure only partisans were present at Harper's daily events, this is the kind of detail that is easily lost when watching him being applauded day after day, newscast after newscast. It serves as a graphic example of the power of visual images over the spoken word, which the Conservatives used skillfully throughout the campaign, assisted by the media, who regularly and predictably put those images on the air.

To a lesser degree, coverage of the NDP also included positive audience response to leader Jack Layton's messages about jobs and unemployment, financial security for seniors, and protecting the health care system. That came after generally negative coverage in the campaign's first two weeks focused on Layton's health after cancer surgery and a hip fracture, the absence of campaign energy, small crowds at NDP events, and criticism of the party for re-announcing past policies. That changed sharply with Quebec opinion poll results after April 20. From that point forward, visual images more than story content propelled the NDP, starting with an April 23 story about the party's largest rally ever in Quebec, held right in the Montreal riding of Gilles Duceppe. Large cheering crowds met a smiling Layton as he shook hands with supporters while carrying his ever-present cane, then spoke to a sea of sign-waving partisans. Those visual images played almost nightly on all three networks during the last week of his cross-country campaign, a push that concluded with a final weekend send-off in Montreal for a bus trip to Toronto, stopping halfway in Kingston, where he was met by a crowd so large that police were forced to close city streets to traffic.

The Liberals were left as the campaign's visual victims. The damage was largely self-inflicted and came from what appears to be a lack of understanding about the power of visuals and a failure to execute (or develop) strategies that would counter the problems television images can create. Ignatieff began the campaign already typecast through more than a year of Conservative pre-election negative advertising that claimed he had primarily his own interests at heart and was "just visiting" after living outside Canada for more than three decades. The ads were misleading, harsh, and arguably unfair — but they also contained just enough truth to get voters thinking about the Liberal leader as a character with questionable motives, long before the Conservative government's defeat in Parliament at the hands of what was then a confident Ignatieff and Liberal opposition.

The stage positioning of the party leaders in the English-language television debate (chosen through a draw) was one example of the obvious televisual challenges Ignatieff faced. Harper was on the viewer's left with Layton, Ignatieff, and Duceppe in that order across the stage. It was a perfect visual representation — one against three — of Harper's daily argument that the opposition parties would gang up on the Conservatives with a coalition if he didn't get a majority mandate. Harper spoke directly to this issue and, during the televised debates, directly through the camera to voters. The debate also heightened Layton's symbolic importance, standing between Harper and Ignatieff, which the NDP leader exploited with a confident performance and an equally strong performance the next night in French. That, in particular, caught the eye of agenda-setting observers such *Toronto Star* columnist and CBC At Issue panelist Chantal Hebert, who noted never before having seen an NDP leader play as central a role in the French language leaders' debate.

By contrast, Ignatieff appeared unaware of the visual straitjacket in which he had been placed and made no apparent effort to look or act prime ministerial or otherwise to differentiate himself from the other opposition leaders. More than that, his interjections right from the start sounded like an extension of the daily House of Commons Question Period with an overriding focus on the same narrow issues that had been failing to produce notable gains in support for the Liberals during the previous eighteen months and which arguably had been part of why voters increasingly reported higher levels of ambivalence about politics and politicians. The Liberal leader never got around to explaining to viewers in the English-language debate why they should vote for his party and make him prime minister. It was a crippling performance that helped confirm in voters' minds what the Conservative ads had been saying all along.

The Liberals appeared no better at understanding the power of images in constructing their daily campaign events. When Ignatieff appeared in the town hall set that all parties used, his remarks were often strong even though they rarely touched on the economic challenges facing voters. Instead Ignatieff regularly attacked Conservative spending, crime policies, and lack of respect for Parliament and democratic institutions. Media on his tour reported he was turning out solid performances. That made it even harder for reporters and the Liberal campaign team to figure out why the negative nightly stories about Harper, his government, and his campaign met with so much voter indifference. While Ignatieff's campaign may have been operating smoothly, the images viewers saw every night were radically different than that of Harper or Layton. Most often the Liberal leader appeared either almost alone answering questions or with candidates at his side. Those solo performances were only rarely accompanied by the applause that regularly greeted Harper's majority government exhortation on network newscasts night after night.

Much of what Ignatieff did, as portrayed on television newscasts, made little sense, whether it was his overdramatic exhortations to "rise up" against the Conservative government, which captured his campaign for three or four days after April 15, or the obvious contradictions of campaigning as a first-time leader of the Liberal party who had never been a member of any government warning Canadians about the dangers of voting for the NDP because it had no experience in government. Yet when criticizing the Conservatives Ignatieff sounded just like the NDP, asking Global National anchor Dawna Friesen in an April 25 interview, "Do you want a Canada where we are focusing on what the banks, insurance companies, or oil companies want or do we to focus on what Canadian families need in order to succeed?" The next night in his Global interview Layton told Friesen, "We're asking ourselves who can we trust to put the interests of our families first. We know the well-connected are well taken care of — banks and oil companies keep getting their tax cuts — but most folks can't make ends meet at the end of the month."

The most obvious Liberal television error came with the party's approach to Ignatieff's interview with the CBC's Peter Mansbridge. The network allowed each party to choose the setting for leader interviews, which each ran about eighteen minutes on *The National*. For his April 18 appearance, the NDP placed Layton and Mansbridge in a series of informal settings: in the back of a van driving between events, talking in the aisle of the NDP campaign jet, and standing on a wharf in St. John's. It strikingly highlighted the NDP leader's openness, informality, industriousness, and personable nature, driving home precisely the characteristics at the core of the party's message that Canadians had a choice beyond just the Conservatives and Liberals. The Conservatives, meanwhile, had Harper on the ice in a hockey rink in Conception Bay, Newfoundland, for his April 21 interview, standing toe-to-toe with the CBC anchor wearing the black Team Canada jacket from the Vancouver Olympics Harper wore almost daily during the campaign (visually reinforcing the link between Conservatives and Canada that the Liberals once owned). Any rink is a familiar surrounding for the small-town and suburban families with hockey-playing children whose votes the Conservatives needed and courted to get their majority. Harper played to that image, speaking casually and colloquially as if he were just talking with another hockey parent and not being interviewed on television.

The Liberals decided Ignatieff should be interviewed in the CBC studio in Toronto on April 19. It can only be described as a terrible decision. In both style and content it felt like just another of the many interviews he had done during his two and a half years as Liberal leader. As well, it was conducted on the anchor's home turf, giving the interviewer an obvious advantage. It was stiff, formal, and offered nothing visually that might engage viewers, particularly when compared to the Layton interview. Ignatieff spent much of the time repeating criticisms of Harper and his government and then was forced into a lengthy exchange about coalitions and what he would do if faced with the opportunity of forming a government. For viewers who care about the details of constitutional matters, it might have been a strong performance. But for the majority of the news audience, the content of the interview gave credence to everything Harper had been claiming on the campaign trail about the possibility of a coalition and the Liberal leader's inconsistent position in relation to it. Ignatieff's stiff and professorial demeanour made for poor television, and it visually reinforced Conservative claims that he simply wasn't an ordinary guy. That Ignatieff spent barely any time explaining to viewers how his government would differ in policy from the Conservatives contributed to his communication problems.[3]

CTV and Global covered issues and party platforms within the body of leaders' tour stories. CBC, with more time in the hour-long *National*, used the same "Reality Check" feature it has employed in past campaigns, trying to fact check or explain comments and policy announcements from the campaign trail. Of the fifteen Reality Checks during the campaign, four focused on the Conservatives, four on the Liberals, and three on the NDP, mostly related to party policies. The CBC also used Reality Checks to compare party positions on job creation and support for seniors. On May 1, the night before voting, the CBC compared each party's approach to helping people care for aging parents and to helping the unemployed. It was an example of the extent to which the networks treated party policies as an afterthought to the regular campaign trail coverage.

As always, the horse race and opinion polls played a major role in television coverage, particularly in the campaign's final week. In recent campaigns the CBC has not commissioned its own polls, unlike its two competitors, but CBC stories and its expert panels spent a great deal of time talking about poll results. Indeed, "the state of the polls" framed some of the discussion in all seven editions of its At Issue election panels and played a large role in newscast reporting of the Bloc campaign. CTV (and the *Globe and Mail*) had Nanos Research as its polling partner, regularly using president Nik Nanos to report results, while Global worked with Ipsos-Reid and CEO Darryl Bricker. Global reported poll results in the campaign's early days, and both Global and CTV featured post-debate poll results. That was perhaps the first sign that the election was going to come down to a Conservative-NDP race. Global reported 42 percent of respondents thought Harper had won the English-language debate, while 25 percent named Layton and only 13 percent named Ignatieff.

Further bad news for the Liberals came as only 11 percent of respondents picked Ignatieff as the leader with whom they would most like to have a coffee or beer (a proxy question for gauging character and likability). The influence of Layton's personality in the NDP's ultimate success first emerged here as 55 percent selected him while 24 percent named Harper. For much of the rest of the campaign the networks concentrated on the horse race in their poll reporting, including almost nightly reporting of tracking polls on CTV and Global in the campaign's last week.

Two others elements of the election on television deserve mention. First, the CBC began the campaign by introducing an interactive game, Vote Compass, on its news website that invited Canadians to log in and answer thirty policy-related questions. The game would assess the responses and suggest which party's policies were closest to the participant's views. The public broadcaster heavily promoted the feature on radio and television, which also attracted a range of critics who variously claimed the questions and/or answers were weighted to make the Liberal party the default choice for most players. That didn't slow down public interest, as by April 16 CBC reported on *The National* that the game had been played almost 1.5 million times, reaching almost 2 million by May 2. Despite the critics, it clearly captured public imagination and stood out as an engaging and worthwhile innovation in a campaign in which innovative coverage was hard to find.

The second element had numbers that didn't come close to Vote Compass. After months of hype about the creation of "Fox News North" and right-wing television coming to Canada, Quebecor launched its SunTV all-news channel in mid-campaign on April 18. As Canadian Press reported on April 27, Sun's flagship evening show had 31,000 viewers for its premiere, but that soon fell to under 20,000, with fewer than 4,000 viewers in some time periods. Any new television venture takes time to try to build an audience, and with those numbers Sun had no impact on this campaign. If anything, a last-weekend attempt by Sun to reverse NDP momentum by broadcasting a sixteen-year-old story about Jack Layton being found by police but not charged in a massage parlour and suspected bawdy house, produced as much if not more debate about the ethics of Sun media's reporting standards as about Layton's personal ethics.

In many respects this review of how television covered the 2011 campaign could have been written in 2004, 2006, or 2008. Little has changed in how television covers federal elections in Canada. While it still dominates as a source of news for the public, it is facing challenges from upstart media that feature instant dissemination of opinions and information and the potential for two-way or multi-way discussions and debates about everything that takes place in a campaign. The 2011 campaign offered the first opportunity to assess how successfully social media is transforming that potential into reality.

TWEET, FRIEND, VOTE: THE CAMPAIGN ON SOCIAL MEDIA

Parties and political hopefuls have become excited by the potential of social media such as Facebook, Twitter, YouTube, and geosocial networking platforms (which allow users to register their location and interact with others based on position) such as FourSquare and Gowalla to mobilize support and to frame campaign issues and perceptions. Tuning in to social media has the potential to give campaigns a better idea of what voters might want or like, and in this respect serves as an adjunct to existing environmental scanning activities. It also gives campaigns a potential means of reaching a greater number of supporters (and thus donors) than ever before. Whether or not the 2011 election was in fact Canada's first social media election is debatable, but one thing is clear — social media were certainly part of many campaigns during this latest federal election. There are many different types of social media, and while all rely on the Internet and, increasingly, on mobile technology, their defining feature is interactivity. Unlike traditional media technologies (print, radio, television, etc.), social media have the capacity to support one-to-one and many-to-many digital conversations. Among the most commonly used social media platforms in Canada are Facebook, YouTube, and Twitter. Canadians are considered world leaders in their use of social media. According to Bryan Segal, Canadian vice-president of comScore, a leading digital media marketing and research firm, "when it comes to Facebook, when it comes to a lot of these web 2.0 tools … Canadians are highly sophisticated." But how sophisticated are their political leaders? In what follows, we provide a brief snapshot of how some of these more popular media were used by politicians and voters alike during the 2011 federal election campaign.

Facebook is the world's most popular social networking site, with more than 500 million users worldwide. The average Facebook user has 130 friends in her network, spends approximately 55 minutes a day within Facebook's network, becomes a fan of 4 new pages each month, posts approximately 25 comments per month, and is a member of 13 groups. According to the popular web traffic measurement site Alexa. com, Facebook is second only to Google as the most visited website by Canadians. Canadians are world leaders in Facebook adoption, with a total penetration of approximately 83 percent of Canadian Internet users.[4] According to Abacus Data, a Canadian market research firm, in 2011 more than 90 percent of Canadians between the ages of eighteen and twenty-nine had a Facebook account, followed by 77 percent of thirty- to forty-four-year-olds and more than 60 percent among Canadians forty-five years and older.[5] This kind of demographic information makes Facebook incredibly attractive to political campaigns. Although Facebook's design makes data collection difficult, we know that it was widely used by parties and individual candidates alike. According to politwitter.com, the Liberal Party had the greatest number of candidates with Facebook pages.[6] It also had the highest number of followers and posts, followed by the NDP, Green, Conservative, Bloc, and Pirate parties respectively.

A survey of the features found on the leaders' Facebook pages show that they largely served as a means of informing people about campaign activities. For example, Jack Layton's page invited "Friends" to attend offline and online rallies and events where they could meet the leader. It was also used to share video and photos of campaign activities. Other campaigns used their sites for similar purposes. Liberal leader Michael Ignatieff's page offered users the greatest opportunity to engage with the leader and with one another. He offered a "Questions" section where users could weigh in on queries posed by his campaign, such as "What does Canada need most to succeed?" Although only two questions were actually posed, it demonstrates some initial innovative thinking by the campaign about the potential of social media. The page also offered a "Discussion" section, which hosted 610 discussion boards on a range of topics. Ignatieff and the Liberals were the only campaign to make use of this feature.

Ignatieff's page also offered an application that was developed for the Liberal Party called "Commit to Vote Liberal." It enabled users to declare their intention of voting Liberal and posting a "digital lawn sign" on their personal page. Here users could choose from a variety of signs emblazoned with a range of messages (e.g. "I am voting for health care," accompanied by the Liberal logo). Once selected, the digital lawn sign would replace the user's existing profile photo. The application also offered the opportunity for the user to create a "vote mob." Users had the option of sending any or all of the people on their friend list the following message: "On May 2nd I'm committing to vote Harper out and Liberals in. I hope you will join me."

In contrast to Ignatieff's page, which had the most features and the highest opportunity for interactivity, Gilles Duceppe's was virtually a shell. It offered no applications, discussion, invitations, photos, or links to other social networking tools. It simply offered the Wikipedia entry on the leader, his life, and his political career. Stephen Harper's page also lacked interactivity. Users could do little more than read some basic information about the leader and follow posts to his wall made by him and his staff. In short, it was little more than another means of broadcast.

According to comScore, Canadians watch more YouTube than anyone in the world. Approximately 71 percent of Canadian Internet users, or 17.6 million people, visit YouTube every month.[7] Each of the five main parties has its own YouTube channel. Here users have the opportunity to view, comment on, and share videos uploaded by the parties. They also have the option of becoming a subscriber of the channel. In most cases the videos found on these channels have are similar to the more traditional broadcast campaign advertisements. They serve as additional means of advertising and communicating endorsements with the public.

More interesting and innovative use of video did not come from the party campaigns themselves, but from citizens. Here we saw a number of viral videos, including those of vote mobs — videos where participants break into a choreographed dance, often urging people, particularly youth, to vote. Other viral videos were more satirical in nature, such as those found on the site shitharperdid.ca. The site received 1.5 million hits on its first day alone.

Canadians are also among the world's most active Twitter users: comScore reports that 13.7 percent of Canadians use the micro-blogging site every day (compared to 11.3 percent of Americans). In comparison with other social networking sites, Twitter received the highest level of media attention during the campaign as it was widely used by media, candidates, and voters alike. Not surprisingly, therefore, increasing numbers of federal politicians are registering Twitter accounts and experimenting with Twitter as a tool to engage citizens, to build their own profiles, and to enhance the digital presence of their parties. According to politwitter.ca, 193 MPs and 479 of the candidates running for office used Twitter at the time the election was called. Its data show a total of 960,521 tweets about the election during the campaign — an average of 13,528 per day. Of these 23,049, or 2.4 percent, were contributed by candidates for office.

An interesting new campaign use of social media involved geosocial networking. Users of FourSquare were able to log in to the service, register their location, and participate in GeoPollster. Billed by the *National Post* (FourSquare's project partner) as "part real-world election game, part mobile polling experiment," this application prompted users to identify their political preferences in the event of an imminent election and offered them the opportunity to share their check-in vote with others on Twitter. Check-in votes would represent the influence of the main parties in various social venues such as coffee shops, pubs, or university residences, as well as cities and provinces. As check-in data increased in volume, GeoPollster would map voter preferences of users to produce a visual representation of Canada's political landscape. Although by no means scientific, the GeoPollster experiment offered an innovative attempt to model political interest and voter preference on the basis of aggregated social data.

It's clear that social media were a factor in the party campaigns and, as we discuss further below, influenced news reporting during the election. Yet to be truly "Canada's First Social Media Election," as it was hailed by the *Hill Times*, citizens must also have not only used social networking in significant numbers, but used it in a way that influenced the course and outcome of the campaign. Gauging the reach and significance of Facebook, YouTube, or Twitter use by Canadian voters during the election is difficult. A tool we used to attempt to do so was Viralheat.[8] It collects data from a range of social media sites and blogs based on a string of provided search terms. Data were collected through creating separate profiles for the Conservative, Liberal, New Democratic, Bloc Québécois, and Green parties. Each profile contained a multitude of search strings including the name of the party's leader as well as synonyms. For example, the profile for the Conservative Party included Conservative Party of Canada, CPC, Stephen Harper, and Tories in its search string. Terms that might have caused confusion or inaccurate results were excluded from the search string. For example, CPC is the acronym for a range of other organizations, such as the Canadian Police College. As much as possible, Viralheat was instructed not to pull data regarding such non-related institutions. Using these terms, it was possible to compose a snapshot of the "chatter" occurring around the election. It should, however, be reinforced that the data gathered highlights only a portion of the online discussion by focusing on the names of parties and leaders. It doesn't capture all mentions and discussions around the election in general.

Viralheat enables researchers to measure and compare how frequently search terms are mentioned, and with coder training can provide measurements of user sentiment. For example, it would allow us to know which federal leader was mentioned most often and whether he was mentioned positively or negatively. Looking at the measurement of mentions alone, it is clear that the federal election was a significant topic of conversation in the social media sphere. Mentions of the parties and leaders averaged approximately 11,000 per day in the weeks following the election call and peaked around 15,000 per day on April 30/May 1 leading up to the May 2 election day. Interestingly, social media activity dropped off significantly in the days after the election, remaining in the 500 to 2,000 range in the month following the election.

Social media activity during the campaign followed a pattern very similar to television coverage. The three main parties and leaders consistently received greater mentions than the Green Party or the Bloc, which peaked around 2,500 and 2,000, respectively, immediately following election day. While the Greens and Bloc didn't generate a lot of mentions in the social media sphere, the NDP was a popular topic of conversation. It dominated the other parties in terms of the number of mentions received both during the election and in the weeks following. The most activity can be seen starting on April 30 with mentions nearing the 10,000 mark. This follows reports from mainstream media on April 29 indicating that the Liberals and Conservatives had dropped in the polls while the NDP had gained. This spike in activity lasted through election day to May 4.

Looking at the various social media tools measured by Viralheat (Facebook pages, YouTube, Google Buzz, and the real time web, which includes blogs), it is apparent that some tools are more conducive to chatter and frequent activity than others. Twitter was by far the dominant source of activity both during the campaign and in the weeks following. Using just the leaders' names in a Viralheat search string in the twelve hours before the polls closed on election day produced a result that isn't dissimilar from the entire campaign in terms of identifying where activity is taking place. During this short time there were more than 7,800 mentions of the leaders on Twitter, twenty-six mentions on publicly accessible Facebook pages, 315 real time web and blog URLs identified, along with fifty-nine videos identified with a total of 2,757 views. Twitter's dominance is not surprising given that its platform is built on conversation and the real-time sharing of information, both of which lend themselves well to ongoing events with frequent changes in content and focus. Posts to a Facebook page or a blog, by comparison, often remain long after they have been created for users to comment on or view. In a sense they are simply reincarnations of earlier forms of social media, notably online discussion boards. Twitter, on the other hand, enables a faster pace for discourse construction, and without effective tracking software it is difficult to capture and archive the full range of tweets, making parts of a conversation easy to miss.

THE MAINSTREAM MEETS SOCIAL MEDIA

The final part of this assessment of the media and the campaign considers how the mainstream media covered the role played by social media.[9]

Social networking sites such as Facebook and Twitter create opportunities for organizations and individuals to engage in two-way communication. Some scholars view interactive communication as more ethical: it's deliberative, involves taking the needs or interests of others into account, and is believed to lead to the formation of more durable relationships.[10] Yet, at the same time, engaging others in a dialogue can be messy and occasionally unpredictable. For political actors, communicating directly with supporters and constituents also means opening yourself to critics and other onlookers, such as journalists and opponents. This potential loss of control over the content of conversations is an issue of concern for all who operate with strategic goals and interests. In other words, social media "holds promise and peril" for politicians.[11]

It is for this latter reason that many organizations (including established political parties) often try to utilize social technologies not to generate deliberative discourse, but as tools to command and control the conversations that affect and involve them. We were therefore interested in exploring to what extent media coverage about the role of social networking sites in the election conformed to an instrumentalist or deliberative/conversational paradigm: did it discuss how Facebook, Twitter, and other social media could be used to create or sustain relationships that might yield more citizen engagement in politics? Or was it framed as merely another instrument in a politician's PR toolbox to be used only to persuade voters and win the election?

Table 1: Issue Themes in Election News Coverage of Social Networking (%)

Impact on Voter Behaviour	19.2
Democratization	16.4
Tools and Tactics	16.4
Surveillance/Intelligence Gathering	12.3
Engagement	9.6
Risk	8.2
Other	17.8
TOTAL	N=73

As shown in Table 1, the election news coverage of social media addressed a diversity of themes. Almost 20 percent of the coverage focused on the extent to which social networking tools could improve voter turnout, particularly among youth who are more regular users of Facebook, Twitter, and YouTube but who vote in low numbers. Most of the time, and typically in stories written by full-time reporters, the coverage addressed the impact of social media on voter turnout in positive terms. For example, speaking to the Sarnia *Observer* in late March, Tim van Bodegom, a candidate seeking a Green Party nomination, remarked, "When we've got turnouts as low as we have in past federal elections, it would really be nice to see more people actively involved. And if that means diving into Twitter and Facebook and that sort of thing, then yes … I certainly don't want to muddy the waters with 140 characters of what I had for breakfast. Although, it's important to note that what I have for breakfast is organic and fair trade."[12] There were other times, however, when the argument about a positive impact of social media on voter behaviour was challenged. In a guest column published in the *National Post*, communications consultant Patrick Thorburn argued,

"Whoever tweets the best, or gets the most 'Likes' on their Facebook page will not necessarily win the election." While social media may have a role to play, Thorburn claimed, traditional advertising was likely to do the heavy lifting in terms of influencing the election outcome.[13] A front-page *Hamilton Spectator* report offered a similar analysis, citing research that concluded, "Social media isn't as popular with seniors, who are the most likely to vote."[14]

Many social media consultants and academics argue that social platforms make the conversations we have about issues of public importance more equal because they enable individuals to be more than just passive recipients of content produced for a mass audience. They also allow them to produce, share, and distribute their ideas with others. Linked to the generally optimistic tone of the voter impact theme, the coverage also focused strongly on the theme of democratization. In 16 percent of the stories examined, social media were talked about as a democratizing technology that would provide a broader range of actors with opportunities to contribute to the conversation Canadians were having about the election. Twitter, Facebook, YouTube, and blogs were framed as vehicles that would reduce the gap between producers and consumers of content and thus upset the traditional balance of power between those who set the media agenda and those who follow it. When news broke that Elections Canada would attempt to impose an embargo on tweeting election night results, Twitter was described by NYU journalism professor and media commentator Jay Rosen as the "ideal system for organizing a protest to this law."[15] Linking the Canadian situation to pro-democracy movements in North Africa and the Middle East, a Postmedia report concluded it was "only a matter of time before the Twitterverse ... started discussing ways to rebel. This is, after all ... occurring in a world where Twitter helped Egyptian protesters organize their efforts to overthrow the regime of Egyptian President Hosni Mubarak."[16]

The coverage talked about the range of social media tools and tactics being deployed by parties and candidates, and to a lesser extent by activists and voters. Focusing on Twitter, social media consultant Mark Blevis wrote in the *Ottawa Citizen*, "Twitter will play an important role in communicating and canvassing the public and co-ordinating volunteers. Used well, it could help win a riding or two … The most successful campaigns will benefit from integrating traditional and digital tactics in a single campaign core."[17] Stories that focused on the national campaign discussed the NDP's popular iPhone app (a tool later copied by the Green Party), the Conservatives' networking site *www.torynation.ca*, the Liberal Party's novel use of the web to launch its policy platform, and the ways in which the Green Party drove the Twitter conversation with its "#emayin" hashtag on the day its leader Elizabeth May was excluded from the leadership debate. For the most part the coverage did not suggest that social media would, themselves, tip the scales of victory for any one candidate or party, but rather that they would help "enhance traditional networking, such as door knocking and pavement pounding."[18] The tone of coverage tended to be more promotional and service-oriented than analytical, offering readers tips on ways of keeping up with the election, staying connected to the campaigns, and where to vote, rather than deep analyses that might offer insight into how different tools were affecting campaign decision-making or influencing outreach strategies.

The focus on tools and tactics was not all positive, however. Slightly more than 12 percent of coverage of social networking focused on how new technologies were being used by the political parties for surveillance, monitoring, and intelligence-gathering. A feature segment on *The National* examined "the dark side of Twitter," and explored other examples of how social media were being "manipulated" on the campaign trail. Interviews with political strategists and social media consultants confirmed a "massive business behind the social media war."[19] The story emphasized the vast amounts of money being spent by the parties hiring consultants who, behind the scenes, attempted to influence voter behaviour through social media sites. CBC News online also published a story on a study by University of Indiana researchers that was tracking "abusive activity" on Twitter in order to "document and reveal smear campaigns and the spreading of misinformation."[20] Although most of the examples from both stories pointed more to mischief by exuberant supporters than organized party efforts, they usefully illustrated not only the degree to which social networking is altering the electoral landscape but also how it remains almost entirely unregulated, offering tremendous opportunities for engaging in election period black ops.

The ability to engage in nefarious social media activity relies in part on the built-in surveillance capabilities of modern communications technology, which don't always reveal anti-democratic goals or practices. Social networking sites utilize sophisticated software programs that can be customized to enable users to monitor and track user content. For market researchers this can produce a gold mine of data that enables businesses and others to target effectively their marketing activities. For political analysts they can yield equally valuable intelligence about the sentiments and political interests and persuasions of voters. In some cases this intelligence can be used to adjust an organization's own position to align better with the values and viewpoints of their stakeholders. There was no evidence, or at least reporting, of this kind of activity during the election. In other cases, it is used to develop persuasive strategies that attempt to change the mindsets of others. A Postmedia story noted how the federal political parties would be "all a-Twitter identifying voters and monitoring opinions,"[21] while the *Globe and Mail* explained how "parties with the proper tracking software" would be capable of obtaining from social media sites "real-time feedback on the campaign to find out what's working and what isn't."[22] A feature article published by *The Hill Times* went into more detail, documenting how campaign teams were using social networking sites such as Twitter to observe what journalists were saying publicly. Since reporters occasionally "let their guard down on Twitter," social networking sites could provide campaigns with valuable evidence to challenge reporters who profess to cover the election neutrally.[23]

Was this Canada's first social media election? To varying degrees the campaigns did make use of Facebook, Twitter, and YouTube. The traditional news media reported and followed its use and, as the Viralheat analyses demonstrated, there was a fairly active group of citizens who were engaged in conversations online about the election. Nevertheless, despite the active and engaged nature of social media discourse about the election, participants were small in number overall and were most likely already committed partisans or voters who would have been more likely to cast ballots whether the technology existed or not. However, it is clear that social media is now recognized as a legitimate component of election campaigns and will certainly figure more prominently in the future. We are therefore confident in concluding that social media did not play as important a role in terms of influencing the results of the election as traditional media did, notably television. It did, however, influence the tenor and tone of the media coverage and became part of the election narrative.

CONCLUSIONS

The complaint is often made that television coverage of election campaigns is superficial. It concentrates on incidents or events, such as gaffes by leaders and parties, and the horse race to the exclusion of party policies and any examination of the complexity of the issues confronting the country. That was certainly true of the vast majority of newscast content on the three English-language networks in this election, and these events were amplified in the social mediascape. For users of social media sites, this had the impact of appearing to make these incidents more significant than they really were to the vast majority of voters. As for the television coverage itself, there was almost no talk of the challenges of financing health care into the future, the debate about climate change, the coming infrastructure crisis, or the fact that Canada for the first time in its history has troops fighting in two concurrent wars, among a host of other important public policy issues. Yet stories away from the leaders' tours did often catch Canadians' anxiety about the economy and their concern about issues that weren't on the news yet appeared to influence how they voted on May 2.

At the same time, there is no question that the leaders' tours are vitally important for the parties that know how to use the media and television. The Conservatives turned the media on Harper's tour into accomplices, using party-designed images to drive home the Conservative leader's message nightly to Canadians about the links between stability, the economy, and a majority government, all the while leaving reporters thinking they were telling stories that would damage Harper's prospects of winning a majority. The NDP also benefited from television images, as Layton's performance in both debates set him apart from the other leaders, attracting interest from Quebec voters. They liked what they saw, and within a week polls showed NDP support climbing in Quebec. That led to tougher questions from reporters about the NDP platform, but, particularly in the final week, the newscast visuals offered compelling, action-oriented images of crowd enthusiasm that helped build a sense of momentum and inevitability ultimately producing their surprising second-place finish. It was the Liberals who suffered from their apparent inability to understand the power of television. The Liberals became captives of the media on their leader's tour, listening as reporters recounted that their campaign and leader were doing well, even in the absence of any external corroboration. In the final week, campaign coverage centred on speculating about how poorly the Liberals would do and whether it would cost Ignatieff his leadership. In the end, after leading the Liberals to a historic defeat and losing his own Toronto seat, Ignatieff resigned as party leader the day after the election and almost immediately accepted a position at the University of Toronto. Although surely not by design, in a curious way this actually validated the very message of the Conservative attack ads.

The focus on the leaders' tour by the television networks certainly benefits political parties, but it also shows how little value comes from the tour coverage for viewers. It is long past time for television to reconsider how it covers election campaigns. Reporters and television crews can meet leaders when they visit communities, but there is no value in flying around with them for thirty-six days. As long as the networks still do that, they are placing the interests of the people they cover well ahead of the interests of their audiences.

The tension and relationship between mainstream media and social media was also apparent in this election. It is clear that older media such as television still play an important role and are not taken lightly by campaigns. However, the chatter in the social media sphere also warrants attention. There are active and ongoing conversations taking place among an increasing number of Canadians, particularly partisans and committed voters. Failing to acknowledge and be part of such digital conversations is not an option for political campaigns today. In many ways, this recent election was Canada's first *experimental* social media election. The parties did not invest tremendous resources into organizing voters. Instead, both parties and candidates tended to ignore the "social" part of social media, using Facebook, Twitter, and YouTube instead as yet another way of distributing information to voters rather than taking the more risky but potentially fruitful route of opening up two-way debate about policies and issues. A generous interpretation might suggest this is simply a sign of nervousness — instead of innovating, the parties are playing things safe for the most part until they can develop a better understanding of possibilities for future use. That level of risk avoidance and reluctance is equally true for the mainstream. Just as they share their enthusiasm for the leaders' tours with the political parties, the networks also share the largely one-way approach to social media. For the mainstream media, social media offer another way of delivering news and information to audiences, but there is little evidence that news organizations, like the parties, are much interested in opening themselves up to the challenges and criticism that two-way social media debate can produce.

The 2011 election broke the cycle of federal elections approximately every two years. The next campaign will be in 2015, and the pace of change in both mainstream and social media makes it impossible to predict which tools the parties will use and how they will use them. It is also difficult to know how the public and the traditional media will participate in and cover that campaign. Yet, it also seems hard to avoid the conclusion that the mainstream media have to change how they cover campaigns and must do a better job of integrating the two-way nature of new media into their campaign activities. That is equally true for the parties. If politicians and the news media want to retain their traditional pre-eminent roles in shaping the debates Canadians have about politics and those who seek the highest office, they will need to show a clearer commitment to making bold and innovative decisions.

NOTES

1. Patricia Aufderheide and Jessica Clark, Public Media 2.0: Dynamic, engaged publics. 2009:1. *http://dspace.wrlc.org/bitstream/1961/4947/1/whitepaper.pdf*
2. Clay Shirky, "How Television Ratings Portend the Death of Mass Media." October 14, 1999. *www.shirky.com/writings/television_ratings.html.*
3. Demonstrating the difference a setting can make, Ignatieff gave a much more relaxed (although shorter) interview on Global with Dawna Friesen while walking in a park in Thunder Bay on April 25. Global ran its three leader interviews on consecutive evenings starting with Harper on April 24, while CTV spread the interviews out over two weeks, with Layton on April 14, Ignatieff on April 20, and Harper on April 27. That approach gave Harper a distinct advantage, as he was the only leader interviewed in the campaign's final week. Arguably, the CTV interview placed Layton at a disadvantage. Its timing so early in the campaign seemed to assume he wouldn't be a player in the final outcome as it took place right after the debates and before his campaign had gathered momentum.
4. *www.digitaljournal.com/article/301903#ixzz1C4omw8f1.*
5. *http://abacusdata.ca/2011/01/13/facebook-is-changing-the-way-canadians-communicate/.*
6. Politwitter is a non-partisan site that tracks and aggregates data regarding the use of social media, Twitter in particular, by Canadian politicians and political candidates. It also allows you to follow and read the tweets posted by both federal and provincial legislators.
7. *http://blogs.marketwatch.com/canada/2011/01/26/canadians-youtube-twitter-facebook-usage-surpasses-americas/.*
8. *www.viralheat.com.*
9. In examining how they did so, we focused on a representative sample of forty newspaper, web, and television reports that were published or broadcast between March 25 and May 5, 2011. Approximately half of the newspaper articles we examined were published in several other papers that are part of the small number of media chains that comprise the Canadian news landscape. The news sample included coverage from national, regional, and local media. Sample items were selected for analysis using the Factiva, Lexis-Nexis, and Canadian Newsstand databases, using a keyword search string that included references to the following terms: Twitter (or Facebook or YouTube or blogs) and election, or "Social Media Election." Among the forty news items we examined, thirty-four were written by full-time reporters, two by regular columnists or freelancers, and four were columns published by experts not employed by the news organization (three were by communication consultants and one by an academic).
10. See, for example, Josh Greenberg and Maggie MacAulay, "NPO 2.0: Exploring the Web Presence of Environmental Nonprofit Organizations in Canada," *Global Media Journal* — Canadian Edition, 2(1) (2009): 63–88.
11. *http://thecaucus.blogs.nytimes.com/2011/06/02/for-politicians-social-media-holds-promise-and-peril/.*

12. "Candidates Embrace Social Media; Pat Davidson Slow to Join 'Twitter Nation.'" *The Observer*, March 29, 2011.

13. "This Is Not the 'Social Media' Election," *National Post*, April 1, 2011, A14.

14. "All A-Twitter Over Election," *Hamilton Spectator*, April 2, 2011, A1.

15. "Protest 'Absurd' Law Barring Election Night Tweeting: American Commentator," *National Post*, April 21, 2011.

16. "Twitter Troops Rally Against Law; Digital Rebellion Looms to Defy Election-Night Results-Sharing," *Edmonton Journal*, April 22, 2011, A5.

17. "This Is Not the 'Twitter Election,'" *Ottawa Citizen*, March 29, 2011, A13.

18. "Social Networking Plays Key Role for Federal Candidates," *Nanaimo Daily News*, March 31, 2011, A3.

19. "Online Election Wars: The Social Media Campaign," *The National*, CBC Television, April 6, 2011.

20. "Project Takes Aim at Election 'Astroturfing.'" CBC News Online, 26 April 2011.

21. "They'll Be Tweeting All the Way to the Polls," *Windsor Star*, March 25, 2011, A7.

22. "Canada's First Social Media Election Clicks On," *Globe and Mail*, March 28, 2011, A4.

23. "Twitter New, Influential, but Political Parties Not Using its Fullest Potential," *The Hill Times*, April 18, 2011.

CHAPTER 10

Ideology and Discipline in the Conservative Party of Canada
James Farney | Jonathan Malloy

This chapter examines the nature of the party that has governed Canada since 2006. Under Stephen Harper, the Conservative Party has articulated a conservative vision while often implementing policies that run against long held conservative beliefs. This is the opposite of the long-standing Liberal strategy of "campaigning from the left and governing from the right." There are many possible explanations for the choice by the Harper Conservatives to pursue a largely centrist path: parliamentary minorities, a commitment to winning office above all else, the nature of coalition politics, or the moderate political beliefs of Canadians. We argue that a crucial piece of the puzzle is the way in which Harper consciously knit back together a conservative coalition in Canada with connections to the Tory past of Diefenbaker and Stanfield as well as the populist Reform Party ideology in which Harper began his political career[1] and which, too often, critics continue to see defining his vision. However, this does not mean the post-2003 Conservative Party is merely a restoration of the Progressive Conservative Party. Rather, the Conservative Party should be understood as an amalgam of the two traditions that, in combining them, has created something distinctively new in Canadian politics and government.

THE PUZZLE OF THE CONSERVATIVE PARTY OF CANADA

A key question in Canadian politics is the extent to which the Conservative Party of Canada (CPC), formed in 2003, is simply a restoration of the

pre-1993 Progressive Conservative (PC) party as opposed to a significantly or even fundamentally different political party. For some, the CPC
is "essentially the same" as the PCs;[2] for others, it puts "at least some of
the old pieces back together."[3] Yet the Conservative Party under its one
and only leader so far, Stephen Harper, also displays distinct differences
from its predecessors, most notably an extraordinary discipline in both
campaigning and governing, a different regional basis of support, and
a more professionalized party organization. Less clear is the role of ideology in the new party; there is evidence of traditional PC centre-right
moderation, but also flashes of a harder ideological core.

The CPC is clearly far more disciplined than its predecessors. The
Progressive Conservative Party of Canada was long plagued by what
Perlin infamously called "the Tory Syndrome" of infighting, parochi-
alism, and undermining of leaders.[4] Leaders such as Robert Stanfield
and Joe Clark found it difficult to control their parliamentary caucuses,
much less the larger party. In contrast, the Reform Party was, despite its
grassroots image, tightly controlled by its founder and leader Preston
Manning. However, even Manning had to deal with significant organized opposition in his efforts to transform the Reform Party into the
Canadian Alliance.[5] His successor, Stockwell Day, was less successful
at controlling the Canadian Alliance, in part because of discontented
Manning loyalists in that party.

The post-2003 Conservative Party under Harper is much closer to
the Manning/Reform model of top-down control than the sprawling and
decentralized PCs. This is partly structural; while the CPC is built on the
PC principle of equality of electoral district associations, rather than a
single mass membership like Reform, it follows other Reform practices
such as centralized membership lists and fundraising, without youth
wings or other subgroups. This all provides greater leverage for leaders
and the national office. But control extends beyond party structures.
CPC parliamentary caucuses are highly disciplined even by normal
Canadian standards[6]; mavericks and dissenters are rare and, in the
case of Garth Turner or Helena Guergis, vulnerable to not only caucus
expulsion but denial of re-nomination as Tory candidates. (In contrast,
attempts in 2009 by one Calgary association to deny nomination to a

sitting MP loyal to Harper were overruled by the central party.) While this control and discipline may be partly explained by the exigencies of minority government, it remains a far cry from the open factionalism of the Tory Syndrome.

Much of the "Tory Syndrome" of the 1960s and 1970s was rooted in struggles over leadership which were sometimes, though not always, also struggles between moderate Red and more right-wing Blue Tories for ideological primacy within the party. But even more dangerous were regional schisms that emerged under Mulroney's leadership. As Johnson has argued,[7] these schisms were the result of the traditional Conservative pattern of winning majority governments with the support of an "ends against the middle" coalition of disaffected Westerners and Quebecers. Inherently unstable, the implosion of the Mulroney coalition in 1993 was just the last in a long parade of such coalitions breaking down. In turn, neither Reform nor the Canadian Alliance had much luck at breaking into Central Canada. Initially — perhaps until after the 2006 election — it seems that the dominant strategy pursued by the new party was one of seeking to add Quebec to a Western base as the PCs had before. The 2008 and 2011 elections have seen a new strategy, one focused on winning seats in Ontario (especially Ontario outside of Toronto), reaching out to ethnic and immigrant communities, and ameliorating the traditional Liberal advantage amongst Roman Catholics. It is on this basis that it has succeeded in winning a majority government. While Conservatives have done well historically in Ontario provincial elections, the alliance between Ontario and Western Canada is unprecedented as a base for a Conservative government and suggests a more stable future for the party than it has heretofore enjoyed.

This change in electoral base and the adherence to a newly rigorous party discipline have been linked by a change in the style of party organization. Even in its heyday, the PCs had a remarkably weak and ephemeral central organization.[8] Following the classic Canadian model, little effort was made to reach out to individual members between elections and — except when an election was expected — little by way of enhanced party organization was created. From Diefenbaker onward, there was a national party office, but it was a very weak organization bypassed, even as an instrument, by the party leader. Rather, the party operated through informal networks of local notables, provincial chieftains, and the leader's kitchen cabinet. The new party has — in the fashion of Reform — crafted a central organization that provides the leader with a powerful tool. To date completely loyal to Harper, the staff resources and fundraising machine embodied in this organization have provided the instrument by which discipline can be ensured in policy discussions, campaign strategy, and even local nomination meetings.

The role of ideology in the Conservative Party of Canada is more difficult to assess. Stephen Harper's own writings and speeches prior to assuming office seem to signify a strong libertarian and decentralizing vision for Canada. Yet as we will see below, it is more difficult to document a consistent ideological vision for the Conservative Party. As prime minister, Harper has overseen a considerable growth in the size, personnel, and spending of the federal government, and sent mixed messages on social conservative issues, for example by opposing international development funding for abortion, yet pledging not to reopen the debate about Canadian abortion laws. We suggest in this chapter that the Conservative Party of Canada is somewhat more ideologically cohesive than its Progressive Conservative predecessor. But much of this apparent cohesion may be the product of its intense discipline, reflecting a larger strategy of winning office and overcoming the Tory Syndrome once and for all.

CANADIAN ALLIANCE AND PROGRESSIVE CONSERVATIVE: RELUCTANT PARENTS OF A PRODUCTIVE HYBRID

Brian Mulroney's commanding 1984 and 1988 election victories, coming at the end of the third party system,[9] embodied both the features of all governing parties during the post-war period and the specific features that made Conservative governments during that period inherently unstable. Mulroney made multiple policy promises, especially to address constitutional concerns emanating from Quebec and the West, reduce government intervention in the economy, balance the federal budget, and implement free trade with the United States, although he was successful only on the final item on his agenda. Mulroney's election victories were based on strong support from Western Canada and Quebec, as was the previous Conservative majority elected under John Diefenbaker in 1958. These were inherently unstable arrangements, for they bound together two groups dissatisfied with their place in the Canadian federation whose demands pulled the party in different directions. This "coalition of the unhappy"[10] meant that the Tories could win enough support to push the Liberals out of office when regional tensions were running high, but had great difficulty finding common ground to sustain this unstable arrangement — a problem exacerbated by the "Tory Syndrome" of being a poorly disciplined party, occasionally in ideological discord. The collapse of the PCs in 1993 represented the nadir of this instability, as Mulroney's coalition sundered into three parts — Quebec nationalists in the Bloc Quebecois, Western populists in the Reform party, and the remnants of the PC party itself. The challenge facing all right-wing party leaders since then — one only Harper has successfully met — has been how to knit these fractious groups back together in such a way as to win government.

The most important of these efforts was by Preston Manning. The Reform Party is often treated as a classic protest or third party,[11] but its leaders believed that it could win office by articulating the mix of conservatism and populism that its activists believed in. It was not that its ideology needed to be moderated, they believed, but that the right organizational form and slogans would let it reach out to voters across the country.[12] By the 1997 election, however, this strategy seemed to have only ensured continued Liberal governments as vote splitting between Reform and the PCs meant neither party was a serious contender for office. Manning attempted to change this through the United Alternative initiative that eventually became the Canadian Alliance, but it failed in its chief objective to attract federal PCs to the new party, and Manning lost the new party's leadership race to Stockwell Day. A good part of Day's appeal was that he seemed more electable than Manning, and especially more appealing in Ontario. At the same time, Day promised many in the party — especially religiously motivated activists and social conservatives — that he would ensure that their desires would not be watered down as they had been under Manning. But in an election that quickly followed his selection as leader, he proved less than appealing to the public, gaffe-prone, and with a tendency to wear his religious beliefs on his sleeve to an extent most saw as a liability for a Canadian politician.[13] The expected breakthrough in Ontario did not happen and the PCs, under the leadership of Joe Clark, enjoyed something of a resurgence. Perhaps the most lasting legacy of the transition from the Manning-led Reform Party to the Day-led Canadian Alliance was that the Alliance was far less of a populist enterprise than Reform had been.[14] Henceforth, the ideological spectrum Canadian conservatives would be placing themselves on would run from more to less conservative, rather than being two-dimensional — running from more to less conservative and more to less populist.

Stephen Harper, even more than Day, had his roots deep in the Reform tradition. Although he had first become involved in politics as a PC staffer, he had risen to prominence as one of the brightest thinkers and speakers of the nascent Reform Party. He was unquestionably committed to free-market economics and to populist institutional reforms and was widely seen as the second figure in the party, behind Manning, from the party's early days until his decision in January of 1997 to resign his seat in the Commons. After his resignation, he became Vice-President (and later President) of the National Citizens Coalition, a conservative lobby group and think-tank.[15] No Canadian prime minister since Pierre Trudeau has left such an intellectual trail prior to assuming office — either in his own writings or through his long-time collaboration with academic and campaign manager Tom Flanagan. Writing under the National Citizens Coalition umbrella or with various co-writers including Flanagan, Harper put forward a number of ideas and positions in this period which have been subsequently cited, usually by opponents, as evidence of his true ideological colours. Many of these have focused on federalism and provincial rights, such as Harper's attack on the 1996 Calgary Declaration approved by the nine English-Canadian premiers as an appeasement of separatism, and his signature on the 2001 "firewall" letter that advocated a maximization of provincial powers for Alberta including withdrawal from the Canada Pension Plan and the provisions of the Canada Health Act. Running for the Canadian Alliance leadership in 2003, Harper gave a speech titled "Federalism and all Canadians" that emphasized "a strict division" between federal and provincial powers and respect for provincial autonomy as the solution for Quebec separatism.[16]

On the matter of uniting the right, Harper argued, in a 1996 article co-written with Tom Flanagan and alluding to the Three Sisters mountain near Banff, that "Canadian conservatism ... is a family of three sisters fated to perish in isolation unless they descend from the mountain tops and embrace more realistic expectations."[17] The three sisters were Prairie populists, Ontario and Atlantic moderate conservatives, and Quebecers who opposed separatism but advocated strong provincial autonomy. Harper and Flanagan argued that these "fragments of Canadian conservatism must recognize that each represents an authentic aspect of a larger conservative philosophy."[18] The "three sisters" vision seems at times incompatible with this single ideological core. But Flanagan argues that Harper's plan comprised a "minimum connected winning coalition" that, rather than trying to be all things to all people in the style of Mulroney, sought a more discrete and focused coalition that maintained internal balance and compatibility.[19]

Harper's accession to the Canadian Alliance leadership was paralleled by Joe Clark's resignation as Progressive Conservative leader and his replacement in June 2003 by Peter MacKay. Though MacKay made a guarantee to a rival that he would not seek a merger with the Canadian Alliance, he soon initiated such talks with Harper, and by October 2003 the two agreed to unite their parties. The terms of the merger largely favoured the Progressive Conservatives, starting with the retention of the Conservative name, a weighting of party structures in favour of individual ridings rather than a single mass membership, and a benign set of party principles drawn more from the PC centrism than Reform populism, all building the sense of restoration and the healing of long-open wounds. Nearly all major figures from both parties endorsed the merger, most with seeming enthusiasm, the most notable exception being Joe Clark and a few of his loyalists who refused to join the new party.[20] And while the subsequent leadership race offered reasonably distinct choices between Harper as former Alliance leader, Belinda Stronach as the choice of many PCs, and Tony Clement as a provincial Progressive Conservative and long-time advocate of merging the two parties, Harper's relatively easy victory over both gave a further sense of restoration and a healing of old wounds.

The 2004 election offered a tantalizing opportunity for the new party, given the damaging revelations of the sponsorship scandal for the Liberal Party, already weakened by its own internal battles. But despite moments during the campaign when the Conservatives seemed to have overtaken the Liberals, they were unable to overcome both Liberal attack ads portraying Harper as Canada's George W. Bush and a set of serious gaffes by Conservative candidates and the central office that suggested the comparison might hold water. The Conservatives focused more on Liberal ills and less on their own platform, which was vague and promised both tax cuts and greater spending, especially on health care.[21] This seeming incoherence reflected the newly merged entity, still healing wounds after ten years of civil war, but the vagueness left the party vulnerable to missteps and misstatements. Conservative candidates questioned the wisdom of official bilingualism and the Canadian status quo on abortion while the party as a whole identified itself as opposing same-sex marriage. Harper himself began to speak of forming a majority government, and in the final week of the campaign, an ill-advised press release accused Martin and the Liberal leadership of abetting child pornography.[22] These episodes exposed Harper and the Conservatives' vulnerability to speculations of a "hidden agenda," allowing the Liberals to eke out a minority government (see also Chapter 12).[23]

Given the short time between the unification of the two parties and the election, the poorly disciplined campaign was perhaps not overly surprising — though it also pointed to worrisome similarities between the new party and the old Progressive Conservatives, who had never been able to challenge the federal Liberals' "Big Red Machine."[24] Importantly, though, leading figures in the party immediately took action to fine-tune the organizational machine, to ensure sufficient funding, and to put it on a footing where it could move into campaign mode very quickly given the short expected lifespan of the Liberal minority.[25] This work on the electoral machinery was very important and would lay the groundwork for the exceptionally disciplined central party of 2006 onwards.

Ideology served discipline in the new party, rather than the other way around. The party leadership hoped to resolve problems of principle by holding a policy convention that would bring together both former CA/ Reform activists and former PCs to decide what the new party stood for. Forestalled by the 2004 election, this convention was held in Montreal in March 2005. Tightly managed, the process was designed to ensure that the party's grassroots element had voice and that nothing was said that would appear extreme. Holding the convention in Montreal was a part of this new image, but it also raised the stakes — outspoken conservatism in Montreal would endanger the party's chances in Quebec in a way that outspoken conservatism in, for example, Calgary would not. While passing resolutions committing the party to opposing same-sex marriage, including property rights in the Charter of Rights and Freedoms and ending minimum sentences and statutory release for serious offenders showed that ideological conservatives were important, an emerging moderation was apparent in the rejection of motions to re-engage the abortion debate, create a Royal Commission on Euthanasia, and develop a package of populist reforms including recall, a citizen's assembly on electoral reform, referenda, and citizen-sponsored initiatives.[26] The convention did support official bilingualism and a limitation on the federal spending power. Combined with the presence of notables from both sides of the party's heritage, the 2005 convention suggested that the party's character was very much in the PC tradition — clearly of the right, but moderate and reaching out to Quebec. But new was the emerging strong discipline, which was partly the result of the work being done after the 2004 election, but also the product of the Reform experience of managing populism through a strong leader.

This ideological moderation was seemingly challenged in the spring of 2005 when parliamentary manoeuvring around same-sex marriage dominated the political landscape. Here, the party broke with tradition and took a clear stand on a moral issue. While technically a free vote, that only three MPs supported the Liberal motion was a striking display of ideological commitment in keeping with the party's principles. It was soon downplayed by Harper, however, who promised that were he to lead a government, he would only introduce a motion to re-open the debate. As we see below, the party's social conservatism continues to be carefully managed in government.

The 2006 Conservative election platform reflected the party's determined commitment to control its message, reversing the failures of 2004. While the "Stand Up for Canada" platform offered sixty policies grouped into six planks, the party emphasized five main commitments: passing the Federal Accountability Act, reducing the GST to 5 percent, cracking down on violent crime, creating a childcare subsidy, and reforming health care in accordance with the principles of the Canada Health Act.[27] These were designed to appeal particularly to middle-class suburban families and Quebec voters, and would not have been out of place in the old Progressive Conservative party. The more divisive pledge to vote on reopening same-sex marriage was quickly made on the first day of the campaign, intentionally to get it out of the way.[28] And while discipline in the final days of the campaign slipped, not only with controversial statements by social conservative candidates but Harper's own misstatement that "a Liberal Senate, a Liberal civil service ... and courts that have been appointed by the Liberals" would restrain his government,[29] the Conservatives were rewarded with a minority government of 124 seats. Crucially, the party was able to win 10 of Quebec's 75 seats (up from zero) and 40 of Ontario's 106 (up from 24), marking a real breakthrough in Central Canada.

Thus, by the time of its 2006 victory, the new Conservative Party had built on elements of the Reform Party's transition to become a tightly disciplined political machine. (New financing rules for political parties also gave it a significant fundraising advantage over its competitors.) From the Progressive Conservative side of its heritage, one could point to a solid breakthrough in Central Canada, with the potential for growth in Quebec, and signs — if not always definite ones — of ideological moderation. In short, Harper seemed to have answered one question that had troubled previous Conservative leaders (how to organize their party) and had tentatively answered two other questions (which regions to appeal to and how ideologically motivated to be).

THE CONSERVATIVES IN GOVERNMENT: MODERATE OR IDEOLOGICAL?

In the following section, we consider the policies of the Conservative party in power since 2006. Do they suggest a continuation of traditional Canadian brokerage politics in the PC vein, or a stronger ideological vision? Looking at economic policy, federalism and foreign policy, and religious and "family" values, we suggest the picture is mixed. In general the Conservatives have taken a moderate and incremental approach to governing, maintaining their focus on middle-class suburban voters, while shifting other aspects of their regional and demographic strategy. Yet at times there appears to be a more ideological approach at work, one that favours a more constrained federal government.

Big or Small Government?

One of the key explanations to suggest the Conservative government has been ideologically moderate and essentially a reincarnation of the Progressive Conservatives has been in its economic policies and the growth of government since 2006. Government hiring and spending has increased under the Conservatives; federal government expenditures increased 19 percent between 2005–06 and 2008–09 (and then leaped a further 18 percent in one year with the 2009 economic stimulus),[30] and federal public service employment increased by 13 percent between 2006 and 2010,[31] hardly indicating a right-wing or libertarian agenda of small government. The Conservatives have been noticeably reluctant to pursue any changes to Canada's public health care system, carefully matching opponents' promises and overseeing significant additional transfers of 6 percent annually since 2006 along with other provincial transfers. It is difficult to distinguish the overall macroeconomic and fiscal policies of the Harper Conservatives from previous Liberal or Progressive Conservative governments.

The infamous November 2008 economic update remains an outlier in Conservative economic policy, with its call for a hard line in public sector bargaining, no stimulus spending to combat the global economic crisis, and a sudden end to the public financing of political parties.[32] But these policies were quickly dropped in the constitutional uproar that followed, and in 2009 the Conservatives embarked on a massive stimulus campaign, a restructuring of the auto sector that included purchasing parts of General Motors and Chrysler, and other expenditures and interventions similar to other western countries — again suggesting a government not unlike its predecessors. The question of whether the 2008 update was an aberration or an indicator of true Conservative intentions remains unanswered.

But while the Conservatives appear generally willing to oversee the growth of the state as a whole, they appear less comfortable with some of its more regulatory and intrusive elements. The most symbolic aspect is the 2010 cancellation of the mandatory long-form census, a decision that surprised many but is consistent with libertarian resistance against an intrusive state and suspicion of "social engineering." More substantive is the Conservative resistance against most climate change regulatory changes, and its general lack of interest in pursuing environmental priorities. It also cancelled the 2005 Liberal national child care plan, saying it was unaffordable and favoured certain parenting choices, substituting it with direct payments to parents to use as they wished — again reducing the direct role of the state. And while it did not end the long-gun registry in its first two stints in office, the government has clearly indicated its interest in doing so, implicitly endorsing a private members' bill in 2010 and pledging abolishment in the 2011 campaign.

Conservative tax policy has been similarly complex. The government was elected in 2006 on a pledge to reduce the GST, at the cost of cancelling Liberal income-tax cuts, but also pursued harmonization with BC and Ontario sales taxes, extending the overall tax burden for most citizens. It has reduced corporate taxes, to the point of being willing to fight the 2011 election campaign partly on the issue. But its most interesting tax policies have been tax expenditures, rather than program spending. While its anti-regulatory stance focuses on curbing the state's demand for certain actions, tax expenditures allow the government to privilege certain actions and values without prohibiting others. And it is very interesting to contemplate Conservative tax expenditures:

credits for dependent children; credits for children's athletic activities (and more recently arts activities as well); public transit passes; home renovations; and in the 2011 election campaign, income-splitting that favours single-breadwinner families. This policy of tax expenditures has been widely criticized, both for further complicating the tax system and only rewarding existing behavior rather than influencing new actions. But if these can be taken as indicators of Conservative priorities, we see an interesting picture that favours middle-class home-owning families with stay-at-home mothers, children, and commuters (as well as other transit users). As Tom Flanagan says, "The pattern of innovations is rather messy, but taken together they have helped to make the Canadian personal income tax system more generous to those who undertake the responsibility of being parents."[33] But whether this is done primarily out of ideological priority or because this is a key swing group of voters is unclear; presumably both objectives are at work.

In short, Conservative economic policy does not follow a single ideological pattern, and in many ways appears consistent with historic Canadian brokerage politics and its tendency to promote continuing state growth. Yet there are patterns that suggest a weakening of the regulatory state and a privileging of middle-class families, especially through the indirect favouritism of tax credits.

Defining Canada: Federalism and Foreign Policy

As with economic policy, it can be difficult to sort out the Harper Conservative vision for other policy areas. However, we can extend the concept of a limited state in two seemingly opposite directions — federalism and foreign policy. While the Harper Conservatives have again not differed dramatically from other parties and governments in these arenas, we again suggest there is a limited ideological pattern at work — one that favours a more focused and constrained role for the Government of Canada. Yet even this is subject to regional political calculations and considerations.

As mentioned above, Stephen Harper's most notable intellectual trail has been in the area of federalism, with his endorsement of an Alberta firewall and strict interpretations of federal jurisdiction. Yet the

Harper government has taken a largely ad hoc and even asymmetrical approach to federalism, pursuing individual agreements with provinces over equalization payments, the harmonized sales tax (HST), and other areas. Decisions often appear reactive and driven by regional political considerations, such as its quick agreement to give Quebec the same HST package as B.C. and Ontario, two decades after Quebec harmonized its provincial sales tax. They are also noticeably sector-by-sector rather than comprehensive — while federal-provincial-territorial ministers' conferences are common, not a single first ministers' meeting has been held under Harper. While in the 1990s Harper took a hard line against Quebec nationalism, such as his opposition to the Calgary Declaration, in 2006 his government endorsed a House of Commons declaration that Quebec is "a nation within Canada" — itself a reaction to a Bloc Québécois motion that excluded the last two words. In general the Conservative approach to Quebec has been erratic and at times seemingly impulsive, playing for votes by respecting provincial jurisdiction, and yet possibly losing support through other actions such as the arts funding controversy in the 2008 election. But despite this seemingly ad hoc approach, we can see elements of a vision that generally eschews new federal programs and intrusions and maintains or expands provincial transfers with few strings. (The notable exception is the federal push to establish a national securities regulator, supported by Ontario but opposed by other provinces.) This is again consistent with an ideological vision of a smaller or reduced state, yet also within the mainstream of Canadian federalism and designed to attract regional political support.

Turning to foreign policy, there appears at times to be a clearer outlook. Foreign policy under the Harper Conservatives has generally eschewed the "soft power" approach attributed to elements of the Liberal party, with a strong commitment to military defence and new and controversial policies such as the planned purchase of advanced fighter aircraft and other military equipment. The federal government has asserted its security presence in the Arctic, with the Prime Minister making regular northern pilgrimages to assert Canadian sovereignty. But much of this has been a relatively bland patriotism, devoid of specific content. In particular, while the Harper government has clearly indicated its warmth toward the United States, it has not distinguished itself particularly from previous governments in terms of Canada–U.S. relations. (Of course, in 2003, prior to the CPC merger, Harper's Canadian Alliance strongly criticized Canada's decision to stay out of the Iraq war, but upon coming to office in 2006 the Conservatives ruled out joining the Iraq effort.) And unlike the famed Mulroney-Reagan friendship, Stephen Harper has not pursued a noteworthy personal relationship with American presidents. The one foreign policy area where the Harper government noticeably stands out is its clear tilt in favour of Israel. While Canada remains committed to a two-state solution for Israel and Palestine, Harper and his ministers have been outspoken in their support of Israel, at times beyond even the United States, Israel's traditional ally.

The Conservative approach to Afghanistan deserves special mention here. The previous Liberal government committed Canadian troops to a combat mission in 2005 (without parliamentary approval) and the Conservatives consistently declared that Parliament would decide on its future. A narrow 149–145 vote was held in 2006 to extend the mission until 2009, and a 2008 vote decided by a wider margin on a final extension until 2011. Since then, the government has remained committed to ending the direct military mission, although Canadian forces have shifted to a training function. Given that these votes represent the most direct parliamentary involvement in a mission abroad since 1939, it suggests a government committed to consensus and the will of Parliament. On the other hand, the votes may be interpreted more tactically as a blow against the Liberal party, since that party split in the 2006 vote and remained divided on the Afghanistan mission. Again, political expediency may be as equally important as principle here. More recently, Harper committed Canada to the 2011 NATO mission against Libya without a parliamentary vote, suggesting no precedent was set by the Afghanistan votes; but he also indicated following the 2011 election that Parliament would be "consulted" about further commitments.

The common element here for both federalism and foreign policy is the idea of a more restrained Government of Canada in both provincial or international affairs. The Harper government is cautious about intervention and involvement in areas not clearly within its jurisdiction. With occasional exceptions, such as Harper's poisonous relationship with former Newfoundland premier Danny Williams, the Conservatives seek engagement over assertive confrontation — whether over equalization payments, the HST, or international agreements. An interesting exception, however, is when the two areas collide, such as the attempted take-over of the Potash Corporation of Saskatchewan by the multinational firm BHP. The Harper government indicated it would not approve this takeover, which was heavily opposed by the Saskatchewan government. In this case, it appears that provincial preferences trumped any commitment to unfettered international trade — and again was likely a wise domestic political move for the Conservatives.

A Question of Values: Church and Hearth

Perhaps the most interesting and potentially explosive aspect of the Conservative Party is the role of religious and social conservatism. While religious and social conservatives were active in both the Progressive Conservative and Reform parties, they often had great difficulty influencing policy agendas and priorities, especially for the key issues of reproductive and gay rights.[34] In a famous 2003 line often noted by critics, Harper approvingly quoted a statement by Ted Byfield that a successful uniting of the right required both economic "neo-cons" and socially conservative "theo-cons." Too often, however, this has been projected into a hidden religious agenda and dire contemplations of an apocalyptic vision.[35] In reality, the evidence is again mixed. We suggest that again the Conservatives have taken a largely moderate path that privileges "the family" without directly confronting other groups.

Many Conservative MPs and activists are religious, but it is difficult to systematically measure their presence, and easy to overstate their zealotry or assume they act in lockstep. Harper's own beliefs are unclear — early studies of the Reform party suggest he was not a religious conservative at the time,[36] and he has been circumspect about his private beliefs throughout his political career.[37] However, there is certainly evidence of social conservative opposition to abortion and gay rights in the Conservative party. Harper and most Tories voted against the legalization of same-sex marriage in 2005, promising to hold a vote on whether to reopen the issue, which they did in 2006 — the answer being negative. In 2009 the Conservatives cut funding to pride parades, and moved to exclude references to homosexuality in citizenship guides (later restored). And in 2010 the government announced a major increase in international development aid for maternal health, but with the explicit exclusion of abortion and contraceptive funding.

But on the other hand, Harper has repeatedly said he will not pursue new abortion laws in Canada — a pledge reiterated in the 2011 campaign — nor will he revisit same-sex marriage. Many in the Conservative government and party continue to strongly oppose abortion and same-sex marriage, but often without the direct support of Harper and other senior figures. A number of backbench Tory MPs have introduced private member's bills, such as Rod Bruinooge's "Roxanne's Law," which would create special penalties for coercing women to have an abortion. But this bill was defeated in the Commons, noticeably with Harper and many cabinet ministers voting against it, and Harper also vowed in the 2011 election to oppose similar backbench bills that tried to reopen the abortion debate. Other backbenchers have spoken out against actions such as awarding the Order of Canada to Dr. Henry Morgentaler, but the Prime Minister's Office was quick to issue a statement of disinterest on the matter. And even on issues above like the cutting of gay pride funding, the government has been evasive and careful not to attribute it as opposition to sexual orientation — to the point of denying a backbencher's claim that it was.[38]

So where is religious and social conservatism in the new Conservative Party? We suggest it is buried within a wider agenda. In a more recent 2009 speech, Harper identified conservatism as resting on three "f"s: "freedom, family, and faith."[39] While again we must be careful not to read too much into a single phrase, this trio suggests an outlook that prioritizes a limited state along with traditional institutions such as the family and religion. But "family values" need not be limited to narrow restrictions on reproductive and sexuality rights. It also encompasses broader concepts of middle-class suburbia, with instruments like tax expenditures discussed above. Again, Tom Flanagan provides guidance here, noting that "in spite of strenuous efforts, Reform and its successors lost every battle over high-profile issues of social conservatism [such as same-sex marriage.] ... In another sense, however, Reform's pro-family position has led to real results," such as the childcare allowance and tax expenditures.[40] The Conservative party appears to have adopted this flexible agenda of both narrow and broader conceptions of family values, generally downplaying the former in favour of the less controversial, and potentially vote-richer, latter approach. At times it has been able to blend the two, most notably in raising the age of sexual consent laws in 2007 from fourteen to sixteen. This was a priority for many social conservatives, but attracted little opposition and was broadly supported by other parties. The childcare allowance and income-splitting proposals can also be seen as especially, yet not exclusively, appealing to traditional families with stay-at-home mothers. In general, it appears that the Conservatives will pursue only social conservative priorities that fit within the larger suburban middle class "family agenda." This family-friendly and limited-state approach is also key to the Conservative outreach to traditionally Liberal Catholic voters, as well as ethnic communities and New Canadians, who increasingly act as a new pillar of Conservative strategy.

The Liberal and NDP parties also place a heavy emphasis on families, such as the Liberal "Family Pack" in its 2011 election platform. Despite having a few social conservative MPs of their own, these parties broadly support abortion and sexual orientation rights, and their platforms promote new state programs rather than the Tory approach of tax breaks and direct transfers. However, they are all appealing to the same suburban middle-class voters. Does this suggest the Harper Conservatives have managed to shift the political spectrum to favour this group and traditional conceptions of families? We suggest not, given that "family" rhetoric is widespread in political discourse at the provincial level as well as outside Canada among political figures of all stripes. (For example, Barack Obama struck a "Task Force on Middle-Class Working Families" immediately after taking office.) If there is a "family agenda" shift in Canada, it can at most be only partly attributed to the Harper Conservatives.

In short, the Harper Conservatives again present us with mixed evidence. While there is clearly a social conservative ideological presence in the party and government, its "family" policies have generally leaned more to the centre or at least centre-right, and are at least partly consistent with mainstream policy and political trends. The party is clearly willing to deliver on some issues to social conservatives, but only at minimal political cost. And as we have seen throughout this section, ideology in the Conservative government is elusive. While sometimes undeniably present, much of government policy remains distinctly moderate and consistent with historic patterns and/or contemporary trends.

BACK TO THE FUTURE?
TOWARD THE CONSERVATIVE VISION OF CANADA

This chapter has discussed the curious character of the Conservative Party of Canada in 2011. We suggest that the CPC in many ways replicates the old Progressive Conservative coalition — but with a more discernible ideological centre, an electoral strategy focused on particular regional, ethnic, and social groups, and an impressive centralized discipline that is a far cry from the historic Tory Syndrome. In this concluding section, we ask three interrelated questions: What will the Conservative party look like after Stephen Harper? Does it represent a long-term shift in the Canadian party system? And is the Conservative party implementing a new "conservative" paradigm for Canada?

It is almost impossible to discuss the Conservative Party of Canada apart from its founding and so far only leader. Yet at some point Harper will move on, and we can only speculate about possible successors and how the party will fare under them. A future leader may either emphasize the more moderate, brokerage elements of Harper's strategy or play more to its ideological aspects, balancing its libertarian and more social conservative wings, all while keeping the various regional, ethnic, and social aspects of the new party base. It may be that no leader can fully emulate Harper's successful balancing act, and the party may even descend back into a renewed Tory Syndrome of bickering factions. But alternatively, Harper may have already shifted the terrain of Canadian politics to make the Conservatives the new natural governing party of Canada.

Various sources suggest Stephen Harper's goal has always been to challenge the Liberal Party's claim to the above title. While leaders like Clark and Mulroney attempted to copy the long-time Liberal brokerage strategy through unstable coalitions of the unhappy, Harper has been more disciplined and selective in his coalition building, and more willing to polarize rather than accommodate on some issues. This has produced — again, drawing from Tom Flanagan — a "minimum connected winning coalition" that maximizes internal cohesion and does not overreach and try to please all the people all the time. (Flanagan also clarifies the modified strategy, writing in June 2011, "When he reentered electoral politics in 2002, Stephen Harper wanted to reconstitute Brian Mulroney's coalition of western populists, traditional Tories and francophone nationalists; but when the francophone pillar of the coalition proved unstable, he was able to replace francophones with sizable elements of Canada's ethnic communities."[41])

This has paid off in slowly increasing electoral victories, aided of course by the Liberals' own missteps. But it is perhaps unwise to even speculate about the long-term outlook here. Canadian party politics have been in constant ferment since the collapse of the established "third party system" in 1993,[42] with five parties in the 1990s, a seemingly steady four in the mid-2000s, and an entirely new set of dynamics in 2011 with the Liberal collapse, NDP surge, and virtual decimation of the Bloc Québécois. Attempts to explain the Canadian "fourth party system," other than one characterized by instability, have often been eclipsed by new developments. And at the heart of much of this instability is the disciplined yet ideologically blurry Conservative Party of Canada under Stephen Harper.

However, a final question asks whether the Conservatives have already changed Canada, or are on their way to do so especially with a new majority government. Have they shifted Canadian politics, policies, and discourse toward a "conservative" vision of Canada? This is perhaps the most difficult to answer. Not only is it hard to define what "conservative" really means here, but we must view the Harper government and Conservative party in context with other governments and global trends.

We have seen above how the Harper government oversaw a general growth of the Canadian federal state while at times curbing more intrusive elements, taking a somewhat more circumspect and ad hoc approach in provincial and international affairs that again suggests a vision of limits on the federal state. And while it has clear social conservative elements that support an increased federal role in the regulation of reproductive and sexuality rights, this has been largely subsumed by a broader middle class "family" agenda. While some of these actions may be distinctly different from past Canadian governments and party positions, they do not necessarily stand out compared to the Harper government's contemporaries, especially following the global economic crisis of the late 2000s. International interest in public sector reform is at its highest since the early 1990s, and other governments in Britain, the United States, and elsewhere are likely to enact much more radical fiscal and economic policies than anything seen in Canada under the Harper Conservatives. We also noted above the prevalence of "family" rhetoric well beyond the Harper Conservatives and other Canadian parties. Yet at the same time the Harper government does show unusual stubbornness on certain issues, from the long-form census to international maternal health and abortion to support for Israel. It is difficult to discern how this fits into a larger picture and the extent to which the Conservatives have been able to contribute independently of larger structural forces to the shaping and shifting of Canadians' views and expectations. For this and other reasons, the Conservative Party of Canada under Stephen Harper remains a fascinating and complex entity whose long-term future remains to be written.

NOTES

1. For general accounts of the creation of the Conservative Party of Canada under Stephen Harper, see Bob Plamondon, *Full Circle: Death and Resurrection in Canadian Conservative Politics* (Toronto: Key Porter, 2006) and Tom Flanagan, *Harper's Team:*

Behind the Scenes in the Conservative Rise to Power, 2nd Edition (Montreal and Kingston: McGill-Queen's University Press, 2009).

2. R. Kenneth Carty and William Cross, "Political Parties and the Practice of Brokerage Politics" in *The Oxford Handbook of Canadian Politics,* eds. John C. Courtney and David Smith (Toronto: Oxford University Press, 2010).

3. Lawrence LeDuc, Jon Pammett, Judith I. McKenzie, Andre Turcotte, *Dynasties and Interludes: Past and Present in Canadian Electoral Politics* (Toronto: Dundurn Press, 2011), 525.

4. George Perlin, *The Tory Syndrome: Leadership Politics in the Progressive Conservative Party* (Montreal and Kingston: McGill-Queen's University Press, 1980).

5. Faron Ellis, *The Limits of Participation: Activists and Leaders in Canada's Reform Party* (Calgary: University of Calgary Press, 2005).

6. Jonathan Malloy, "High Discipline, Low Cohesion? The Uncertain Patterns of Canadian Parliamentary Party Groups," *Journal of Legislative Studies,* 2003.

7. Richard Johnston, "Polarized Pluralism in the Canadian Party System," *Canadian Journal of Political Science* 41 (December 2008): 815.

8. Peter Woolstencroft, "The Progressive Conservative Party, 1984–1993: Government, Party, Members" *Party Politics in Canada* (Seventh Edition), ed. Hugh G. Thorburn (Scarborough: Prentice-Hall, 1996).

9. R. Kenneth Carty, William Cross, and Lisa Young, *Rebuilding Canadian Party Politics* (Vancouver: UBC Press, 2000), 214–16.

10. Johnston, "Polarized Pluralism," 815.

11. Carty, Cross, and Young, *Rebuilding Canadian Party Politics,* 62.

12. Tom Flanagan, *Waiting for the Wave: The Reform Party and the Conservative Movement,* 2nd edition (Montreal and Kingston: McGill-Queen's University Press, 2009), 24–36.

13. Trevor Harrison, *Requiem for a Lightweight: Stockwell Day and Image Politics* (Montreal: Black Rose Books, 2002).

14. Ellis, *The Limits of Participation.*

15. William Johnson, *Stephen Harper and the Future of Canada* (Toronto: McClelland and Stewart, 2005).

16. Johnson, *Stephen Harper,* 299.

17. Lloyd Mackey, *The Pilgrimage of Stephen Harper* (Toronto: ECW Books, 2005), 151.

18. Mackey, *The Pilgrimage,* 151.

19. Tom Flanagan, "The Emerging Conservative Coalition," *Policy Options* (June–July 2011): 106.

20. Plamandon, *Full Circle,* 217–19.

21. LeDuc *et al., Dynasties and Interludes,* 489.

22. *Ibid.,* 492.

23. See Jon H. Pammett and Christopher Dornan, eds., *The Canadian General Election of 2004* (Toronto: Dundurn, 2004).

24. Stephen Clarkson, *The Big Red Machine: How the Liberal Party Dominates Canadian Politics* (Toronto: University of Toronto Press, 2005).

25. See Flanagan, *Harper's Team*, 195–228 for an excellent first-person discussion of this period.
26. Faron Ellis and Peter Woolstencroft, "A Change of Government, Not a Change of Country: The Conservatives and the 2006 Election" in *The Canadian Federal Election of 2006*, eds. Jon H. Pammett and Christopher Dornan (Toronto: Dundurn, 2006), 65.
27. Ellis and Woolstencroft, "A Change of Government," 76–77.
28. Ellis and Woolstencroft, "A Change of Government," 77; Flanagan, *Harper's Team*, p 233.
29. Ellis and Woolstencroft, "A Change of Government," 85.
30. Government of Canada, Department of Finance, *Fiscal Reference Tables* (October 2010), 9. However, during this period government expenditures remained steady at about 13 percent of GDP (rising with the 2009 stimulus package).
31. Government of Canada, Treasury Board Secretariat. Office of the Chief Human Resources Officer. "Demographic Snapshot of the Public Service, 2010," last accessed June 18, 2011. *www.tbs-sct.bc.ca/res/stats/ssen-ane-eng.asp*.
32. Michael Valpy, "The 'Crisis': A Narrative," in *Parliamentary Democracy in Crisis*, eds. Peter H. Russell and Lorne Sossin (Toronto: University of Toronto Press, 2009).
33. Tom Flanagan, *Waiting for the Wave: The Reform Party and the Conservative Movement*, Revised Edition (Montreal and Kingston: McGill-Queen's University Press, 2009), 215.
34. James H. Farney, "Social Conservatives And The Boundary Of Politics In Canada and The United States" (PhD diss., Department of Political Science, University of Toronto, 2009).
35. Marci McDonald, *The Armageddon Factor: The Rise of Christian Nationalism in Canada* (Toronto: Random House, 2010).
36. Trevor Harrison, *Of Passionate Intensity: Right-Wing Populism and the Reform Party of Canada* (Toronto: University of Toronto Press, 1995); Flanagan, *Waiting for the Wave*.
37. Colin Campbell, "The Church of Stephen Harper," *Maclean's*, March 30, 2006.
38. Kevin Libin, "Grants and Drag Queens Don't Mix," *National Post*, May 11, 2010.
39. David Akin, "Spendthrift Consumers Caused Global Recession: Harper," *National Post*, March 12, 2009.
40. Flanagan, *Waiting for the Wave*, 214.
41. Flanagan, "The Emerging Conservative Coalition," 106.
42. Carty, Cross and Young, *Rebuilding Canadian Party Politics*.

CHAPTER 11

Winners and Losers:
Voters in the 2011 Federal Election

Harold D. Clarke | Thomas J. Scotto | Jason Reifler | Allan Kornberg

By producing a majority government, the 2011 federal election ended a lengthy period of instability in Canadian national politics. That period began in 2004 when the then new Conservative Party of Canada had nearly upset the Liberals. Reducing the Liberals to a minority government in 2004, the CPC defeated them in 2006. However, the Conservatives could not win a majority in either that election or in the subsequent one in 2008. Throughout much of the 2011 campaign, it looked as if the result would be yet another Conservative minority. But history did not repeat itself a third time. Although their vote share was only 2 percent greater than it had been in 2008, the Conservatives benefited from a very strong performance by the NDP and very weak ones by the Liberals and the Bloc Québécois. The result was two big winners and two big losers. The CPC and the NDP were the big winners — the former got its majority and the latter became the official opposition party in Ottawa for the first time since its predecessor, the CCF, was founded in 1932. The big losers were the Liberals and the Bloc. The Liberals were reduced to "third party" status for the first time in history with a meagre contingent of thirty-four MPs, and the Bloc returned only four MPs. Both Liberal Leader Michael Ignatieff and BQ Leader Gilles Duceppe lost their seats.

The dynamics of party choice was not the only story in 2011. Turnout was a major issue as well. Over the past two decades, participation in Canadian federal elections has fallen substantially, reaching a historic low of 59.1 percent in 2008. Some analysts have argued that the decline is not simply a product of changes in the party system or fatigue produced by holding several elections over a relatively short time span. Rather, the decline reflects a generational change; unlike their elders, many young people simply do not see electoral participation as an important aspect of their duty as Canadian citizens. If so, it is unlikely that turnout will rebound quickly.[1]

When the 2011 election was called, it was feared that these generational effects would be compounded by disaffection — perhaps even disgust — engendered by the continuing inability of the national political system to produce a decisive electoral outcome. There had already been three federal elections in the preceding six years, and there was no compelling reason to believe things would be different this time. As it happened, the 2011 turnout was 61.4 percent. Perhaps reflecting excitement associated with the NDP surge in the polls during the last two weeks of the campaign or the closer inter-party competition in ridings where New Democrats were seriously challenging one or more rival parties, the small increase in turnout in 2011 could be only mildly gratifying for all those concerned about the erosion of citizen engagement in Canadian democracy. Only 2 percent above the record low that occurred in 2008, turnout in 2011 remained far below the 75-percentage range that was typical of most twentieth-century federal elections.

At the outset of the 2011 campaign, the principal opposition parties, the Liberals and the NDP, announced that they would focus on two issues. The first of these was their widely publicized contempt of Parliament charge, and the second was a hardy perennial for left-of-centre parties, namely the failure of a Conservative government to provide adequate financial support for health care and other cherished social services. Data gathered in the 2011 Political Support in Canada (PSC) study's pre- and post-election surveys indicate that the first of these issues resonated with the electorate.[2] As Table 1, Panel A shows, a clear majority (56 percent) of the survey respondents agreed that it was right to hold the Harper government in contempt of Parliament, and only a small minority (17 percent) disagreed. A plurality, albeit much smaller, also disagreed with the idea that the contempt of Parliament charge was "just a political smear." In addition, although the PSC respondents were quite evenly divided on whether Prime Minister Harper had been right to prorogue Parliament, a large plurality (42 percent) agreed with the more general charge that he had "run rough-shod over Canadian democracy." Only 25 percent disagreed.

Table 1: Harper Government's Treatment of Parliament and the Health Care System (Horizontal Percentages)

	Agree	Neither	Disagree	Don't Know
A. Treatment of Parliament				
i. Parliamentary committee was right to hold Conservative Government in contempt of Parliament	56%	18	17	9
ii. Contempt of Parliament charge just a political smear	33%	21	34	12
iii. Prime Minister Harper right to prorogue Parliament	30%	24	34	12
iv. Prime Minister Harper has run rough-shod over Canadian democracy	42%	22	25	11
B. The Health Care System				
i. Given present economic circumstances, can't afford to spend more on health care	17%	18	61	4
ii. Generally speaking, health care system works well	48%	19	31	2
iii. Should spend more on health care and less on military operations like Afghanistan and Libya	72%	16	9	3
iv. Overall, the federal government is doing a good job providing health care for Canadians	49%	25	23	3

Note: N for all questions is 2,500
Source: 2011 Political Support in Canada pre-election survey.

Opinion on health care was less clear-cut. On one hand, Liberal Leader Michael Ignatieff had seemingly struck a sympathetic cord when he demanded that the federal government should spend more on health care and less on "jets and jails." More than 70 percent of the PSC respondents agreed with the proposition that more should be spent on health care rather than military operations in places like Afghanistan and Libya, and only 9 percent disagreed (see Table 1, Panel B). Less than one person in five agreed that Canada could not afford to spend more on health care given present economic circumstances and more than three in five disagreed. However, these opinions should not be read as an unqualified condemnation of how the federal government was handling the health system — almost half of the PSC respondents judged the federal government's performance on health care positively, and less than one in four was displeased (see Table 1, Panel B). Similarly, nearly half of those surveyed said that they were generally pleased with how the health system was working, and less than one in three held the contrary opinion.

For his part, Prime Minister Harper was not purely on the defensive at the outset of the campaign. When his government was defeated in Parliament, Harper immediately proclaimed that it was clear that Canadians did not want yet another federal election. However, since an election was being forced on them, they should opt for a single-party, majority government that would provide long-term stability in Ottawa. According to the Prime Minister, only the Conservatives had the potential to form such a government. Survey data indicates that he had read public opinion quite accurately. As illustrated in Figure 1, 49 percent of PSC respondents favoured single-party rather than multi-party government, and only 34 percent favoured a multi-party (coalition) government. Sentiments in favour of majority government were even stronger; 56 percent preferred a majority government, and only 26 percent preferred minority government. These figures suggest that many voters might have responded positively to Harper's call that they should install a CPC majority on the government benches in Parliament.

Calling for majority government was not the only trump card in Harper's hand. Public attitudes towards the economy and his government's stewardship of it provided him with a major advantage. In 2008, a Harper-led minority government had been re-elected, despite the onset of the most serious recession in several decades. At that time Harper had benefited from widespread perceptions that he was best able to handle the crisis. Rather than simply blaming Harper and his colleagues for the ailing economy and "throwing the rascals out," many Canadians hesitated because it appeared that none of the other party leaders had the "right stuff" to deal with the problem.[3]

Figure 1. Opinions About Single-Party Versus Multi-Party Government and Majority Versus Minority Government

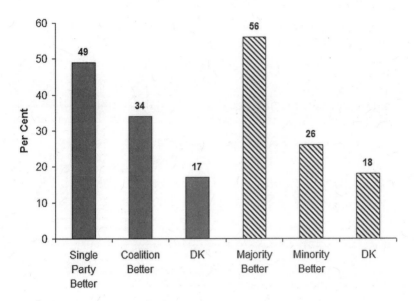

Source: 2011 Political Support in Canada pre-election survey.

Three years later, things had changed and the Conservatives were positioned to reap political benefits from a reviving economy. Although times had been tough for many people, the Canadian economy had fared relatively well during the recession. Unlike the American and British cases, no Canadian banks or other major financial institutions had failed. Also — and especially important for electoral politics — the unemployment rate was now falling. After rising to 8.7 percent in August 2009, joblessness had dropped to 7.6 percent when the 2011 election was called — well below the 9 percent figure bedeviling the United States.

Canadian public opinion reflected the improving situation. In 2008, fully two-thirds of the PSC respondents had concluded that the economy had deteriorated over the past year and only one in ten thought that it had improved. In sharp contrast, 43 percent of the 2011 respondents believed the economy had gotten better over the past year and only 26 percent thought it had worsened (see Figure 2). Also, optimism about the future was growing with 45 percent of those surveyed in 2011 stating

Figure 2. National Economic Evaluations, 2008 and 2011

A. *Canadian Economy Last Year*

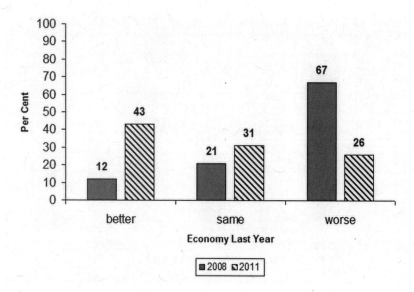

B. *Canadian Economy Next Year*

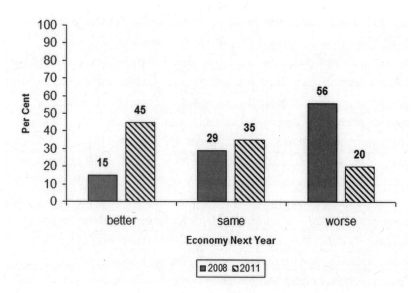

Source: 2008 and 2011 Political Support in Canada pre-election surveys.

that the economy would be better in the year ahead, and only 20 percent saying it would be worse. These figures contrast sharply with data gath-. ered in 2008. Then, only 15 percent were sanguine about Canada's economic future and fully 56 percent were pessimistic. Such a sharp upturn in economic optimism is always good news for a governing party preparing to fight an election. A healthy economy is a sturdy political fundamental and, as we shall see below, large numbers of Canadians credited Harper and his party for astute economic stewardship.

ISSUES, PARTIES, AND LEADERS

Issues

Although numerous factors can influence the choices voters make, among the most important are judgments regarding which party is best able to handle what political scientists call valence issues. The economy is a quintessential example; virtually everyone wants vigorous, sustainable economic growth coupled with low levels of unemployment and inflation. Opinion distributions about heath care, education, and the environment are similarly one-sided — high quality, affordable, and accessible health care and educational systems and an attractive, healthy environment receive virtually unanimous endorsement from people in all walks of life. Security is another important example, with vast majorities placing high value on protection from threats posed by ill-intentioned rogue states, international terrorists, common criminals, and miscellaneous miscreants. For all of these issues, political debate centres not on *what*, but rather *how* and, especially, *who*.

In contrast to valence issues, position issues are ones upon which public opinion is divided, sometimes deeply. In contemporary Canada, abortion, immigration, same-sex marriage, and the gun registry are all good examples of position issues. Many Canadians favour abortion on demand, increased immigration, same-sex marriage, and the registration of all guns, but it is also the case that many others wish to restrict abortion, decrease immigration, forbid same-sex marriage, and end gun registration. Such divisions in public opinion make position issues attractive to media commentators looking for stories that will engage, and perhaps enrage, their audiences. Controversy is good copy. As a result, position issues often get a great deal of play in the print and electronic media, and observers are tempted to conclude that they have major effects on how people vote. Indeed they might, if such issues were the stuff of the public's evaluations of the parties. However, research in Canada and other major democracies such as Great Britain and the United States indicates that, although there are occasional exceptions such as the 1988 federal election when sharp disagreements about the Canada–U.S. free trade agreement dominated the campaign, position issues typically are not as important as valence issues.[4]

The dominance of valence issues in the 2011 federal election is clearly apparent in the survey data. In the post-election wave of the PSC survey, respondents were asked to rank what they considered to be the top three of eleven issues. Figure 3 shows which issues were ranked first. The importance of the economy is signalled by the fact that 39 percent gave top billing to the economy, unemployment, or government debt. The only other issue with a substantial number of first mentions is health care, at 23 percent. All other issues receive few first mentions, with the lack of emphasis on widely publicized position issues being noteworthy. Specifically, only 1 percent of those surveyed ranked the gun registry first, and even fewer gave top priority to gay and lesbian marriage, Afghanistan, Libya, or Quebec sovereignty. Nor were these position issues often ranked second or third in importance. On average, fully 97 percent of respondents did not rank any of the position issues among the three most important. A sizable minority of people (27 percent) did not rank any of the eleven issues as particularly important in 2011, but of those who did, valence issues dominated.

The power of issues to influence electoral choice derives from judgments about which party (if any) is best able to deal with the issues voters care about. In 2011, a large plurality of Canadians chose the Conservatives as most competent. As illustrated in Figure 4, the CPC's "issue-edge" over their closest rival, the NDP, was sixteen points, with 40 percent choosing the Conservatives and 24 percent selecting the New

Figure 3. Top-Ranked Issues, 2011

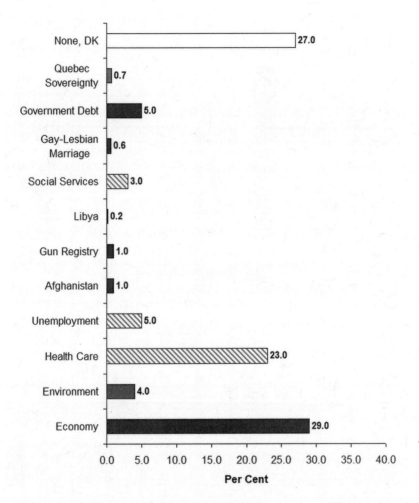

Source: 2011 Political Support in Canada post-election survey.

Democrats. The Liberals trailed badly, with only 11 percent selecting them as best on the top-ranked issue. Similarly, only 6 percent selected the Greens or the BQ; 19 percent did not choose any party.

The numbers displayed in Figure 4 are for party preferences on all top-ranked issues. More detailed analyses of preferences on specific issues confirm that the Conservative Party dominated on the economy,

Figure 4. Party Best Able to Handle Top-Ranked Issue

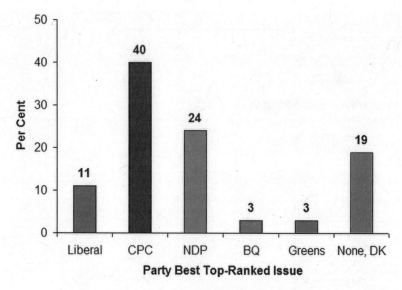

Source: 2011 Political Support in Canada post-election survey.

being selected as best by 58 percent of those choosing the "economy generally" as most important (data not shown). The CPC also did well among those mentioning government debt or unemployment, receiving the endorsements of 50 percent of the former group and 28 percent of the latter one. And although the NDP led among those selecting health care as most important with a 32 percent share, almost as many (29 percent) chose the CPC. These analyses also reinforce the conclusion that the Liberals did very poorly on the issues in 2011. Indeed, they did not lead the other parties on a single issue, and their maximum share was 20 percent among the minuscule group (0.6 percent of all PSC respondents) who chose gay and lesbian marriage as the top-ranked election issue. On the key issues of the economy and health care, the Liberal shares were 9 percent and 15 percent, respectively. As for other parties, the Greens led with 31 percent among the 4 percent choosing the environment as the most important issue (the NDP were a close second on the environment at 28 percent), and the BQ led with 77 percent among the tiny 0.7 percent primarily concerned with Quebec sovereignty.

Parties

Political scientists have long recognized that many voters form psychological attachments to political parties and that these attachments can strongly influence voting behavior. Pioneering studies conducted in the United States in the 1950s characterized these attachments as "party identifications" akin to the identifications people form with religious, ethnic, or regional groups in the population.[5] Just as some people think of themselves as Presbyterians, or Scottish, or Albertans, they think of themselves as Liberals, or Conservatives, or New Democrats. As originally conceived, such party identifications were said to be highly stable attachments that typically formed during childhood or adolescence and then strengthened as people aged. Party identifications provided voters with important cues about how to cast their ballots in successive elections.

Research in Canada has confirmed the significance of partisanship for explaining vote choices made at any particular point in time, but challenged the idea that party identifications are necessarily strong and stable psychological attachments. Although some Canadians do have durable partisan attachments, many others demonstrate partisan flexibility, being willing to change their party identifications in reaction to changing perceptions of the performance of parties and their leaders.[6] In addition, there is substantial partisan inconsistency across levels of the federal system, with sizable numbers of people identifying with one party in federal politics and a different one in provincial politics. The presence of large numbers of flexible partisans means that political parties, even ones that historically have been highly successful, can quickly lose substantial numbers of supporters. Equally, erstwhile minor parties can gain strength quickly. Both of these processes have been at work in federal politics in recent years, and they had important consequences for voting in the 2011 election.

The dynamics of federal party identification over the twenty-three-year period from 1988 to 2011 are displayed in Figure 5. Viewed generally, the figure clearly shows that the percentages of people identifying with various parties have shifted substantially over time. Such changes in party support have been very much in evidence in recent years. Perhaps most noteworthy is Liberal partisanship, which has drifted downwards over the past decade from a high point of 40 percent in 2000 to 28 percent immediately after the 2008 election. The slide did not stop there, but rather continued such that only 20 percent of the 2011 pre-election respondents identified themselves as Liberals. In the post-election survey, only 18 percent did so. In little more than ten years, the Liberal Party has lost well over half of its identifiers.[7]

Figure 5. Federal Party Identification, 1988–2011

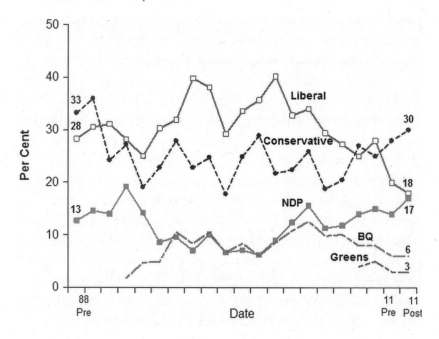

Source: 1988–2011 Political Support in Canada pre- and post-election surveys.

Conservative partisanship has manifested consequential dynamics too. After crashing in the early 1990s alongside the virtual annihilation of the old Progressive Conservative (PC) Party in the 1993 federal election, Conservative partisanship (considered as the sum of identifications with the PCs, Reform Alliance, and CPC parties) has slowly revived. However, at the time of its minority victory in the 2006 federal election, only 21

percent of the Canadian electorate identified with the CPC. Party identification data gathered from the mid-1960s onwards indicates that 21
percent is an extremely small partisan share for a winning party, and it
is indicative of the shallowness of CPC support in the electorate when
the party first came to power.[8] Since then, Conservative partisanship has
gradually increased: 27 percent identified with the party before the 2008
election, and 28 percent did so before the 2011 election. Even achieving
a majority victory in the latter contest, the CPC's partisan share stood at
a mediocre 30 percent, well below what used to be typical for winning
parties in federal elections.

The absence of large numbers of Liberal and Conservative identifiers in the run-up to the 2011 election constituted an ideal context for
a strong surge by a third party such as the NDP. And, indeed, this is
what occurred. However, as Figure 5 illustrates, the growth in NDP support at the polls was not accompanied by major gains in NDP party
identification. Right after the 2008 election, 15 percent identified themselves as New Democrats. Before the 2011 election, 14 percent did so,
with this figure climbing to 17 percent afterwards. Much as the CPC
had done in 2006, the NDP made a major move in 2011 without a pro-
portionate increase in its partisan share. Green and BQ partisanships
also are noteworthy, with the former party making no discernible gains
between 2008 and 2011, and the latter one seeing its cohort of identifiers decrease by about one-third — from 35 percent to 24 percent of
the Quebec electorate.

Finally, what is not shown in Figure 5 is the percentage of people
who say that they do not identify with any of the federal parties. This
number stood at 29 percent for the 2011 PSC pre-election survey and 25
percent for the post-election one. These percentages are typical of those
gathered in the 2008 and other recent PSC election surveys. With over a
quarter of voters lacking a psychological attachment to any of the federal
parties and numerous others willing to shift their identifications, there
is strong, ongoing potential for dramatic movements in party support
during the course of a federal election campaign. That potential was realized in 2011.

Leaders

Party leader images typically have significant effects on electoral choice in Canada and elsewhere.[9] However, some analysts believe that it is irrational for voters to pay attention to leaders, and that they should focus all of their attention on the policies parties propound. In contrast, we contend that voters are in a sense "smart enough to know that they are not smart enough" to make their choices purely on the basis of the merits of alternative policy proposals. Operating in a political world of high stakes, cheap talk, and abundant uncertainty, voters rely on the cues provided by leaders (and parties) to help them decide. In the language of cognitive psychology, leader images constitute "fast and frugal heuristics" for making political choices.[10]

Over the years, political scientists have posed a variety of questions on election surveys to study voters' images of party leaders. Analyses indicate that affective (like-dislike) feelings are especially important. Using data gathered in the 2008 and 2011 PSC post-election surveys, Figure 6 displays average scores on 0–10 "dislike-like" scales for each of the federal party leaders. These scores are interesting in several respects. First, it is evident that media commentary about how much Canadians liked NDP Leader Jack Layton was not just empty hype propagated by reporters seeking to enliven an otherwise dull campaign. Layton's 2011 score (6.2) is well above what he had achieved in 2008 (5.4) and far above those for any of the other party leaders. Indeed, his closest rival is Green Party Leader Elizabeth May, whose 2011 average score is 4.8. To place Layton's score in perspective, we note that it is the highest score for any party leader since 1968 when Pierre Trudeau recorded a 6.8. Layton also is unusual in that feelings about him have become increasingly positive in successive elections. Average scores above 6 on the 10-point scale are extremely unusual, and Layton's 6.2 is strong evidence of his success in "connecting" with Canadians.[11]

Scores for the other leaders are also of interest. Figure 6 testifies that Conservative Leader Stephen Harper did not generate much enthusiasm among the voters in either 2008 or 2011. Nevertheless, his 2011 score (4.7) is over half a point higher than it was in 2008. In sharp contrast, the

Figure 6. Feelings About Party Leaders, 2008 and 2011

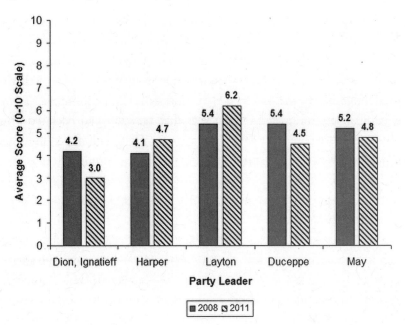

Note: Duceppe's scores are from Quebec only.
Source: 1988–2011 Political Support in Canada pre- and post-election surveys.

score for Liberal Leader Michael Ignatieff is only 3.0 — a truly dismal number for someone aspiring to lead a political party to national power. Again, perspective is provided by noting that Ignatieff's score was more than full point below that recorded by his predecessor, Stéphane Dion, in 2008 (4.2). At that time, Dion's number had been taken as evidence of the chilly reception many voters gave him.[12]

After the 2008 election, many observers speculated that Dion had been poorly received by the Canadian electorate in part because the Conservatives had run highly effective attack ads portraying him as "not a leader." When Ignatieff replaced Dion, the Conservatives repeated the ploy, attempting to frame the new Liberal leader as not a true Canadian, but rather someone who was "just visiting." Ignatieff was open to this charge because he had spent much of his adult life as a student, university professor, and broadcaster, first in the United States, then in Great

Britain, and then in the United States again. Indeed, he had only returned to Toronto from Harvard's Kennedy School in time to run in the 2006 federal election, in response to signals from several senior Liberals that they viewed him as a potential future party leader. To add punch to their "not a Canadian" characterization of Ignatieff, the Conservatives ran a short video clip of him talking to a group in which he said that the United States was their country "just as much as it's mine." There were also reports posted on the web that Ignatieff had declared himself "an American Democrat" who had voted for John Kerry in the 2004 American presidential election.

Well before the 2011 election, Ignatieff had tried to parry these attacks with his own publicity campaign, which included extensive media exposure and writing a book, *True Patriot Love*.[13] These efforts to improve his image were largely unsuccessful, and he received an extremely chilly reception from Canadian voters. Even BQ chieftain Gilles Duceppe, who shared Ignatieff's embarrassing fate of losing his own seat in 2011, fared comparatively well. Although Duceppe's like-dislike score was well below what it had been in 2008, his 2011 score (among Quebecers) was 4.5, a full point and a half above that given to the hapless Ignatieff. Similarly, Green Leader Elizabeth May scored a 4.8, down from the 5.2 recorded in 2008, but placing her ahead of all the other leaders except the highly popular Jack Layton.

Above, we have discussed the importance of the economy as a political fundamental, and the leverage that parties and their leaders can obtain by developing a reputation for being able to manage the country's economic affairs competently. As we also observed, Stephen Harper and the CPC had benefited from an image of competence on the economy to mute the potentially highly damaging effects of the world financial crisis that occurred during the 2008 federal election campaign. Figure 7 testifies that Harper had retained this competence edge in 2011. When the PSC respondents were asked which leader is best able to handle the economy, 37 percent chose Harper, 21 percent chose Jack Layton, 11 percent chose Michael Ignatieff, 2 percent designated Gilles Duceppe, and another 2 percent opted for Elizabeth May. As in 2008, a quarter of the respondents said none of the leaders were competent on the economy or that they simply didn't know who was best.

Harper's economic competence percentage was two points higher than it had been in 2008, whereas Layton's number had increased by six points. Thus, although he was considerably more popular than Harper, Layton remained well back of his Conservative rival when it came to managing the economy. However, as with overall popularity, another important component of the economic competence story in 2011 concerns public reactions to Michael Ignatieff. His 11 percent share as best leader on the economy was seven points down on the already weak 18 percent his predecessor, Stéphane Dion, had recorded three years earlier. With only one voter in ten judging him best able to take care of the country's economy, the unpopular Ignatieff was very poorly positioned to lead his party to victory.

Figure 7. Best Leader on the Economy, 2008 and 2011

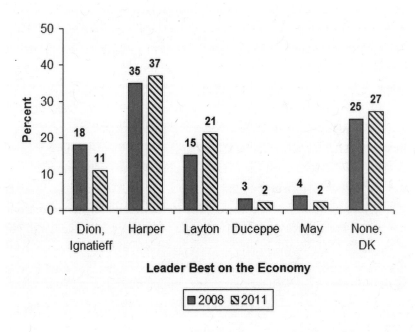

Source: 2011 Political Support in Canada post-election survey.

DEBATES AND DYNAMICS

Party leader debates have been a feature of Canadian federal elections since 1968. As is the norm, two debates, one in English and one in French, took place in 2011. The first debate was held on April 12 and the second, one day later, on April 13. Although not everyone watches or listens to the debates, the audience is typically very large. In the 2011 PSC post-election survey, 47 percent said that they had watched or heard at least part of one or both debates. The "effective audience" may have been even larger, as others saw or heard portions of the debates replayed on the media, or were exposed to post-debate commentaries about the leaders' performance.

The cast of characters in the 2011 debates differed from the lineup three years earlier. Michael Ignatieff had replaced Stéphane Dion as Liberal Leader. Also, Green Leader Elizabeth May, a participant in 2008, was not invited in 2011. The stated reason was that the Green Party did not have any seats in Parliament and if May was asked to participate, leaders of the many other small parties at the fringes of the Canadian political land-scape should also be allowed to take part, creating an unworkable format. Behind this stated rationale lay political calculations that May would prove detrimental to all of the other parties' prospects. At several points in the 2008 debates May had led the charge against Stephen Harper, ques-tioning his ability and values. Clearly, Harper did not relish a replay, and the more general prospect of having four, rather than three, opponents piling onto him did not appeal. The Liberals and NDP also had reasons not to roll out the welcome mat for May. The Green Party's agenda might resonate with environmentally concerned Canadians, and there was a risk that May would use the debates to poach these voters from the Liberals or the NDP. Keeping May at bay would reduce the risk of this happening.

Although the format of the 2011 debates was somewhat different from that used in 2008, the content was basically familiar. Opposition leaders used every opportunity to attack Prime Minister Harper and his government as incompetent and uncaring, and Harper responded again and again that the charges were false or misleading. To make their points, the opposition leaders employed strong rhetoric. Liberal Leader

Michael Ignatieff's criticisms were particularly harsh. He reiterated his charge that Harper and his colleagues were in contempt of Parliament and had attempted to subvert Canadian democracy. Ignatieff also repeatedly characterized Harper as being afraid of the Canadian people — someone who would "shut down" anything he could not control. Turning to another of his campaign themes, the Liberal leader said Harper was poised to waste taxpayers' dollars on "jets and jails," rather than investing it in health care and other social services. BQ Leader Gilles Duceppe also was very negative, issuing several charges that Harper had squandered tax money while not doing enough to help Quebec industries recover from the recession. Adhering to his sovereignist script, Duceppe repeatedly distinguished between how much Harper was doing for Canada and how little he was doing for Quebec.

Although no friend of Harper, NDP Leader Layton appeared considerably more positive and relaxed. Letting Ignatieff and Duceppe be the "heavies" in the attack on the Prime Minister, Layton used more of his allotted time to emphasize the many benefits his party's policies would provide for Canadians. When Harper tried to pin Layton down on specific measures he would employ to reach his lofty goals, Layton simply ignored him. Layton also shrewdly recognized that there was political capital to be accumulated by tarnishing Ignatieff's image. Soon after Ignatieff issued one of his several complaints about how Harper had shown disrespect for Parliament in particular and Canadian democracy more generally, Layton pointed out that the Liberal leader had missed 70 percent of the House of Commons votes, and added: "[M]ost Canadians, if they don't show up for work, they don't get a promotion." Indignant, Ignatieff attempted to rebut, but Layton struck again, saying that the Liberal leader needed to learn more about how "our democracy works." A number of observers believed the exchange was the highlight of the debates, and a defining moment for both leaders.

Certainly, the 2011 PSC survey data indicate that many Canadians were positively impressed by Layton's debate performance. As Figure 8 illustrates, a large plurality (46 percent) of those who watched or listened to the debates judged that the NDP leader had won. Harper also did reasonably well, with one-third choosing him as the winner. Ignatieff and Duceppe fared very poorly—only 5 percent and 7 percent, respectively, chose one of them as the winner. Responses about who had lost the debates were a mirror image. Fully 41 percent believed Ignatieff had lost the debates, and another large group (32 percent) thought Duceppe had lost. In sharp contrast, only 16 percent selected Harper as the loser, and hardly any (3 percent) selected Layton.

Figure 8. Best and Worst Performances in the Leader Debates

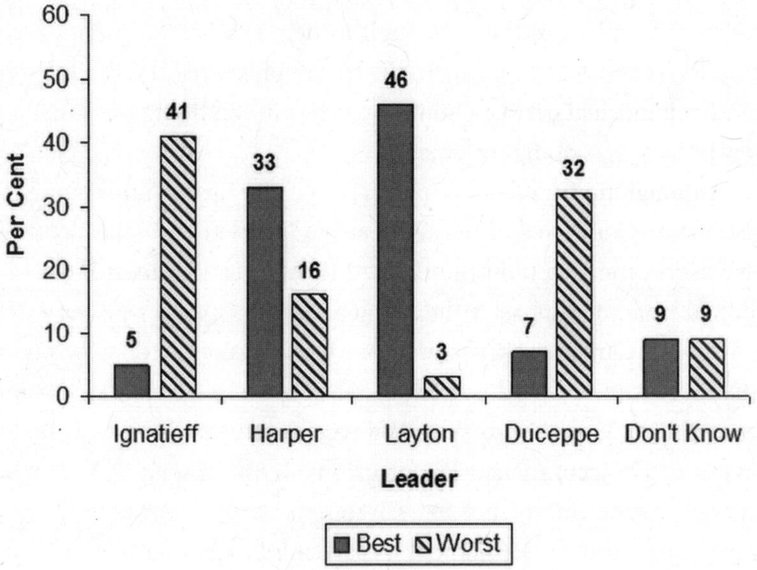

Source: 2011 Political Support in Canada post-election survey.

Statistical analyses suggest that perceptions of debate winners and losers influenced voters' images of the party leaders. For example, controlling for party identification and party chosen as best on voters' most important issue, people who thought that Jack Layton had won the debates rated him 1.2 points higher on the 0–10 point like-dislike scale than did people who thought some other leader had won the debates, or who thought that no one had won (data not shown). Comparable effects for Harper, Ignatieff, and Duceppe are increases of 1.1 points, 2.9 points, and 2.7 points, respectively. There is also evidence that perceptions of being a loser are influential.

Thus, other things being equal, people who thought Layton had lost the debates scored him 2.3 points lower on the 0–10 like-dislike scale. Again, the pattern for Harper, Ignatieff, and Duceppe is the same: Harper is scored 1.5 points lower among people judging him the loser, Ignatieff .30 points lower, and Duceppe .30 points lower. Finally, there is evidence that perceiving another leader as the loser increases support for particular leaders. For example, Ignatieff's like-dislike score is 1.8 points higher among respondents who thought Harper had lost the debates, 1.4 points higher among those who thought Layton had lost, and 1.0 point higher among those who thought Duceppe had lost. Comparable patterns appear in the analyses of Harper's, Layton's, and Duceppe's like-dislike scores. Taken together, these results suggest that the leaders' images were affected by perceptions of how they had performed in the debates.

More dramatic evidence that the debates mattered comes from public opinion polls tracking vote intention dynamics. To this end Figure 9 presents a "poll of polls" conducted from January 1, 2011, to election day. As the figure shows, in the wake of the leaders' debates, support for the NDP began a sharp upward climb, moving from 18 percent to 32 percent at the end of the campaign. The pattern for the Liberals is exactly the opposite. At the time of the debates, the Liberal vote intention share stood at 28 percent, one point above what it had been at the campaign's outset. However, after the debates, the Liberal slide began, with the party's support falling to 20 percent on the eve of the election.

Debate effects for other parties appear much smaller. The BQ lost a great deal of its support over the course of the campaign, and the slide depicted in Figure 9 is quite steady. Starting at 10 percent when the campaign began, BQ support was at 8 percent at the time of the debates, before finishing at 6 percent. Green support was also on a protracted downward trend. Starting at 9 percent at the beginning of 2011, the Green vote intention share had already fallen to 7 percent when the campaign began. Still at 7 percent when the debates were held, Green support dropped another point by the time of the election.

The Conservative support pattern was different again. Although a third of the public believed that party leader Stephen Harper won the debates, and less than one person in six thought he had lost them, his

Figure 9. Trends in Federal Party Support, January 1–May 1, 2011

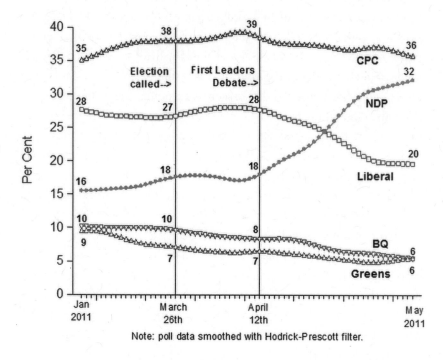

Note: poll data smoothed with Hodrick-Prescott filter.

Source: Sixty-eight public opinion polls published between January 1 and May 1, 2011.

party did not move upwards after the debates. Rather, it lost three points, trending downward from 39 to 36 percent by the end of the campaign. This difference was not great, but statistical models designed to convert popular vote totals into parliamentary seat totals indicated that being in the 39–40 percent range was crucial for the CPC to win a majority. Accordingly, looking at polls conducted in the last week of the campaign, a number of analysts concluded that the game was lost for the Conservatives, and that Canada would once again have a minority government.

However, these minority government forecasts were wrong. As noted in the introduction, on election day the Conservatives received 39.7 percent of the vote, enough to get 166 seats and a parliamentary majority. Final NDP and the Liberal poll numbers were somewhat closer to the mark, with the NDP getting just over 30 percent of the vote and the Liberals just over 18 percent. Late polls showing a BQ debacle were on target as well — as widely anticipated, Duceppe and his party were swept away by the NDP tsunami that engulfed Quebec. As for the Greens, late polls slightly exaggerated their vote; rather than being 6 percent, it came in just below 4 percent. On election night, Elizabeth May's victory in Saanich–Gulf Islands was the only result for Greens to cheer about. In the next section, we present the results of multivariate analyses that assess the strength of various factors influencing voting in 2011.

MAKING POLITICAL CHOICES 2011

Studies have repeatedly shown that party leader images, perceptions of parties as best able to handle issues deemed important by voters, and (flexible) partisan attachments have major effects on voting behaviour.[14] The importance of voters' views of parties and leaders is suggested by the data in Figure 10. When asked which factor was most important for determining their vote, pluralities of Canadians participating in a series of election surveys conducted since 1974 have always reported "parties as a whole." However, sizable minorities have always said "party leaders" or "local candidates," with the number citing leaders being largest in the 1970s and early 1980s, and then again in 2008 and 2011, with the 2011 number perhaps reflecting the very positive reception given NDP Leader Jack Layton. In an analysis of voting in the 2008 federal election,[15] we speculated that the relative importance in the earlier period might be attributed to the presence of the charismatic Pierre Trudeau.[16] We also hypothesized that the growing strength of "parties as a whole" in the 1980s and 1990s might have reflected the breakup of the old "two-party-plus" federal party system and the rise of Reform and Bloc Québécois, two ideologically distinctive parties with strong regional bases. The validity of these conjectures aside, as Figure 10 illustrates, the combined strength of leaders and parties in reports of what influenced voting behaviour is always readily apparent. *Circa* 2011, more than eight PSC respondents in ten said that one of these two factors was most important for their vote.

Figure 10. Importance of Party Leaders, Local Candidates, and
Parties as a Whole in Vote Decisions, 1974–2011 Federal Elections

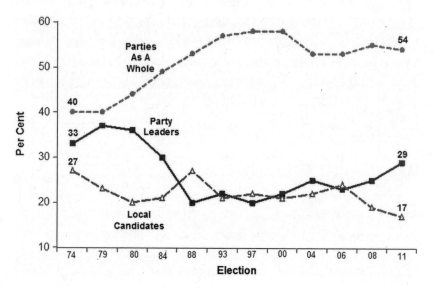

Source: Pammett and Dornan, 2006, 2008, and 2011 Political Support in Canada post-election surveys.

A more comprehensive analysis of the factors influencing voting
behaviour in 2011 is presented in Table 2. Numbers in this table illustrate the ability of several predictor variables to affect the probability of
voting for various parties. The presence of a large number of significant
effects emphasizes that a variety of forces are at work. The five strongest
effects on voting for each party are shown in boldface.

As anticipated, leader images had powerful effects on electoral choice
in 2011. We illustrate the point by manipulating the like-dislike scores
voters gave to the party leaders. For example, when we increased Harper's
score on the "like-dislike" scale across its range from 0 to 10, the probability of voting Conservative increased by fully .66 points. In contrast,
increasingly positive feelings towards NDP leader Jack Layton reduced
the probability of choosing the Tories by .41 points. Increasingly positive
support for the Green Party Leader Elizabeth May and opposition to Bloc
Leader Gilles Duceppe also reduced the probability of a voter choosing
the Conservatives — by .20 and .13 points, respectively.

Table 2. Significant Predictors and Changes in Probabilities of Voting for Various Parties

| | | Changes in Probabilities of Voting for Various Parties | | | | |
| | | Party | | | | |
Predictor Variable		CPC	Liberal	NDP	Green	BQ
Leader:	Ignatieff	--	**.45**	**-.27**	--	--
	Harper	**.66**	--	--	--	--
	Layton	**-.41**	**-.23**	**.60**	--	**-.74**
	Duceppe	-.20	-.12	--	--	.62
	May	-.13	--	--	.32	--
Party ID:	Liberal	--	.22	-.10	-.06	--
	CPC	.22	-.12	-.20	-.05	--
	NDP	--	-.09	.17	--	--
	BQ	-.23	-.19	-.20	--	--
	Green	--	--	--	--	-.28
Party Best on Top Ranked Issue:	Liberal	-.32	.31	-.23	--	-.19
	CPC	.30	-.11	-.25	--	--
	NDP	-.16	-.09	.13	-.05	--
	BQ	--	--	-.40	--	.61
	Green	--	--	-.42	.28	-.21
Single Party Majority Government:		.15	--	--	--	--
Contempt of Parliament		-.41	.17	.34	-.17	--
Health care Performance		--	--	--	--	--
Health care Spending		-.29	--	--	--	-.43
Positional Issues:						
	Economic	--	--	--	.23	.76
	Social	--	--	--	--	--
	Quebec Sovereignty	xx	xx	xx	xx	.28
Region/Ethnicity:						xx
	Atlantic	--	.15	--	-.03	xx
	Quebec-French	--	--	--	--	--

	Quebec- Non French	-.10	--	--	-.04	xx
	Prairies	--	--	--	--	xx
	British Columbia	--	-.13	.12	--	xx
Age		--	--	-.25	-.05	.55
Education		--	--	--	--	--
Gender		--	--	--	--	--
Income		--	--	-.12	--	--

boldface	— five largest effects on voting for a particular party.
--	— effect not statistically significant, p<0.05 or less.
xx	— predictor variable not included in model.

Note: Probabilities are calculated as the ability of a statistically significant ($p \leq .05$) pre-dictor variable to change the probability of voting for a party from its achieved vote share in the election with other predictor variables held at their mean values. Parameters in voting models are estimated using binomial logit analyses.

Reading across the columns in Table 2, one sees that feelings about NDP leader Jack Layton significantly influenced four of the five voting choices, whereas support for Harper was only relevant for the decision of whether to vote Conservative. Highly positive feelings about the NDP leader greatly increased the probability of voting for his party *and* decreased the chances of voting for any of the opposition parties except the Greens. It appears that Layton's attractiveness played a pivotal role in his party's major breakthrough in Quebec; increasingly positive feelings about the NDP leader were capable of reducing the chances of voting for the once potent Bloc by fully .74 points.

Sanguine images of Liberal leader Michael Ignatieff were also important, having the capacity to significantly increase the probability of voting Liberal (by .45 points) and reduce the probability of voting for the NDP (by .27 points). Unfortunately for the Liberals, these effects did little to help them because, as discussed earlier, in contrast to being enthusiastic about Jack Layton, most voters were genuinely sour about Ignatieff. Finally, increasingly positive feelings about Green and BQ party leaders May and Duceppe mattered too, significantly enhancing propensities to cast ballots for these parties. Both effects were large —.32 and .62 points, respectively.

As anticipated, judgments about party performance on important issues also had a variety of significant effects. Believing that the Conservatives were best able to handle one of these issues increased the probability of a CPC vote by .30 points and decreased the likelihood of voting Liberal and NDP by .11 and .25 points, respectively. The Liberals also garnered a sizable increment in support (.31 points) if they were seen as best on a most-important issue. Again, the Liberals' problem in 2011 was that only 11 percent of the electorate preferred them on such issues. Supporting the Bloc on an issue that mattered most had potent effects as well. It both increased the chances of supporting the BQ by .61 points *and* reduced the likelihood of voting for the NDP by .40 points. Again, the small number of people who listed the Greens as best able to handle the most important issue were significantly more likely to vote for that party (by .28 points).

As is also the norm for Canadian elections, partisanship also exerted a variety of predictable effects. As documented in Table 2, thirteen of twenty-five possible partisan effects were statistically significant and all of them were in the expected direction. For example, compared to people without a party identification, those with a CPC identification were .20 points more likely to vote Conservative, those with a Liberal identification were .22 points more likely to vote Liberal, and those with an NDP identification were .17 points more likely to vote New Democrat. Switches in partisanship were even more consequential; for example, if a voter moved from being a Conservative to being an NDP partisan, the probability of casting a New Democratic ballot increased by .37 (from -.20 to .17) points. NDP balloting also was predictably and negatively affected by identifications with the Liberals (-.10 points), the CPC (-.20 points), and the BQ (-.20 points).

Controlling for of the effects discussed above, opinions about the contempt of Parliament charges that precipitated the 2011 election mattered. Moving from thinking the charges were not serious at all to thinking that the charges were very serious reduced the probability of a Conservative vote by .41 points and increased the probability of voting Liberal or NDP by .17 and .34 points, respectively. These figures suggest that the Liberals' attack on Harper and his party for undemocratic behaviour had traction. However, it appears that the NDP, not the Liberals, were major beneficiaries from this issue.

Several other factors also influenced voting for various parties. For example, although positions on economic issues concerning wealth (re) distribution did not affect CPC, Liberal, or NDP voting, moving from a very negative to a very positive position on such issues helped the Greens (by .23 points) and strongly enhanced the probability of casting a ballot for the Bloc (.76 points). This effect was considerably more potent than the sovereignty issue (.28 points) in motivating BQ support in 2011. Regarding other factors, although positions on a social issue dimension defined by opinions about gay rights, abortion, and the gun registry did not exert significant effects on voting for any of the parties, the issue of majority versus minority government mattered for CPC balloting. But the effect was not particularly large; Canadians who were tired of the parliamentary deadlock were more likely (.15 points) to throw their support to the Conservatives than those who favoured minority government or were not concerned with the matter. This result indicates that despite the emphasis Prime Minister Harper placed on the majority government issue, it was not a key factor motivating people to support his party in 2011.

The effects of other factors are worth noting as well. Support for additional spending on health care, although very widespread, had an influence on election-day decisions only in the cases of the Bloc (-.43 points) and the Conservatives (-.29 points). Moreover, and likely to the detriment of the Liberals who emphasized the issue in their campaign, opinions about the federal government's performance in delivering health care were not significant predictors of voting for any of the parties. Finally, in the small number of instances where demographic factors (age, education, gender, income, region/ethnicity) were significant, most effects were quite small. The only exception was the relationship between age and BQ support. The effect was strong (.55 points) and positive, suggesting that other things being equal, elderly people were more likely to cast their ballots for the Bloc. What this relationship says about the BQ's future prospects remains to be seen.

CONCLUSION

As is typical in Canadian elections, a powerful combination of party leader images, judgments about party and leader performance on valence issues, and flexible partisan attachments did much to drive the vote. Although many voters remained less than enthusiastic about Stephen Harper, they believed that he was the most capable leader on the issue that mattered most, the economy. Many judged that he had done a good job in guiding Canada through the recent economic crisis, and, in sharp contrast to 2008, they expressed optimism about the future. Layton was in some sense a mirror image of Harper; although he had not made a convincing case that he was best able to deal with the economy or most other important issues, he was extremely well liked.

In sharp contrast to his rivals, Liberal Leader Michael Ignatieff was neither loved nor trusted. Ignatieff had correctly concluded that there were political gains to be had by charging that Prime Minister Harper was a "control freak" who had held Parliament in contempt and run roughshod over Canadian democracy. However, Ignatieff was unable to capitalize on these charges. Framed by Conservative attack ads as an arrogant, self-centred Harvard professor who was "just visiting" Canada on the prospect of becoming prime minister, Ignatieff received an extremely chilly reception from the electorate. Nor was he able to establish his bona fides on the economy or the traditional Liberal strong suit, health care, or, for that matter, on any other issues that Canadians cared about. Snookered by his street-smart NDP rival in the first leader debate, Ignatieff never recovered, and Liberal fortunes went downhill in the last two weeks of the campaign. The day after the election he announced his resignation as Liberal leader and quickly returned to academic life.

Operating quietly in the background was partisanship, the third in the triumvirate of explanatory variables that animate the valence politics model of electoral choice that does much to explain why Canadians vote as they do. Since its initial foray into the national electoral arena in 2004 the Conservative Party has gradually increased its share of party identifiers to 30 percent of the electorate. By historical standards, this is very a modest number to use as a base for winning a parliamentary majority, but its power in 2011 was magnified by the sharp erosion in the number of Liberal partisans. A decade ago, fully two in five Canadians identified themselves as federal Liberals; coming into the 2011 election only one in five did. Half the Liberals' partisan base had disappeared. The missing Liberals have not been replaced by large groups of identifiers with any of the other federal parties. As a result, the Conservatives found themselves fighting the 2011 campaign in the unprecedented position of having a sizable lead in the number of party identifiers. This, in turn, made it easier for them to leverage their strength on the campaign's major valence issue, the economy, and related strength flowing from Harper's image as the leader best able to restore the Canadian economy to its full good health.

NOTES

1. For analyses of turnout in Canadian federal elections, see Jon H. Pammett and Lawrence LeDuc, *Explaining the Turnout Decline in Canadian Federal Elections: Evidence from a New Survey of Non-Voters* (Ottawa: Elections Canada, 2003) and Harold D. Clarke, Allan Kornberg, and Thomas J. Scotto, *Making Political Choices: Canada and the United States* (Toronto: University of Toronto Press, 2009), Chapter 8.
2. The 2011 PSC study (version 1.0 data release) interviewed 2,500 respondents via the Internet in the three weeks leading up to the election. Shortly after the election, 1,810 of these respondents were re-interviewed in a follow-up Internet survey. Fieldwork was carried out by Polimetrix, and funding for the survey was provided by a National Science Foundation RAPID grant to Jason Reifler and a faculty research grant to Thomas J. Scotto (with Ailsa Henderson) from the Canadian High Commission, London. All interpretations of the election and the data belong to the authors.
3. For an analysis of the relationship between evaluations of the economy and support for Prime Minister Harper in 2008, see Harold D. Clarke, Thomas J. Scotto, and Allan Kornberg, "Valence Politics and Economic Crisis: Electoral Choice in Canada, 2008," *Electoral Studies* (2011) 30: 438–39.

4.   On the distinction between valence and position issues, see Donald E. Stokes, "Spatial Models of Party Competition," *American Political Science Review* 57 (1963): 368–77. Studies that emphasize the role of valence politics in Canada include Harold D. Clarke, Jane Jenson, Lawrence LeDuc, and Jon Pammett, *Absent Mandate: Canadian Politics in an Era of Restructuring*, 3rd edition (Toronto: Gage Educational Publishing, 1996) and Clarke et al., *Making Political Choices.*

5.   The social-psychological conception of party identification was developed in Angus Campbell, Philip E. Converse, Warren E. Miller, and Donald E. Stokes, *The American Voter* (New York: Wiley, 1960).

6.   On the instability of partisan identification in Canada, see Clarke et al., *Absent Mandate*, and Harold D. Clarke and Allan McCutcheon, "The Dynamics of Party Identification Reconsidered," *Public Opinion Quarterly* 73 (2009): 704–28. On the propensity of Canadians to have different partisan identifications in federal and provincial politics, see Marianne C. Stewart and Harold D. Clarke, "The Dynamics of Party Identification in Federal Systems: The Canadian Case," *American Journal of Political Science* 42 (1998): 97–116.

7.   The question used to ascertain respondents' party identification on the PSC studies is "Thinking about *federal politics*, do you *usually* think of yourself as Liberal, Conservative, NDP, Bloc Québécois, or what?"

8.   Clarke et al., *Absent Mandate.*

9.   Clarke et al., *Absent Mandate* and Clarke et. al, *Making Political Choices.*

10. See, for example, Paul M. Sniderman, Richard A. Brody, and Philip Tetlock, *Reasoning and Choice: Explorations in Political Psychology* (Cambridge: Cambridge University Press, 1991) and Gerd Gigerenzer, *Rationality for Mortals* (Oxford: Oxford University Press, 2008).

11. Information regarding the PSC surveys including question wording, answer choice options, and variable construction can be found on Scotto's homepage (*www.thomasjscotto.co.uk*). Statistical analyses used to estimate the probabilities shown in Table 2 are also located on this site.

12. Harold D. Clarke, Allan Kornberg, and Thomas J. Scotto, "None of the Above: Voters in the 2008 Federal Election," in *The Canadian Federal Election of 2008*, ed. Jon H. Pammett and Christopher Dornan (Toronto: Dundurn Press, 2009).

13. Michael Ignatieff, *True Patriot Love: Four Generations in Search of Canada* (Toronto: Viking Canada, 2009).

14. Clarke et al., *Making Political Choices.*

15. Clarke, Kornberg and Scotto, 2009.

16. Clarke et al., "Valence Politics and Economic Crisis."

CHAPTER 12

The Evolution of the Harper Dynasty

Lawrence LeDuc | Jon H. Pammett

The Conservative majority government produced by the 2011 federal election ultimately came as something of a surprise, although the potential for such an outcome was always present. Achieved with just 39.6 percent of the total vote (the second smallest in Canadian history), the Conservative victory was nevertheless a convincing one. Adding a net gain of twenty-one seats in Ontario to its strong base in the West, the Harper Conservatives benefited both from the collapse of the Liberals and the splitting of votes between opposition parties as the NDP surged in Central Canada. Only in Quebec, where they lost five seats (including three Cabinet ministers) and saw their total vote reduced to 16.5 percent, did the Conservatives experience any decline from the vote share that the party had obtained in the two previous elections (see Table 1). The question therefore to be addressed in this chapter is whether the 2011 outcome represents merely another election victory for the Harper Conservatives or the establishment of a "Harper dynasty." We will argue that the conditions for the latter interpretation have already been met.

DYNASTIES AND INTERLUDES

At fifty-two years of age, Stephen Harper has now been prime minister for slightly more than five years. The 2011 election result all but guarantees that he will remain in office for at least another four. By the time of the next federal election, Harper's tenure in office will begin to approach that of Jean Chrétien. Another election victory would place Harper firmly

Table 1. Results of the 2006, 2008, and 2011 Federal Elections, by Province

		CPC			LIB			NDP			Bloc		
		2006	2008	2011	2006	2008	2011	2006	2008	2011	2006	2008	2011
Newfoundland	votes (%)	43	16	28	43	47	38	14	34	33			
	seats (#)	3		1	4	6	4		1	2			
Prince Edward Island	votes (%)	33	36	41	53	48	41	10	10	15			
	seats (#)		1	1	4	3	3						
Nova Scotia	votes (%)	30	26	37	37	30	29	30	29	30			
	seats (#)	3	3	4	6	5	4	2	2	3			
New Brunswick	votes (%)	36	39	44	39	32	23	22	22	30			
	seats (#)	3	6	8	6	3	1	1	1	1			
Quebec	votes (%)	25	22	17	21	24	14	7	12	43	42	38	23
	seats (#)	10	10	5	13	14	7		1	59	51	49	4
Ontario	votes (%)	35	39	44	40	34	25	19	18	26			
	seats (#)	40	51	73	54	38	11	12	17	22			
Manitoba	votes (%)	43	49	54	26	19	17	25	24	26			
	seats (#)	8	9	11	3	1	1	3	4	2			

Saskatchewan	votes (%)	49	54	56	22	15	9	24	26	32			
	seats (#)	12	13	13	2	1	1						
Alberta	votes (%)	65	65	67	15	11	9	12	13	17			
	seats (#)	28	27	27					1	1			
British Columbia	votes (%)	37	44	46	28	19	13	28	26	33			
	seats (#)	17	22	21	9	5	2	10	9	12			
Yukon / NWT / Nunavut	votes (%)	23	35	36	41	30	26	30	25	28			
	seats (#)		1	2	2	1		1	1	1			
TOTAL CANADA	votes (%)	36	38	40	30	26	19	17	18	31	10	10	6
	seats (#)	124	143	166	103	77	34	29	37	103	49	51	4

One Independent was elected in 2006, and two in 2008. One Green Party in 2011.

among Canada's longest enduring and most politically successful leaders. This is therefore an appropriate time to look both forward and backward in order to better understand the rise of the Harper dynasty. By examining the outcome of not just the 2011 election but also those of 2006 and 2008, we can identify some of the factors that have led to Harper's electoral success. And a closer examination of the 2011 results utilizing currently available data can also provide clues to the Conservatives' future prospects.

FIGURE 1
Dynasties and Interludes in Canadian politics
(adapted from *Dynasties and Interludes*, p. 523)

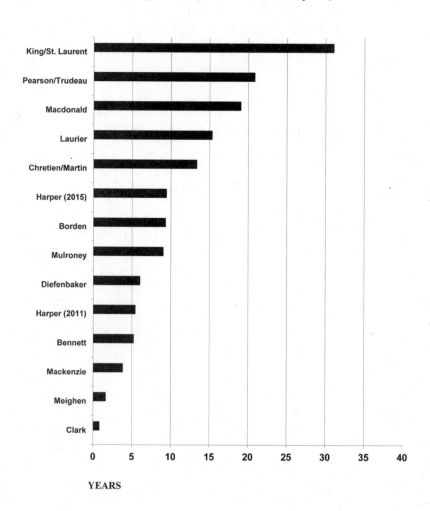

YEARS

As documented in our new book, *Dynasties and Interludes: Past and Present in Canadian Electoral Politics*, only five of Canada's most politically successful prime ministers built electoral dynasties that endured for long periods of time. John A. Macdonald, Wilfrid Laurier, William Lyon Mackenzie King (followed by Louis St. Laurent), Pierre Trudeau (preceded by Lester B. Pearson), and Jean Chrétien (with Paul Martin) were the only leaders who managed to create periods of sustained political dominance (see Figure 1). This group was certainly not unique in winning resounding electoral victories. Alexander Mackenzie, Robert Borden, R.B. Bennett, John Diefenbaker, and Brian Mulroney, despite opportunities to build on their election victories, ultimately presided over interludes between the dynasties created by others. And some (e.g. Arthur Meighen and Joe Clark) lost power after even briefer periods at the helm.

Canadian federal politics has repeatedly followed this pattern — long periods of political hegemony under successful political leaders, punctuated by short, sharp interludes. The Harper dynasty, which would become the sixth such period of dominance and only the second Conservative dynasty, may or may not extend beyond the next four years. But with three consecutive election victories, it clearly fits the definition of a dynasty according to the criteria that we have applied to earlier periods — a point that we will develop further in the next section of this chapter. The dynasties achieved their preeminence and longevity not by the personal appeal of their leaders, though this often played a part, but rather by their ability to capture a degree of public trust on the three main issue areas that are nearly always present in Canadian electoral politics. These three "keys to victory" have been: to be perceived by the public as the leader and party best positioned to solve the key economic questions of the time; to have the ability to ensure national unity; and (at least since the early twentieth century) to gain public confidence on the issue of expanding or preserving the social safety net provided by the key elements of the modern welfare state — e.g. health care, pensions, unemployment insurance — on which large numbers of Canadians depend.

In the first Canadian dynasty, John A. Macdonald combined his ability to bridge the interests of the different regions of the country with his National Policy of industrial protection and railway construction.

On Macdonald's death, Wilfrid Laurier assumed the mantle of French-English harmony, and pursued economic policies of freer trade and economic growth in a period of industrial expansion. Both Macdonald and Laurier were masters of political patronage, which they used effectively to deliver benefits to groups and regions that supported their parties in the era before the rise of the welfare state. William Lyon Mackenzie King and his successor, Louis St. Laurent, likewise established the Liberal party as the champion of national unity, the steward of economic growth, and added to these the early building blocks of the Canadian welfare state through pensions and unemployment insurance. Pierre Trudeau, although he ended his political career as a divisive figure, embodied national unity by promoting bilingualism and confronting the threat of Quebec separatism, and also sustained social welfare measures through his "Just Society." It was Trudeau's struggles with the economic downturns, inflation, and unemployment of the 1970s and '80s that interrupted and ultimately ended the Trudeau dynasty. Finally, Jean Chrétien and Paul Martin restored economic stability and concentrated on preserving social welfare measures — particularly health care. They struggled to establish their credentials on national unity, but were helped immeasurably in that area by the rise of the Bloc Québécois and the inability of the Progressive Conservatives to hold together the Quebec-West coalition that had been constructed by Brian Mulroney.

Has Stephen Harper captured these three pillars of Canadian electoral success and thereby established the basis for a second Conservative dynasty? After the 2004 failure, his successful 2006 campaign seemed to point in that direction. Helped by the collapse of the Martin regime and the sponsorship scandal, the Conservatives made short-term but realistic commitments in the economic realm (GST cuts) and the welfare area (money to cut hospital wait times and support child care), and courted Quebec sufficiently successfully to elect ten members in that province in 2006, thus positioning the Conservatives as a party of national reach, if not national unity. In 2008, however, despite winning more seats and slightly improving their total vote share, the Conservatives experienced setbacks in their mastery of all three issue areas. Only the economy appeared to continue to work in their favour, although the uncertainties wrought by the global economic crisis placed even that area at risk as the financial crisis in the United States accelerated during the campaign.[1] In the 2011 campaign, the modest economic recovery and program of fiscal stimulus (the Economic Action Plan) worked more clearly in their favour, and they managed to at least neutralize any advantage that the other parties may have held in the social welfare area with repeated commitments to protecting health care. Only in the national unity area, with their continued weakness in Quebec, did the Conservatives fall short of meeting the standards established by other successful dynasties. This weakness clearly has the potential to undermine the Harper dynasty, just as a similar failure prevented the establishment of a Diefenbaker dynasty in the 1960s.[2] But for the present, the Conservatives' dominance in two regions — the West and Ontario — together with the Liberals' inability to re-establish their position in Quebec, has at least neutralized this factor. With a majority

Table 2. Six Elections that Established New Political Dynasties
(adapted from *Dynasties and Interludes*, p. 27)

	Macdonald	Laurier	King	Trudeau	Chrétien	Harper
ESTABLISHING	1867	1896	1921	1968	1993	2006
TESTING	1872 1874[1] 1878	1900	1925	1972	1997	2008
CONFIRMING	1882 1887 1891	1904 1908	1926 1930[2] 1935 1940 1945 1949[5] 1953	1974 1979[3] 1980	2000 2004[4]	2011

1. Mackenzie interlude 1949
2. Bennett interlude
3. Clark interlude
4. Liberal party led by Paul Martin
5. Liberal party led by Louis St. Laurent

Table 3. Six Elections that Failed to Establish New Dynasties
(from *Dynasties and Interludes*, p. 27)

	Mackenzie	Borden	Bennett	Diefenbaker	Clark	Mulroney
ESTABLISHING	1874	1911	1930	1957–58	1979	1984
TESTING	1878	1917[1]	1935	1962	1980	1988
NOT CONFIRMING		1921[2]		1963		1993[3]

1. Union government
2. Conservative party led by Arthur Meighen
3. Progressive Conservative party led by Kim Campbell

government and four years to work on establishing themselves as *the* party of national unity, the Harper Conservatives may be able to overcome this weakness. Alternatively, either Harper's continued inability to appeal to Quebec voters, or events beyond his control (such as a third referendum) could eventually place the Harper dynasty at risk. And, of course, the NDP, with its breakthrough in Quebec and strong performance in *all* regions of the country, may now be well placed to compete effectively in this area.

ESTABLISHING A DYNASTY

The establishment of the five earlier dynasties described above was not a simple matter. While each of the dynasties started with a decisive election victory, the new electoral pattern established in that election was tested in the one following. Often, given the inherent volatility of Canadian electoral politics, the existence of the dynasty could not be confirmed until a third election demonstrated the staying power of both the party and its leader (see Table 2). In the cases of both Mackenzie King and Trudeau, the test that occurred after their initial election was a dramatic one. King lost the election of 1925 but managed to remain in power for eight months before yielding to Arthur Meighen, whom he defeated more decisively in the subsequent election (1926). Trudeau's election victory in 1968 was followed by near defeat in 1972. Only after his political recovery in the 1974 election would it have been possible to discern the shape and durability of the Trudeau dynasty. Such patterns suggest that, to understand electoral politics in Canada, it is essential not to put too much emphasis on the interpretation of a single election. Instead, it is important to place elections within the context of a longer and more complex process of political and social change.

The six periods that we classify as interludes (see Table 3) also contain many elements of complexity. A few, such as the single-term governments of Alexander Mackenzie (1874–78) or R.B. Bennett (1930–35), are readily demarcated. Likewise, the nine-month administration headed by Joe Clark (1979–80) represents a temporary break, with Pierre Trudeau returning to power decisively in the election of 1980. But others are not so readily classified. The Borden government of 1911 might not have lasted so long had its term not been extended first by the war and subsequently by the election of a wartime Unionist government in 1917. Historically, it now appears as an extended interlude, in spite of the decisiveness of the 1911 and 1917 elections. The Diefenbaker and Mulroney periods are likewise complicated segments of Canadian electoral history. Given their one-sided election victories (Diefenbaker in 1958, Mulroney in 1984), both of these leaders had the potential to establish new political dynasties. Mulroney in particular had the clear determination to do so. But, for a number of reasons specific to the periods in which they governed or the political choices that they made, neither Diefenbaker nor Mulroney was able to translate his dramatic election victory into the type of lasting political success attained by Mackenzie King or Trudeau. Despite the 1958 landslide, Diefenbaker failed a crucial electoral test in the election of 1962, and his government was defeated a year later. Mulroney, in contrast, won a difficult re-election in 1988, but was ultimately unable to either hold on to power himself or to pass the leadership on to a successor who could do so.

As is shown in Table 2, we now include the Harper period as a sixth dynasty according to this classification, showing how it has met the electoral test that we applied to earlier dynasties.[3] The fact that two of the

Conservatives' recent election victories produced minority governments is only a limited qualification. Mackenzie King's initial victory in 1921 was likewise a minority, and his outright loss of the 1925 election would have made his political future appear uncertain indeed to his contemporaries. Likewise, Trudeau's reduction to a minority in 1972 would have caused many at the time to interpret the 1968 victory as a one- time wave of "Trudeaumania."[4] Yet both King and Trudeau, in spite of their electoral setbacks, went on to lead successful dynasties. Harper's beginnings are at least as convincing as either of these former leaders at a comparable stage of their political careers. Diefenbaker and Mulroney, in contrast, would have been prone to a different kind of misinterpretation in the context of their times. The sheer size of their initial electoral victories made them appear invincible. Yet neither was able to translate electoral victory alone into the kind of political longevity needed to establish a dynasty.

PAST AND PRESENT

Canada's most politically successful prime ministers built electoral dynasties that endured for long periods of time. William Lyon Mackenzie King served a total of twenty-two years as prime minister before handing power over to Louis St. Laurent, who served another nine years. Jean Chrétien served more than ten years before handing the job over to Paul Martin, who, for most of that time, had been his Minister of Finance. These periods of electoral dominance, which in Canada are often identified with the fortunes of individual political leaders, are truly long ones by most comparative standards. In Britain — perhaps the most useful comparison because of institutional similarities — only a few leaders have approached these degrees of political longevity. Winston Churchill, for example, served two terms in office spanning a total of nine years, but these were separated by one stunning electoral defeat (1945). Margaret Thatcher won three consecutive elections, serving a total of eleven years as prime minister. Tony Blair served ten before handing power over to Gordon Brown. While William Gladstone served longer (fourteen years), his tenure was spread across four interrupted terms in office. American presidents, of course, are now constitutionally limited to two four-year terms, but even before the enactment of the 22nd Amendment, only Franklin D. Roosevelt served longer than eight years. The first question that we posed in *Dynasties and Interludes*, therefore, was: What explains these patterns of enduring success enjoyed by Canadian political leaders and by the parties that they led? As Stephen Harper now appears poised to join this elite group, understanding the basis for such continued electoral success becomes even more pertinent.

The interludes that we encounter periodically over the course of Canadian political history have been, with a few exceptions, short and sharp. The stark contrast between these brief interludes and the successful political dynasties tells much of the story of Canadian federal politics as it has evolved over nearly a century and a half. A second question, therefore, is: Can we explain how and why these brief interludes occurred, even in some instances when the dynasties that they toppled appeared secure?

Part of the answer to these questions is found in the cases that do not fit so neatly into our typology of dynasties and interludes. Lester Pearson, for example, served six years as prime minister, and his tenure in the office is highly regarded by historians today, in part because of the significant policy achievements of his administration. But Pearson endured one of the worst electoral defeats in Canadian history at the hands of John Diefenbaker in 1958, and he never succeeded in obtaining a majority of parliamentary seats in the two elections that he won (1963 and 1965). Yet, unlike Borden, he *did* manage to pass the reins of power along to a successor who presided over one of the more enduring political dynasties of recent times. Do we think then of a Pearson interlude or a Pearson/Trudeau dynasty, as is suggested by the configuration employed in Figure 1 and as we have argued in *Dynasties and Interludes*? Neither term captures with total accuracy the high and low points, the successes and failures, of the Pearson and Trudeau eras. But, with the benefit of hindsight, we can now see that the longevity of the Pearson/ Trudeau dynasty rivals those of Macdonald and Laurier, even though neither Pearson nor Trudeau enjoyed unqualified political success over the course of their political careers.

The fortunes of two other political leaders who fell short of establishing dynasties can also help us to formulate part of the answer to the questions posed above. John Diefenbaker and Brian Mulroney led the Progressive Conservative Party to two of its greatest electoral victories, in 1958 and 1984 respectively, but neither was able to found a political dynasty based on this initial success. Diefenbaker's six-year tenure as prime minister ended ignominiously with his defeat in the 1963 election and his ouster from the party leadership in 1967. Mulroney's two terms culminated in the near destruction of his party in the disastrous 1993 election. However, both leaders left a political legacy that endured long after their time in office had ended. Diefenbaker bequeathed to his successors a solidly Conservative West and Mulroney a nationalist Quebec. In part, the huge and unwieldy electoral coalitions that these two leaders built explain both their initial success and their ultimate failure. In the longer term, holding these diverse coalitions together proved more difficult than constructing them in the first place.

The construction of the Harper dynasty has been more incremental. It was Preston Manning who established the dominance of the Reform party in the West, but he was unable to extend that success significantly beyond his regional base. Under the banner of Reform's successor party, the Canadian Alliance, Stockwell Day did somewhat better, obtaining 24 percent of the vote in Ontario in the 2000 federal election, but only two seats in the province. With the merger of the Alliance and Progressive Conservatives in 2003, Harper was well positioned to build on this base. Aided by the "sponsorship scandal" in 2004, the Conservatives' vote share in Ontario improved to 31 percent, yielding twenty-four parliamentary seats. Nearly all of these were in rural areas of the province. The 2006 election, which brought the party to power, added a breakthrough in Quebec, with the Conservatives obtaining 25 percent of the vote and ten seats in that province. Thus, each election saw another building block added, while at the same time retaining all or most of the gains realized previously. One of the weaknesses of the Conservatives in the 2006 and 2008 elections had been their failure to win a seat in any of Canada's three largest cities. This was overcome in 2011 with the party's breakthrough in metropolitan Toronto, taking a number of urban seats previously held by Liberals.

There was thus no stunning electoral victory like that of 1958 or 1984 that inaugurated the Harper era. Rather, like Mackenzie King in the 1920s, it gradually took shape as new electoral alignments consolidated and old ones further weakened. It remains to be seen, of course, whether all or most of these patterns will remain in place in a future election. We do not know whether either the Bloc or the Liberals can recover, or whether the NDP can build upon its 2011 feat. However, whether any of these things occur or not, the building blocks that have brought about the Harper dynasty appear to be more than transient phenomena.

THE KEYS TO VICTORY

The main argument in *Dynasties and Interludes* centres not around partisan alignments per se but rather the various ways that Canadian political parties structure the choices available to the voter in an election.[5] Canadian parties have always had considerable freedom in this regard because they have typically tended to eschew long-term ideological commitments and are thus better able to manoeuvre strategically in choosing issues and emphases in any given election campaign.[6] The particular ways in which parties attempt to structure the voting choice in any given election often depend on short-term strategic choices of issues and the appeal of the current party leaders. However, the parties are not totally free to structure electoral choice in any way that they wish. They are constrained by a set of factors traditionally associated with the Canadian political landscape, which commonly recur in electoral appeals.[7] They must be well positioned on the key economic questions of the time, have public confidence on issues of national integration, and, since the Depression, be in favour of expanding or at least preserving the welfare state.

Lest we think that these factors are of recent vintage, consider the views of André Siegfried, writing at the beginning of the twentieth century about elections in Canada.

In all electioneering programmes [in Canada] there are certain points upon which the politicians lay stress, instinctively as it were, because they know them to be calculated to impress public opinion; and nothing throws more light upon the real spirit of a constituency than the kind of language addressed to it by the candidates, its licensed flatterers. In this chapter we shall study the arguments of a general character which the Canadian election organizers are most given to invoking, and which ensure victory to their party when they can make out their claim with sufficient plausibility. They are four in number: the defence of one of the two races or of one of the two religions against the other; the prosperity of the country; the promise of public works or material local advantages; and the personal prestige of the party leader.[8]

The "prosperity of the country," the need to promote economic growth, and a pledge to attack any problems that may appear to be threatening it have always been an important part of Canadian electoral discourse. In every election, parties will attempt to structure choices to their advantage around economic issues. To some extent, they are free to espouse the specific economic policies they consider advantageous, as the Conservative Party did with the National Policy under Macdonald in 1878, the Little New Deal under Bennett in 1935, Wage and Price Controls under Stanfield in 1974, and the Free Trade Agreement under Mulroney in 1988. In many cases, however, these were responses to larger economic problems that had thrust their way onto the electoral stage. American domination, recession or depression, inflation, unemployment, government debt — whatever the threat to Canadian economic prosperity, political parties promise solutions, whether specific or general, in order to persuade the public that they are the ones who should be trusted to deal with the complex matters of economic policy.

The defence of race or religion identifies a second constraint on Canadian electoral politics, though not necessarily in the way invoked in Siegfried's quotation. We can reconceptualize this constraint as a necessity for parties to decide whether to appeal along or across racial, ethnic, religious, or regional lines. Often in the past, parties, whether defending their principles or seeking short-term electoral advantage, have opted to structure their appeal *across* cleavage lines, in particular to accommodate Quebec. The accommodation of Quebec has provided some vestiges of internal structuring in Canadian parties, placed constraints on Cabinet selection, and influenced strategic decisions on election issues. For a considerable part of Canadian electoral history, the success of one party in appealing to Quebec as part of a national community (first the Conservatives, then the Liberals) has been an important component of federal electioneering. The appeal of the Bloc Québécois to represent the province (or at least the francophone majority thereof) along cleavage lines in elections since 1993 reversed this historic pattern, and caused other parties to react by making strategic decisions of their own to deal with ethnic and linguistic relations, either in an accommodating manner or in a more antagonistic one.

Attempts by the major parties to accommodate the West have over time been less successful than with Quebec, and that region has spawned several new parties that have from time to time altered or disrupted the Canadian party system. Starting in 1921 with the Progressives, then in 1935 with the CCF and Social Credit, and later in 1993 with Reform, several new political parties have arisen as representatives of the West and structured their appeals along regional lines.[9] The strategic question of whether to continue to act as a regional party or to aspire to become a national entity has bedeviled all of these parties. The Canadian Alliance's attempt to break out of this pattern in the 2000 election was only marginally successful. Its Conservative successor did better in this regard in elections after 2004, but still faced the dilemma of balancing its desire to act as a true representative of western grievances with its ambition to form a national government. The decision to act solely as a regional party is a momentous one, since it would appear to involve abandoning the ultimate ambition of gaining power. In fact, such political movements of the past (e.g. Social Credit, the Progressives) have generally faded over time or been absorbed by the major parties. Reform's quest to find a "united alternative," beginning in 1997 and continuing under the Alliance banner in 2000 and the Conservative one after the 2003 merger, eventually came to display an awareness of the fact that even successful regional parties in Canada must grow and change in order to survive. The Bloc, of course, unlike the Alliance, did not have the option of transforming itself into a Canadian national party. Thus its seeming demise in 2011 leaves the door wide open to new electoral possibilities in Quebec. It is not impossible that the Bloc may revive, particularly if the PQ comes to power provincially in Quebec. A Liberal revival under a francophone leader is likewise not inconceivable, in spite of the party's many problems. Whether the NDP can be an effective voice for Quebec in federal politics is problematic, despite its fifty-nine seats in the province. And finally, a return to the 2006 strategy could over time produce a second Conservative breakthrough in Quebec, thereby enhancing the party's "national unity" credentials.

A third important factor in the electoral campaigns of all major Canadian parties is the need to extend, maintain, improve, or defend the welfare state. This factor represents a more modern extension of the emphasis that Siegfried, in the era in which he was writing, placed on "public works." The modern variation on this theme stems from the policy consensus that developed after the Great Depression of the 1930s, establishing that it was a responsibility of the state to provide a "social safety net."[10] During and after the Second World War, a number of programs were put in place to create such a framework for social policy — unemployment insurance, welfare, health insurance, medicare, and pensions. Not all of these programs were established by the federal government, and their implementation often involved controversy. However, their popularity with the public meant that their acceptance needed to be stated with assurance by political parties during election campaigns, regardless of any desires they might harbour for substantially changing or even replacing such programs. Brian Mulroney's reference to social programs as a "sacred trust" during the 1984 election campaign provided such assurance to voters at the time, but came back to haunt him later when he sought to implement changes in pension and welfare policies. The accusation by the Liberals in the 2004 election campaign that the new Conservatives under Stephen Harper had a "hidden agenda" favouring tax cuts at the expense of social programs was in part directed toward this same end. Any attack on the welfare state, even in the name of financial prudence, cannot easily be acknowledged in elections without serious repercussions. The incorporation of welfare state measures into their electoral programs is the price that mainstream parties have had to pay to prevent sharp class divisions from arising in Canadian elections.[11]

THE CREATION OF THE HARPER DYNASTY

Stephen Harper was chosen as leader of the Conservative Party of Canada in March 2004, shortly after the founding of the party as a merger of the PCs and the Alliance. A June election was forced on the new party more quickly than they might have desired, but they were not as disadvantaged as might have been the case in more normal circumstances. Having finally attained the Liberal leadership, Paul Martin was beset by the sponsorship scandal and struggled to reassert control of the agenda. The Martin government maintained some advantages from the Chrétien dynasty, but the dimensions of the scandal in Quebec, and the relentless publicity from the Gomery inquiry, meant that Liberal warnings about the new Conservatives were met with some skepticism.[12]

Because of some prior positions adopted by the Reform Party, the Conservatives were vulnerable to attack on values and fear of what actions they might take in power. The Conservatives, Martin claimed, had the goal of making Canada into a carbon copy of the United States. In the foreign policy realm, the Liberals argued that a Conservative Canada would have followed the United States into the "coalition of the willing" in Iraq. Furthermore, the Liberals exploited public doubts about alleged Conservative intentions to re-open debates on moral issues such as abortion. But nowhere were the Liberal attacks on Conservative "values" more concentrated than in the realm of social policy.

The 2004 Liberal campaign saw an emphasis on "fixing health care for a generation" by investing billions of dollars a year in the health care system. While health care as a federal election issue had the disadvantage of being limited in its ability to influence health policy because of the provincial jurisdiction over health care delivery, the Liberals were building on past strengths in emphasizing this issue. They had been responsible for bringing in medicare during the Pearson administration, and also the Canada Health Act, which established guidelines for the expenditure of federal money in the health field. Furthermore, the seeming willingness of the Reform and Alliance parties to consider some privatization of health care allowed the Liberals to exploit public doubts about the intentions of the Harper Conservatives.

The Conservative campaign in 2004 was well aware that the Liberals had an advantage in the social policy realm and would attempt to make the most of it. They made a decision, therefore, to counter the Liberal financial plan by offering even more money for health care than the Liberals did. The Conservative health policy promise reflected the Harper strategy of presenting a moderate image for the party by underlining a commitment to public provision of health services. As it played out during the campaign, the commitment to increased spending on health coexisted uneasily in 2004 with a continuation of the party's economic policy of offering tax cuts. The Liberals were able to point out the "black hole" which existed between promises of increased spending and decreased revenues.

The Conservative 2004 campaign experimented with a tactic that was to become more prominent over the decade: promising small but targeted policies in an effort to make direct personal connections with voters. In 2004, the Conservatives promised to raise the child tax credit and to establish tax-free savings plans. Although these initiatives in the realm of economic policy generated some positive comment, they were dwarfed by the larger issues of tax cuts and increased spending. But the lesson was quickly learned that the public reacted well to such pocket-book promises.

In 2004, the Conservatives' principal appeal to a right of centre clientele centred on promises to be tougher on criminals. Much of the anti-crime agenda was symbolic. In 2004, the self-righteousness that marked this anti-crime policy undermined its effectiveness. Not content with proclaiming that they were against child pornography, the Conservatives claimed that Martin favoured it, because he had not brought in legislation specifically to combat it. Once again, the Conservatives were to learn from their 2004 missteps. In subsequent campaigns the anti-crime agenda was made more credible and specific.

Similarly unrefined in 2004 was the nature of the party's appeal on national unity. Harper established in the election debate in that year that he was capable in French. However, the main Quebec appeal of the Conservatives was to promise greater accountability in government in the aftermath of the sponsorship scandal.

The Conservatives were defeated in 2004, but acquired ninety-nine seats, which put them solidly into the official opposition position. The bulk of those seats were in the West, as had been the case with the Reform and Alliance parties before them, but they added twenty-four seats on 31 percent of the vote in Ontario and a handful of seats in the Atlantic region. The party was well on its way to establishing itself as a credible national alternative to the Liberals.

The Conservative campaign in 2006 demonstrated the many lessons that Stephen Harper and his associates had learned from their 2004 experience. For one thing, they knew they needed to take on the "values" issue. At the outset of the campaign, Harper announced that the party's policy opposing gay marriage would be put to a free vote in Parliament, with the clear implication that this would decide the issue and that it would not be pursued if defeated. There was some negative publicity on the issue, but the announcement effectively neutralized the values question in the face of the emphasis of the campaign on economic and social issues. The fact that the Conservatives were perceived as unlikely to win a majority, which might allow them to proceed with a social conservative agenda, meant that their values positions could be put aside by many of those who might be attracted to the party for other reasons.

In the social and economic policy areas, the Conservatives retreated from the large-scale funding and tax cut pledges which had caused them so much grief in 2004 and announced smaller-scale targeted promises in both areas. On health care, there was to be new funding, but specifically for a guarantee to reduce waiting times for various types of surgery or treatment. On daycare for children, the Conservatives proposed to pay each family with a child under six years old a stipend of $100 per month per child to help with daycare expenses. These were simple and concrete pledges, calculated to be sensible, achievable, and affordable steps in areas where the Liberals had failed to achieve much traction with grandiose promises to fix the health and daycare situations once and for all. For one thing, they were actions that the federal government could take without long and protracted negotiation with the provinces.

The same approach was extended to the economic policy area. The unimplemented budget of the defeated Martin government had proposed reductions in income taxes, but the Conservatives decided to concentrate on the Goods and Services Tax (GST). This ubiquitous and disliked tax, although introduced by the Mulroney Conservatives, had been criticized by the Chrétien Liberals but not removed by them after they assumed power in 1993. Harper proposed in 2006 to begin reducing the amount of the GST by two percentage points over five years. Once again, this was a concrete and visible approach to reducing taxation, which would be noticeable in every transaction at the store.

Finally, when it came to Quebec, the Conservatives saw a major opportunity because of the continuing problems the sponsorship scandal was causing the Liberals. The party had inherited from the Mulroney years an image of favourability toward greater provincial autonomy. To this they added a promise to give the provincial government more occasions to participate in Canadian representation abroad, as part of cultural delegations to international institutions such as UNESCO. Thus, the Conservative minority government was achieved in 2006 by the party gaining a moderate advantage in all of the three issue areas essential to success in Canadian federal elections: the economy, social policy, and national unity.

The incremental gains of the Conservatives between 2004 and 2006 to achieve a modest victory persuaded Stephen Harper that the same techniques would produce a majority two years later. It was with this goal in mind that an election was suddenly called in the fall of 2008. Having launched attack advertising against the new Liberal leader, Stéphane Dion, portraying him as bumbling and incompetent, they felt they could sustain this theme during the campaign when the Liberals proposed a scheme of carbon taxation (the "Green Shift"). Ridiculing this plan as a "tax on everything," the Conservatives concentrated on portraying the

Liberal campaign negatively and did not develop their own platform in any significant manner. What proposals they did outline were a continuation of the small-scale concrete benefits approach of 2006 on an even smaller scale, such as removing the tax on jet fuel. They contented themselves with asserting their general competence on the economy and offering assurances that a Harper administration would continue to pursue balanced budgets, lower taxes, and job creation. These platitudes were quickly overtaken by the global economic crisis, when the Conservatives appeared to have no plans for bailouts of important companies and economic stimulus such as was being undertaken in the United States and affected European countries.

The tactic of targeting specific promises to appeal to certain groups also appeared to backfire when proposals to cut funding to arts groups and programs were criticized as unnecessary and mean-spirited. In Quebec, these proposals were interpreted as attacks by anglophones on Quebec's freedom of artistic expression, seriously compromising the party's Quebec strategy. Similarly, the Conservative efforts to expand the "tough on crime" agenda by jailing young offenders for long periods had no appeal in Quebec. The national unity pillar of Canadian electoral success did not yield the Conservatives any additional seats in Quebec in 2008: they kept the ten they had achieved in 2006, but their popular vote in Quebec declined to 22 percent. What gains the Conservatives made in 2008 came mainly in Ontario, where they increased their vote by 4 percent and their seat total by eleven.

In government, the Harper Conservatives continued to undertake small-scale program actions and proposals — the census, gun registry, criminal justice. Tax cuts for corporations, but not individuals, limited their appeal but allowed them to maintain a pro-business/economic growth posture in the economic area. A renewal of the attack advertising against new Liberal leader Michael Ignatieff kept the focus on the negative characteristics of the opposition and away from the sparseness of the governmental legislative output and the limited nature of its vision.

The Liberal determination to bring down the government ultimately turned out to be a disastrous decision, one that must be attributed to Ignatieff himself. If the government had been allowed to run its course until 2012, the Conservative claims that a "coalition of losers" was plotting to replace it would have been more difficult to establish, and much more planning might have gone into the Liberal campaign, which appeared unfocused. After initially deciding to campaign on ethical transgressions of the Conservatives (not producing documents for Parliamentary committees dominated by the opposition), the Liberal campaign focused on social policy, with some small proposals (education credits) and a promise to continue augmenting health care funding. There was also a renewal of the long-standing pledge for a daycare program. The Liberal platform was a combination of small-scale pledges of their own (echoing the Conservative strategy) with a renewal of big plans to fund health care. Notable by its absence was anything substantial to follow up on the Liberal strategy of the 2008 campaign — climate change. Ignatieff was fulsome in his praise of the oil sands, and made no mention of carbon taxation (a major plank of his, not Dion's, in his unsuccessful campaign for the Liberal leadership in 2006).

Even though the Conservative government was not defeated over its budget, this document played a role in the campaign. Although it appeared rather innocuous, the Liberals had signalled even before the budget was delivered that they were not going to support it. Being more cautious, NDP leader Jack Layton stated several conditions for his party's support of the budget — conditions that were not fully met. But the budget never came to a vote. Thus, the whole economic policy area in the election was effectively ceded to the Conservatives. They took full credit for the Economic Action Plan, a stimulus measure that originated in the threatened defeat of the government after the ineffective economic statement of fall 2008. The Conservatives could have avoided an election by including a few more measures in the budget to satisfy the opposition, but felt that an election would be to their advantage. Any danger that the Bloc Québécois would support the budget was averted when the Conservatives decided not to accede to BQ demands to provide money to Quebec to support its harmonization of the federal and provincial sales taxes, as had been made available to Ontario and British Columbia. Following the parliamentary vote of non-confidence, the Conservatives reversed this position and indicated in the election campaign that they would in fact provide such support — a measure that was implemented in their first budget following the election. Once again, a series of small measures was targeted to particular groups in the electorate. Tax reductions for low-income seniors, tax credits for volunteer firefighters, money for doctors who locate in rural areas: these were all designed for immediate appeal without jeopardizing the overall position that a period of restraint was needed to offset the stimulus spending of the Economic Action Plan. The announced goal was to balance the budget in five years, with unspecified austerity measures, attrition in the public service, and no major cuts to essential services.

The Harper dynasty has some similarities to previous dynasties, as well as some differences. It differs from previous dynasties in that it was deliberately achieved on a diminished scale, with minor issue adjustments rather than larger moves to capture valence issue areas. This approach was most visible in the social policy area, the last remaining area of Liberal strength. Small-scale benefits were emphasized: for example, there is to be a new tax credit for enrolling children in an arts program. While the Liberals and NDP directed attention during the campaign to the social policy area, they were not able to establish a clear advantage in this area. The Liberal "learning passport" plan, for example, was a small-scale program that appeared designed for the publicity it might attract rather than to be an adequate solution to the problem of access to higher education for those with limited incomes.

The national unity area was least amenable to the Harper incrementalist approach. The party had little sustained appeal inside Quebec and little credibility outside the province that it could deal with Quebec. Indeed, their campaign in Quebec appeared to be mostly a holding operation, designed to maintain the ten seats won in 2006. The large-scale shift away from the Bloc did not lead to increased support for the Conservatives; indeed, the party lost five of the ten seats that it had won in 2006. The NDP contingent that has replaced the BQ will be severely tested in its ability to represent public opinion from Quebec, particularly that of Quebecers who favour sovereignty. Federalist leadership in the province is quite fluid, but it seems unlikely that the Conservatives can reassert themselves as the main representatives of this option. Eventually their problems in doing so may become an issue in the rest of Canada as well, since ownership of the national unity issue involves credibility both inside and outside Quebec.

Table 4. Vote and Vote Change in Eighteen GTA Ridings

	% vote in 2011			Net change from 2008		
	CPC	NDP	LIB	CPC	NDP	LIB
Eglinton–Lawrence	48.6	11.6	38.4	9.3	3.2	-5.6
York Centre	48.5	15.9	33.3	10.5	3.8	-10.2
Brampton–Springdale	48.3	19.6	27.9	9.0	8.0	-13.1
Mississauga South	46.5	12.8	37.2	6.9	3.9	-7.0
Brampton West	44.8	17.7	35.0	4.9	4.1	-5.3
Mississauga–Brampton South	44.7	17.9	35.2	11.7	6.1	-12.5
Richmond Hill	44.1	16.9	35.3	8.4	7.0	-11.7
Ajax–Pickering	44.1	18.7	38.3	6.1	9.6	-6.2
Mississauga–Streetsville	43.9	15.5	37.0	8.1	5.6	-8.8
Don Valley West	42.9	11.7	41.8	4.1	1.5	-2.6
Willowdale	41.7	18.4	39.9	9.2	8.2	-8.8
Etobicoke Centre	41.2	14.7	41.2	3.7	6.4	-7.7
Etobicoke–Lakeshore	40.3	20.3	35.1	5.4	8.6	-11.0
Pickering–Scarborough East	40.1	18.6	37.6	7.6	8.0	-12.1
Mississauga East–Cooksville	40.0	18.8	38.5	7.4	7.4	-11.7
Don Valley East	36.8	25.2	34.6	5.8	11.9	-3.5
Scarborough Centre	35.6	30.1	31.7	5.5	14.3	-17.0
Bramalea–Gore–Malton	34.4	33.5	28.4	-2.7	21.5	-16.7
Mean	42.6	18.8	35.9	6.7	7.7	-9.5

The Harper dynasty is similar to some other dynasties, particularly that of Chrétien, in that it depended in part for its creation on a divided and relatively weak opposition. The Conservatives owe their majority outcome largely to the party's substantial gains in Ontario, with a net gain in the province of twenty-one seats over the 2008 result.[13] Of these twenty-one seats, eighteen were in the Toronto region,[14] a highly significant breakthrough in comparison with the party's rather dismal showing in urban areas in its three previous elections. As is seen in Table 4, the surge in Conservative support in these ridings, all of which had been won by Liberals in 2008, was substantial. In all but three of the ridings, the Conservative vote topped 40 percent. In several, it was substantially higher, coming close to 50 percent in Eglinton–Lawrence, York Centre, and Brampton–Springdale. The NDP share of the vote also increased in all of these ridings, with an average increase over 2008 of just under 8 percent. There was a decline in the Liberal vote, on average, of nearly 10 percent, although there was also considerable variation in the level of Liberal support. In several ridings (e.g. Don Valley West), the Liberal decline was quite modest. In others (e.g. Scarborough Centre), it was much higher.

This means that the Conservative success in the Greater Toronto Area cannot be attributed to any single factor such as vote splitting. Certainly, the vote splitting among the three parties contributed to the result. But it is not the sole explanation, as the surge in Conservative support alone would have allowed the party to capture some of these ridings even without the rise in the NDP vote. Neither does the Liberal collapse fully explain the outcome, as the party's overall vote, at nearly 36 percent, held up better in Toronto generally than it did elsewhere. But taken together, these three factors — the Conservative gains and the strength of the NDP, combined with Liberal weakness — allowed the Conservatives to take more seats in the GTA than might have been the case otherwise. This, in turn, accounts largely for the party's winning 73 of Ontario's 106 seats (compared with 51 in 2008), and with that level of dominance in Canada's largest province came a national majority. Without the Toronto breakthrough, the distribution of Conservative seats across the country would have looked much more similar to that of 2008.

Data on the support bases for the Canadian federal parties in the 2004–2011 period are presented in Tables 5 and 6. They show some changes and some continuity when the 2011 election is compared to previous years. First, a pattern of gender difference in party support seems to have more or less disappeared in the 2011 election. Previously, women had been less likely to support the Conservatives. The differences in

Table 5. Party Support by Gender, 2004–2011, by Percentage

	2004		2006		2008		2011	
	Male	Female	Male	Female	Male	Female	Male	Female
Liberal	35	35	28	29	26	25	19	17
Conservative	33	31	40	36	40	35	42	41
NDP	16	18	16	20	15	21	30	31
BQ	11	13	10	11	12	13	6	6
Green	5	3	5	5	6	8	3	5

Source: 2004–2008 Canadian Election Studies; 2011 Political Support in Canada Study.

Table 6. Party Support by Age Group, 2004–2011, by Percentage

	2004			2006			2008			2011		
	18–34	35–54	55+	18–34	35–54	55+	18–34	35–54	55+	18–34	35–54	55+
Liberal	29	35	40	27	26	32	20	27	26	17	17	20
Conservative	27	31	37	29	40	42	32	35	44	27	40	50
NDP	23	18	11	21	19	16	25	18	16	40	33	34
BQ	15	11	9	15	10	9	15	14	10	9	6	4
Green	6	5	2	8	6	3	8	7	5	7	4	3

Source: 2004–2008 Canadian Election Studies; 2011 Political Support in Canada Study.

2006 and 2008 were about 5 percent, while the Conservative vote in 2011 was very similar between the sexes. Age, however, tells a different story. The Conservative vote in 2011 was even more likely to come from older Canadians than had been the case in previous elections. Young people were more likely to choose the NDP. The Bloc Québécois and Green party vote were stronger among the youngest age group in the above table, but both of these parties were of course weaker overall in 2011 than in the two previous elections. The fact that their age profile is younger is both good and bad news for the NDP. On the positive side for the party, if these younger supporters can be persuaded to continue voting NDP, the party could increase support in the future. On the negative side, younger citizens are less likely to cast ballots, and support dependent on them can lead to disappointment.

The Conservative majority in 2011 was a narrow one, but a majority nevertheless. The overall gain in the Conservative vote was only about 2 percent, but they benefited from where their gains and losses were realized, in part a function of the party's targeting of specific constituencies, particularly in the GTA. The loss of 5 percent of the vote in Quebec cost the Conservatives five seats, but the gain of 5 percent in Ontario got them twenty-one. The Harper dynasty was established by primacy in only one of the three issue areas that we have identified as vital to Canadian federal electoral success — the economy — but it managed to at least neutralize the other two. The extent of the economic recovery in the next four years will determine whether this economic primacy can sustain the Harper dynasty. But there are signs of potential vulnerability in the other two areas, particularly that of national unity, that have in the longer term undermined previous dynasties. Its ability to manage these may ultimately determine both the length and durability of the Harper dynasty.

NOTES

1.	See Jon H. Pammett and Christopher Dornan, eds., *The Canadian Federal Election of 2008* (Toronto: Dundurn, 2009), 45–55, 237–49, and 259–66.
2.	See Lawrence LeDuc, Jon H. Pammett, Judith I. McKenzie, and Andre Turcotte, *Dynasties and Interludes: Past and Present in Canadian Electoral Politics* (Toronto: Dundurn Press, 2010), Chapter 4.
3.	This line of argument is developed more extensively in *Dynasties and Interludes*, Chapter 1.
4.	See *Dynasties and Interludes*, chapter 6.
5.	This section is a synthesis of the argument put forward in *Dynasties and Interludes* (35–41). On the theme of structuring electoral choices more generally, see also Peter Mair, "Party Systems and Structures of Competition," in *Comparing Democracies: Elections and Voting in Global Perspective*, eds. Lawrence LeDuc, Richard G. Niemi, and Pippa Norris (Thousand Oaks, CA: Sage, 1996) and Leon Epstein, *Political Parties in Western Democracies* (New Brunswick, NJ: Transaction Books, 1980).
6.	This argument is developed extensively in Harold D. Clarke, Jane Jenson, Lawrence LeDuc, and Jon H. Pammett, *Absent Mandate: Canadian Electoral Politics in an Era of Restructuring* (Toronto: Gage, 1996). See especially Chapter 2.
7.	On the topic of constraints on political parties, see William L. Miller and Richard G. Niemi, "Voting Choice, Conditioning, and Constraint," in *Comparing Democracies 2: New Challenges in the Study of Elections and Voting*, eds. Lawrence LeDuc, Richard G. Niemi, and Pippa Norris (London: Sage, 2002).
8.	André Siegfried, *The Race Question in Canada* (London: Eveleigh Nash, 1907), 207.
9.	On changes in the Canadian party system, particularly those that occurred in the aftermath of the 1993 election, see R. Kenneth Carty, William Cross, and Lisa Young, *Rebuilding Canadian Party Politics* (Vancouver: University of British Columbia Press, 2000).
10.	See Raymond Blake, Penny Bryden, and J. Frank Strain, eds., *The Welfare State in Canada: Past, Present and Future* (Concord, ON: Irwin, 1997).
11.	Janine Brodie and Jane Jenson, *Crisis, Challenge and Change: Party and Class in Canada Revisited* (Ottawa: Carleton University Press, 1988).
12.	See Jon H. Pammett and Christopher Dornan, eds., *The Canadian General Election of 2004* (Toronto: Dundurn, 2004) for a more detailed account of the issues and events of the 2004 election.
13.	Twenty-two if Vaughan, which was won in a 2010 by-election, is included.
14.	The others were London North Centre (41.4 percent), Nipissing-Timiskaming (36.7 percent), and Sault Ste. Marie (37.0 percent).

KEY TO APPENDICES

AAEV	Animal Alliance Environment Voters Party of Canada/ Animal Alliance Environment Voters Party of Canada
BQ	Bloc Québécois/Bloc Québécois
CA	Canadian Action Party/Parti action canadienne
CHP	Christian Heritage Party of Canada/Parti de l'Héritage Chrétien du Canada
COMM	Communist Party of Canada/Parti communiste du Canada
Cons	Conservative Party of Canada/Parti conservateur du Canada
FPNP	First Peoples National Party of Canada/First Peoples National Party of Canada
GP	Green Party of Canada/Le Parti Vert du Canada
Liberal	Liberal Party of Canada/Parti libéral du Canada
Libert	Libertarian Party of Canada/Parti Libertarien du Canada
MP	Marijuana Party/Parti Marijuana
NDP	New Democratic Party/Nouveau Parti démocratique
PPP	Pirate Party of Canada/Parti Pirate du Canada
PCP	Progressive Canadian Party/Parti Progressiste Canadien
RP	Rhinoceros Party/Parti Rhinocéros
UPC	United Party of Canada/Parti Uni du Canada
WBP	Western Block Party/Western Block Party
IND	Independent/Indépendant
No Affiliation	No Affiliation/Aucune appurtenance

APPENDIX A: The Results in Summary

	Canada		N.L.		P.E.I.		N.S		N.B.		Que.		Ont.		Man.		Sask.		Alta.		B.C.		Y.T.		N.W.T.		Nun.	
	# seats	% votes	# seats	% votes	# seats	% votes	# seats	% votes	# seats	% votes	# seats	% votes	# seats	% votes	# seats	% votes	# seats	% votes	# seats	% votes	# seats	% votes	# seats	% votes	# seats	% votes	# seats	% votes
AAEV	0	0																							0	0.6		
BQ	4	6.1									4	23.4																
CA	0	0																										
CHP	0	0.1			0	0.1	0	0.1	0	0.1			0	0.2		0.3			0	0.2		0.1						
COMM	0	0														0.1						.						
Cons	166	39.6	1	28.3	1	41.2	4	36.7	8	43.8	5	16.5	73	44.4	11	53.5	13	56.3	27	66.8	21	45.6	1	33.8	0	32.1	1	49.9
FPNP	0	0																										
GP	1	3.9	0	0.9	0	2.4	0	3.9	0	3.2	0	2.1	0	3.8	0	3.6	0	2.6	0	5.2	1	7.7	0	18.9	0	3.1	0	2
Liberal	34	18.9	4	37.9	3	41	4	28.9	1	22.6	7	14.2	11	25.3	1	16.6	1	8.5	0	9.3	2	13.4	0	32.9	0	18.4	0	28.7
Libert	0	0											0	0.1							0	0.1						
MP	0	0																										
ML	0	0.1									0	0.1	0	0.1					0	0.1	0	0.1						
NDP	103	30.6	2	32.6	0	15.4	3	30.3	1	29.8	59	42.9	22	25.6	2	25.8	0	32.3	1	16.8	4	32.5	0	14.4	1	45.8	0	19.4
PPP	0	0																			0	0.1						
PCP	0	0									0	0.1	0	0.1					0	0.1								
RP	0	0											0	0.1					0	0.1								
UPC	0	0																										
WBP	0	0																										
IND	0	0.4	0	0.3					0	0.5	0	0.6	0	0.2	0	0.1	0	0.2	0	1.3	0	0.2						
No Affiliation	0	0.1											0	0.2														
	308		7		4		11		10		75		106		14		14		28		28		1		1		1	

APPENDIX B

The Results by Constituency

District and Party	Vote %
NEWFOUNDLAND	
AVALON	
Liberal	44.0
Conservative	40.5
New Democratic Party	14.2
Independent	0.8
Green Party	0.6
BONAVISTA–GANDER–GRAND FALLS–WINDSOR	
Liberal	57.7
Conservative	27.6
New Democratic Party	13.8
Green Party	0.9
HUMBER–ST. BARBE–BAIE VERTE	
Liberal	57.0
Conservative	25.2
New Democratic Party	15.8
Independent	1.1
Green Party	0.8
LABRADOR	
Conservative	39.8
Liberal	39.1
New Democratic Party	19.8
Green Party	1.3

District and Party	Vote %
RANDOM–BURIN–ST. GEORGE'S	
Liberal	49.7
Conservative	32.0
New Democratic Party	17.2
Green Party	1.2
ST. JOHN'S EAST	
New Democratic Party	71.2
Conservative	20.9
Liberal	6.9
Green Party	1.1
ST. JOHN'S SOUTH–MOUNT PEARL	
New Democratic Party	47.9
Liberal	28.5
Conservative	22.8
Green Party	0.7
PRINCE EDWARD ISLAND	
CARDIGAN	
Liberal	49.6
Conservative	38.4
New Democratic Party	10.2
Green Party	1.8
CHARLOTTETOWN	
Liberal	39.5
Conservative	32.7
New Democratic Party	25.1
Green Party	2.3
CHP Canada	0.5

District and Party	Vote %	District and Party	Vote %
EGMONT		**HALIFAX**	
Conservative	54.6	New Democratic Party	51.6
Liberal	31.3	Liberal	25.6
New Democratic Party	12.4	Conservative	18.0
Green Party	1.7	Green Party	4.4
		Marxist-Leninist	0.3
MALPEQUE			
Liberal	42.4	**HALIFAX WEST**	
Conservative	39.1	Liberal	35.9
New Democratic Party	14.6	Conservative	30.5
Green Party	3.9	New Democratic Party	29.3
		Green Party	4.3
NOVA SCOTIA			
		KINGS–HANTS	
CAPE BRETON–CANSO		Liberal	39.6
Liberal	46.4	Conservative	36.6
Conservative	30.6	New Democratic Party	20.0
New Democratic Party	19.7	Green Party	3.8
Green Party	3.2		
		SACKVILLE–EASTERN SHORE	
CENTRAL NOVA		New Democratic Party	54.1
Conservative	56.8	Conservative	30.5
New Democratic Party	24.8	Liberal	11.2
Liberal	14.8	Green Party	4.2
Green Party	3.7		
		SOUTH SHORE–ST. MARGARET'S	
CUMBERLAND–COLCHESTER–		Conservative	43.1
MUSQUODOBOIT VALLEY		New Democratic Party	36.1
Conservative	52.5	Liberal	16.9
New Democratic Party	23.2	Green Party	3.8
Liberal	18.1		
Green Party	5.3	**SYDNEY–VICTORIA**	
CHP Canada	0.9	Liberal	39.9
		Conservative	37.8
DARTMOUTH–COLE HARBOUR		New Democratic Party	19.0
New Democratic Party	36.3	Green Party	3.2
Liberal	35.1		
Conservative	24.8	**WEST NOVA**	
Green Party	3.8	Conservative	47.0
		Liberal	36.4
		New Democratic Party	13.1
		Green Party	3.5

District and Party	Vote %	District and Party	Vote %

NEW BRUNSWICK

MONCTON–RIVERVIEW–DIEPPE
Conservative	35.7
Liberal	31.3
New Democratic Party	28.8
Green Party	4.1

ACADIE–BATHURST
New Democratic Party	69.7
Conservative	16.2
Liberal	14.1

NEW BRUNSWICK SOUTHWEST
Conservative	56.6
New Democratic Party	23.2
Liberal	13.5
Green Party	5.2
CHP Canada	1.4

BEAUSÉJOUR
Liberal	39.1
Conservative	33.3
New Democratic Party	23.4
Green Party	4.3

FREDERICTON
Conservative	48.4
New Democratic Party	23.8
Liberal	23.2
Green Party	4.0
Independent	0.6

SAINT JOHN
Conservative	49.7
New Democratic Party	30.7
Liberal	16.1
Green Party	2.7
Independent	0.8

FUNDY ROYAL
Conservative	58.1
New Democratic Party	27.0
Liberal	10.1
Green Party	4.8

TOBIQUE–MACTAQUAC
Conservative	62.7
New Democratic Party	19.0
Liberal	15.9
Green Party	2.5

MADAWASKA–RESTIGOUCHE
Conservative	40.6
Liberal	35.2
New Democratic Party	18.8
Independent	3.7
Green Party	1.7

QUEBEC

ABITIBI–BAIE-JAMES–NUNAVIK–EEYOU
New Democratic Party	44.8
Conservative	22.7
Bloc Québécois	18.0
Liberal	10.5
Green Party	3.9

MIRAMICHI
Conservative	52.4
New Democratic Party	23.1
Liberal	22.1
Green Party	2.4

ABITIBI–TÉMISCAMINGUE
New Democratic Party	51.2
Bloc Québécois	31.6
Conservative	9.9
Liberal	5.9
Green Party	1.4

District and Party	Vote %	District and Party	Vote %
AHUNTSIC		**BEAUHARNOIS–SALABERRY**	
Bloc Québécois	31.8	New Democratic Party	43.8
New Democratic Party	30.3	Bloc Québécois	33.2
Liberal	27.9	Conservative	12.9
Conservative	8.0	Liberal	8.3
Green Party	1.3	Green Party	1.8
Rhinoceros	0.6		
		BEAUPORT–LIMOILOU	
ALFRED–PELLAN		New Democratic Party	46.1
New Democratic Party	42.1	Conservative	26.2
Bloc Québécois	22.8	Bloc Québécois	19.4
Liberal	22.0	Liberal	6.0
Conservative	11.2	Green Party	1.8
Green Party	1.5	CHP Canada	0.2
Independent	0.4	Marxist-Leninist	0.2
ARGENTEUIL–PAPINEAU–MIRABEL		**BERTHIER–MASKINONGÉ**	
New Democratic Party	44.3	New Democratic Party	39.6
Bloc Québécois	29.0	Bloc Québécois	29.4
Liberal	12.2	Liberal	14.2
Conservative	11.1	Conservative	14.0
Green Party	2.6	Green Party	2.1
Independent	0.6	Rhinoceros	0.7
Marxist-Leninist	0.2		
		BOURASSA	
BAS-RICHELIEU–NICOLET–		Liberal	40.9
BÉCANCOUR		New Democratic Party	32.3
Bloc Québécois	38.3	Bloc Québécois	16.1
New Democratic Party	35.6	Conservative	8.8
Conservative	13.0	Green Party	1.6
Liberal	10.1	Marxist-Leninist	0.3
Green Party	3.0		
		BROME–MISSISQUOI	
BEAUCE		New Democratic Party	42.6
Conservative	50.7	Liberal	22.1
New Democratic Party	30.0	Bloc Québécois	21.3
Liberal	11.0	Conservative	11.9
Bloc Québécois	6.7	Green Party	2.1
Green Party	1.6		

District and Party	Vote %
BROSSARD–LA PRAIRIE	
New Democratic Party	41.0
Liberal	27.3
Bloc Québécois	17.5
Conservative	12.6
Green Party	1.4
Marxist-Leninist	0.2
CHAMBLY–BORDUAS	
New Democratic Party	42.7
Bloc Québécois	27.7
Independent	11.3
Liberal	8.9
Conservative	7.8
Green Party	1.5
CHARLESBOURG–HAUTE-SAINT-CHARLES	
New Democratic Party	45.0
Conservative	30.3
Bloc Québécois	16.3
Liberal	6.5
Green Party	1.6
CHP Canada	0.4
CHÂTEAUGUAY–SAINT-CONSTANT	
New Democratic Party	52.0
Bloc Québécois	26.7
Conservative	10.3
Liberal	9.0
Green Party	1.6
Marxist-Leninist	0.3
CHICOUTIMI–LE FJORD	
New Democratic Party	38.1
Bloc Québécois	28.8
Conservative	25.3
Liberal	5.6
Green Party	1.5
Rhinoceros	0.7

District and Party	Vote %
COMPTON–STANSTEAD	
New Democratic Party	47.6
Bloc Québécois	26.0
Liberal	12.1
Conservative	11.8
Green Party	2.5
DRUMMOND	
New Democratic Party	51.6
Bloc Québécois	22.0
Conservative	15.9
Liberal	8.4
Green Party	2.1
GASPÉSIE–ÎLES-DE-LA-MADELEINE	
New Democratic Party	33.8
Bloc Québécois	31.6
Conservative	17.1
Liberal	15.0
Green Party	2.5
GATINEAU	
New Democratic Party	61.8
Bloc Québécois	15.1
Liberal	14.0
Conservative	7.9
Green Party	1.1
HAUTE-GASPÉSIE–LA MITIS–MATANE–MATAPÉDIA	
Bloc Québécois	36.1
Liberal	25.6
New Democratic Party	21.4
Conservative	15.0
Green Party	2.0

CANADIAN FEDERAL ELECTION OF 2011

District and Party	Vote %	District and Party	Vote %
HOCHELAGA		JONQUIÈRE–ALMA	
New Democratic Party	48.2	New Democratic Party	43.4
Bloc Québécois	31.2	Conservative	35.2
Liberal	10.9	Bloc Québécois	18.1
Conservative	6.7	Liberal	2.0
Green Party	1.7	Green Party	1.2
Rhinoceros	0.5		
Communist	0.4	LAC-SAINT-LOUIS	
Marxist-Leninist	0.3	Liberal	34.1
		New Democratic Party	30.0
HONORÉ–MERCIER		Conservative	28.5
New Democratic Party	36.4	Green Party	4.3
Liberal	30.4	Bloc Québécois	3.1
Bloc Québécois	18.5		
Conservative	12.4	LA POINTE-DE-L'ÎLE	
Green Party	1.6	New Democratic Party	48.3
Rhinoceros	0.4	Bloc Québécois	32.5
Marxist-Leninist	0.4	Liberal	9.2
		Conservative	7.7
HULL–AYLMER		Green Party	1.9
New Democratic Party	59.2	Marxist-Leninist	0.4
Liberal	20.3		
Conservative	10.2	LASALLE–ÉMARD	
Bloc Québécois	8.4	New Democratic Party	42.1
Green Party	1.9	Liberal	26.6
		Bloc Québécois	14.7
JEANNE–LE BER		Conservative	13.1
New Democratic Party	44.7	Green Party	2.3
Bloc Québécois	24.2	Marxist-Leninist	0.7
Liberal	19.3	Rhinoceros	0.5
Conservative	9.0		
Green Party	2.6	LAURENTIDES–LABELLE	
Marxist-Leninist	0.2	New Democratic Party	43.8
		Bloc Québécois	31.5
JOLIETTE		Liberal	12.7
New Democratic Party	47.3	Conservative	9.3
Bloc Québécois	32.9	Green Party	2.5
Conservative	9.7	Marxist-Leninist	0.3
Liberal	6.2		
Green Party	3.9		

District and Party	Vote %	District and Party	Vote %
LAURIER–SAINTE-MARIE		**LOTBINIÈRE–CHUTES-DE-LA-**	
New Democratic Party	46.6	**CHAUDIÈRE**	
Bloc Québécois	35.9	Conservative	39.9
Liberal	9.9	New Democratic Party	38.5
Conservative	3.5	Bloc Québécois	14.9
Green Party	2.6	Liberal	5.1
Rhinoceros	0.8	Green Party	1.7
Communist	0.3		
Marxist-Leninist	0.2	**LOUIS-HÉBERT**	
Independent	0.1	New Democratic Party	38.7
		Bloc Québécois	24.2
LAVAL		Conservative	21.8
New Democratic Party	43.3	Liberal	13.4
Bloc Québécois	22.7	Green Party	1.6
Liberal	18.5	CHP Canada	0.2
Conservative	12.5		
Green Party	2.5	**LOUIS-SAINT-LAURENT**	
Marxist-Leninist	0.4	New Democratic Party	39.9
		Conservative	37.6
LAVAL–LES ÎLES		Bloc Québécois	14.4
New Democratic Party	47.6	Liberal	6.4
Liberal	20.6	Green Party	1.5
Conservative	15.9	CHP Canada	0.3
Bloc Québécois	13.0		
Green Party	1.8	**MANICOUAGAN**	
Pirate Party	0.7	New Democratic Party	48.9
Marxist-Leninist	0.4	Bloc Québécois	31.2
		Conservative	11.5
LÉVIS–BELLECHASSE		Liberal	5.6
Conservative	43.9	Green Party	2.7
New Democratic Party	33.8		
Bloc Québécois	14.9	**MARC-AURÈLE-FORTIN**	
Liberal	5.8	New Democratic Party	49.7
Green Party	1.5	Bloc Québécois	26.4
		Liberal	12.0
LONGUEUIL–PIERRE-BOUCHER		Conservative	9.8
New Democratic Party	51.9	Green Party	2.1
Bloc Québécois	27.2		
Liberal	10.2		
Conservative	8.3		
Green Party	2.0		
Marxist-Leninist	0.4		

District and Party	Vote %
MÉGANTIC–L'ÉRABLE	
Conservative	49.1
New Democratic Party	26.2
Bloc Québécois	16.8
Liberal	5.8
Green Party	1.5
CAP	0.6
MONTCALM	
New Democratic Party	53.0
Bloc Québécois	30.2
Conservative	7.9
Liberal	5.4
Green Party	3.6
MONTMAGNY–L'ISLET–KAMOURASKA–RIVIÈRE-DU-LOUP	
New Democratic Party	36.4
Conservative	36.3
Bloc Québécois	20.1
Liberal	5.8
Green Party	1.5
MONTMORENCY–CHARLEVOIX–HAUTE-CÔTE-NORD	
New Democratic Party	37.3
Bloc Québécois	34.9
Conservative	20.5
Liberal	5.6
Green Party	1.7
MOUNT ROYAL	
Liberal	41.4
Conservative	35.6
New Democratic Party	17.9
Bloc Québécois	2.9
Green Party	1.8
Marxist-Leninist	0.3
No Affiliation	0.2

District and Party	Vote %
NOTRE-DAME-DE-GRÂCE–LACHINE	
New Democratic Party	39.7
Liberal	31.9
Conservative	14.6
Bloc Québécois	8.8
Green Party	4.2
Independent	0.5
Marxist-Leninist	0.3
OUTREMONT	
New Democratic Party	56.4
Liberal	23.7
Conservative	8.8
Bloc Québécois	8.2
Green Party	2.2
Rhinoceros	0.4
Communist	0.4
PAPINEAU	
Liberal	38.4
New Democratic Party	28.3
Bloc Québécois	25.9
Conservative	4.7
Green Party	1.9
Marxist-Leninist	0.5
No Affiliation	0.2
PIERREFONDS–DOLLARD	
New Democratic Party	34.1
Liberal	30.5
Conservative	26.9
Bloc Québécois	5.0
Green Party	3.6
PONTIAC	
New Democratic Party	45.7
Conservative	29.5
Liberal	12.8
Bloc Québécois	10.0
Green Party	1.7
Marxist-Leninist	0.3

District and Party	Vote %
PORTNEUF–JACQUES-CARTIER	
New Democratic Party	42.7
Independent	27.8
Bloc Québécois	20.5
Liberal	6.6
Green Party	2.4
QUÉBEC	
New Democratic Party	42.6
Bloc Québécois	28.0
Conservative	17.8
Liberal	9.0
Green Party	2.2
CHP Canada	0.4
REPENTIGNY	
New Democratic Party	51.9
Bloc Québécois	31.1
Liberal	7.8
Conservative	7.4
Green Party	1.7
RICHMOND–ARTHABASKA	
Bloc Québécois	33.8
New Democratic Party	32.5
Conservative	24.7
Liberal	7.0
Green Party	2.1
RIMOUSKI–NEIGETTE–TÉMISCOUATA–LES BASQUES	
New Democratic Party	43.0
Bloc Québécois	30.8
Conservative	14.6
Liberal	9.6
Green Party	2.0

District and Party	Vote %
RIVIÈRE-DES-MILLE-ÎLES	
New Democratic Party	49.2
Bloc Québécois	28.5
Liberal	10.2
Conservative	9.7
Green Party	2.4
RIVIÈRE-DU-NORD	
New Democratic Party	55.3
Bloc Québécois	28.2
Conservative	8.3
Liberal	6.3
Green Party	1.8
ROBERVAL–LAC-SAINT-JEAN	
Conservative	45.7
New Democratic Party	27.7
Bloc Québécois	21.2
Liberal	4.0
Green Party	1.4
ROSEMONT–LA PETITE-PATRIE	
New Democratic Party	51.0
Bloc Québécois	32.8
Liberal	9.1
Conservative	4.3
Green Party	1.7
Rhinoceros	0.8
Marxist-Leninist	0.3
SAINT-BRUNO–SAINT-HUBERT	
New Democratic Party	44.6
Bloc Québécois	28.2
Liberal	13.6
Conservative	10.8
Green Party	2.8

District and Party	Vote %	District and Party	Vote %
SAINT-HYACINTHE–BAGOT		**SAINT-MAURICE–CHAMPLAIN**	
New Democratic Party	52.4	New Democratic Party	39.1
Bloc Québécois	24.6	Bloc Québécois	29.3
Conservative	15.7	Conservative	17.7
Liberal	5.4	Liberal	11.9
Green Party	1.9	Green Party	2.0
SAINT-JEAN		**SHEFFORD**	
New Democratic Party	47.5	New Democratic Party	51.1
Bloc Québécois	30.5	Bloc Québécois	23.4
Conservative	10.7	Conservative	14.7
Liberal	8.8	Liberal	9.0
Green Party	2.5	Green Party	1.9
SAINT-LAMBERT		**SHERBROOKE**	
New Democratic Party	42.6	New Democratic Party	43.1
Bloc Québécois	25.9	Bloc Québécois	35.9
Liberal	19.3	Liberal	9.7
Conservative	10.0	Conservative	9.2
Green Party	2.2	Green Party	1.7
		Rhinoceros	0.4
SAINT-LAURENT–CARTIERVILLE			
Liberal	43.4	**TERREBONNE–BLAINVILLE**	
New Democratic Party	29.3	New Democratic Party	49.3
Conservative	17.5	Bloc Québécois	30.8
Bloc Québécois	7.3	Conservative	9.1
Green Party	2.1	Liberal	8.5
Marxist-Leninist	0.4	Green Party	2.1
SAINT-LÉONARD–SAINT-MICHEL		**TROIS-RIVIÈRES**	
Liberal	42.3	New Democratic Party	53.6
New Democratic Party	32.3	Bloc Québécois	23.8
Conservative	13.8	Conservative	12.3
Bloc Québécois	9.4	Liberal	7.2
Green Party	1.8	Green Party	1.9
Marxist-Leninist	0.4	Independent	0.7
		Rhinoceros	0.5

District and Party	Vote %
VAUDREUIL–SOULANGES	
New Democratic Party	43.6
Bloc Québécois	25.7
Conservative	16.4
Liberal	11.6
Green Party	2.7
VERCHÈRES–LES PATRIOTES	
New Democratic Party	43.3
Bloc Québécois	36.4
Liberal	9.5
Conservative	8.6
Green Party	2.2
WESTMOUNT-VILLE-MARIE	
Liberal	37.2
New Democratic Party	35.6
Conservative	17.5
Bloc Québécois	5.5
Green Party	3.7
Rhinoceros	0.3
Communist	0.2
ONTARIO	
AJAX–PICKERING	
Conservative	44.1
Liberal	38.3
New Democratic Party	14.7
Green Party	2.8
United Party	0.1
ALGOMA–MANITOULIN–KAPUSKASING	
New Democratic Party	51.7
Conservative	30.3
Liberal	14.8
Green Party	3.1

District and Party	Vote %
ANCASTER–DUNDAS–FLAMBOROUGH–WESTDALE	
Conservative	51.3
Liberal	24.7
New Democratic Party	18.6
Green Party	5.0
Libertarian	0.3
Marxist-Leninist	0.1
BARRIE	
Conservative	56.7
New Democratic Party	20.9
Liberal	16.1
Green Party	5.8
Libertarian	0.3
CAP	0.1
Marxist-Leninist	0.1
BEACHES–EAST YORK	
New Democratic Party	41.6
Liberal	30.8
Conservative	22.7
Green Party	4.6
Marxist-Leninist	0.3
BRAMALEA–GORE–MALTON	
Conservative	34.4
New Democratic Party	33.5
Liberal	28.4
Green Party	3.0
Marxist-Leninist	0.6
BRAMPTON–SPRINGDALE	
Conservative	48.3
Liberal	27.9
New Democratic Party	19.6
Green Party	3.8
Communist	0.4

District and Party	Vote %
BRAMPTON WEST	
Conservative	44.8
Liberal	35.0
New Democratic Party	17.7
Green Party	1.9
Independent	0.6
BRANT	
Conservative	48.9
New Democratic Party	28.5
Liberal	18.8
Green Party	3.2
Independent	0.3
Independent	0.2
BRUCE–GREY–OWEN SOUND	
Conservative	56.3
New Democratic Party	17.6
Liberal	16.1
Green Party	10.0
BURLINGTON	
Conservative	54.2
Liberal	23.3
New Democratic Party	18.8
Green Party	3.5
Marxist-Leninist	0.2
CAMBRIDGE	
Conservative	53.4
New Democratic Party	27.7
Liberal	15.1
Green Party	3.6
Marxist-Leninist	0.3
CARLETON–MISSISSIPPI MILLS	
Conservative	57.0
Liberal	24.0
New Democratic Party	14.6
Green Party	4.5

District and Party	Vote %
CHATHAM-KENT–ESSEX	
Conservative	53.8
New Democratic Party	26.3
Liberal	16.5
Green Party	3.4
DAVENPORT	
New Democratic Party	53.7
Liberal	27.9
Conservative	14.2
Green Party	3.4
Communist	0.4
Animal Alliance/Environment Voters	0.3
DON VALLEY EAST	
Conservative	36.8
Liberal	34.6
New Democratic Party	25.2
Green Party	2.8
CHP Canada	0.6
DON VALLEY WEST	
Conservative	42.9
Liberal	41.8
New Democratic Party	11.7
Green Party	3.2
Communist	0.3
DUFFERIN–CALEDON	
Conservative	59.0
Green Party	14.7
New Democratic Party	13.2
Liberal	13.1
DURHAM	
Conservative	54.5
New Democratic Party	21.1
Liberal	17.9
Green Party	5.4
CHP Canada	0.8
Libertarian	0.3

District and Party	Vote %	District and Party	Vote %
EGLINTON–LAWRENCE		**GLENGARRY–PRESCOTT–RUSSELL**	
Conservative	46.8	Conservative	48.8
Liberal	38.4	Liberal	30.7
New Democratic Party	11.6	New Democratic Party	16.6
Green Party	3.2	Green Party	3.5
		Libertarian	0.3
ELGIN–MIDDLESEX–LONDON			
Conservative	57.5	**GUELPH**	
New Democratic Party	24.6	Liberal	43.4
Liberal	13.4	Conservative	32.8
Green Party	3.0	New Democratic Party	16.7
CHP Canada	1.1	Green Party	6.1
CAP	0.3	Libertarian	0.3
		Radical Marijuana	0.3
		Animal Alliance/Environment Voters	0.2
ESSEX		Communist	0.2
Conservative	48.1		
New Democratic Party	35.2	**HALDIMAND–NORFOLK**	
Liberal	14.2	Conservative	50.9
Green Party	2.4	Liberal	24.9
Marxist-Leninist	0.1	New Democratic Party	20.0
		Green Party	3.3
ETOBICOKE CENTRE		CHP Canada	0.9
Conservative	41.2		
Liberal	41.2	**HALIBURTON–KAWARTHA LAKES–BROCK**	
New Democratic Party	14.7		
Green Party	2.6	Conservative	60.0
Marxist-Leninist	0.3	New Democratic Party	22.1
		Liberal	12.9
ETOBICOKE-LAKESHORE		Green Party	5.1
Conservative	40.3		
Liberal	35.1	**HALTON**	
New Democratic Party	20.3	Conservative	54.5
Green Party	4.0	Liberal	25.8
Marxist-Leninist	0.3	New Democratic Party	16.0
		Green Party	3.4
ETOBICOKE NORTH		CHP Canada	0.3
Liberal	42.4		
Conservative	32.1		
New Democratic Party	23.7		
Marxist-Leninist	0.6		
Libertarian	0.6		
CHP Canada	0.6		

District and Party	Vote %	District and Party	Vote %
HAMILTON CENTRE		**KINGSTON AND THE ISLANDS**	
New Democratic Party	57.0	Liberal	39.3
Conservative	26.4	Conservative	34.9
Liberal	14.1	New Democratic Party	21.5
Radical Marijuana	1.9	Green Party	4.2
Marxist-Leninist	0.6		
		KITCHENER CENTRE	
HAMILTON EAST–STONEY CREEK		Conservative	42.4
New Democratic Party	45.2	Liberal	31.3
Conservative	36.2	New Democratic Party	21.6
Liberal	13.2	Green Party	4.0
Green Party	3.0	Independent	0.4
PC Party	1.0	Communist	0.2
Libertarian	0.8	Marxist-Leninist	0.2
Communist	0.3		
Marxist-Leninist	0.2	**KITCHENER–CONESTOGA**	
CAP	0.2	Conservative	54.1
		New Democratic Party	21.8
HAMILTON MOUNTAIN		Liberal	19.9
New Democratic Party	47.2	Green Party	4.1
Conservative	33.1		
Liberal	16.2	**KITCHENER–WATERLOO**	
Green Party	2.8	Conservative	40.9
CHP Canada	0.5	Liberal	37.6
Independent	0.3	New Democratic Party	16.0
		Green Party	4.8
		Pirate Party	0.4
HURON–BRUCE		Independent	0.3
Conservative	54.9	Marxist-Leninist	0.1
New Democratic Party	25.3		
Liberal	16.5	**LANARK–FRONTENAC–LENNOX**	
Green Party	2.7	**AND ADDINGTON**	
Independent	0.5	Conservative	57.3
		New Democratic Party	20.7
KENORA		Liberal	16.9
Conservative	47.0	Green Party	4.6
New Democratic Party	27.9	Independent	0.6
Liberal	21.9		
Green Party	2.6		
Independent	0.6		

District and Party	Vote %	District and Party	Vote %

LEEDS–GRENVILLE

Conservative	60.8
New Democratic Party	18.3
Liberal	15.9
Green Party	5.0

LONDON–FANSHAWE

New Democratic Party	50.9
Conservative	33.5
Liberal	11.5
Green Party	2.8
CHP Canada	1.3

LONDON NORTH CENTRE

Conservative	37.0
Liberal	33.8
New Democratic Party	24.7
Green Party	4.1
Animal Alliance/Environment Voters	0.4

LONDON WEST

Conservative	44.5
Liberal	26.8
New Democratic Party	25.9
Green Party	2.7
United Party	0.1

MARKHAM–UNIONVILLE

Liberal	38.9
Conservative	35.5
New Democratic Party	21.8
Green Party	3.2
Libertarian	0.5

LAMBTON–KENT–MIDDLESEX

Conservative	57.7
New Democratic Party	24.0
Liberal	14.2
Green Party	3.3
CHP Canada	0.8

MISSISSAUGA–BRAMPTON SOUTH

Conservative	44.7
Liberal	35.2
New Democratic Party	17.9
Green Party	2.0
Marxist-Leninist	0.2

MISSISSAUGA EAST–COOKSVILLE

Conservative	40.0
Liberal	38.5
New Democratic Party	18.8
Green Party	2.2
Marxist-Leninist	0.5

MISSISSAUGA–ERINDALE

Conservative	47.0
Liberal	33.9
New Democratic Party	16.3
Green Party	2.7
Marxist-Leninist	0.2

MISSISSAUGA SOUTH

Conservative	46.5
Liberal	37.2
New Democratic Party	12.8
Green Party	3.1
No Affiliation	0.4

MISSISSAUGA–STREETSVILLE

Conservative	43.9
Liberal	37.0
New Democratic Party	15.5
Green Party	3.6

NEPEAN–CARLETON

Conservative	54.5
Liberal	25.2
New Democratic Party	16.2
Green Party	4.1

District and Party	Vote %

District and Party	Vote %

NEWMARKET–AURORA
Conservative	54.3
Liberal	23.9
New Democratic Party	15.3
Green Party	4.5
PC Party	1.7
Animal Alliance/Environment Voters	0.3

NIAGARA FALLS
Conservative	53.3
New Democratic Party	23.5
Liberal	18.9
Green Party	3.9
CHP Canada	0.5

NIAGARA WEST–GLANBROOK
Conservative	57.3
New Democratic Party	21.6
Liberal	14.8
Green Party	4.3
CHP Canada	2.0

NICKEL BELT
New Democratic Party	55.0
Conservative	28.0
Liberal	14.1
Green Party	2.8
Marxist-Leninist	0.1

NIPISSING–TIMISKAMING
Conservative	36.7
Liberal	36.6
New Democratic Party	20.8
Green Party	6.0

NORTHUMBERLAND–QUINTE WEST
Conservative	53.8
Liberal	21.0
New Democratic Party	20.7
Green Party	4.5

OAK RIDGES–MARKHAM
Conservative	51.1
Liberal	28.3
New Democratic Party	16.8
Green Party	2.6
PC Party	1.2

OAKVILLE
Conservative	51.6
Liberal	30.7
New Democratic Party	13.9
Green Party	3.7

OSHAWA
Conservative	51.3
New Democratic Party	37.9
Liberal	7.0
Green Party	3.2
Libertarian	0.5
Marxist-Leninist	0.1

OTTAWA CENTRE
New Democratic Party	52.1
Conservative	21.7
Liberal	20.1
Green Party	5.0
Radical Marijuana	0.5
Independent	0.3
Communist	0.2
Marxist-Leninist	0.1

OTTAWA–ORLÉANS
Conservative	44.6
Liberal	38.4
New Democratic Party	14.2
Green Party	2.9

District and Party	Vote %	District and Party	Vote %
OTTAWA SOUTH		**PARRY SOUND–MUSKOKA**	
Liberal	44.0	Conservative	55.7
Conservative	33.3	New Democratic Party	24.2
New Democratic Party	18.2	Liberal	11.5
Green Party	3.0	Green Party	8.1
PC Party	0.9	Independent	0.4
Pirate Party	0.6	Marxist-Leninist	0.1
OTTAWA–VANIER		**PERTH–WELLINGTON**	
Liberal	38.2	Conservative	54.5
New Democratic Party	29.4	New Democratic Party	21.3
Conservative	27.1	Liberal	18.0
Green Party	5.2	Green Party	4.6
Marxist-Leninist	0.2	CHP Canada	1.7
OTTAWA WEST–NEPEAN		**PETERBOROUGH**	
Conservative	44.7	Conservative	49.7
Liberal	31.5	New Democratic Party	24.9
New Democratic Party	19.7	Liberal	21.4
Green Party	4.0	Green Party	3.6
		No Affiliation	0.3
OXFORD		CAP	0.2
Conservative	58.9		
New Democratic Party	25.6	**PICKERING–SCARBOROUGH EAST**	
Liberal	9.5	Conservative	40.1
Green Party	4.3	Liberal	37.6
CHP Canada	1.6	New Democratic Party	18.6
		Green Party	3.7
PARKDALE–HIGH PARK			
New Democratic Party	47.2	**PRINCE EDWARD–HASTINGS**	
Liberal	32.9	Conservative	53.3
Conservative	15.6	New Democratic Party	23.7
Green Party	3.3	Liberal	18.7
CHP Canada	0.5	Green Party	3.5
Radical Marijuana	0.4	Independent	0.5
Marxist-Leninist	0.2	PC Party	0.3

District and Party	Vote %	District and Party	Vote %
RENFREW–NIPISSING–PEMBROKE		**SCARBOROUGH–AGINCOURT**	
Conservative	53.4	Liberal	45.4
Independent	18.7	Conservative	34.2
New Democratic Party	13.4	New Democratic Party	18.1
Liberal	12.7	Green Party	2.3
Green Party	1.7		
		SCARBOROUGH CENTRE	
RICHMOND HILL		Liberal	31.7
Conservative	44.1	New Democratic Party	30.1
Liberal	35.3	Green Party	2.6
New Democratic Party	16.9		
Green Party	3.7	**SCARBOROUGH–GUILDWOOD**	
		Liberal	36.2
ST. CATHARINES		Conservative	34.4
Conservative	50.9	New Democratic Party	26.5
New Democratic Party	23.8	Green Party	2.2
Liberal	20.6	Independent	0.7
Green Party	3.8		
CHP Canada	0.7	**SCARBOROUGH–ROUGE RIVER**	
Communist	0.2	New Democratic Party	40.6
		Conservative	29.9
ST. PAUL'S		Liberal	27.2
Liberal	40.6	Green Party	1.5
Conservative	32.4	Independent	0.8
New Democratic Party	22.0		
Green Party	4.5	**SCARBOROUGH SOUTHWEST**	
Libertarian	0.5	New Democratic Party	35.0
		Conservative	31.8
SARNIA–LAMBTON		Liberal	29.0
Conservative	52.6	Green Party	4.1
New Democratic Party	29.9		
Liberal	14.0	**SIMCOE–GREY**	
Green Party	2.5	Conservative	49.4
CHP Canada	1.0	New Democratic Party	17.4
		No Affiliation	13.5
SAULT STE. MARIE		Liberal	12.7
Conservative	41.4	Green Party	5.4
New Democratic Party	37.2	CHP Canada	1.2
Liberal	18.9	CAP	0.4
Green Party	2.1		
CHP Canada	0.3		
Marxist-Leninist	0.1		

District and Party	Vote %	District and Party	Vote %
SIMCOE NORTH		**TIMMINS–JAMES BAY**	
Conservative	54.5	New Democratic Party	50.4
New Democratic Party	19.9	Conservative	31.7
Liberal	19.1	Liberal	15.7
Green Party	6.0	Green Party	2.2
CHP Canada	0.6		
		TORONTO CENTRE	
STORMONT–DUNDAS–SOUTH		Liberal	41.0
GLENGARRY		New Democratic Party	30.2
Conservative	62.1	Conservative	22.6
Liberal	17.9	Green Party	5.0
New Democratic Party	17.5	Libertarian	0.5
Green Party	2.2	Communist	0.3
Libertarian	0.3	Independent	0.2
		Marxist-Leninist	0.1
SUDBURY			
New Democratic Party	49.9	**TORONTO–DANFORTH**	
Conservative	28.3	New Democratic Party	60.8
Liberal	18.0	Liberal	17.6
Green Party	3.0	Conservative	14.3
FPNP	0.5	Green Party	6.5
Independent	0.3	Animal Alliance/Environment Voters	0.8
THORNHILL		**TRINITY–SPADINA**	
Conservative	61.4	New Democratic Party	54.5
Liberal	23.7	Liberal	23.4
New Democratic Party	12.0	Conservative	16.8
Green Party	2.6	Green Party	4.4
Animal Alliance/Environment Voters	0.4	Libertarian	0.7
		Marxist-Leninist	0.2
THUNDER BAY–RAINY RIVER			
New Democratic Party	48.7	**VAUGHAN**	
Conservative	27.2	Conservative	56.3
Liberal	21.7	Liberal	29.9
Green Party	2.4	New Democratic Party	11.6
		Green Party	2.2
THUNDER BAY–SUPERIOR NORTH			
New Democratic Party	49.9		
Conservative	29.7		
Liberal	16.7		
Green Party	3.0		
Radical Marijuana	0.7		

CANADIAN FEDERAL ELECTION OF 2011

District and Party	Vote %
WELLAND	
New Democratic Party	42.2
Conservative	40.2
Liberal	14.0
Green Party	2.5
CHP Canada	0.6
Independent	0.3
Marxist-Leninist	0.1
WELLINGTON–HALTON HILLS	
Conservative	63.7
Liberal	16.4
New Democratic Party	13.0
Green Party	6.4
CHP Canada	0.6
WHITBY–OSHAWA	
Conservative	58.4
New Democratic Party	22.3
Liberal	14.1
Green Party	4.9
Libertarian	0.3
WILLOWDALE	
Conservative	41.7
Liberal	39.9
New Democratic Party	18.4
WINDSOR–TECUMSEH	
New Democratic Party	49.9
Conservative	33.6
Liberal	12.9
Green Party	3.0
Marxist-Leninist	0.5
WINDSOR WEST	
New Democratic Party	54.3
Conservative	31.6
Liberal	10.9
Green Party	2.8
Marxist-Leninist	0.4

District and Party	Vote %
YORK CENTRE	
Conservative	48.5
Liberal	33.3
New Democratic Party	15.9
Green Party	2.3
YORK–SIMCOE	
Conservative	63.6
New Democratic Party	19.3
Liberal	10.8
Green Party	5.4
CHP Canada	0.7
United Party	0.3
YORK SOUTH–WESTON	
New Democratic Party	40.1
Liberal	32.8
Conservative	24.3
Green Party	2.8
YORK WEST	
Liberal	47.0
New Democratic Party	27.8
Conservative	22.1
Green Party	1.6
CHP Canada	0.8
CAP	0.6
MANITOBA	
BRANDON–SOURIS	
Conservative	63.7
New Democratic Party	25.2
Green Party	5.7
Liberal	5.4
CHARLESWOOD–ST. JAMES–ASSINIBOIA	
Conservative	57.6
New Democratic Party	20.1
Liberal	18.4
Green Party	3.9

District and Party	Vote %	District and Party	Vote %
CHURCHILL		**SAINT BONIFACE**	
New Democratic Party	51.1	Conservative	50.3
Conservative	26.2	Liberal	30.8
Liberal	20.4	New Democratic Party	· 16.0
Green Party	2.3	Green Party	2.9
DAUPHIN–SWAN RIVER–MARQUETTE		**SELKIRK–INTERLAKE**	
Conservative	63.1	Conservative	65.2
New Democratic Party	26.1	New Democratic Party	26.5
Liberal	6.6	Liberal	4.8
Green Party	4.2	Green Party	3.5
ELMWOOD–TRANSCONA		**WINNIPEG CENTRE**	
Conservative	46.4	New Democratic Party	53.7
New Democratic Party	45.5	Conservative	27.6
Liberal	5.0	Liberal	11.1
Green Party	3.1	Green Party	7.1
		Communist	0.6
KILDONAN–ST. PAUL			
Conservative	58.2	**WINNIPEG NORTH**	
New Democratic Party	30.1	Liberal	35.8
Liberal	8.2	New Democratic Party	35.6
Green Party	2.6	Conservative	26.4
Independent	0.6	Green Party	1.8
Independent	0.4	Communist	0.5
PORTAGE–LISGAR		**WINNIPEG SOUTH**	
Conservative	76.0	Conservative	52.2
New Democratic Party	9.8	Liberal	32.7
Liberal	6.3	New Democratic Party	13.0
Green Party	5.6	Green Party	2.0
CHP Canada	2.3		
		WINNIPEG SOUTH CENTRE	
PROVENCHER		Conservative	38.8
Conservative	70.6	Liberal	37.0
New Democratic Party	17.9	New Democratic Party	19.9
Liberal	6.7	Green Party	3.5
Green Party	3.0	Independent	0.5
CHP Canada	1.3	Independent	0.3
Pirate Party	0.5		

District and Party	Vote %

SASKATCHEWAN

BATTLEFORDS–LLOYDMINSTER

Conservative	66.9
New Democratic Party	27.1
Liberal	3.3
Green Party	2.7

BLACKSTRAP

Conservative	54.4
New Democratic Party	36.8
Liberal	6.3
Green Party	2.4

CYPRESS HILLS–GRASSLANDS

Conservative	69.8
New Democratic Party	21.2
Liberal	6.2
Green Party	2.7

DESNETHÉ–MISSINIPPI–CHURCHILL RIVER

Conservative	47.9
New Democratic Party	44.3
Liberal	5.2
Green Party	2.6

PALLISER

Conservative	47.0
New Democratic Party	44.7
Liberal	5.3
Green Party	3.0

PRINCE ALBERT

Conservative	62.2
New Democratic Party	31.8
Liberal	3.5
Green Party	2.2
CAP	0.4

REGINA–LUMSDEN–LAKE CENTRE

Conservative	53.2
New Democratic Party	36.8
Liberal	7.3
Green Party	2.7

REGINA–QU'APPELLE

Conservative	53.5
New Democratic Party	38.4
Liberal	4.7
Green Party	3.0
Independent	0.4

SASKATOON–HUMBOLDT

Conservative	52.7
New Democratic Party	35.1
Liberal	8.0
Green Party	2.4
Independent	1.8

SASKATOON–ROSETOWN–BIGGAR

Conservative	48.7
New Democratic Party	46.9
Liberal	2.3
Green Party	2.1

SASKATOON–WANUSKEWIN

Conservative	58.4
New Democratic Party	31.4
Liberal	6.7
Green Party	3.4

SOURIS–MOOSE MOUNTAIN

Conservative	74.0
New Democratic Party	18.7
Liberal	4.2
Green Party	3.1

District and Party	Vote %	District and Party	Vote %
WASCANA		CALGARY CENTRE	
Liberal	40.8	Conservative	57.7
Conservative	36.9	Liberal	17.5
New Democratic Party	19.8	New Democratic Party	14.9
Green Party	2.5	Green Party	9.9
YORKTON–MELVILLE		CALGARY SOUTHEAST	
Conservative	68.9	Conservative	76.3
New Democratic Party	21.8	New Democratic Party	10.3
Liberal	6.8	Green Party	6.5
Green Party	2.4	Liberal	6.4
		Independent	0.4
ALBERTA		WBP	0.3
CALGARY EAST		CALGARY SOUTHWEST	
Conservative	67.4	Conservative	75.1
New Democratic Party	14.1	New Democratic Party	11.9
Liberal	11.8	Liberal	7.2
Green Party	5.9	Green Party	5.2
Communist	0.7	Independent	0.5
CALGARY CENTRE-NORTH		CALGARY WEST	
Conservative	56.5	Conservative	62.2
New Democratic Party	16.0	Liberal	17.7
Liberal	14.0	New Democratic Party	10.4
Green Party	13.1	Green Party	9.4
Marxist-Leninist	0.4	Marxist-Leninist	0.4
CALGARY NORTHEAST		CROWFOOT	
Conservative	56.8	Conservative	84.0
Liberal	27.7	New Democratic Party	9.1
New Democratic Party	10.3	Green Party	3.3
Green Party	4.7	Liberal	2.3
Marxist-Leninist	0.5	Independent	0.9
		CHP Canada	0.4
CALGARY–NOSE HILL			
Conservative	70.2		
New Democratic Party	12.5		
Liberal	11.3		
Green Party	6.0		

CANADIAN FEDERAL ELECTION OF 2011

District and Party	Vote %	District and Party	Vote %
EDMONTON–MILL WOODS–BEAUMONT		**EDMONTON–SPRUCE GROVE**	
Conservative	61.0	Conservative	71.1
New Democratic Party	23.8	New Democratic Party	15.8
Liberal	11.1	Liberal	9.3
Green Party	3.0	Green Party	3.8
Pirate Party	0.8		
Communist	0.2	**EDMONTON–STRATHCONA**	
		New Democratic Party	53.5
		Conservative	40.6
EDMONTON CENTRE		Liberal	2.8
Conservative	48.0	Green Party	2.3
New Democratic Party	25.4	Independent	0.4
Liberal	22.4	Marxist-Leninist	0.2
Green Party	3.4	Independent	0.2
Pirate Party	0.6		
Marxist-Leninist	0.2	**FORT McMURRAY–ATHABASCA**	
		Conservative	71.8
EDMONTON EAST		New Democratic Party	13.2
Conservative	52.7	Liberal	10.4
New Democratic Party	37.4	Green Party	4.5
Liberal	6.9		
Green Party	2.9	**LETHBRIDGE**	
		Conservative	56.5
EDMONTON–LEDUC		New Democratic Party	27.2
Conservative	63.6	Liberal	8.4
New Democratic Party	19.3	Green Party	4.4
Liberal	12.2	CHP Canada	3.6
Green Party	4.9		
		MACLEOD	
		Conservative	77.5
EDMONTON–ST. ALBERT		New Democratic Party	10.3
Conservative	63.5	Green Party	4.6
New Democratic Party	21.4	Liberal	3.7
Liberal	10.7	PC Party	3.4
Green Party	4.4	CHP Canada	0.5
EDMONTON–SHERWOOD PARK			
Conservative	44.7	**MEDICINE HAT**	
Independent	29.5	Conservative	71.5
New Democratic Party	14.5	New Democratic Party	13.1
Liberal	7.5	Liberal	10.3
Green Party	3.5	Green Party	4.4
WBP	0.4	CHP Canada	0.7

District and Party	Vote %	District and Party	Vote %
PEACE RIVER		**YELLOWHEAD**	
Conservative	75.8	Conservative	77.0
New Democratic Party	16.1	New Democratic Party	13.1
Green Party	3.5	Green Party	5.1
Liberal	3.1	Liberal	2.9
Independent	0.7	CHP Canada	1.0
Rhinoceros	0.7	CAP	0.9
RED DEER		**BRITISH COLUMBIA**	
Conservative	75.9		
New Democratic Party	15.1	**ABBOTSFORD**	
Green Party	5.1	Conservative	65.0
Liberal	3.8	New Democratic Party	20.2
		Liberal	9.9
VEGREVILLE–WAINWRIGHT		Green Party	4.3
Conservative	79.8	Marxist-Leninist	0.6
New Democratic Party	11.3		
Green Party	5.1	**BRITISH COLUMBIA SOUTHERN**	
Liberal	3.1	**INTERIOR**	
CHP Canada	0.7	New Democratic Party	50.9
		Conservative	38.9
WESTLOCK–ST. PAUL		Green Party	6.4
Conservative	77.8	Liberal	3.8
New Democratic Party	12.2		
Liberal	6.1	**BURNABY–DOUGLAS**	
Green Party	3.9	New Democratic Party	43.0
		Conservative	40.9
WETASKIWIN		Liberal	11.2
Conservative	81.4	Green Party	3.6
New Democratic Party	11.4	Libertarian	0.9
Green Party	4.3	Communist	0.3
Liberal	2.9	Marxist-Leninist	0.1
WILD ROSE		**BURNABY–NEW WESTMINSTER**	
Conservative	74.7	New Democratic Party	49.7
New Democratic Party	11.3	Conservative	35.8
Green Party	7.0	Liberal	10.1
Liberal	6.7	Green Party	3.9
CHP Canada	0.3	Libertarian	0.4
		Marxist-Leninist	0.2

District and Party	Vote %	District and Party	Vote %
CARIBOO–PRINCE GEORGE		**KAMLOOPS–THOMPSON–CARIBOO**	
Conservative	56.2	Conservative	52.2
New Democratic Party	30.2	New Democratic Party	36.9
Green Party	6.2	Liberal	5.3
Liberal	5.1	Green Party	5.2
CHP Canada	1.0	CHP Canada	0.3
Independent	0.9		
Rhinoceros	0.5	**KELOWNA–LAKE COUNTRY**	
		Conservative	57.4
CHILLIWACK–FRASER CANYON		New Democratic Party	22.1
Conservative	57.2	Liberal	11.7
New Democratic Party	25.8	Green Party	8.7
Liberal	10.8		
Green Party	5.5	**KOOTENAY–COLUMBIA**	
Marxist-Leninist	0.4	Conservative	55.9
WBP	0.4	New Democratic Party	33.2
		Green Party	6.0
DELTA–RICHMOND EAST		Liberal	3.5
Conservative	54.2	Independent	1.5
New Democratic Party	23.3		
Liberal	16.9	**LANGLEY**	
Green Party	4.8	Conservative	64.5
No Affiliation	0.5	New Democratic Party	20.5
Libertarian	0.3	Liberal	9.1
		Green Party	5.3
ESQUIMALT–JUAN DE FUCA		Pirate Party	0.6
New Democratic Party	40.9		
Conservative	40.2	**NANAIMO–ALBERNI**	
Liberal	10.0	Conservative	46.4
Green Party	8.3	New Democratic Party	38.3
Independent	0.3	Liberal	7.6
CAP	0.2	Green Party	6.8
		Pirate Party	0.6
FLEETWOOD–PORT KELLS		CHP Canada	0.1
Conservative	47.5	Marxist-Leninist	0.1
New Democratic Party	32.8		
Liberal	16.0	**NANAIMO–COWICHAN**	
Green Party	2.9	New Democratic Party	48.9
Libertarian	0.7	Conservative	38.3
		Green Party	7.8
		Liberal	4.7
		Marxist-Leninist	0.3

District and Party	Vote %
NEW WESTMINSTER–COQUITLAM	
New Democratic Party	45.9
Conservative	41.5
Liberal	8.1
Green Party	4.3
Marxist-Leninist	0.2
NEWTON–NORTH DELTA	
New Democratic Party	33.4
Liberal	31.5
Conservative	31.3
Green Party	3.3
Independent	0.3
Communist	0.3
NORTH VANCOUVER	
Conservative	48.6
Liberal	29.6
New Democratic Party	16.1
Green Party	5.0
Independent	0.6
OKANAGAN–COQUIHALLA	
Conservative	53.6
New Democratic Party	24.1
Liberal	10.9
Green Party	9.4
Independent	1.6
Independent	0.3
OKANAGAN–SHUSWAP	
Conservative	55.4
New Democratic Party	26.4
Green Party	10.7
Liberal	7.5
PITT MEADOWS–MAPLE RIDGE–MISSION	
Conservative	54.3
New Democratic Party	35.5
Liberal	5.2
Green Party	5.0

District and Party	Vote %
PORT MOODY–WESTWOOD–PORT COQUITLAM	
Conservative	56.1
New Democratic Party	30.1
Liberal	8.5
Green Party	4.5
Libertarian	0.9
PRINCE GEORGE–PEACE RIVER	
Conservative	62.1
New Democratic Party	25.6
Green Party	6.0
Liberal	5.2
Pirate Party	1.1
RICHMOND	
Conservative	58.4
Liberal	18.7
New Democratic Party	18.3
Green Party	4.7
SAANICH–GULF ISLANDS	
Green Party	46.3
Conservative	35.7
New Democratic Party	11.9
Liberal	6.1
SKEENA–BULKLEY VALLEY	
New Democratic Party	55.3
Conservative	34.5
Liberal	3.6
Green Party	3.1
CHP Canada	3.0
CAP	0.5

CANADIAN FEDERAL ELECTION OF 2011

District and Party	Vote %

SOUTH SURREY–WHITE ROCK–CLOVERDALE

Conservative	54.6
New Democratic Party	20.3
Liberal	16.7
Green Party	5.5
Independent	1.3
CHP Canada	0.7
PC Party	0.4
Independent	0.3
Independent	0.3

SURREY NORTH

New Democratic Party	39.7
Conservative	35.6
Liberal	18.4
Green Party	3.5
Independent	1.2
CHP Canada	0.8
Libertarian	0.8

VANCOUVER CENTRE

Liberal	31.0
Conservative	26.0
New Democratic Party	26.0
Green Party	15.4
PC Party	0.5
Libertarian	0.5
Pirate Party	0.3
Marxist-Leninist	0.1

VANCOUVER EAST

New Democratic Party	62.8
Conservative	18.9
Liberal	9.9
Green Party	7.6
Marxist-Leninist	0.7

VANCOUVER ISLAND NORTH

Conservative	46.1
New Democratic Party	43.0
Liberal	5.2
Green Party	5.1
Independent	0.5
Marxist-Leninist	0.1

VANCOUVER KINGSWAY

New Democratic Party	50.1
Conservative	28.1
Liberal	16.6
Green Party	4.0
Libertarian	0.6
Communist	0.4
Marxist-Leninist	0.2

VANCOUVER QUADRA

Liberal	42.2
Conservative	38.6
New Democratic Party	13.8
Green Party	5.4

VANCOUVER SOUTH

Conservative	43.3
Liberal	34.7
New Democratic Party	19.0
Green Party	2.6
Marxist-Leninist	0.5

VICTORIA

New Democratic Party	50.8
Conservative	23.6
Liberal	14.0
Green Party	11.6

District and Party	Vote %

WEST VANCOUVER–SUNSHINE
COAST–SEA TO SKY COUNTRY

Conservative	45.5
New Democratic Party	23.6
Liberal	22.5
Green Party	7.1
PC Party	0.5
Libertarian	0.4
WBP	0.2
Marxist-Leninist	0.1
CAP	0.1

YUKON

YUKON

Conservative	33.8
Liberal	32.9
Green Party	18.9
New Democratic Party	14.4

NORTHWEST TERRITORIES

WESTERN ARCTIC

New Democratic Party	45.8
Conservative	32.1
Liberal	18.4
Green Party	3.1
Animal Alliance/Environment Voters	0.6

NUNAVUT

NUNAVUT

Conservative	49.9
Liberal	28.7
New Democratic Party	19.4
Green Party	2.0

NOTES ON CONTRIBUTORS

Éric Bélanger is Associate Professor in the Department of Political Science at McGill University and a member of the Centre for the Study of Democratic Citizenship. His research interests include political parties, public opinion, and voting behaviour, as well as Quebec and Canadian politics. His work has been published in a number of scholarly journals, including *Comparative Political Studies, Political Research Quarterly, Electoral Studies, Publius: The Journal of Federalism*, the *European Journal of Political Research*, and the *Canadian Journal of Political Science*. He is also the co-author of *French Presidential Elections* and *Le comportement électoral des Québécois* (2010 Donald Smiley Prize).

Harold D. Clarke is Ashbel Smith Professor, University of Texas at Dallas, and Adjunct Professor, Department of Government, University of Essex. He is a principal investigator for the British Election Study. Recent publications include *Making Political Choices: Canada and the United States*, with Allan Kornberg and Thomas Scotto (University of Toronto Press) and *Performance Politics and the British Voter*, with David Sanders, Marianne Stewart, and Paul Whiteley (Cambridge University Press).

Christopher Dornan is Director of the Arthur Kroger College of Public Affairs, Associate Dean of the Faculty of Public Affairs, and Associate Professor in the School of Journalism and Communication at Carleton University. He is the co-editor of, and contributor to, this and four previous volumes in the Canadian Election series.

Faron Ellis teaches political science and history at Lethbridge College. His research in Canadian politics focuses on parties and elections and includes *The Limits of Participation: Members and Leaders in Canada's Reform Party* and *Parameters of Power: Canadian Political Institutions, Brief Edition*. In 2010 he was elected as alderman to the Lethbridge City Council.

Jim Farney is an Assistant Professor of Political Science at the University of Regina, having previously been a visiting professor and post-doctoral fellow at Queen's University. His interests include Canadian and American politics, religion and politics, and the politics of education. His *Social Conservatives and Party Politics in Canada and the United States* is forthcoming from the University of Toronto Press and he is currently co-editing (with David Rayside) a volume of essays placing Canadian conservatism in comparative perspective.

Mary Francoli is an Assistant Professor in the School of Journalism and Communication at Carleton University. Her research focuses largely on the impact of new media on governance, the state, and society. She received her Ph.D. in political science from the University of Western Ontario and was the Leverhulme Visiting Fellow in New Media and Internet Politics at Royal Holloway, University of London.

Josh Greenberg is an Associate Professor in the School of Journalism and Communication at Carleton University. His areas of teaching and research interest include media analysis, social media, public relations, social activism, and community-based research. He has explored these topics as they pertain to several areas of public policy: immigration, labour relations, energy, climate change, and crime and surveillance. He is the co-editor of *Communication in Question* (Nelson, 2009), *The Surveillance Studies Reader* (The Open University Press, 2007), and *Surveillance: Power, Problems and Politics* (UBC Press, 2010). He is currently preparing an edited book on research methods for communication and media studies.

Susan Harada is an Associate Professor with the School of Journalism and Communication at Carleton University. A former national news and documentary journalist with the CBC, her posting prior to joining Carleton was that of National Parliamentary Correspondent for CBC News *The National*. She has contributed several chapters to the Pammett and Dornan Canadian Election series since 2004, focusing mainly on the Green Party of Canada.

Brooke Jeffrey is Professor of Political Science at Concordia University and Director of the Masters Program in Public Policy and Public Administration. A former public servant and Director of the Liberal Caucus Research Bureau, she is the author of several books on Canadian federalism, political parties, and public policy. Her most recent book is a history of the Liberal Party, *Divided Loyalties: The Liberal Party of Canada 1984–2008*.

Allan Kornberg is Norb F. Schaefer Professor Emeritus of Political Science at Duke University. His articles on Canadian political behaviour have appeared in the *American Political Science Review*, the *Journal of Politics*, *Electoral Studies* and *Party Politics*. His most recent books on Canadian politics are *A Polity on the Edge: Canada and the Politics of Fragmentation* and *Making Political Choices: Canada and the United States*.

Lawrence LeDuc is Professor of Political Science at the University of Toronto. His publications on Canadian elections include *Political Choice in Canada*, *Absent Mandate*, and *Dynasties and Interludes: Past and Present in Canadian Electoral Politics*. In the comparative field, his publications include *Comparing Democracies 3* (with Richard G. Niemi and Pippa Norris) and *The Politics of Direct Democracy: Referendums in Global Perspective*.

Jonathan Malloy is Associate Professor of Political Science at Carleton University. His research focuses on Canadian political institutions and religion and politics, particularly the politics of evangelical Christians in Canada. He also serves as president of the Canadian Study of Parliament Group, and his recent publications include studies of Parliament under minority government, Parliament's role in the "war on terror," and Canadian prime ministers' relationships with their parties.

Alex Marland is an Assistant Professor with the Department of Political Science at Memorial University. He was the lead editor of *Political Marketing in Canada* (UBC Press, forthcoming) and has published about electioneering in Canada and about politics in Newfoundland and Labrador. He has also worked in the public, private, and political sectors in capacities that exposed him to the practice of media relations, opinion research, and governance.

David McGrane is an Assistant Professor in Political Studies at St. Thomas More College and the University of Saskatchewan. He has published in the *International Journal of Canadian Studies*, the *Journal of Canadian Studies*, the *Canadian Review of Political Science*, and has a contribution in *Constructing Tomorrow's Federalism* (University of Manitoba Press). His most recent research appeared in *Saskatchewan Politics: Crowding the Centre*. His research interests include federal-provincial fiscal relations, social democracy, Québécois nationalism, Western Canadian alienation, immigration, multiculturalism, and child care.

Richard Nadeau is Professor of Political Science at the University of Montreal and a member of the Centre for the Study of Democratic Citizenship. His interests are voting behaviour, public opinion, political communication, and quantitative methodology. A Fulbright Scholar, Professor Nadeau has authored or co-authored more than 120 articles (published in the most prestigious political science journals), chapters, and books including *Unsteady State*, *Anatomy of a Liberal Victory*, *French Presidential Elections*, and *Le comportement électoral des Québécois*.

Jon H. Pammett is Professor of Political Science at Carleton University in Ottawa. He is also co-director of the Carleton University Survey Centre and Canadian delegate to the International Social Survey Programme. He is co-author of *Political Choice in Canada* and *Absent Mandate*, books about voting behaviour in Canadian elections. He is co-editor of, and contributing author to, the previous volumes in the Canadian Election series. His most recent book is *Dynasties and Interludes: Past and Present in Canadian Electoral Politics* (with Lawrence LeDuc, Judith I. McKenzie, and Andre Turcotte).

Jason Reifler is currently an Assistant Professor of Political Science at Georgia State University. His research focuses on voting behaviour, public opinion about foreign policy, and factual misperceptions held by citizens. Dr. Reifler received his Ph.D. from Duke University and his B.A. from Colby College. Prior to graduate school, he worked in Washington, D.C., as a pollster and campaign strategist. His book (with Peter Feaver and Christopher Gelpi) *Paying the Human Costs of War: American Public Opinion and Casualties in Military Conflicts* was published by Princeton University Press in 2009.

Thomas J. Scotto is a Senior Lecturer in the Department of Government at the University of Essex in the United Kingdom. He is the co-author of *Making Political Choices: Canada and the United States* (University of Toronto Press, 2009). His interests lie in the areas of public opinion, polling, and voting behaviour, and his articles on the topics have appeared in *Public Opinion Quarterly*, *International Studies Quarterly*, the *Journal of Politics*, and *Electoral Studies*.

André Turcotte is Associate Professor at Carleton University's School of Journalism and Communication and the Graduate Supervisor of the Clayton H. Riddell Graduate Program in Political Management. Between 1992 and 1993, he was the co-editor of The Gallup Poll. He was part of the polling team for the Chrétien Liberals in the 1993 Federal Election. Between 1994 and 2000, he was the official pollster of the Reform Party of Canada and its leader, Preston Manning. He has also provided advice to several political leaders. He is the co-author of the recent book *Dynasties and Interludes: Past and Present in Canadian Electoral Politics.*

Christopher Waddell is an Associate Professor and Director of Carleton's School of Journalism and Communication. Prior to joining Carleton in 2001 he was Parliamentary Bureau Chief for CBC Television news from 1993 to 2001, senior producer of *The National* from 1991 to 1993, and a reporter, Ottawa Bureau chief, associate editor, and national editor for the *Globe and Mail* from 1985 to 1991. He has authored or co-authored the media chapter in the three previous election books in this series. His research interests include political communication, the media and national politics, elections, public policy as it affects business and the economy, and the business of the media.

Peter Woolstencroft teaches Canadian and comparative politics at the University of Waterloo. He has published essays on various aspects of party politics (including seven contributions to this series), political geography, the politics of education, the federal and Ontario Progressive Conservative parties, and party leadership elections. Ongoing projects include the politics of economic and political integration in North America and the character of contemporary conservatism in Canada.

RECYCLED
Paper made from
recycled material
FSC® C103567

Marquis Book Printing Inc.

Québec, Canada
2011

Printed on Silva Enviro 100% post-consumer EcoLogo certified paper,
processed chlorine free and manufactured using biogas energy.